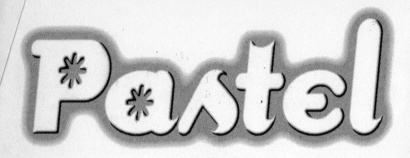

5

TOSHIHIKO KOBAYASHI

Translated and adapted by David Ury

Lettered by Foltz Design

BALLANTINE BOOKS • NEW YORK

Pastel volume 5 is a work of fiction. Names, characters, places, and incidents are the products of the author's imagination or are used fictitiously. Any resemblance to actual events, locales, or persons, living or dead, is entirely coincidental.

A Del Rey Trade Paperback Original

Published in the United States by Del Rey Books, an imprint of The Random House Publishing Group, a division of Random House, Inc., New York.

DEL REY is a registered trademark and the Del Rey colophon is a trademark of Random House, Inc.

Publication rights arranged through Kodansha Ltd.

First published in Japan in 2003 by Kodansha Ltd., Tokyo.

ISBN 978-0-345-49324-8

Printed in the United States of America

www.delreymanga.com

2 3 4 5 6 7 8 9

Translator and Adapter—David Ury
Lettering—Foltz Design

Pastel

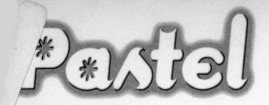

CONTENTS

A Note from the Author

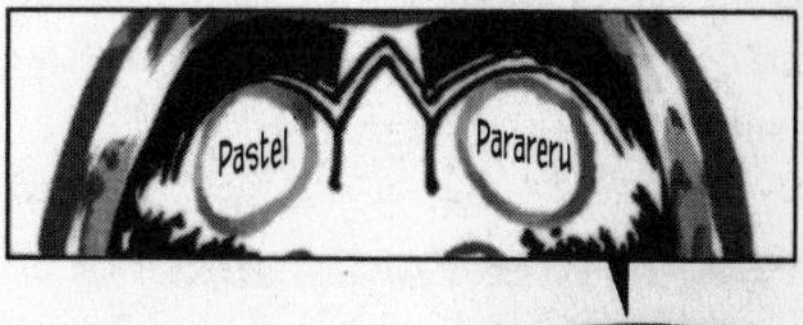
Pastel
Parareru

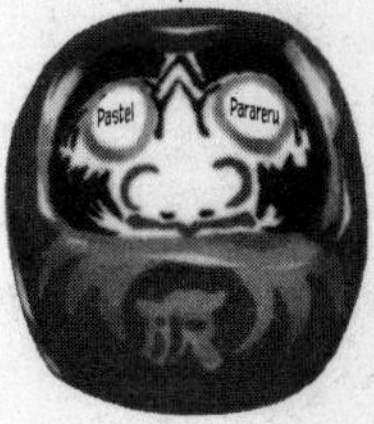
Pastel
Parareru

WHEN I WENT HOME FOR NEW YEAR'S THE OTHER DAY, I FOUND A DARUMA DOLL. WRITTEN ON ONE OF ITS EYES WAS THE NAME OF THIS MANGA, "PASTEL." ON ITS OTHER EYE WAS THE TITLE "PARARERU," ANOTHER MANGA SERIES I WROTE. WHAT THE HECK? ISN'T THIS AGAINST THE RULES OF THE DARUMA? BUT MY DAD (HE'S THE ONE WHO WROTE ON THE DARUMA) SAID, "HEY, IT WORKED DIDN'T IT?" MAYBE THE FACT THAT I HAVE THIS SERIES IS ALL THANKS TO THIS LITTLE DARUMA.

Honorifics Explained

Throughout the Del Rey Manga books, you will find Japanese honorifics left intact in the translations. For those not familiar with how the Japanese use honorifics, and, more important, how they differ from American honorifics, we present this brief overview.

Politeness has always been a critical facet of Japanese culture. Ever since the feudal era, when Japan was a highly stratified society, use of honorifics—which can be defined as polite speech that indicates relationship or status—has played an essential role in the Japanese language. When addressing someone in Japanese, an honorific usually takes the form of a suffix attached to one's name (example: "Asuna-san"), as a title at the end of one's name, or in place of the name itself (example: "Negi-sensei" or simply "Sensei!").

Honorifics can be expressions of respect or endearment. In the context of manga and anime, honorifics give insight into the nature of the relationship between characters. Many English translations leave out these important honorifics, and therefore distort the feel of the original Japanese. Because Japanese honorifics contain nuances that English honorifics lack, it is our policy at Del Rey not to translate them. Here, instead, is a guide to some of the honorifics you may encounter in Del Rey Manga.

-san: This is the most common honorific and is equivalent to Mr., Miss, Ms., Mrs. It is the all-purpose honorific and can be used in any situation where politeness is required.

-sama: This is one level higher than "-san" and is used to confer great respect.

-dono: This comes from the word "tono," which means "lord." It is even a higher level than "-sama" and confers utmost respect.

-kun: This suffix is used at the end of boys' names to express familiarity or endearment. It is also sometimes used by men amongst friends, or when addressing someone younger or of a lower station.

-chan: This is used to express endearment, mostly toward girls. It is also used for little boys, pets, and even among lovers. It gives a sense of childish cuteness.

Bozu: This is an informal way to refer to a boy, similar to the English terms "kid" or "squirt."

**Sempai/
Senpai:** This title suggests that the addressee is one's senior in a group or organization. It is most often used in a school setting, where underclassmen refer to their upperclassmen as "sempai." It can also be used in the workplace, such as when a newer employee addresses an employee who has seniority in the company.

Kohai: This is the opposite of "-sempai," and is used toward underclassmen in school or newcomers in the workplace. It connotes that the addressee is of a lower station.

Sensei: Literally meaning "one who has come before," this title is used for teachers, doctors, or masters of any profession or art.

-[blank]: This is usually forgotten in these lists, but it is perhaps the most significant difference between Japanese and English. The lack of honorific means that the speaker has permission to address the person in a very intimate way. Usually, only family, spouses, or very close friends have this kind of permission. Known as *yobisute*, it can be gratifying when someone who has earned the intimacy starts to call one by one's name without an honorific. But when that intimacy hasn't been earned, it can also be very insulting.

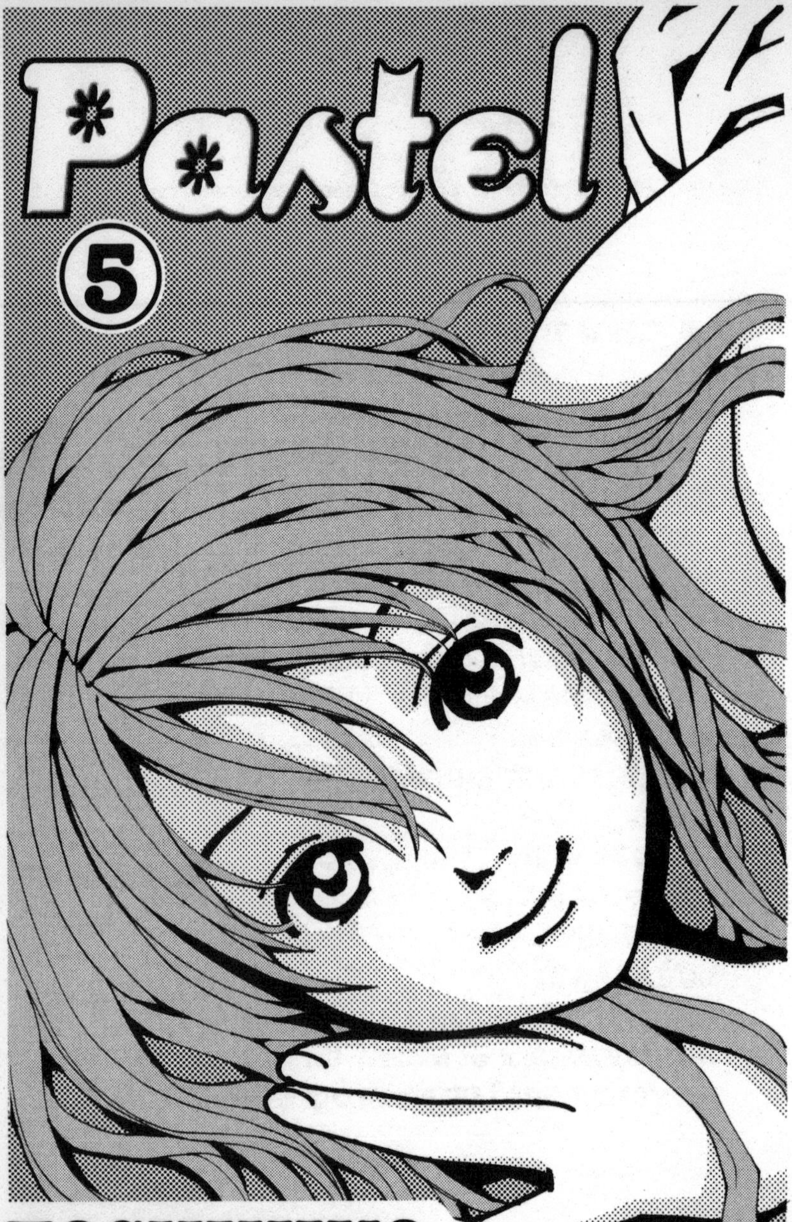
Pastel
5

TOSHIHIKO KOBAYASHI

TRANSLATED AND ADAPTED BY DAVID URY

LETTERED BY FOLTZ DESIGN

Pastel

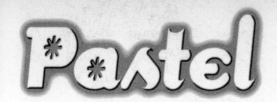

CONTENTS

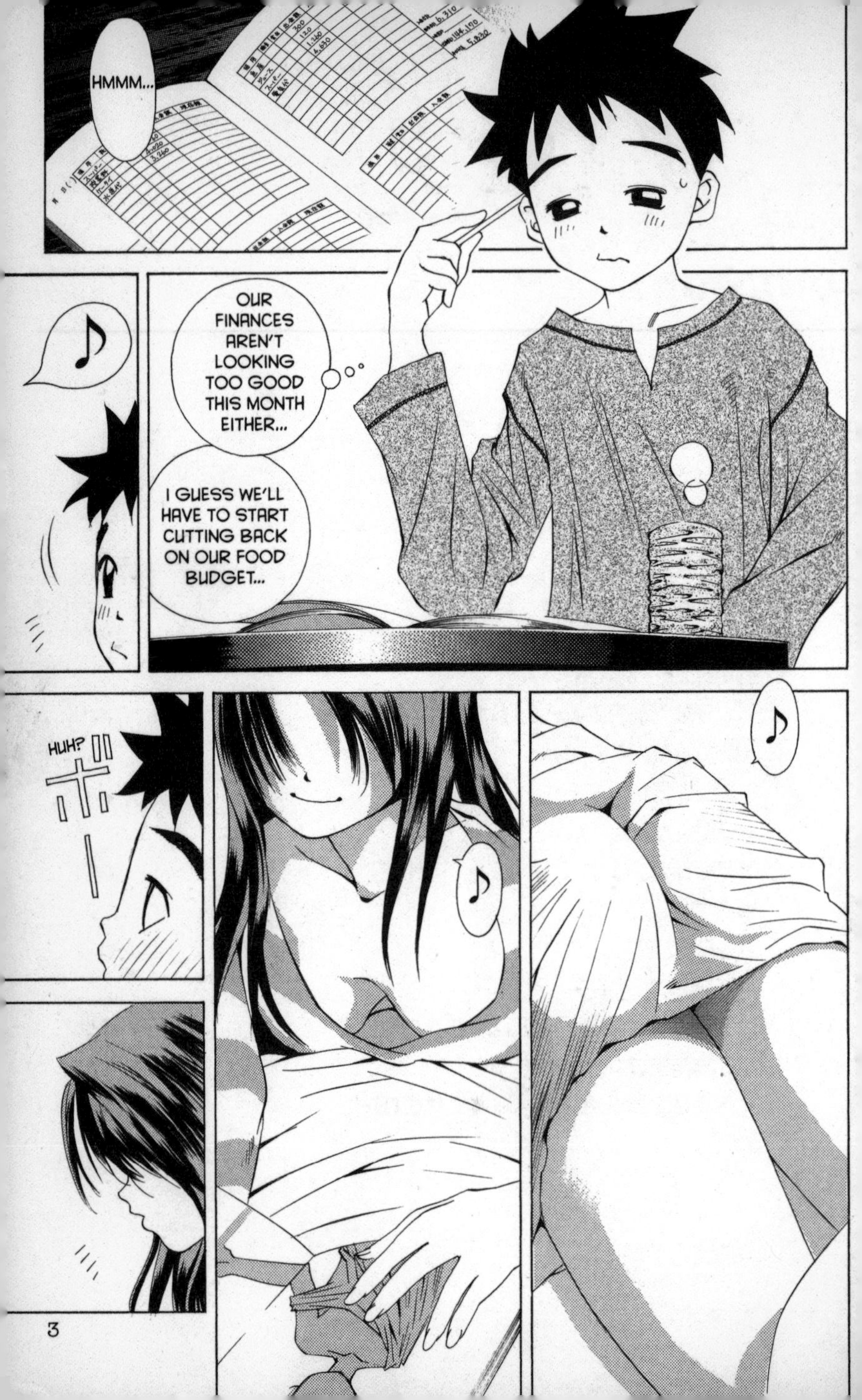
HMMM...
OUR FINANCES AREN'T LOOKING TOO GOOD THIS MONTH EITHER...
I GUESS WE'LL HAVE TO START CUTTING BACK ON OUR FOOD BUDGET...
♪
♪
♪
HUH?
ボー

Pastel

MIRACLE 32: ONLY ONE

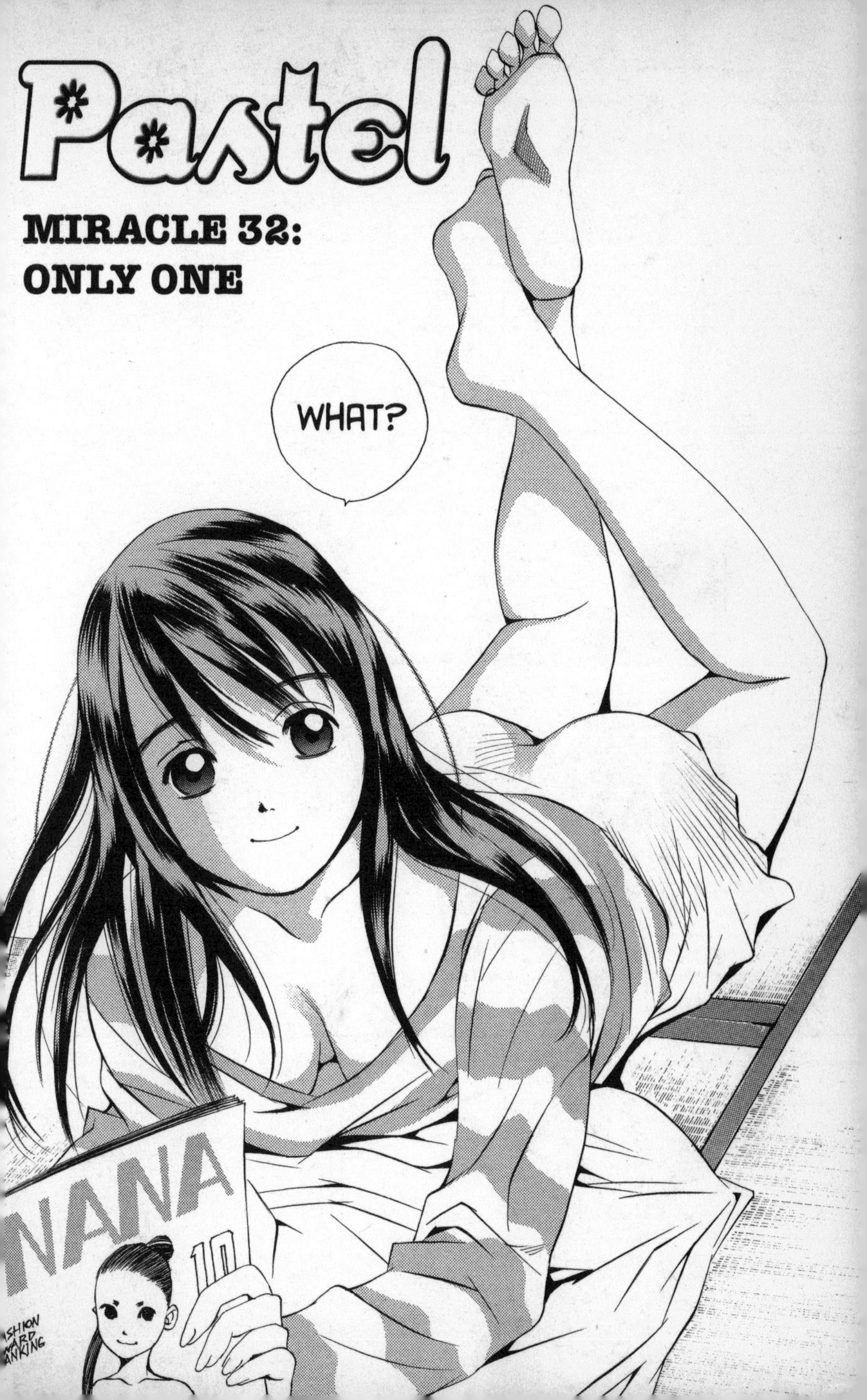
WHAT?
NANA
10

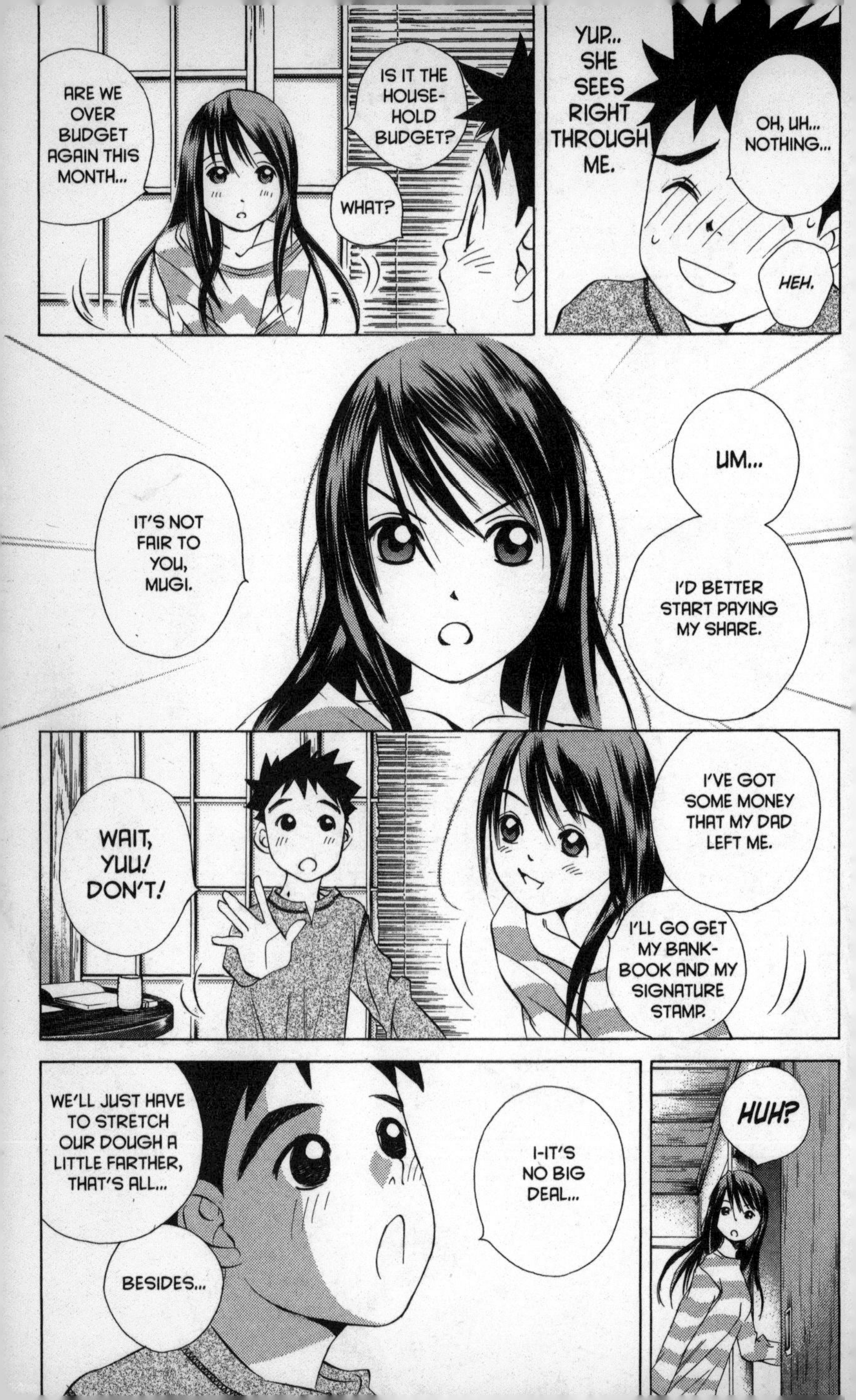
OH, UH... NOTHING...
HEH.
YUP... SHE SEES RIGHT THROUGH ME.
IS IT THE HOUSE-HOLD BUDGET?
WHAT?
ARE WE OVER BUDGET AGAIN THIS MONTH...
UM...
I'D BETTER START PAYING MY SHARE.
IT'S NOT FAIR TO YOU, MUGI.
I'VE GOT SOME MONEY THAT MY DAD LEFT ME.
I'LL GO GET MY BANK-BOOK AND MY SIGNATURE STAMP.
WAIT, YUU! DON'T!
HUH?
I-IT'S NO BIG DEAL...
WE'LL JUST HAVE TO STRETCH OUR DOUGH A LITTLE FARTHER, THAT'S ALL...
BESIDES...

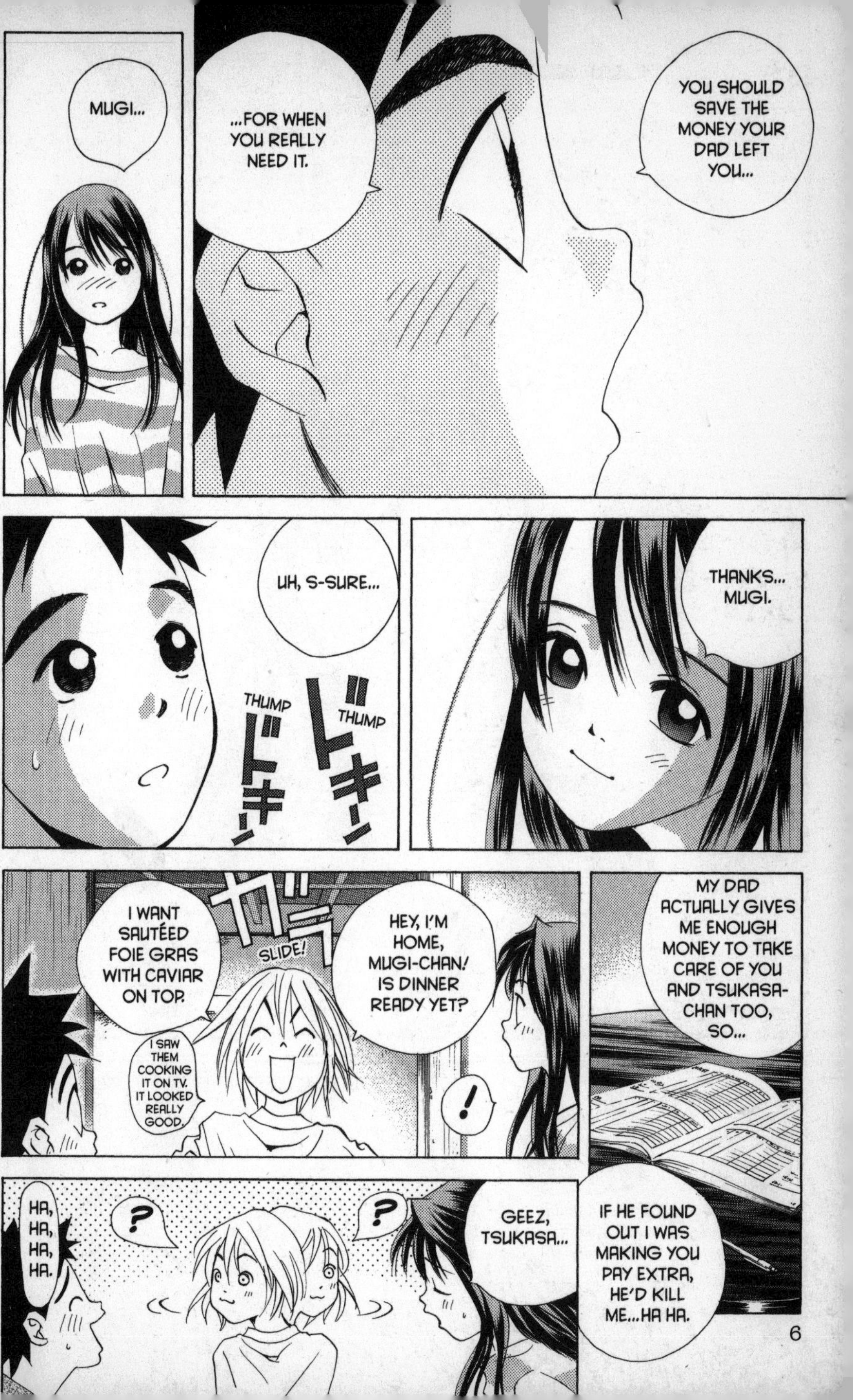
YOU SHOULD SAVE THE MONEY YOUR DAD LEFT YOU...
...FOR WHEN YOU REALLY NEED IT.
MUGI...
THANKS... MUGI.
UH, S-SURE...
THUMP
THUMP
MY DAD ACTUALLY GIVES ME ENOUGH MONEY TO TAKE CARE OF YOU AND TSUKASA-CHAN TOO, SO...
HEY, I'M HOME, MUGI-CHAN! IS DINNER READY YET?
SLIDE!
I WANT SAUTÉED FOIE GRAS WITH CAVIAR ON TOP.
!
I SAW THEM COOKING IT ON TV. IT LOOKED REALLY GOOD.
IF HE FOUND OUT I WAS MAKING YOU PAY EXTRA, HE'D KILL ME...HA HA.
GEEZ, TSUKASA...
?
?
HA, HA, HA, HA.

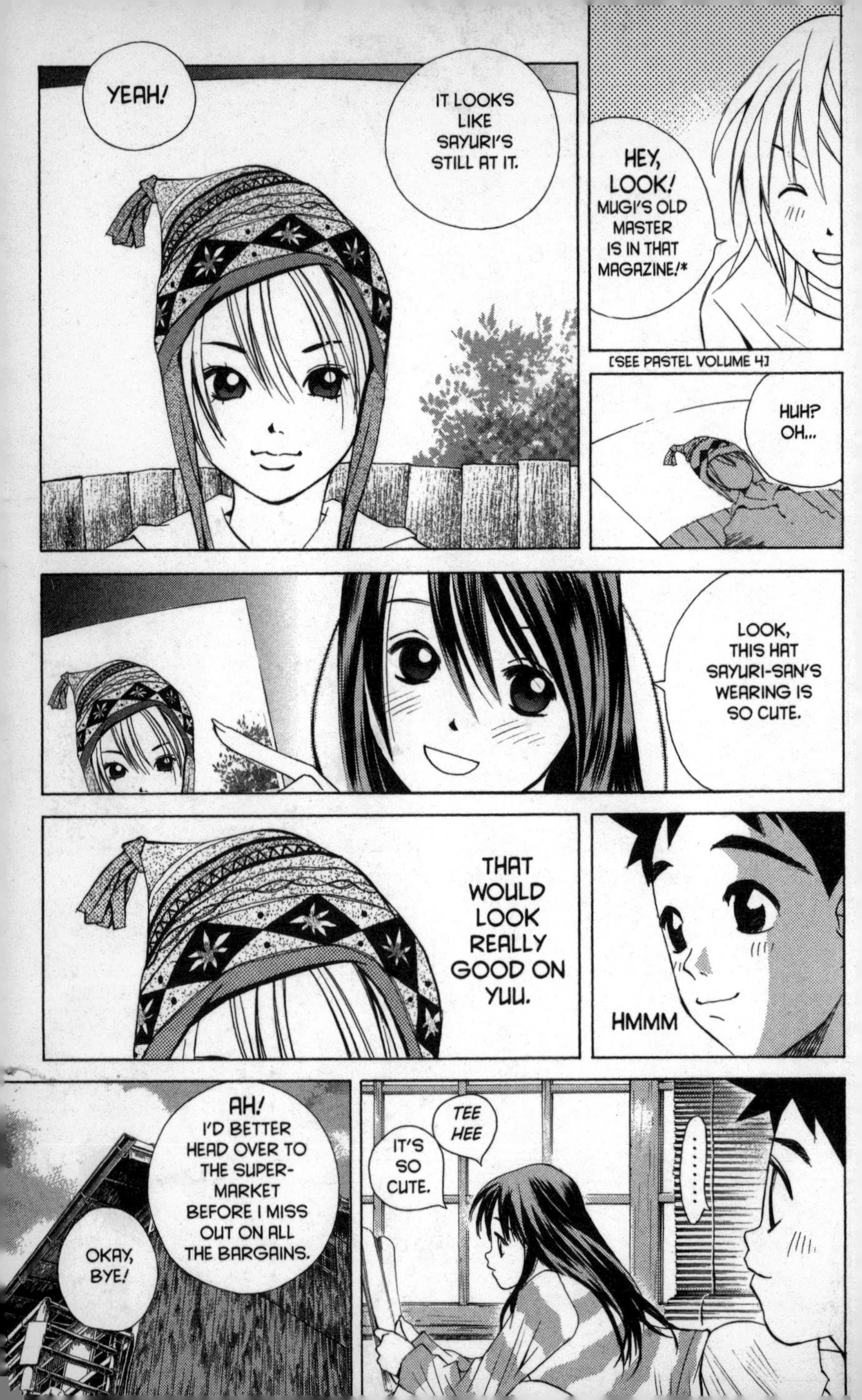
HEY, LOOK! MUGI'S OLD MASTER IS IN THAT MAGAZINE!*
[SEE PASTEL VOLUME 4]
HUH? OH...
IT LOOKS LIKE SAYURI'S STILL AT IT.
YEAH!
LOOK, THIS HAT SAYURI-SAN'S WEARING IS SO CUTE.
HMMM
THAT WOULD LOOK REALLY GOOD ON YUU.
......
TEE HEE
IT'S SO CUTE.
AH! I'D BETTER HEAD OVER TO THE SUPER-MARKET BEFORE I MISS OUT ON ALL THE BARGAINS.
OKAY, BYE!

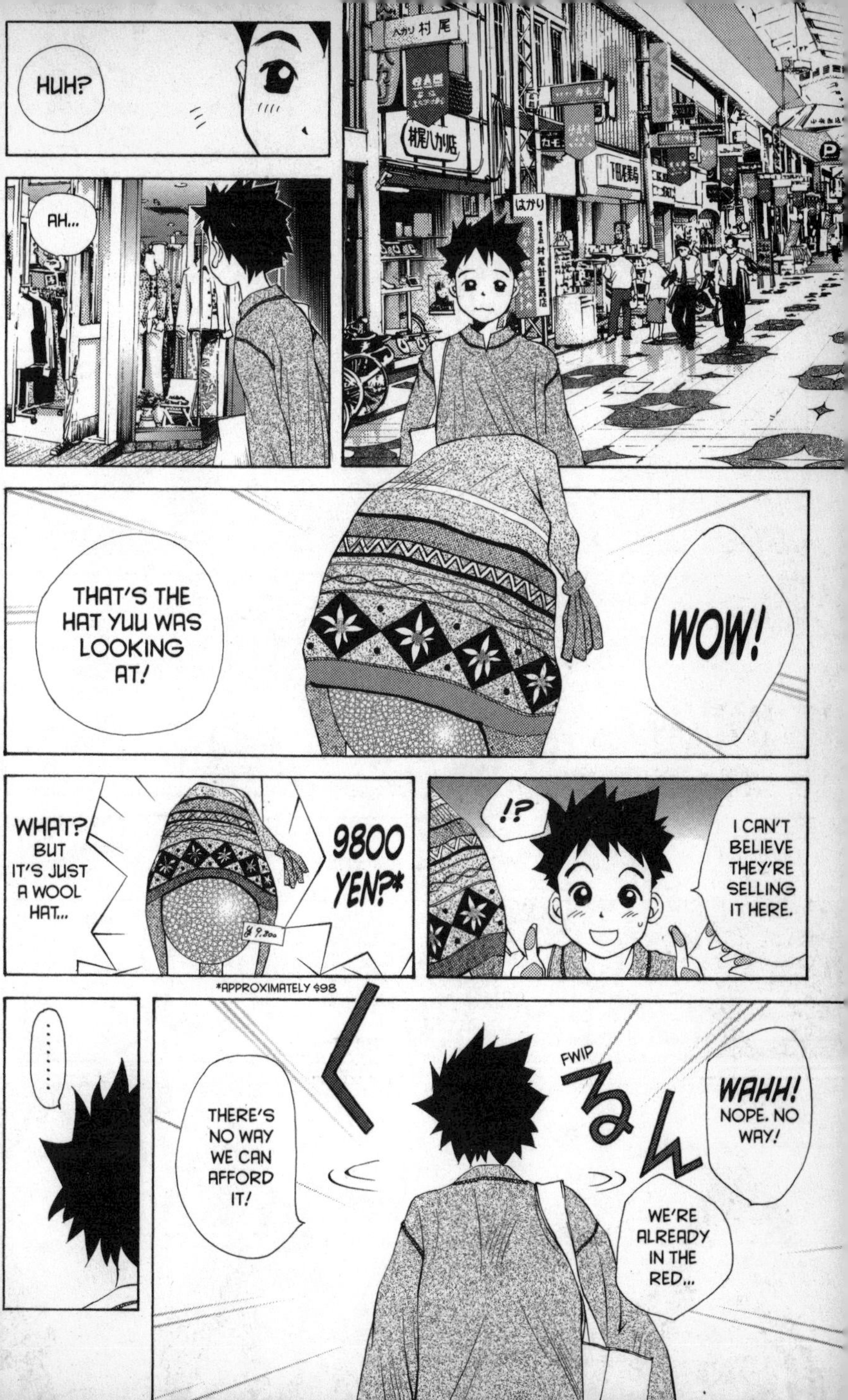
村尾ハカリ店
はかり
HUH?
AH...
WOW!
THAT'S THE HAT YUU WAS LOOKING AT!
!?
I CAN'T BELIEVE THEY'RE SELLING IT HERE.
9800 YEN?*
WHAT? BUT IT'S JUST A WOOL HAT...
¥9,800
*APPROXIMATELY $98
WAHH! NOPE. NO WAY!
FWIP
くるん
WE'RE ALREADY IN THE RED...
THERE'S NO WAY WE CAN AFFORD IT!
....

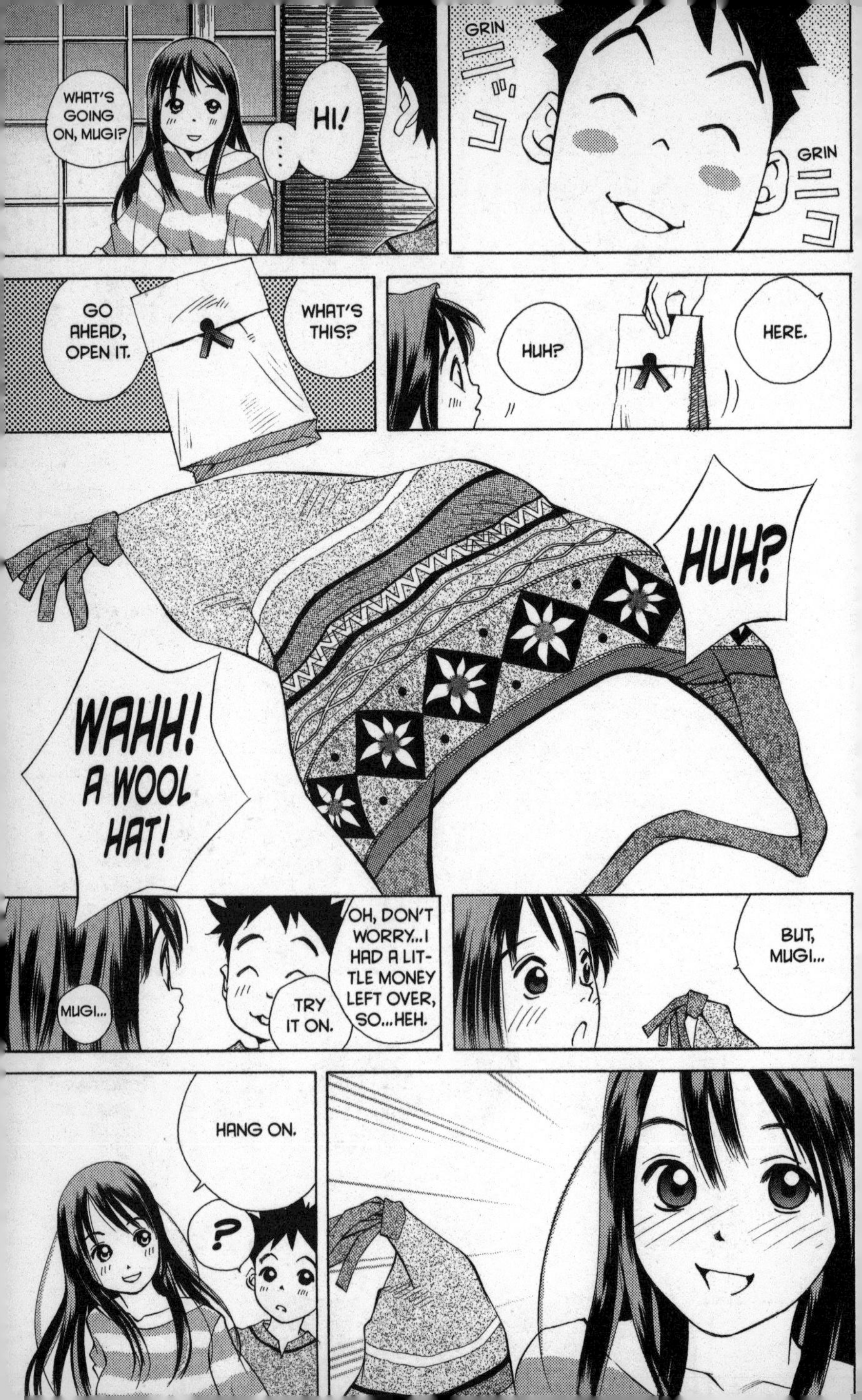
GRIN
GRIN
HI!
....
WHAT'S GOING ON, MUGI?
HERE.
HUH?
WHAT'S THIS?
GO AHEAD, OPEN IT.
HUH?
WAHH! A WOOL HAT!
BUT, MUGI...
OH, DON'T WORRY...I HAD A LIT-TLE MONEY LEFT OVER, SO...HEH.
TRY IT ON.
MUGI...
HANG ON.
?

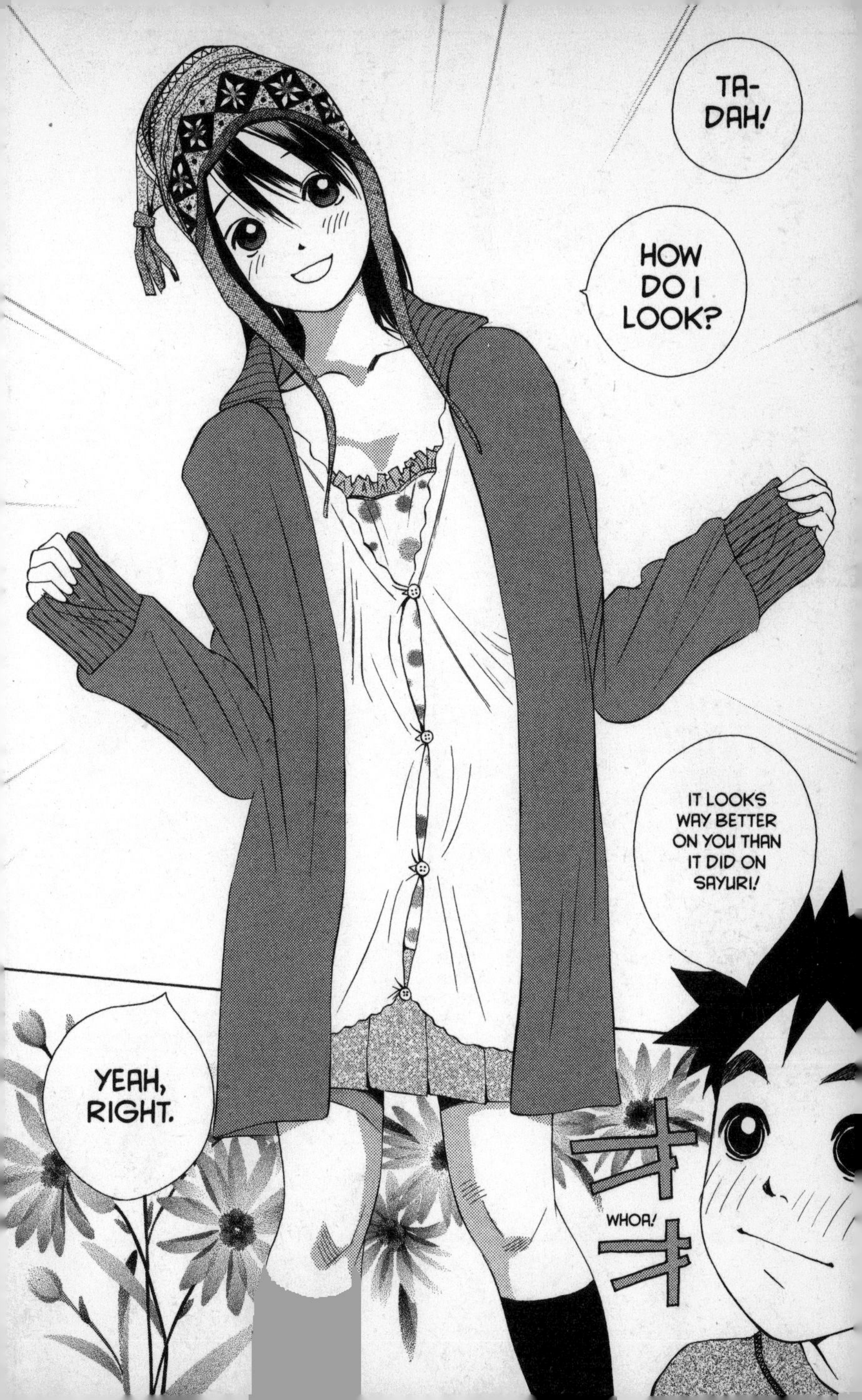
TA-DAH!
HOW DO I LOOK?
IT LOOKS WAY BETTER ON YOU THAN IT DID ON SAYURI!
WHOA!
YEAH, RIGHT.

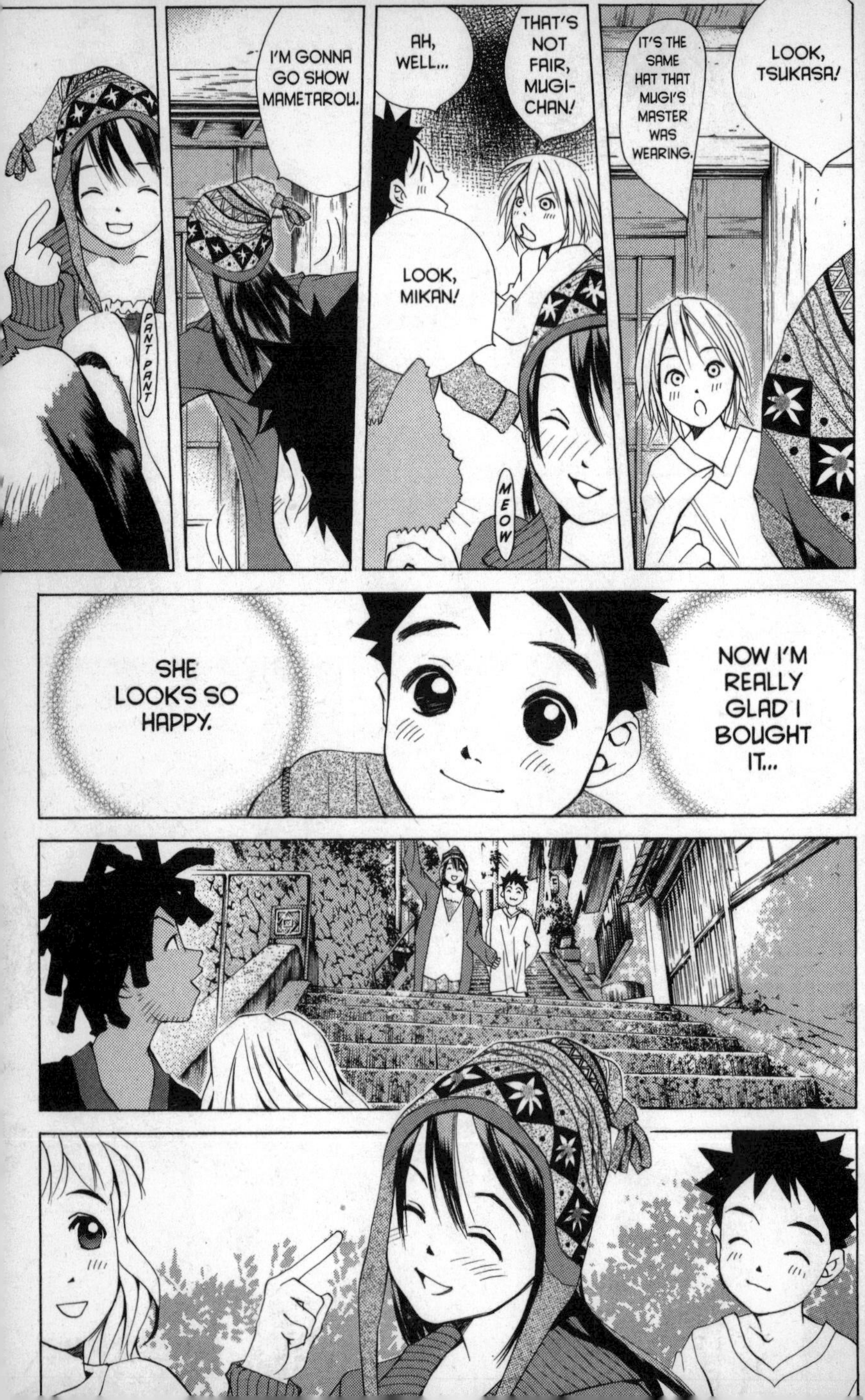
LOOK, TSUKASA!
IT'S THE SAME HAT THAT MUGI'S MASTER WAS WEARING.
THAT'S NOT FAIR, MUGI-CHAN!
AH, WELL...
LOOK, MIKAN!
MEOW
I'M GONNA GO SHOW MAMETAROU.
PANT PANT
NOW I'M REALLY GLAD I BOUGHT IT...
SHE LOOKS SO HAPPY.

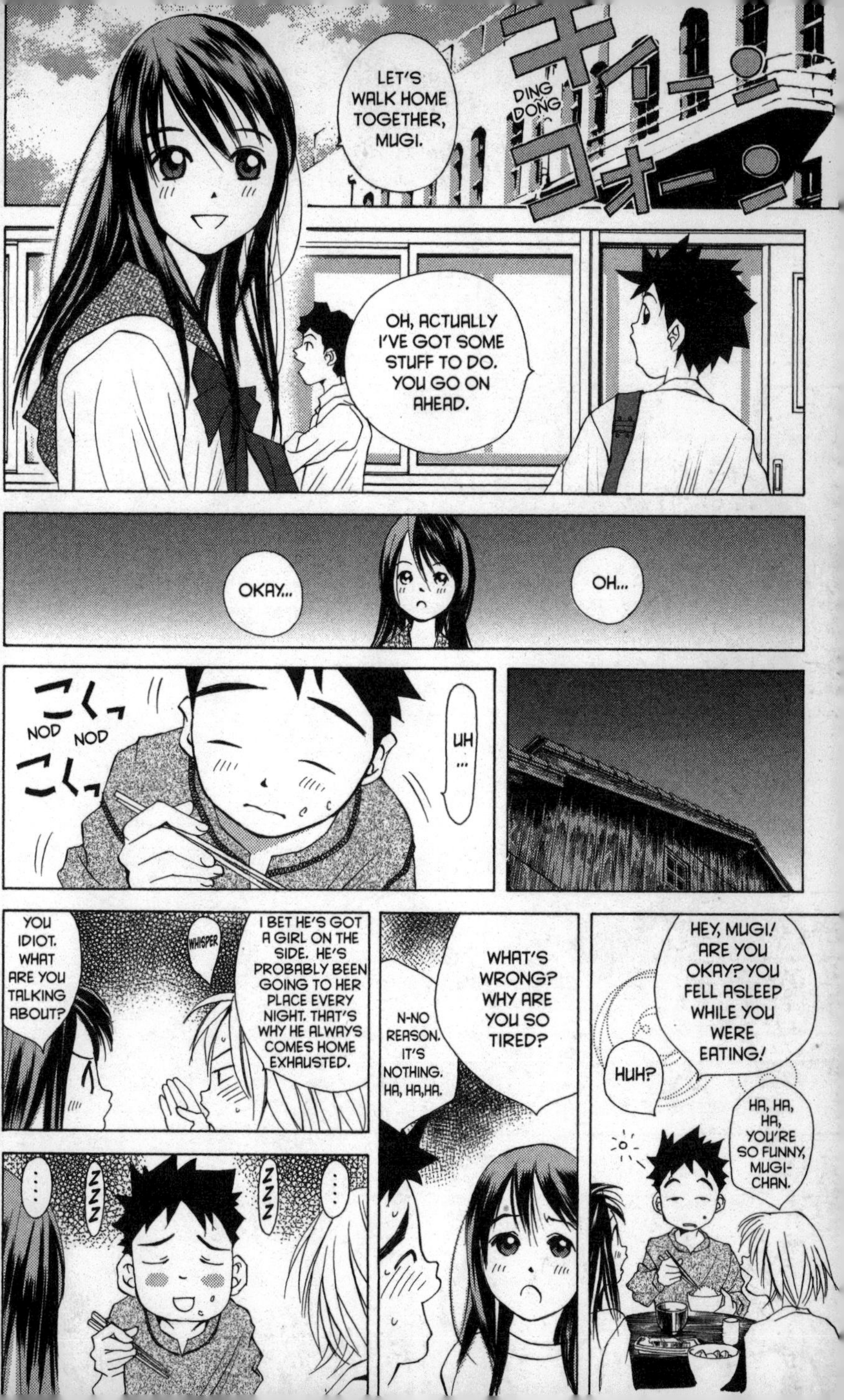
DING DONG
LET'S WALK HOME TOGETHER, MUGI.
OH, ACTUALLY I'VE GOT SOME STUFF TO DO. YOU GO ON AHEAD.
OH...
OKAY...
UH ...
こくっ
NOD NOD
こくっ
HEY, MUGI! ARE YOU OKAY? YOU FELL ASLEEP WHILE YOU WERE EATING!
HUH?
HA, HA, HA, YOU'RE SO FUNNY, MUGI-CHAN.
WHAT'S WRONG? WHY ARE YOU SO TIRED?
N-NO REASON. IT'S NOTHING. HA, HA,HA.
I BET HE'S GOT A GIRL ON THE SIDE. HE'S PROBABLY BEEN GOING TO HER PLACE EVERY NIGHT. THAT'S WHY HE ALWAYS COMES HOME EXHAUSTED.
WHISPER
YOU IDIOT. WHAT ARE YOU TALKING ABOUT?
ZZZ
....
ZZZ
....

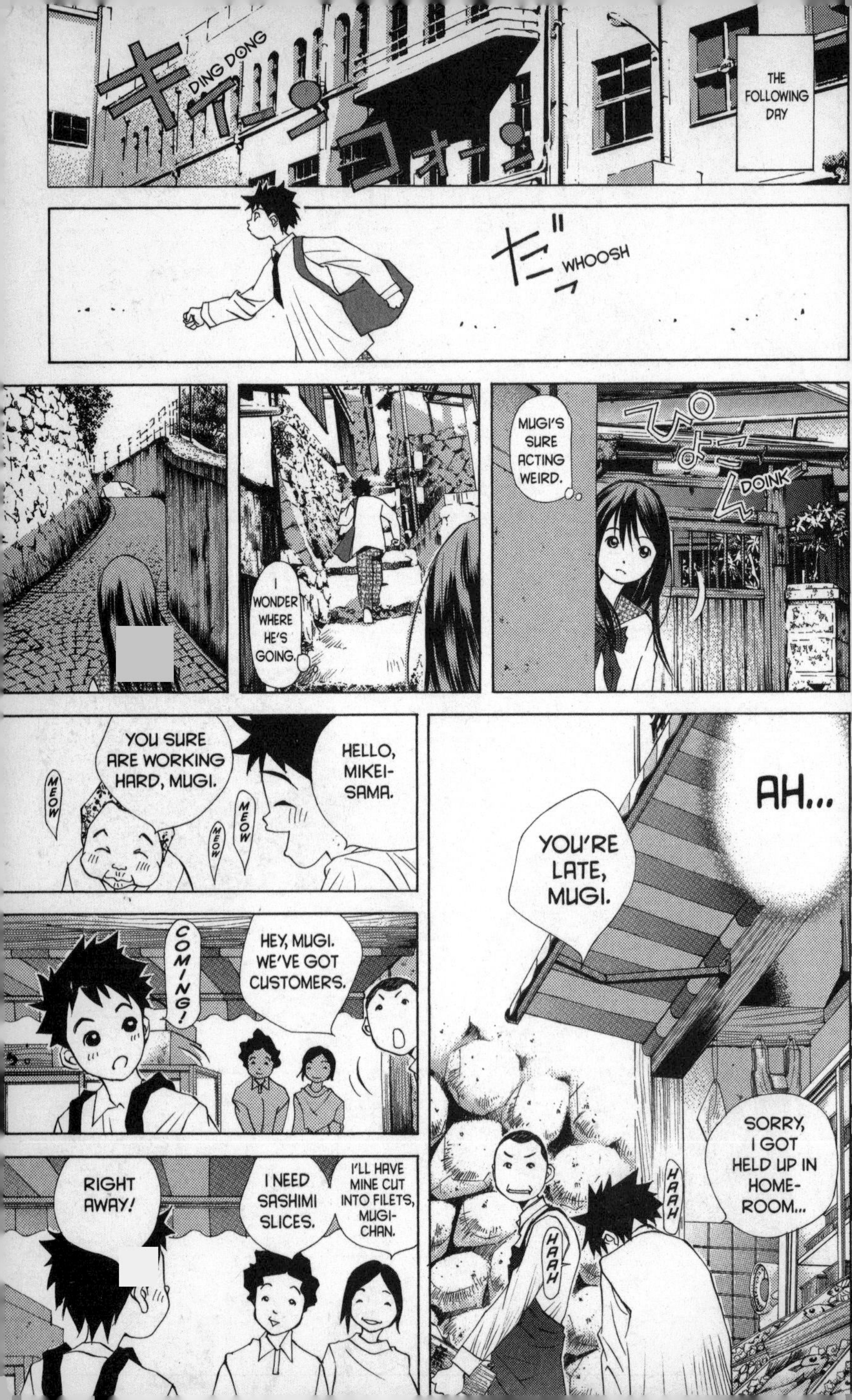
THE FOLLOWING DAY
DING DONG
WHOOSH
DOINK
MUGI'S SURE ACTING WEIRD.
I WONDER WHERE HE'S GOING.
AH...
YOU'RE LATE, MUGI.
SORRY, I GOT HELD UP IN HOME-ROOM...
HAAH
HAAH
HELLO, MIKEI-SAMA.
YOU SURE ARE WORKING HARD, MUGI.
MEOW
MEOW
MEOW
HEY, MUGI. WE'VE GOT CUSTOMERS.
COMING!
I'LL HAVE MINE CUT INTO FILETS, MUGI-CHAN.
I NEED SASHIMI SLICES.
RIGHT AWAY!

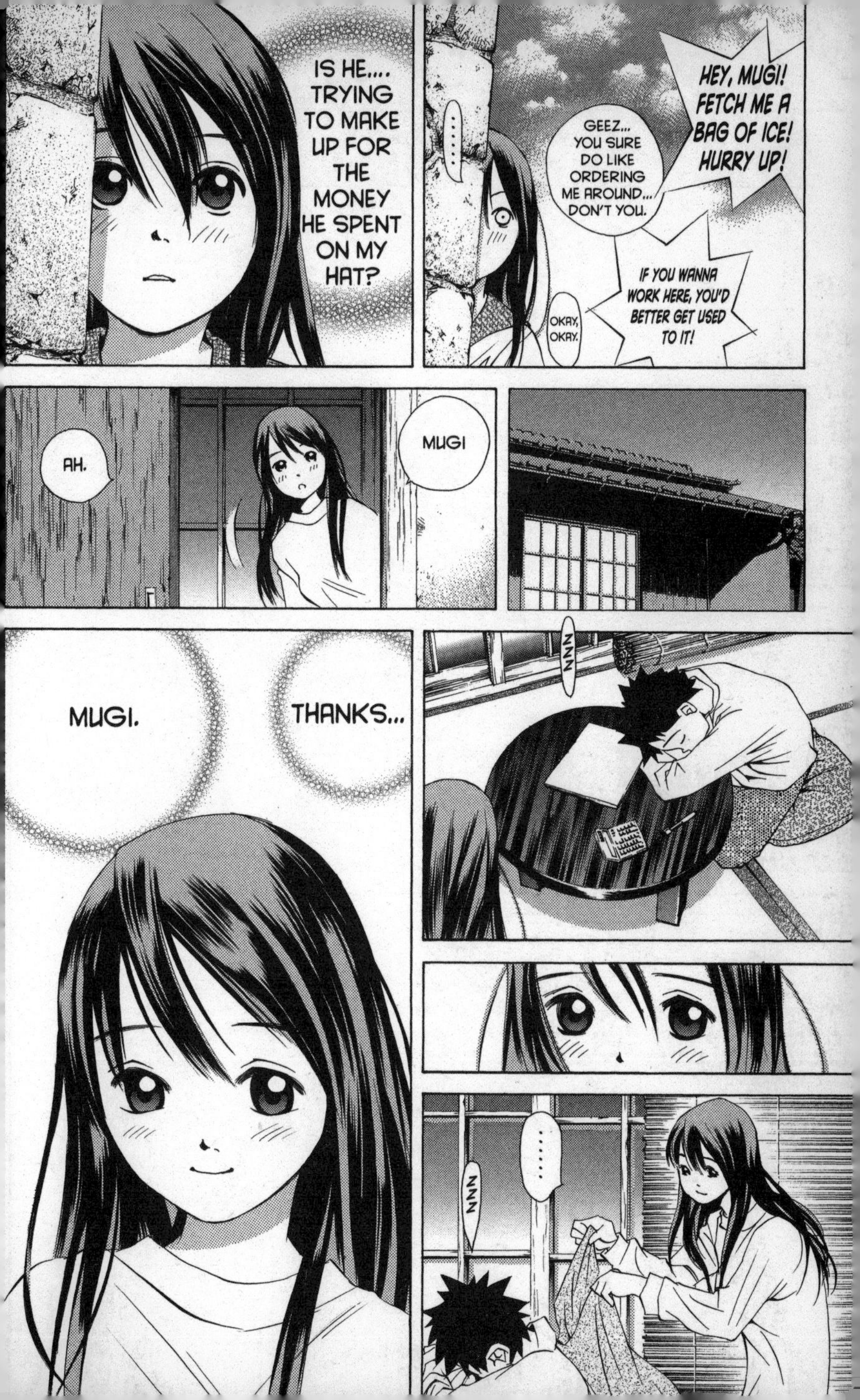
HEY, MUGI! FETCH ME A BAG OF ICE! HURRY UP!
GEEZ... YOU SURE DO LIKE ORDERING ME AROUND... DON'T YOU.
......
IF YOU WANNA WORK HERE, YOU'D BETTER GET USED TO IT!
OKAY, OKAY.
IS HE.... TRYING TO MAKE UP FOR THE MONEY HE SPENT ON MY HAT?
MUGI
AH.
ZZZ
......
ZZZ
THANKS...
MUGI.

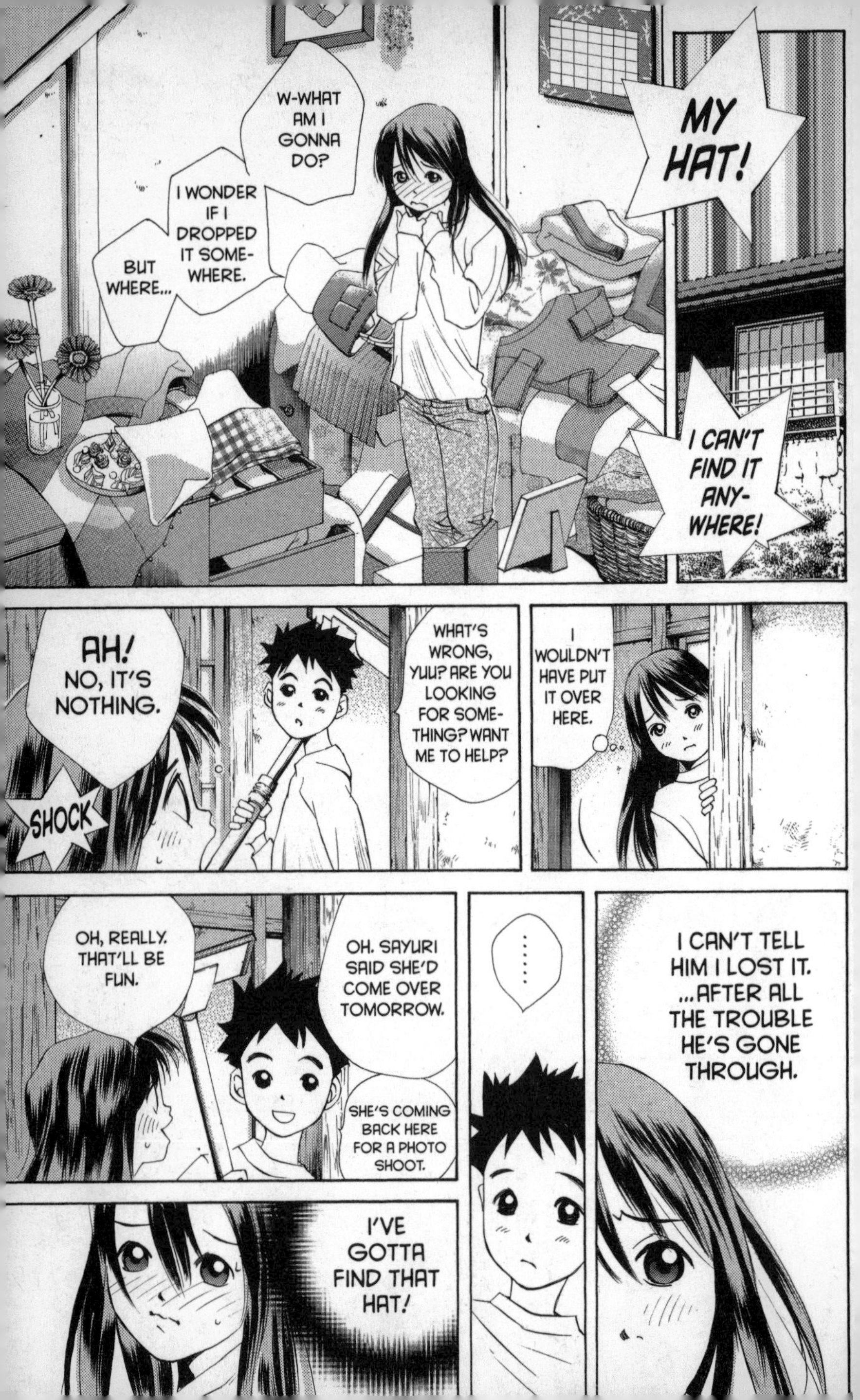
MY HAT!
I CAN'T FIND IT ANY-WHERE!
W-WHAT AM I GONNA DO?
I WONDER IF I DROPPED IT SOME-WHERE.
BUT WHERE...
I WOULDN'T HAVE PUT IT OVER HERE.
WHAT'S WRONG, YUU? ARE YOU LOOKING FOR SOME-THING? WANT ME TO HELP?
AH! NO, IT'S NOTHING.
SHOCK
I CAN'T TELL HIM I LOST IT. ...AFTER ALL THE TROUBLE HE'S GONE THROUGH.
......
OH. SAYURI SAID SHE'D COME OVER TOMORROW.
SHE'S COMING BACK HERE FOR A PHOTO SHOOT.
OH, REALLY. THAT'LL BE FUN.
I'VE GOTTA FIND THAT HAT!

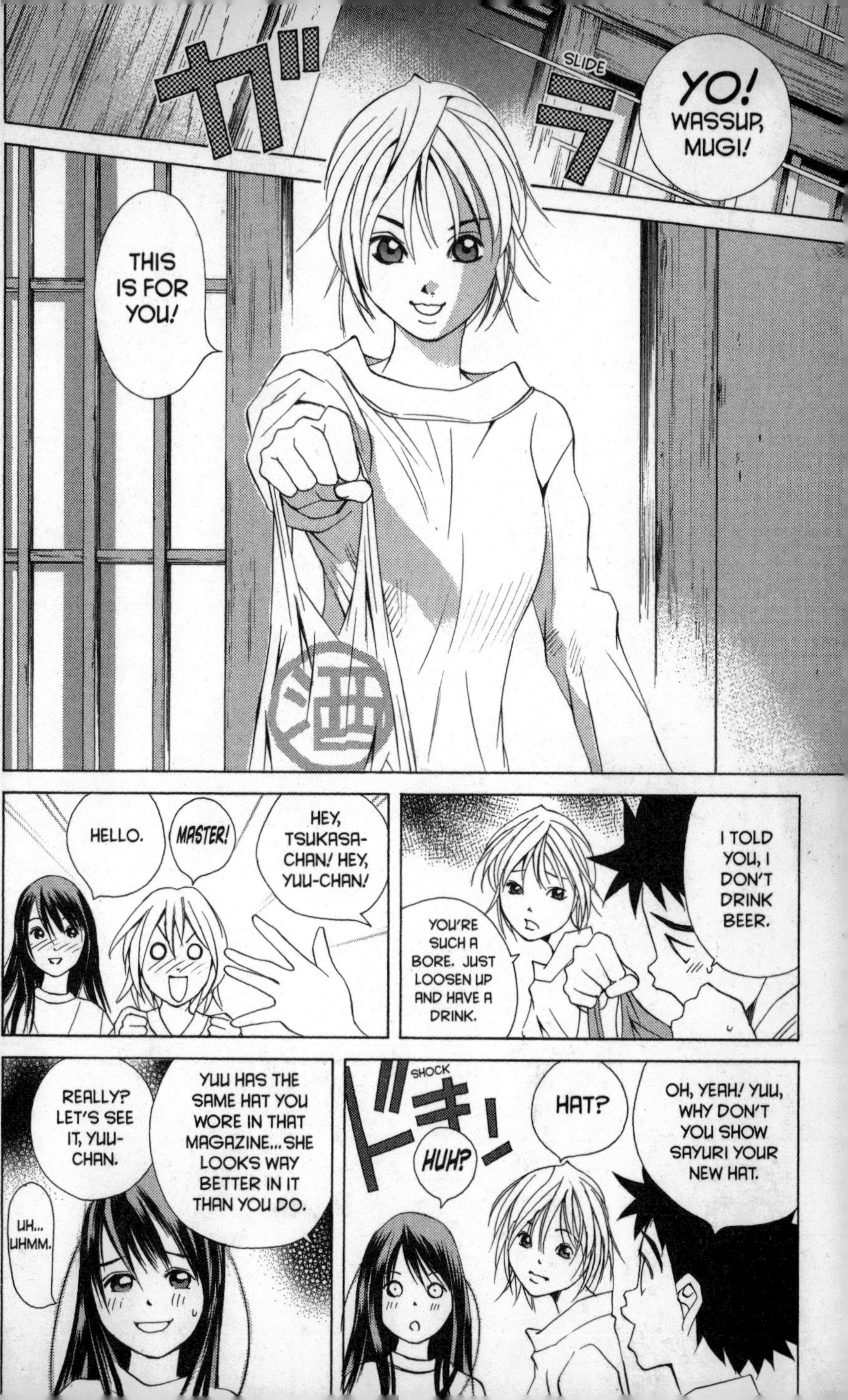
SLIDE
YO! WASSUP, MUGI!
THIS IS FOR YOU!
I TOLD YOU, I DON'T DRINK BEER.
YOU'RE SUCH A BORE. JUST LOOSEN UP AND HAVE A DRINK.
HEY, TSUKASA-CHAN! HEY, YUU-CHAN!
MASTER!
HELLO.
OH, YEAH! YUU, WHY DON'T YOU SHOW SAYURI YOUR NEW HAT.
HAT?
SHOCK
HUH?
YUU HAS THE SAME HAT YOU WORE IN THAT MAGAZINE...SHE LOOKS WAY BETTER IN IT THAN YOU DO.
REALLY? LET'S SEE IT, YUU-CHAN.
UH... UHMM.

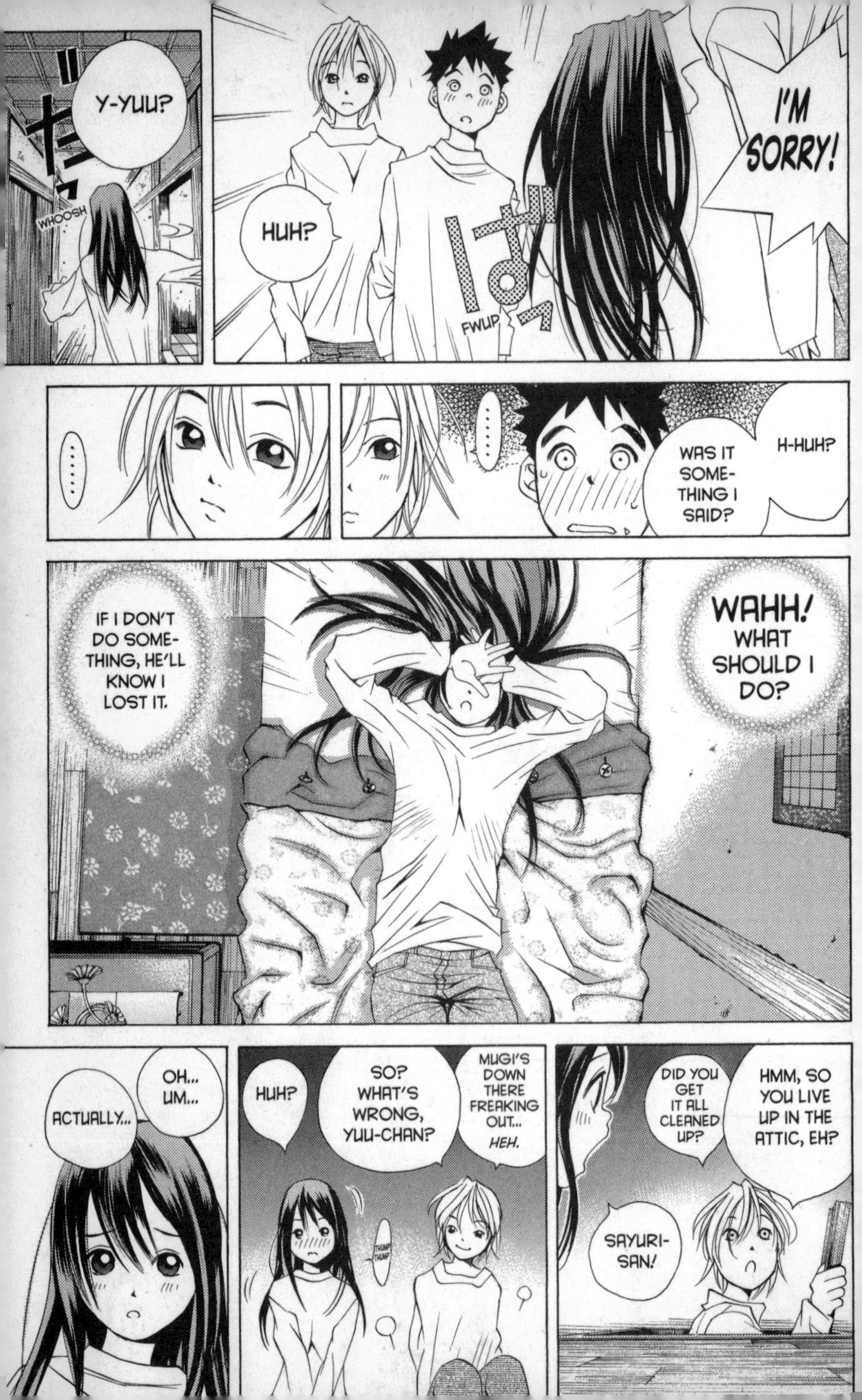
I'M SORRY!
HUH?
FWUP
Y-YUU?
WHOOSH
H-HUH?
WAS IT SOME-THING I SAID?
......
......
WAHH! WHAT SHOULD I DO?
IF I DON'T DO SOME-THING, HE'LL KNOW I LOST IT.
HMM, SO YOU LIVE UP IN THE ATTIC, EH?
DID YOU GET IT ALL CLEANED UP?
SAYURI-SAN!
MUGI'S DOWN THERE FREAKING OUT... HEH.
SO? WHAT'S WRONG, YUU-CHAN?
HUH?
THUMP THUMP
OH... UM...
ACTUALLY...

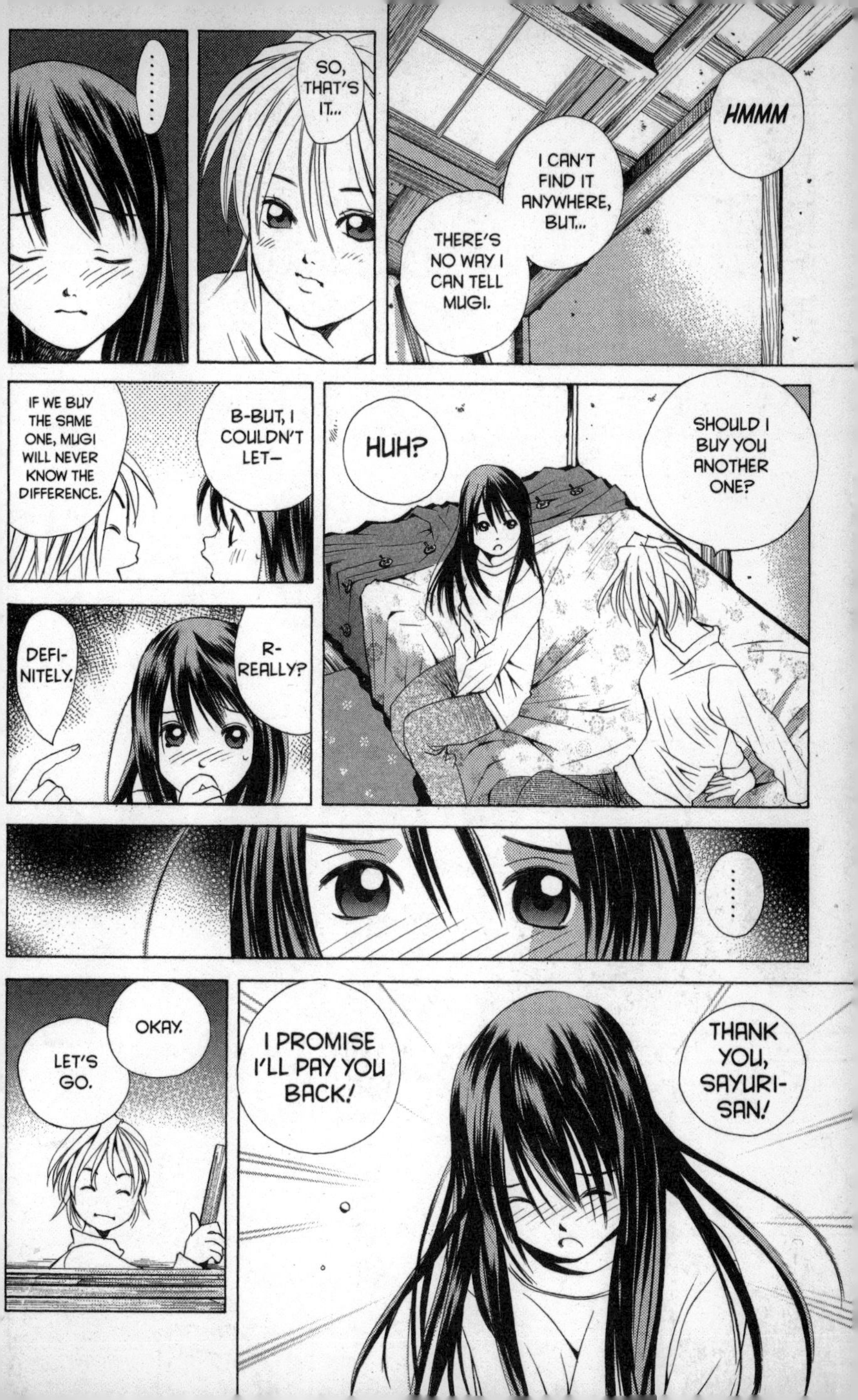
HMMM
I CAN'T FIND IT ANYWHERE, BUT...
THERE'S NO WAY I CAN TELL MUGI.
SO, THAT'S IT...
......
SHOULD I BUY YOU ANOTHER ONE?
HUH?
B-BUT, I COULDN'T LET—
IF WE BUY THE SAME ONE, MUGI WILL NEVER KNOW THE DIFFERENCE.
R-REALLY?
DEFINITELY.
......
THANK YOU, SAYURI-SAN!
I PROMISE I'LL PAY YOU BACK!
OKAY.
LET'S GO.

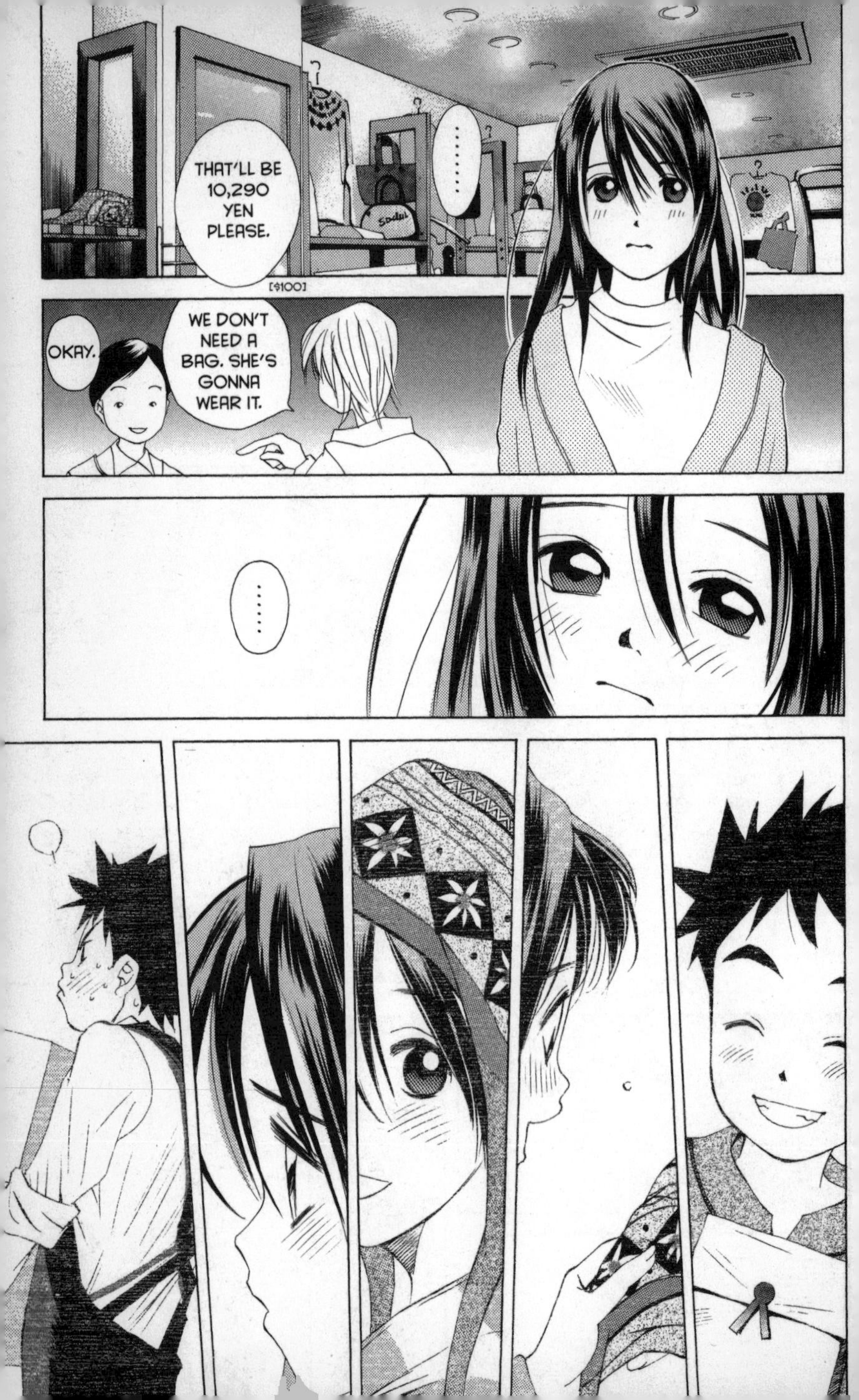
......
THAT'LL BE 10,290 YEN PLEASE.
[$100]
WE DON'T NEED A BAG. SHE'S GONNA WEAR IT.
OKAY.
......

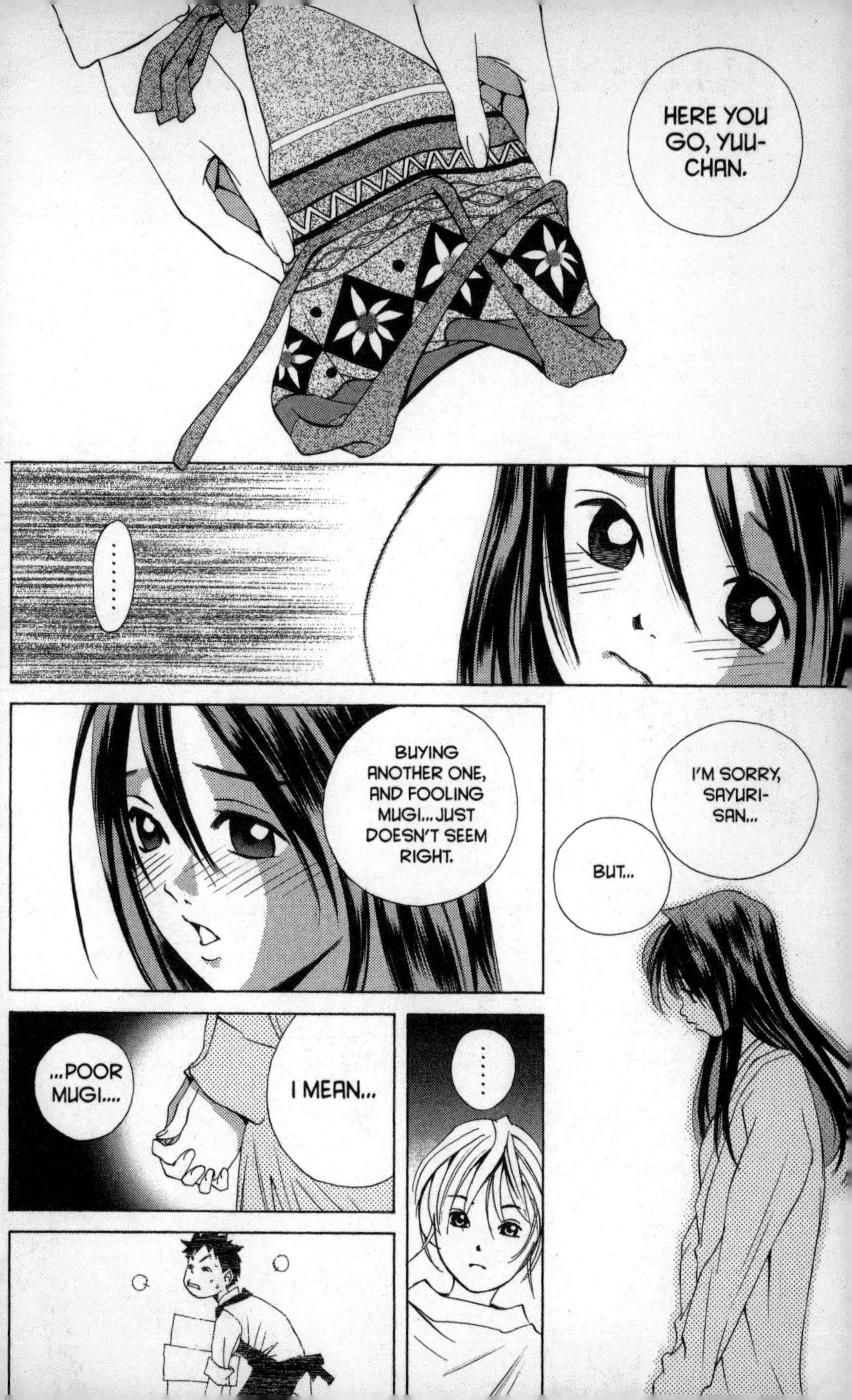
HERE YOU GO, YUU-CHAN.
......
I'M SORRY, SAYURI-SAN...
BUT...
BUYING ANOTHER ONE, AND FOOLING MUGI...JUST DOESN'T SEEM RIGHT.
......
I MEAN...
...POOR MUGI....

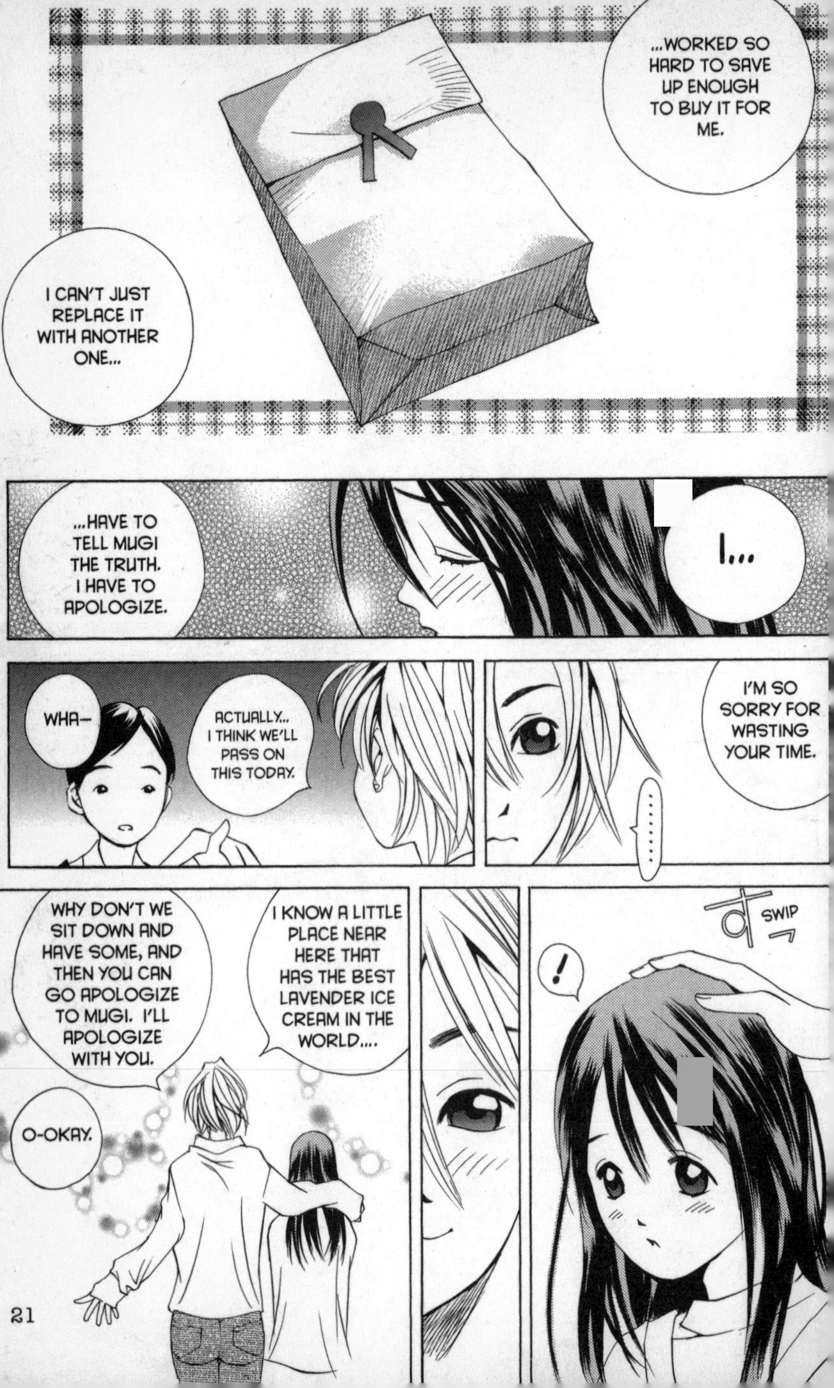
...WORKED SO HARD TO SAVE UP ENOUGH TO BUY IT FOR ME.
I CAN'T JUST REPLACE IT WITH ANOTHER ONE...
I...
...HAVE TO TELL MUGI THE TRUTH. I HAVE TO APOLOGIZE.
I'M SO SORRY FOR WASTING YOUR TIME.
......
ACTUALLY... I THINK WE'LL PASS ON THIS TODAY.
WHA–
SWIP
!
I KNOW A LITTLE PLACE NEAR HERE THAT HAS THE BEST LAVENDER ICE CREAM IN THE WORLD....
WHY DON'T WE SIT DOWN AND HAVE SOME, AND THEN YOU CAN GO APOLOGIZE TO MUGI. I'LL APOLOGIZE WITH YOU.
O-OKAY.

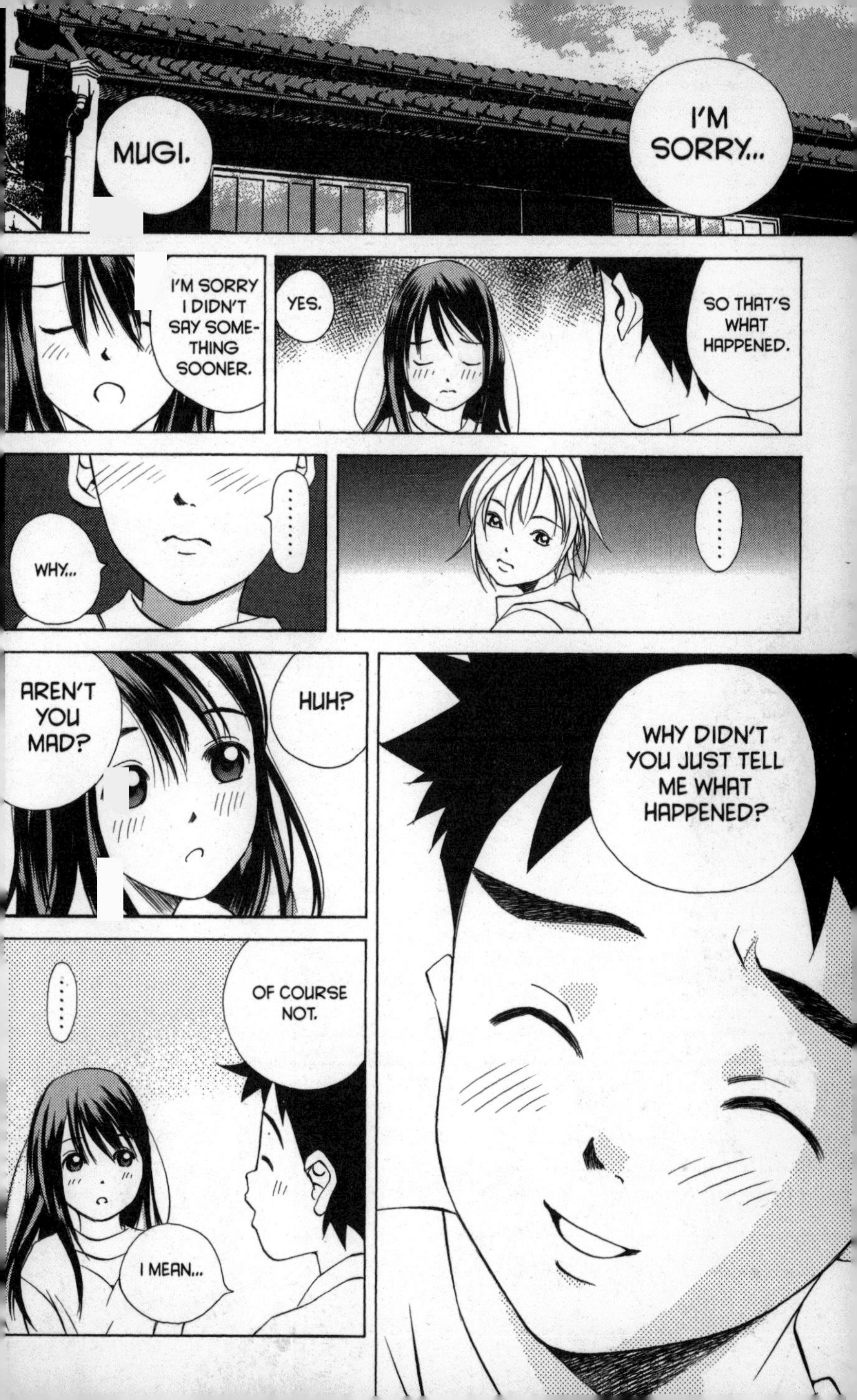
I'M SORRY...
MUGI.
SO THAT'S WHAT HAPPENED.
YES.
I'M SORRY I DIDN'T SAY SOME-THING SOONER.
......
......
WHY...
WHY DIDN'T YOU JUST TELL ME WHAT HAPPENED?
HUH?
AREN'T YOU MAD?
OF COURSE NOT.
......
I MEAN...

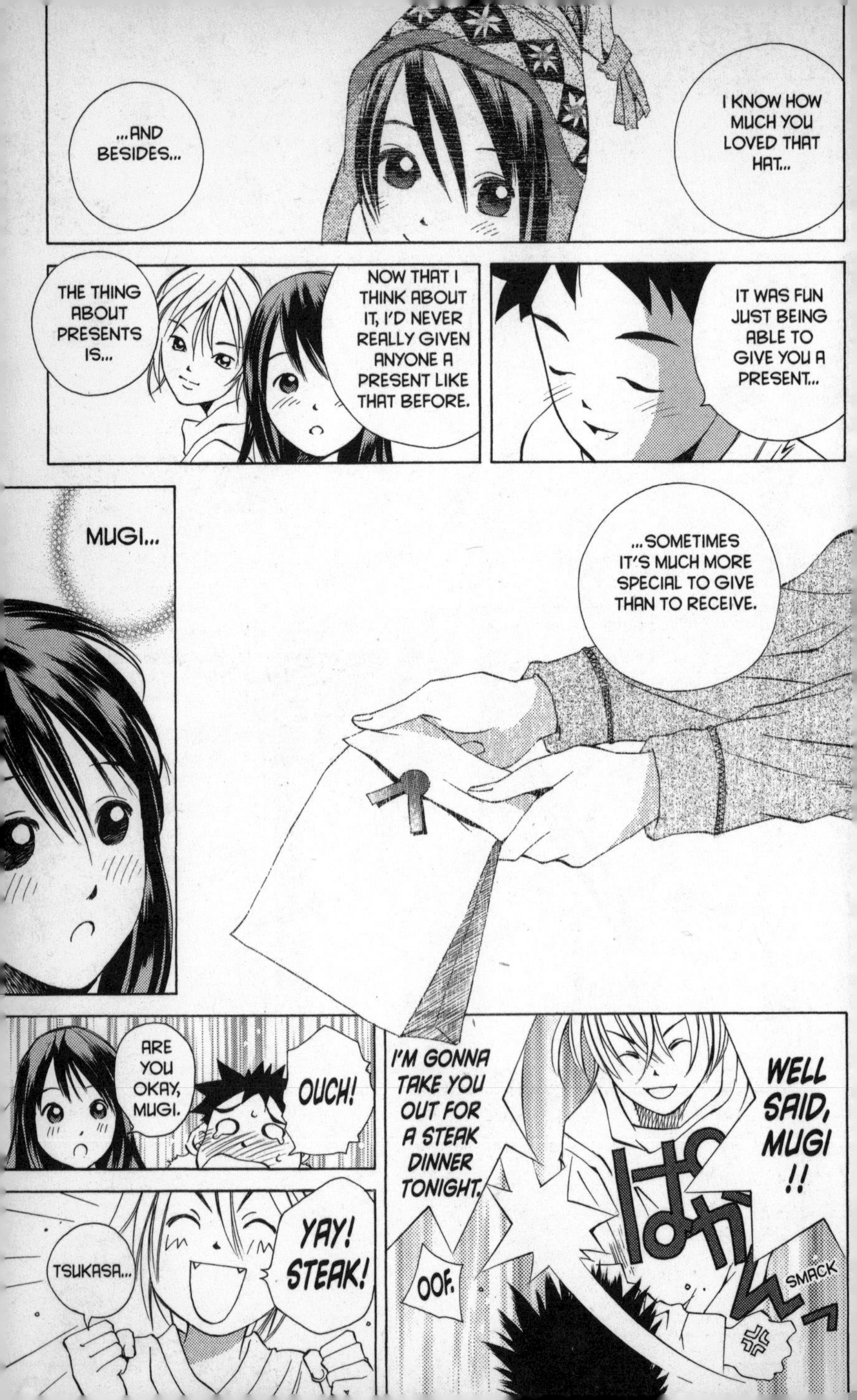
I KNOW HOW MUCH YOU LOVED THAT HAT...
...AND BESIDES...
IT WAS FUN JUST BEING ABLE TO GIVE YOU A PRESENT...
NOW THAT I THINK ABOUT IT, I'D NEVER REALLY GIVEN ANYONE A PRESENT LIKE THAT BEFORE.
THE THING ABOUT PRESENTS IS...
...SOMETIMES IT'S MUCH MORE SPECIAL TO GIVE THAN TO RECEIVE.
MUGI...
WELL SAID, MUGI!!
I'M GONNA TAKE YOU OUT FOR A STEAK DINNER TONIGHT.
SMACK
OOF.
OUCH!
ARE YOU OKAY, MUGI.
YAY! STEAK!
TSUKASA...

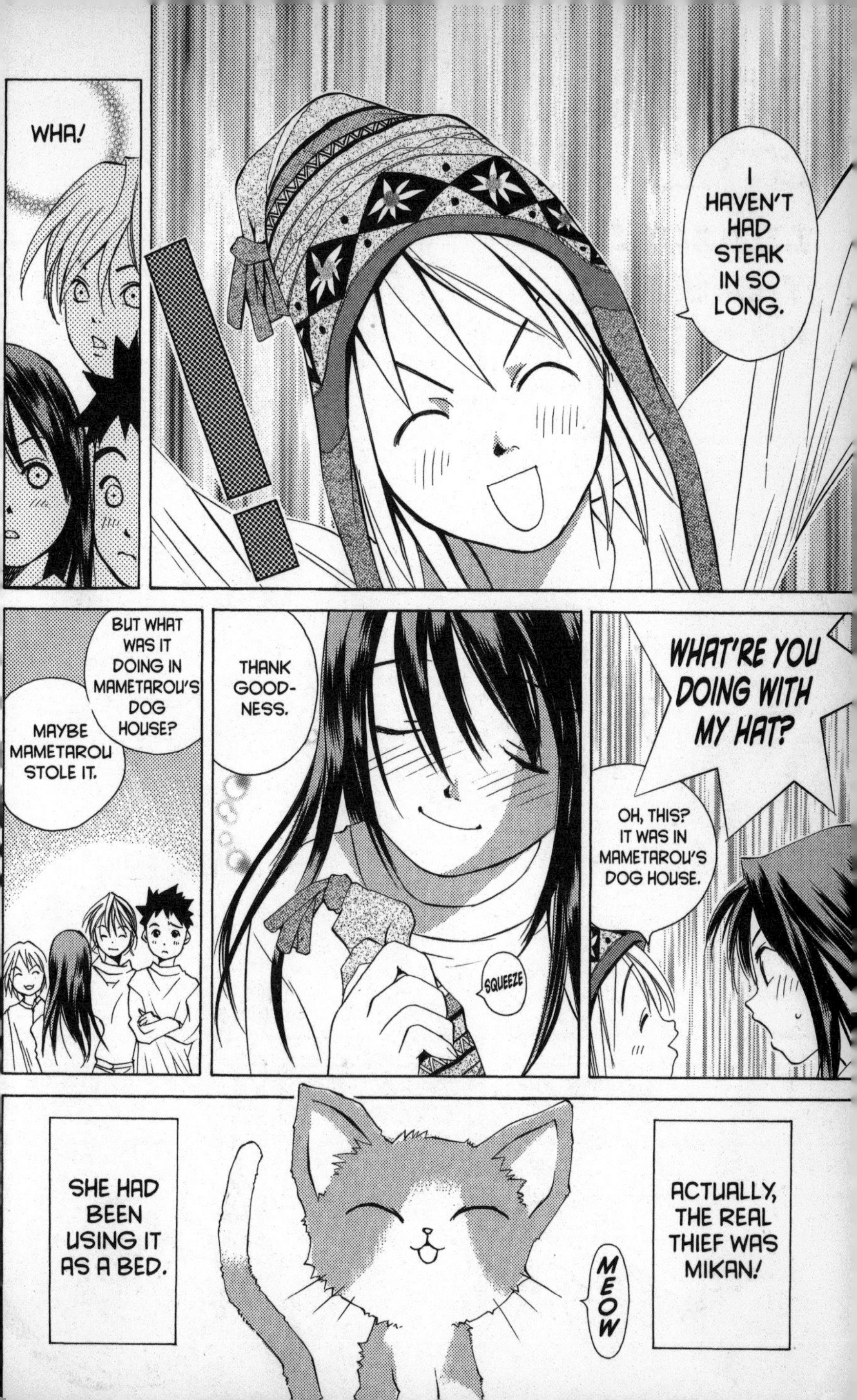
I HAVEN'T HAD STEAK IN SO LONG.
WHA!
WHAT'RE YOU DOING WITH MY HAT?
OH, THIS? IT WAS IN MAMETAROU'S DOG HOUSE.
THANK GOODNESS.
SQUEEZE
BUT WHAT WAS IT DOING IN MAMETAROU'S DOG HOUSE?
MAYBE MAMETAROU STOLE IT.
ACTUALLY, THE REAL THIEF WAS MIKAN!
MEOW
SHE HAD BEEN USING IT AS A BED.

Pastel

MIRACLE 33: THE STEPS OF LOVE

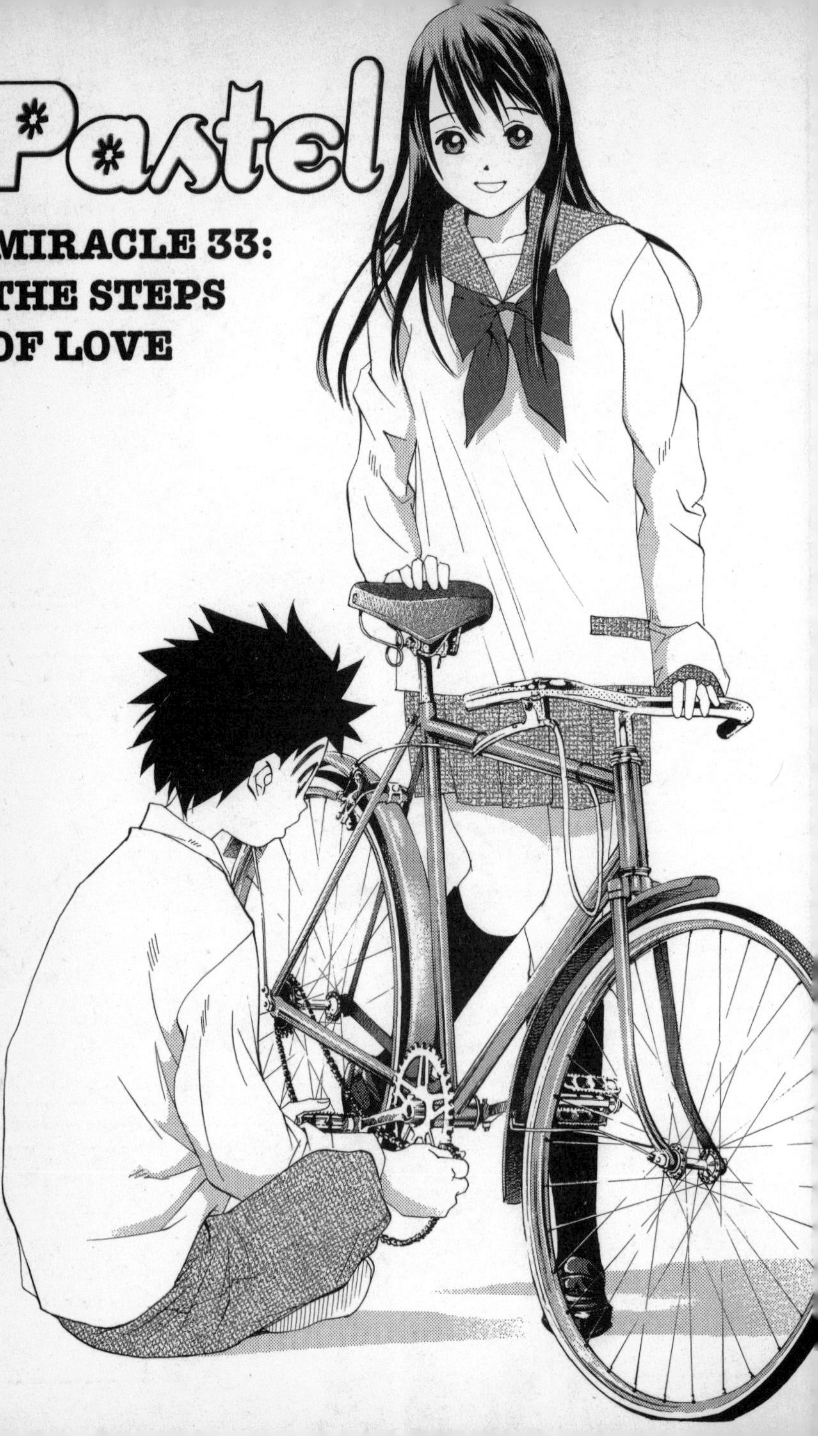

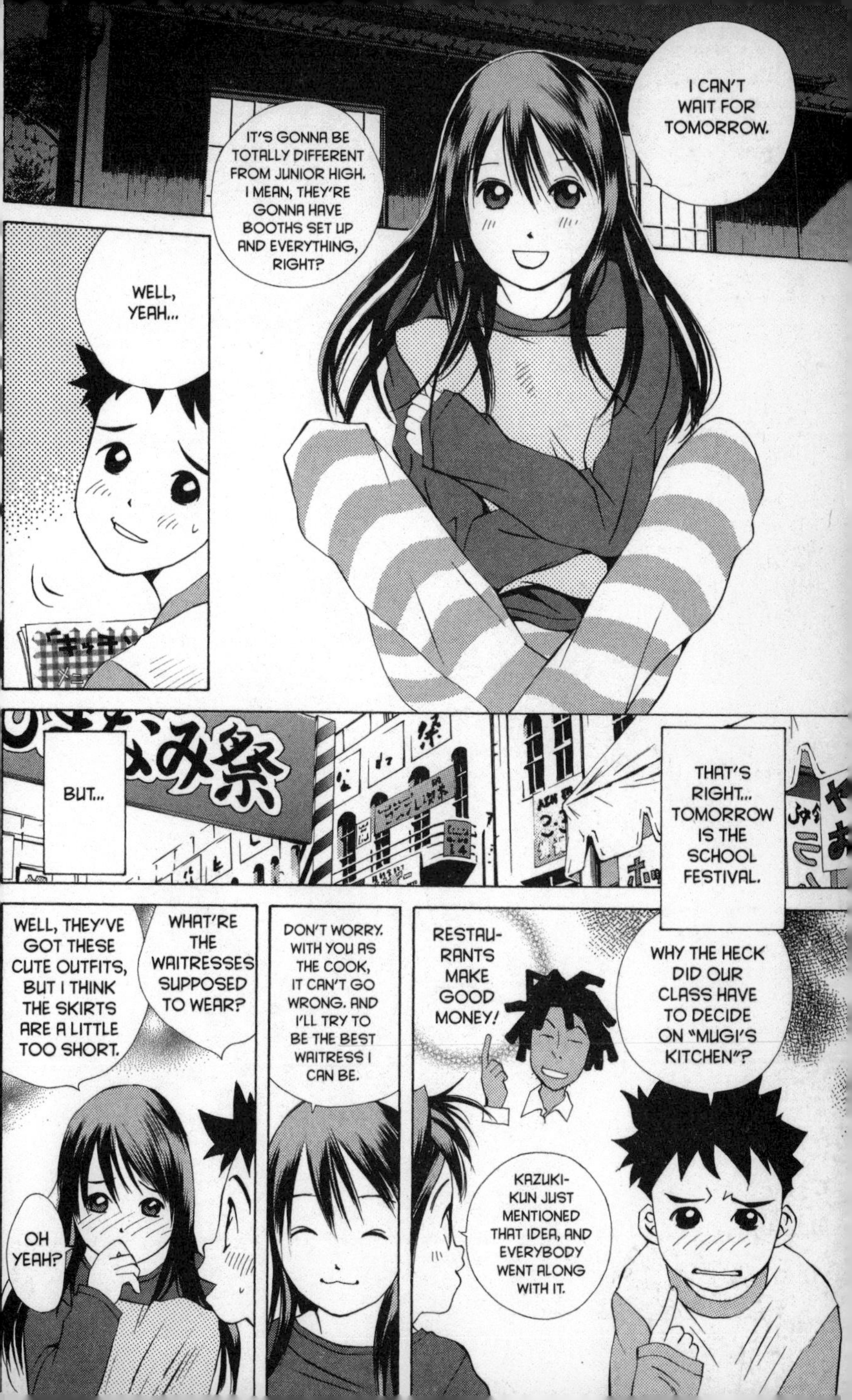
I CAN'T WAIT FOR TOMORROW.
IT'S GONNA BE TOTALLY DIFFERENT FROM JUNIOR HIGH. I MEAN, THEY'RE GONNA HAVE BOOTHS SET UP AND EVERYTHING, RIGHT?
WELL, YEAH...
THAT'S RIGHT... TOMORROW IS THE SCHOOL FESTIVAL.
BUT...
WHY THE HECK DID OUR CLASS HAVE TO DECIDE ON "MUGI'S KITCHEN"?
RESTAU-RANTS MAKE GOOD MONEY!
KAZUKI-KUN JUST MENTIONED THAT IDEA, AND EVERYBODY WENT ALONG WITH IT.
DON'T WORRY. WITH YOU AS THE COOK, IT CAN'T GO WRONG. AND I'LL TRY TO BE THE BEST WAITRESS I CAN BE.
WHAT'RE THE WAITRESSES SUPPOSED TO WEAR?
WELL, THEY'VE GOT THESE CUTE OUTFITS, BUT I THINK THE SKIRTS ARE A LITTLE TOO SHORT.
OH YEAH?

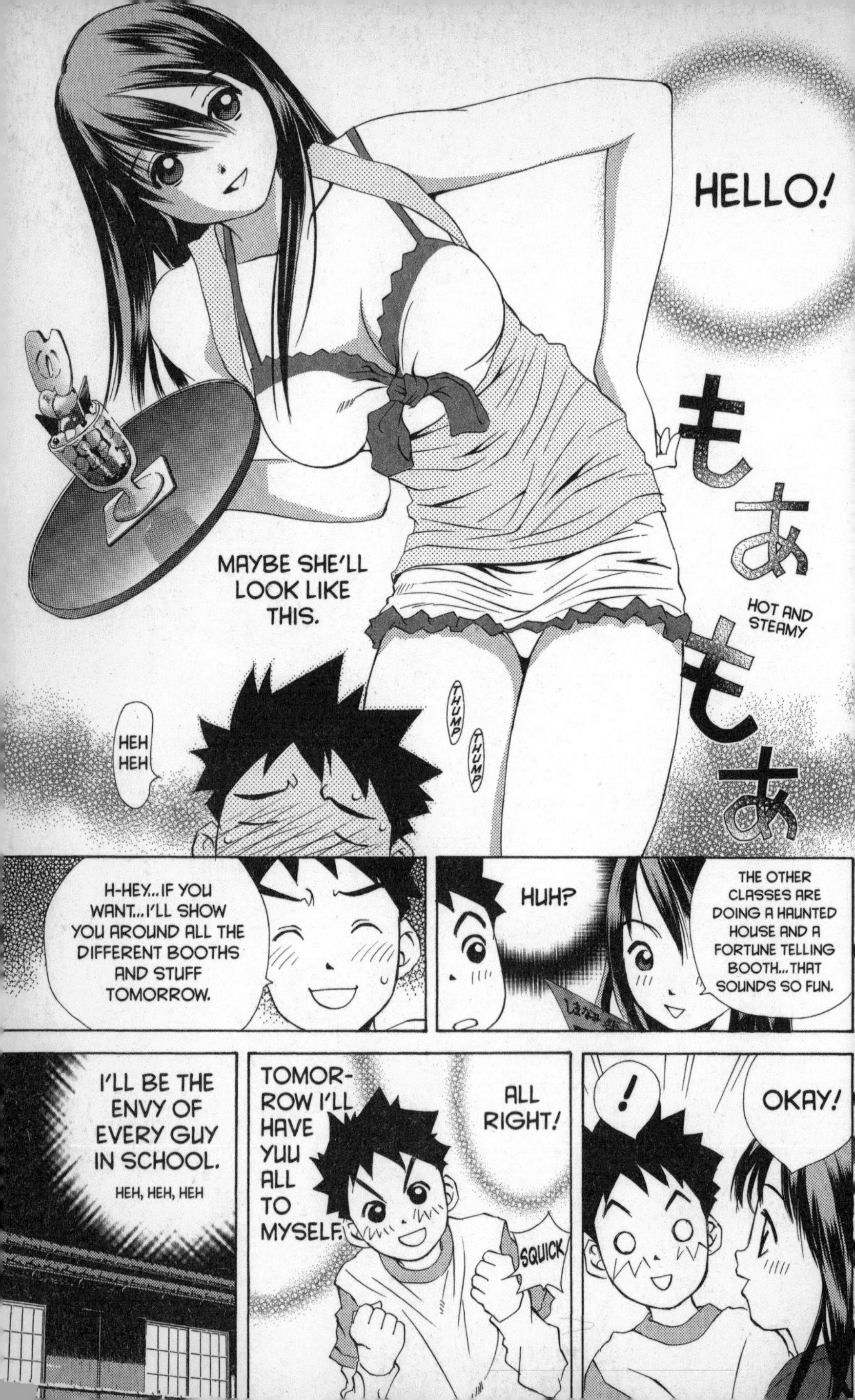
HELLO!
もあ もあ
HOT AND STEAMY
MAYBE SHE'LL LOOK LIKE THIS.
THUMP
THUMP
HEH HEH
THE OTHER CLASSES ARE DOING A HAUNTED HOUSE AND A FORTUNE TELLING BOOTH...THAT SOUNDS SO FUN.
HUH?
H-HEY...IF YOU WANT...I'LL SHOW YOU AROUND ALL THE DIFFERENT BOOTHS AND STUFF TOMORROW.
OKAY!
!
ALL RIGHT!
TOMOR-ROW I'LL HAVE YUU ALL TO MYSELF.
SQUICK
I'LL BE THE ENVY OF EVERY GUY IN SCHOOL.
HEH, HEH, HEH

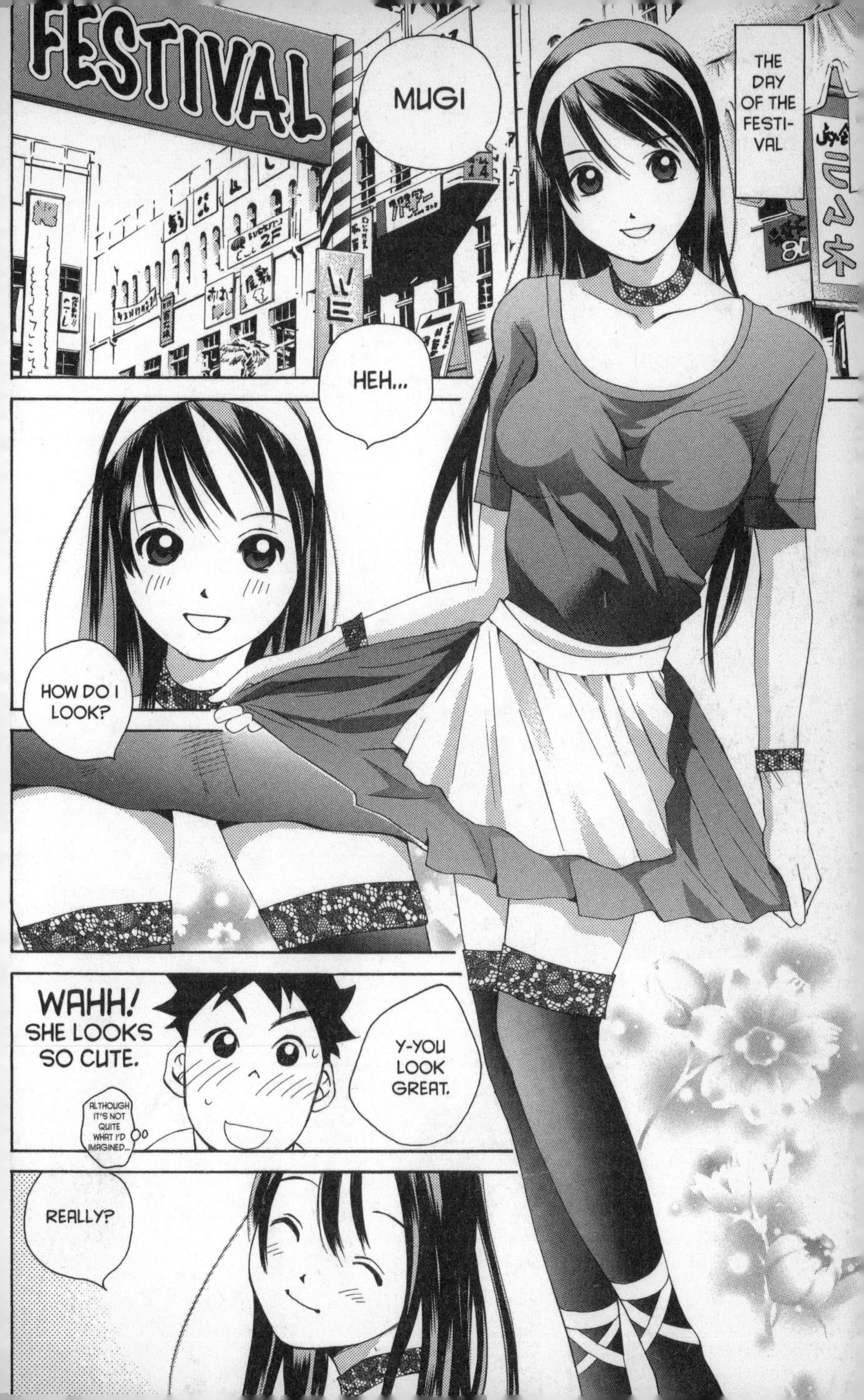
THE DAY OF THE FESTI-VAL
MUGI
FESTIVAL
HEH...
HOW DO I LOOK?
Y-YOU LOOK GREAT.
WAHH! SHE LOOKS SO CUTE.
ALTHOUGH IT'S NOT QUITE WHAT I'D IMAGINED...
REALLY?

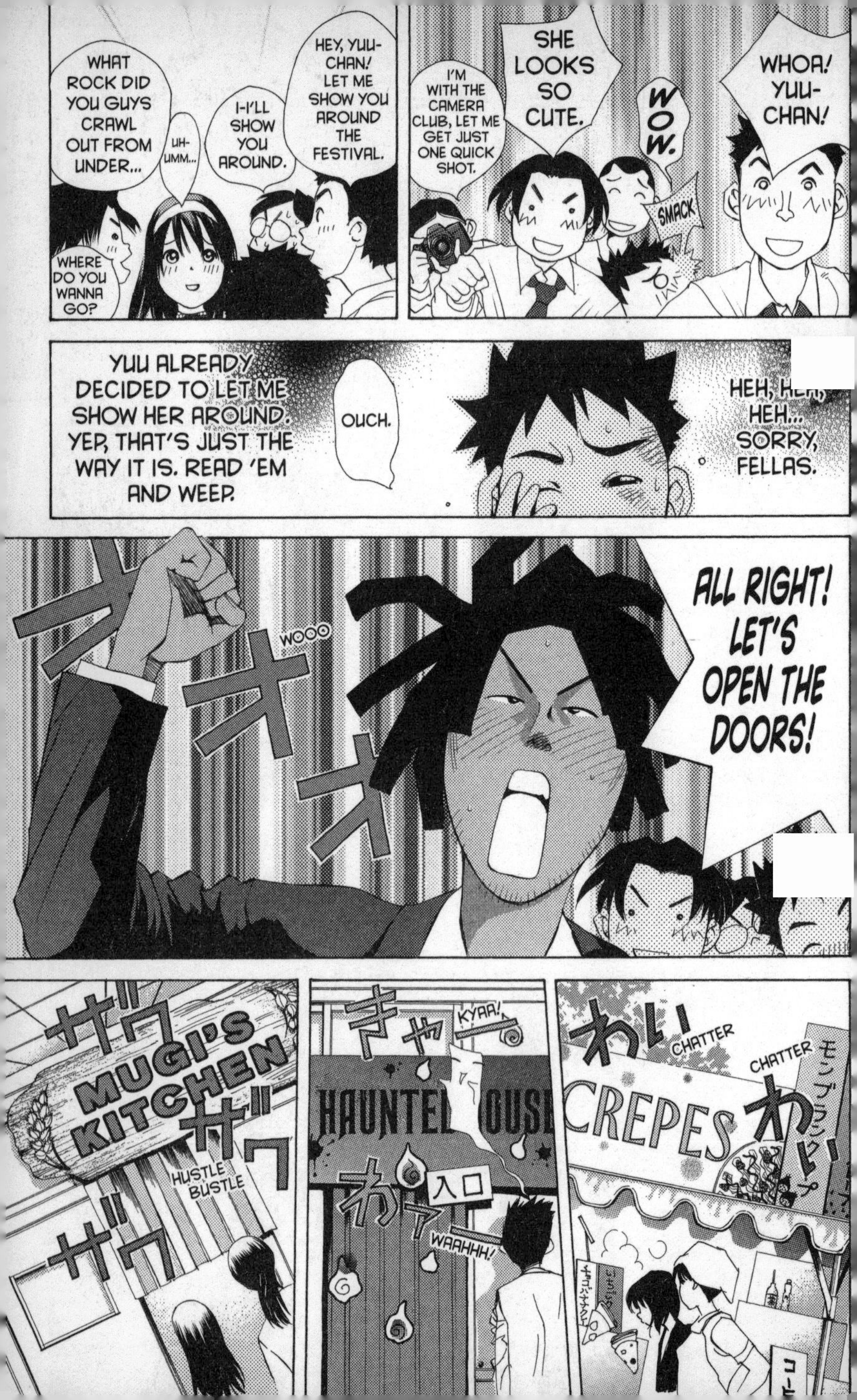
WHOA! YUU-CHAN!
WOW.
SMACK
SHE LOOKS SO CUTE.
I'M WITH THE CAMERA CLUB, LET ME GET JUST ONE QUICK SHOT.
HEY, YUU-CHAN! LET ME SHOW YOU AROUND THE FESTIVAL.
I-I'LL SHOW YOU AROUND.
UH-UMM...
WHAT ROCK DID YOU GUYS CRAWL OUT FROM UNDER...
WHERE DO YOU WANNA GO?
HEH,
HEH... SORRY, FELLAS.
OUCH.
YUU ALREADY DECIDED TO LET ME SHOW HER AROUND. YEP, THAT'S JUST THE WAY IT IS. READ 'EM AND WEEP.
ALL RIGHT! LET'S OPEN THE DOORS!
WOOO
CHATTER
CHATTER
CREPES
KYAA!
入口
WAAHHH!
MUGI'S KITCHEN
HUSTLE BUSTLE

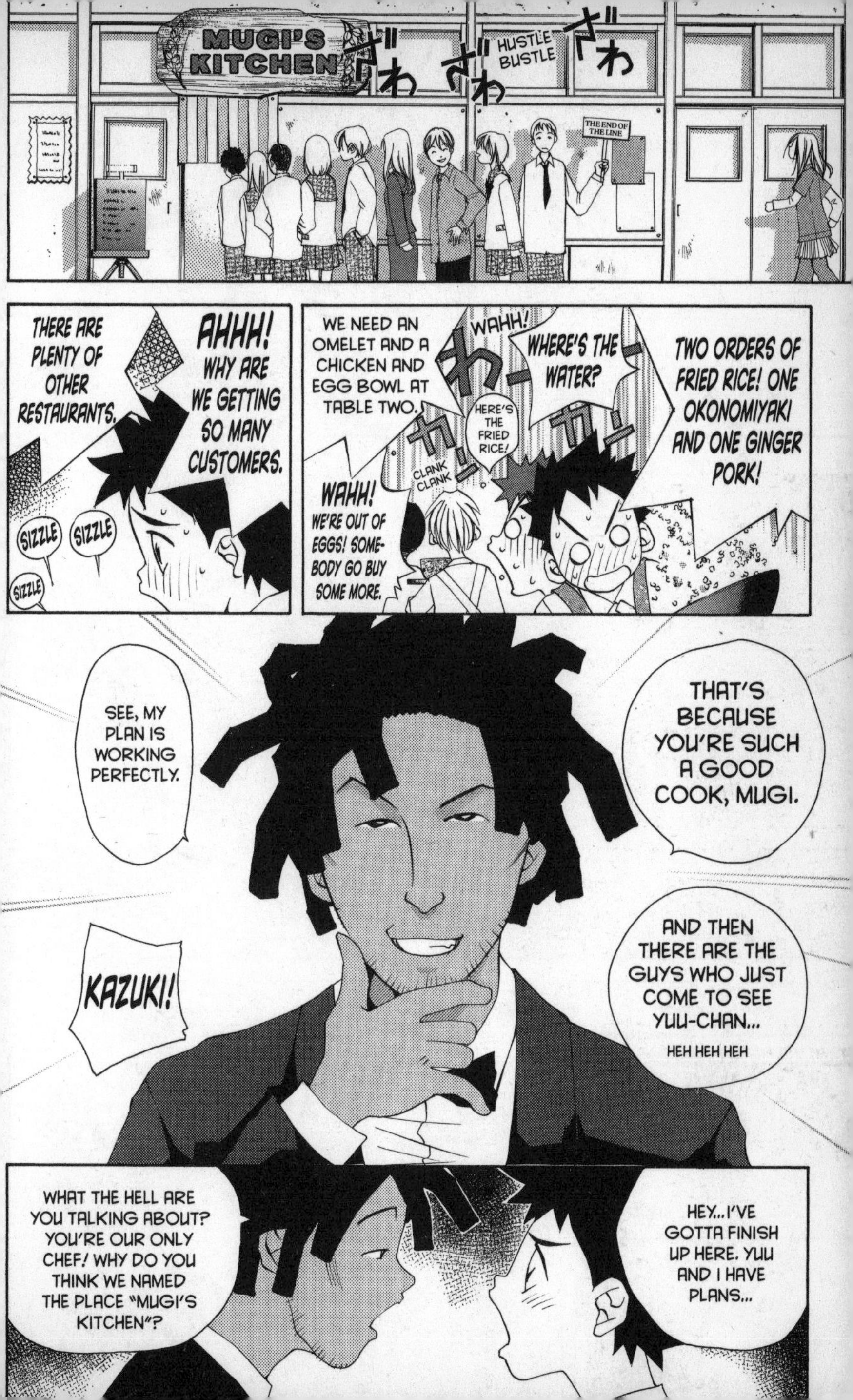
MUGI'S KITCHEN
ざわ ざわ
HUSTLE BUSTLE
ざわ
THE END OF THE LINE
TWO ORDERS OF FRIED RICE! ONE OKONOMIYAKI AND ONE GINGER PORK!
WHERE'S THE WATER?
WAHH!
わー わー
WE NEED AN OMELET AND A CHICKEN AND EGG BOWL AT TABLE TWO.
HERE'S THE FRIED RICE!
CLANK CLANK
WAHH! WE'RE OUT OF EGGS! SOMEBODY GO BUY SOME MORE.
AHHH! WHY ARE WE GETTING SO MANY CUSTOMERS.
THERE ARE PLENTY OF OTHER RESTAURANTS.
SIZZLE
SIZZLE
SIZZLE
THAT'S BECAUSE YOU'RE SUCH A GOOD COOK, MUGI.
SEE, MY PLAN IS WORKING PERFECTLY.
AND THEN THERE ARE THE GUYS WHO JUST COME TO SEE YUU-CHAN...
HEH HEH HEH
KAZUKI!
HEY...I'VE GOTTA FINISH UP HERE. YUU AND I HAVE PLANS...
WHAT THE HELL ARE YOU TALKING ABOUT? YOU'RE OUR ONLY CHEF! WHY DO YOU THINK WE NAMED THE PLACE "MUGI'S KITCHEN"?

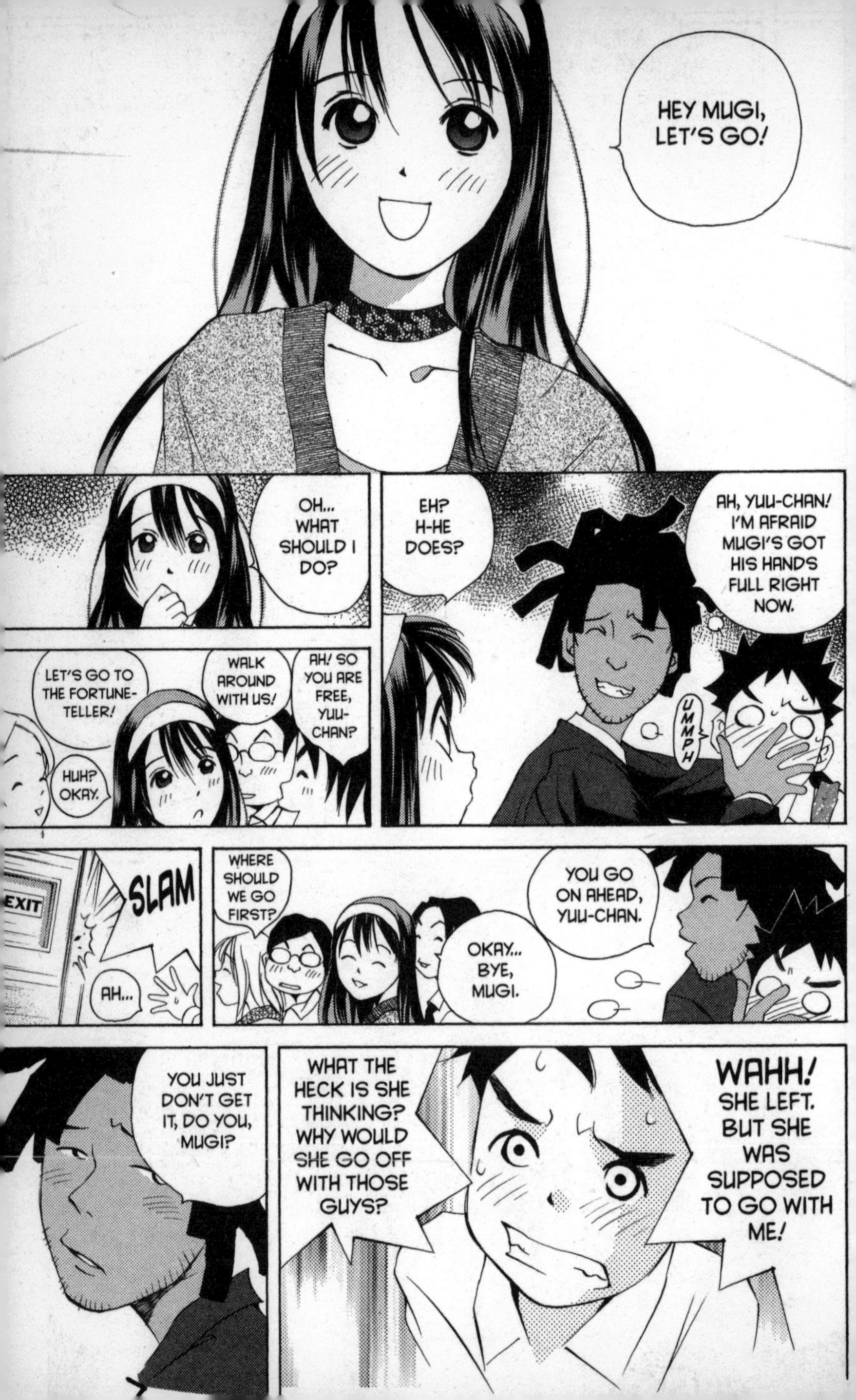
HEY MUGI, LET'S GO!
AH, YUU-CHAN! I'M AFRAID MUGI'S GOT HIS HANDS FULL RIGHT NOW.
UMMPH
EH? H-HE DOES?
OH... WHAT SHOULD I DO?
AH! SO YOU ARE FREE, YUU-CHAN?
WALK AROUND WITH US!
LET'S GO TO THE FORTUNE-TELLER!
HUH? OKAY.
YOU GO ON AHEAD, YUU-CHAN.
OKAY... BYE, MUGI.
WHERE SHOULD WE GO FIRST?
SLAM
EXIT
AH...
WAHH! SHE LEFT. BUT SHE WAS SUPPOSED TO GO WITH ME!
WHAT THE HECK IS SHE THINKING? WHY WOULD SHE GO OFF WITH THOSE GUYS?
YOU JUST DON'T GET IT, DO YOU, MUGI?

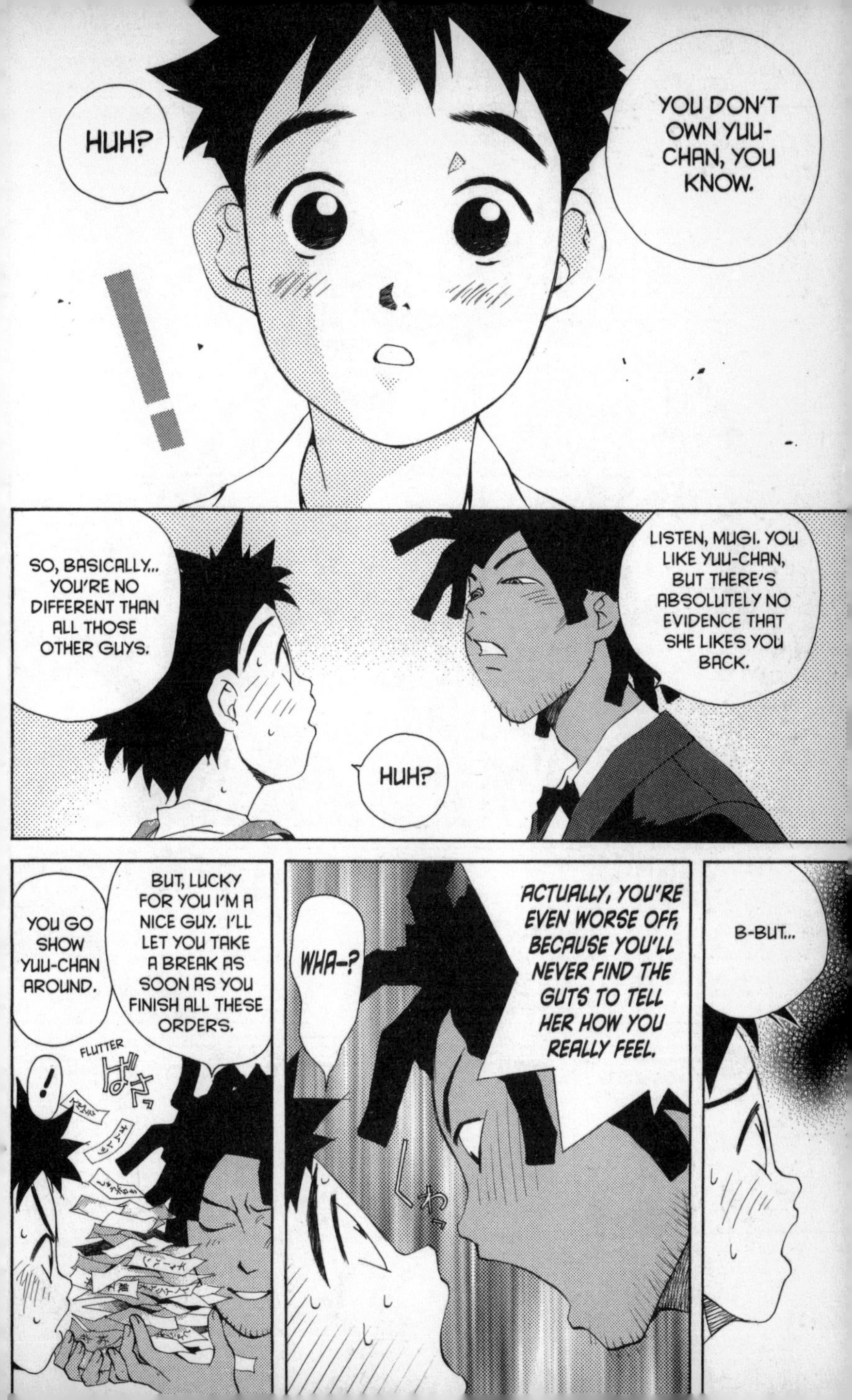
YOU DON'T OWN YUU-CHAN, YOU KNOW.
HUH?
!
LISTEN, MUGI. YOU LIKE YUU-CHAN, BUT THERE'S ABSOLUTELY NO EVIDENCE THAT SHE LIKES YOU BACK.
SO, BASICALLY... YOU'RE NO DIFFERENT THAN ALL THOSE OTHER GUYS.
HUH?
B-BUT...
ACTUALLY, YOU'RE EVEN WORSE OFF, BECAUSE YOU'LL NEVER FIND THE GUTS TO TELL HER HOW YOU REALLY FEEL.
WHA-?
BUT, LUCKY FOR YOU I'M A NICE GUY. I'LL LET YOU TAKE A BREAK AS SOON AS YOU FINISH ALL THESE ORDERS.
YOU GO SHOW YUU-CHAN AROUND.
FLUTTER
!

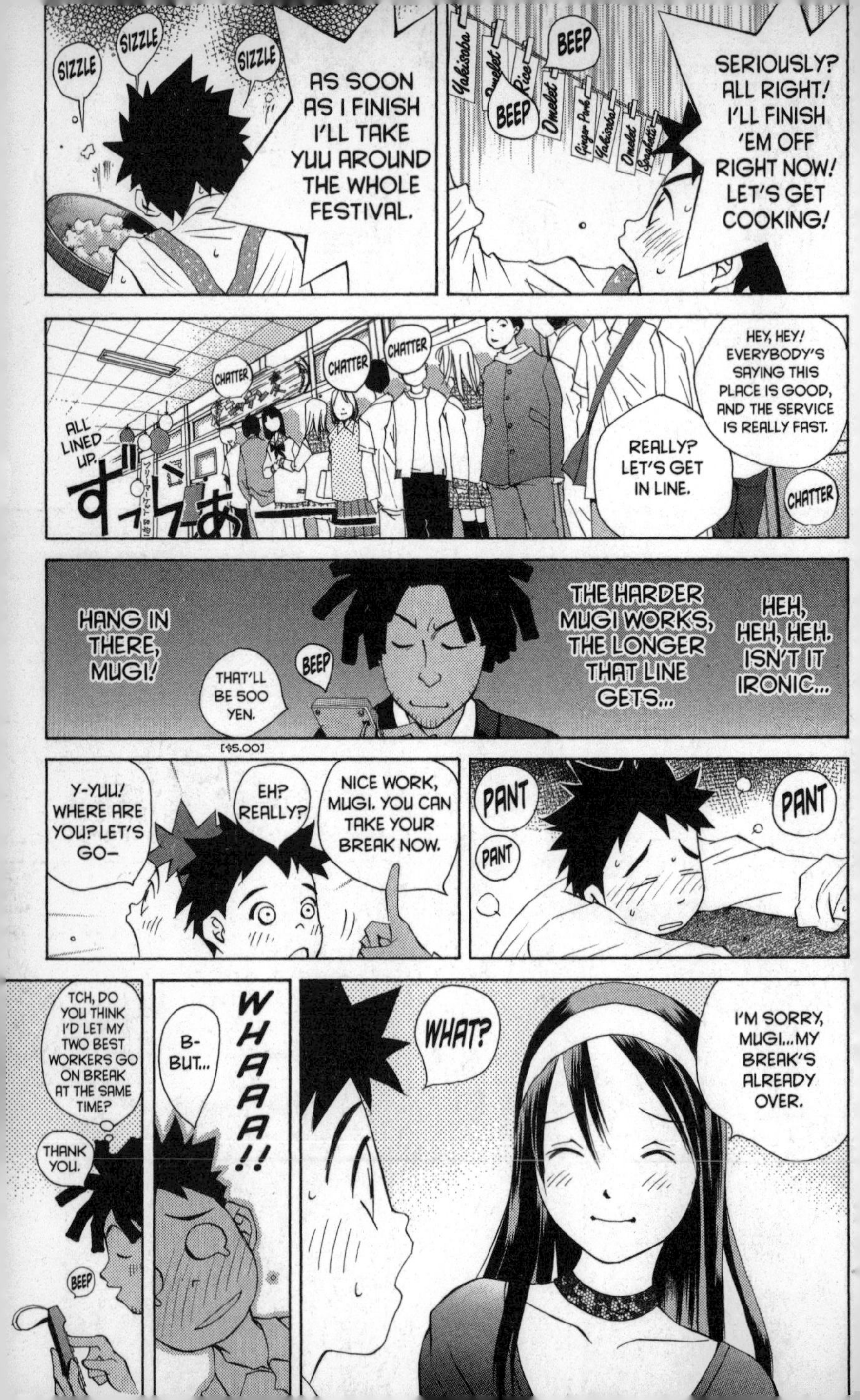
Yakisoba
Omelet
Rice
Omelet
Ginger Pork
Yakisoba
Omelet
Spaghetti
BEEP
BEEP
SERIOUSLY? ALL RIGHT! I'LL FINISH 'EM OFF RIGHT NOW! LET'S GET COOKING!
SIZZLE
SIZZLE
SIZZLE
AS SOON AS I FINISH I'LL TAKE YUU AROUND THE WHOLE FESTIVAL.
HEY, HEY! EVERYBODY'S SAYING THIS PLACE IS GOOD, AND THE SERVICE IS REALLY FAST.
CHATTER
REALLY? LET'S GET IN LINE.
CHATTER
CHATTER
CHATTER
ALL LINED UP.
ずらぁー
HEH, HEH, HEH. ISN'T IT IRONIC...
THE HARDER MUGI WORKS, THE LONGER THAT LINE GETS...
BEEP
THAT'LL BE 500 YEN.
HANG IN THERE, MUGI!
[$5.00]
PANT
PANT
PANT
NICE WORK, MUGI. YOU CAN TAKE YOUR BREAK NOW.
EH? REALLY?
Y-YUU! WHERE ARE YOU? LET'S GO–
I'M SORRY, MUGI...MY BREAK'S ALREADY OVER.
WHAT?
WHAAAA!!
B-BUT...
TCH, DO YOU THINK I'D LET MY TWO BEST WORKERS GO ON BREAK AT THE SAME TIME?
THANK YOU.
BEEP

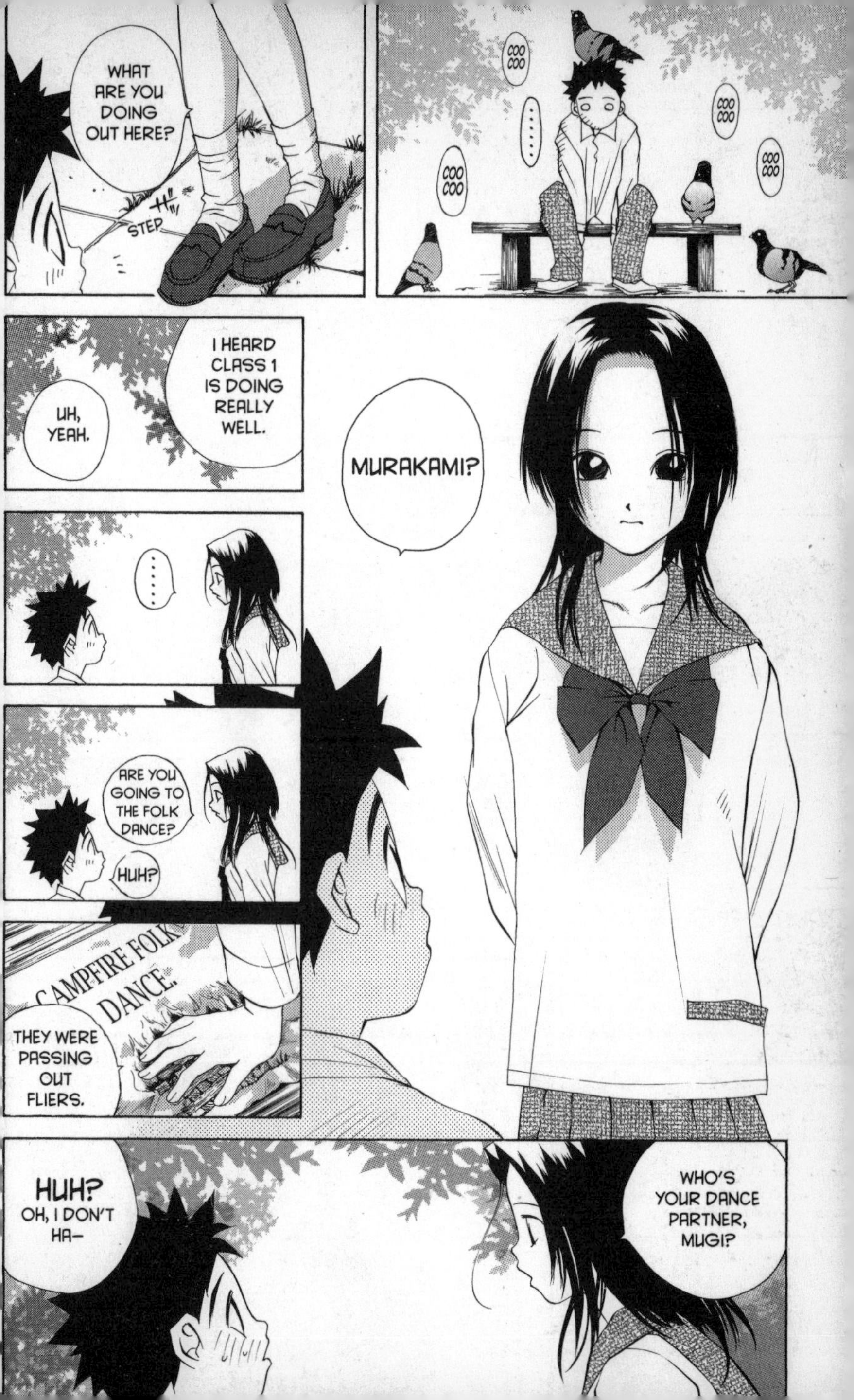
COO COO
......
COO COO
COO COO
COO COO
WHAT ARE YOU DOING OUT HERE?
STEP
MURAKAMI?
I HEARD CLASS 1 IS DOING REALLY WELL.
UH, YEAH.
......
ARE YOU GOING TO THE FOLK DANCE?
HUH?
CAMPFIRE FOLK DANCE.
THEY WERE PASSING OUT FLIERS.
WHO'S YOUR DANCE PARTNER, MUGI?
HUH? OH, I DON'T HA–

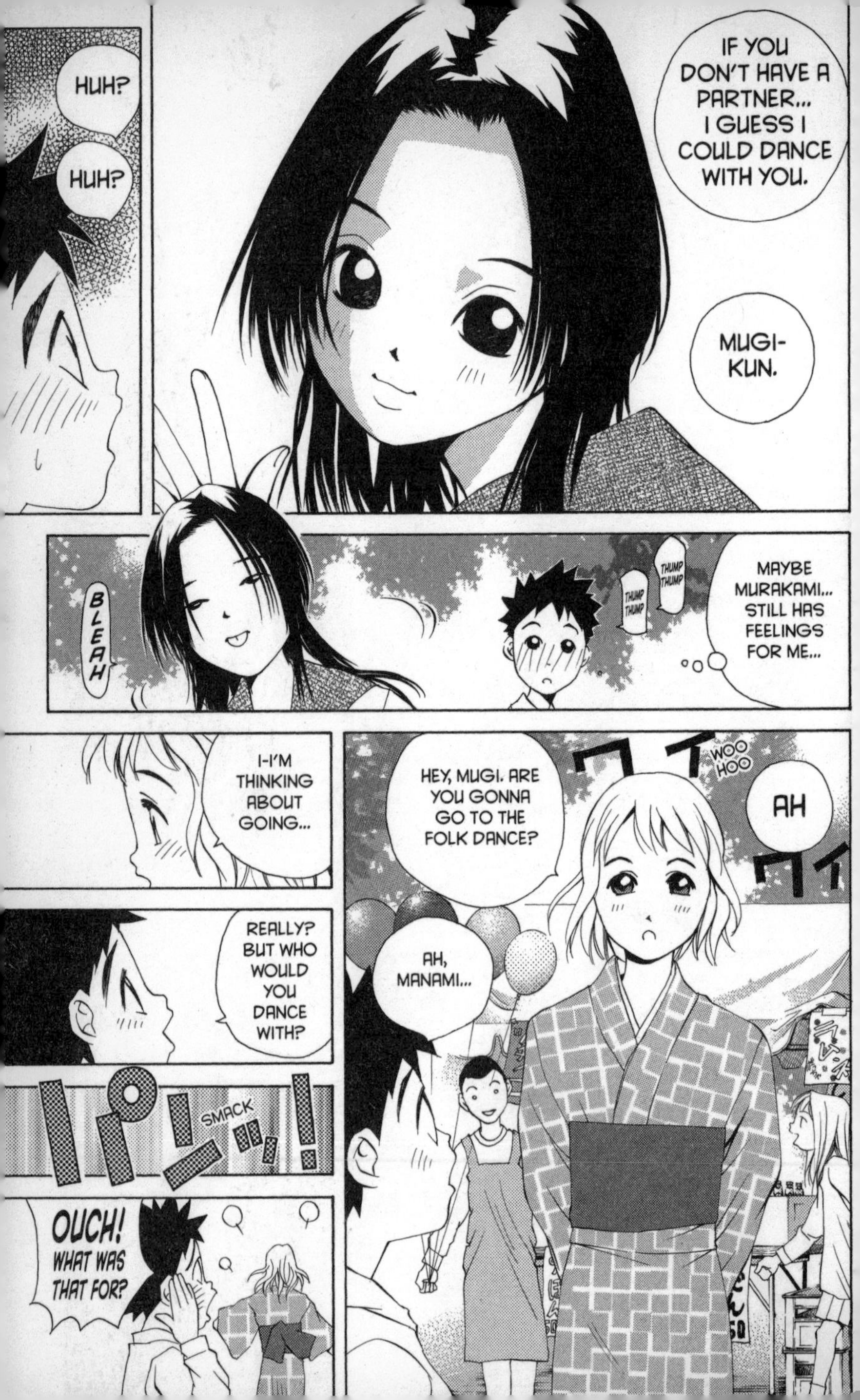
IF YOU DON'T HAVE A PARTNER... I GUESS I COULD DANCE WITH YOU.
MUGI-KUN.
HUH?
HUH?
MAYBE MURAKAMI... STILL HAS FEELINGS FOR ME...
THUMP THUMP
THUMP THUMP
BLEAH
AH
WOO HOO
HEY, MUGI. ARE YOU GONNA GO TO THE FOLK DANCE?
AH, MANAMI...
I-I'M THINKING ABOUT GOING...
REALLY? BUT WHO WOULD YOU DANCE WITH?
SMACK
OUCH! WHAT WAS THAT FOR?

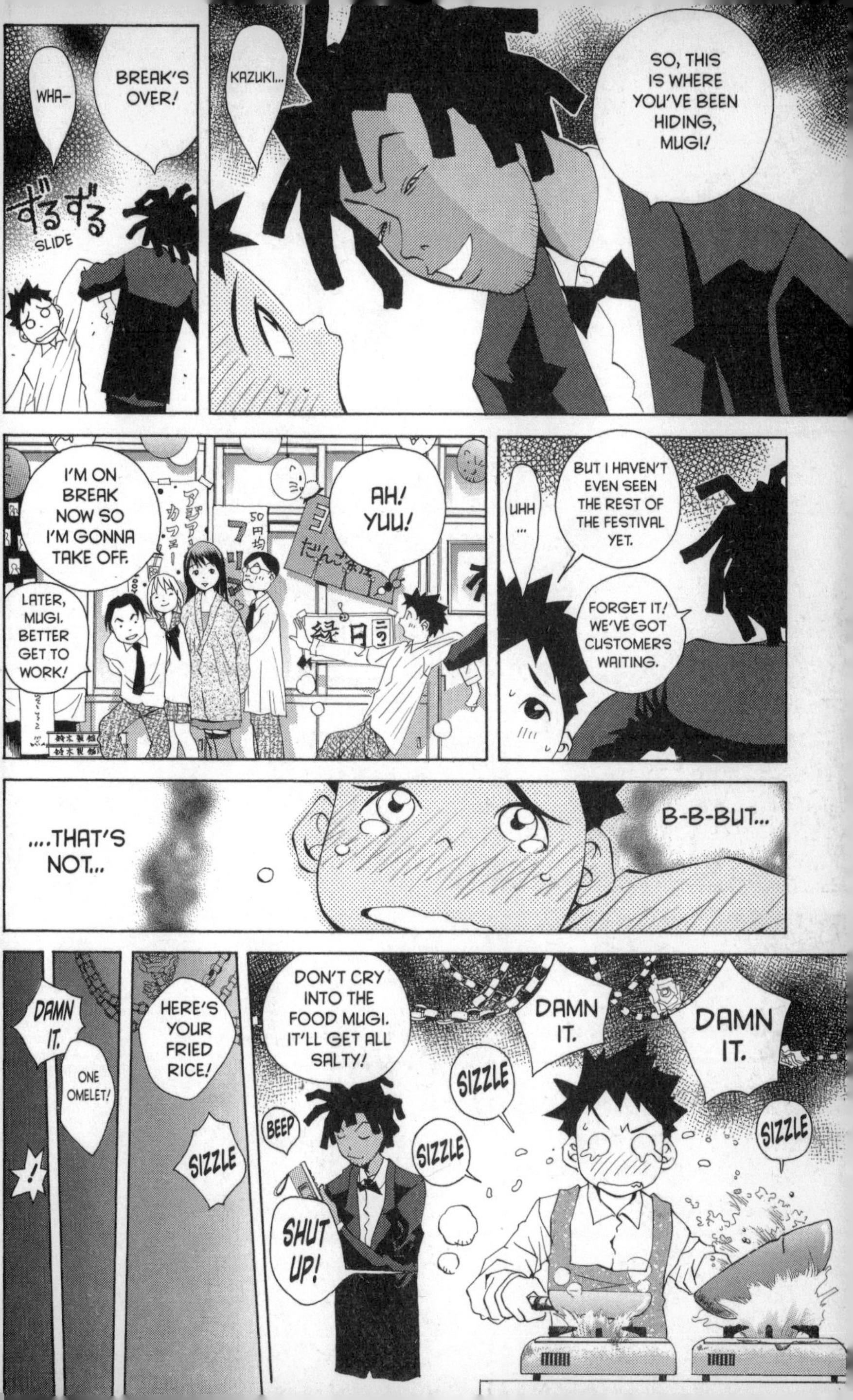
SO, THIS IS WHERE YOU'VE BEEN HIDING, MUGI!
KAZUKI...
BREAK'S OVER!
WHA-
ずるずる
SLIDE
BUT I HAVEN'T EVEN SEEN THE REST OF THE FESTIVAL YET.
UHH ...
FORGET IT! WE'VE GOT CUSTOMERS WAITING.
AH! YUU!
I'M ON BREAK NOW SO I'M GONNA TAKE OFF.
LATER, MUGI. BETTER GET TO WORK!
B-B-BUT...
....THAT'S NOT...
DAMN IT.
DAMN IT.
DON'T CRY INTO THE FOOD MUGI. IT'LL GET ALL SALTY!
SIZZLE
SIZZLE
BEEP
SIZZLE
SHUT UP!
HERE'S YOUR FRIED RICE!
SIZZLE
DAMN IT.
ONE OMELET!
!

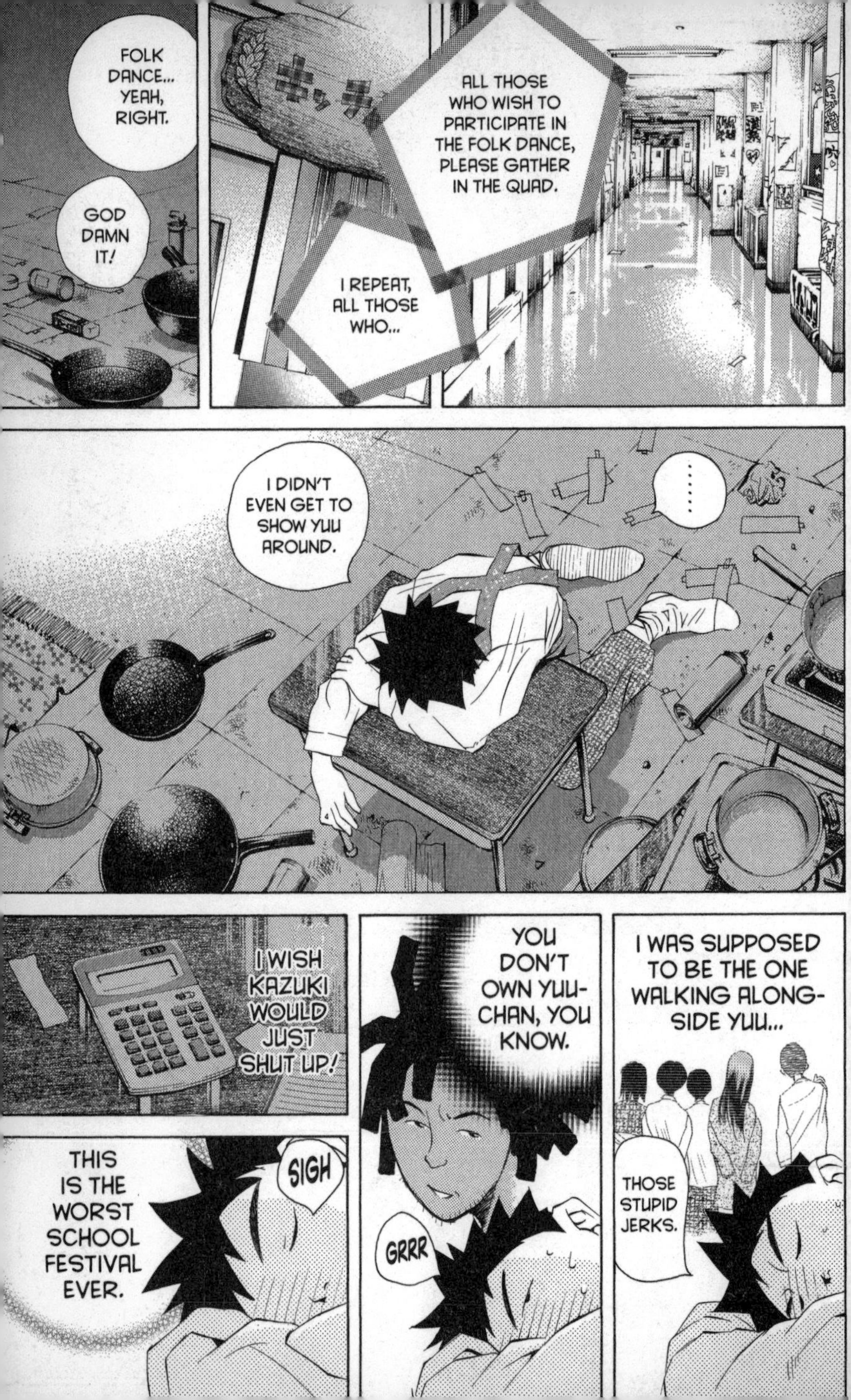
ALL THOSE WHO WISH TO PARTICIPATE IN THE FOLK DANCE, PLEASE GATHER IN THE QUAD.
I REPEAT, ALL THOSE WHO...
FOLK DANCE... YEAH, RIGHT.
GOD DAMN IT!
......
I DIDN'T EVEN GET TO SHOW YUU AROUND.
I WAS SUPPOSED TO BE THE ONE WALKING ALONG-SIDE YUU...
THOSE STUPID JERKS.
YOU DON'T OWN YUU-CHAN, YOU KNOW.
GRRR
I WISH KAZUKI WOULD JUST SHUT UP!
SIGH
THIS IS THE WORST SCHOOL FESTIVAL EVER.

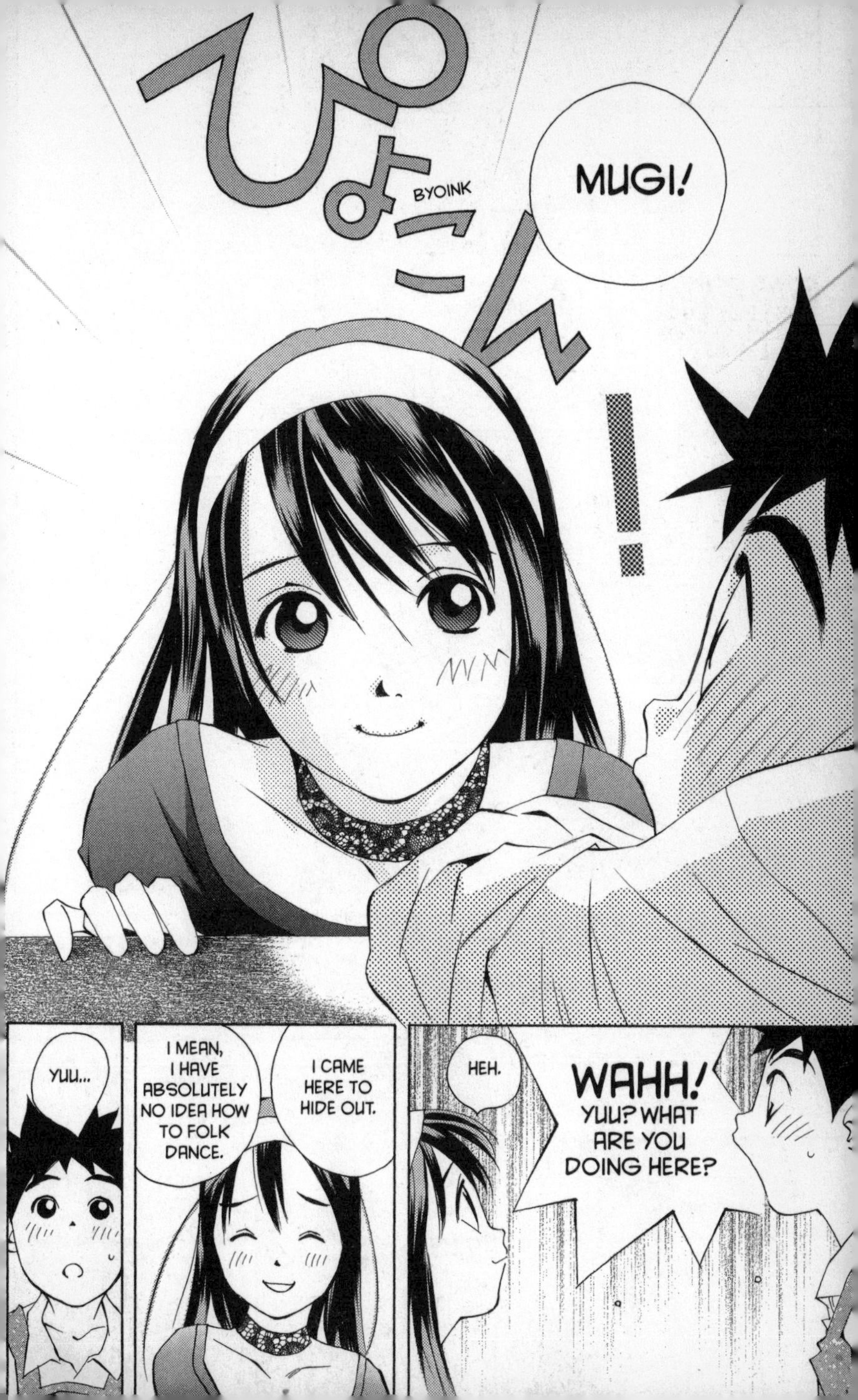

MUGI!
ぴょこん
BYOINK
!
WAHH!
YUU? WHAT ARE YOU DOING HERE?
HEH.
I CAME HERE TO HIDE OUT.
I MEAN, I HAVE ABSOLUTELY NO IDEA HOW TO FOLK DANCE.
YUU...

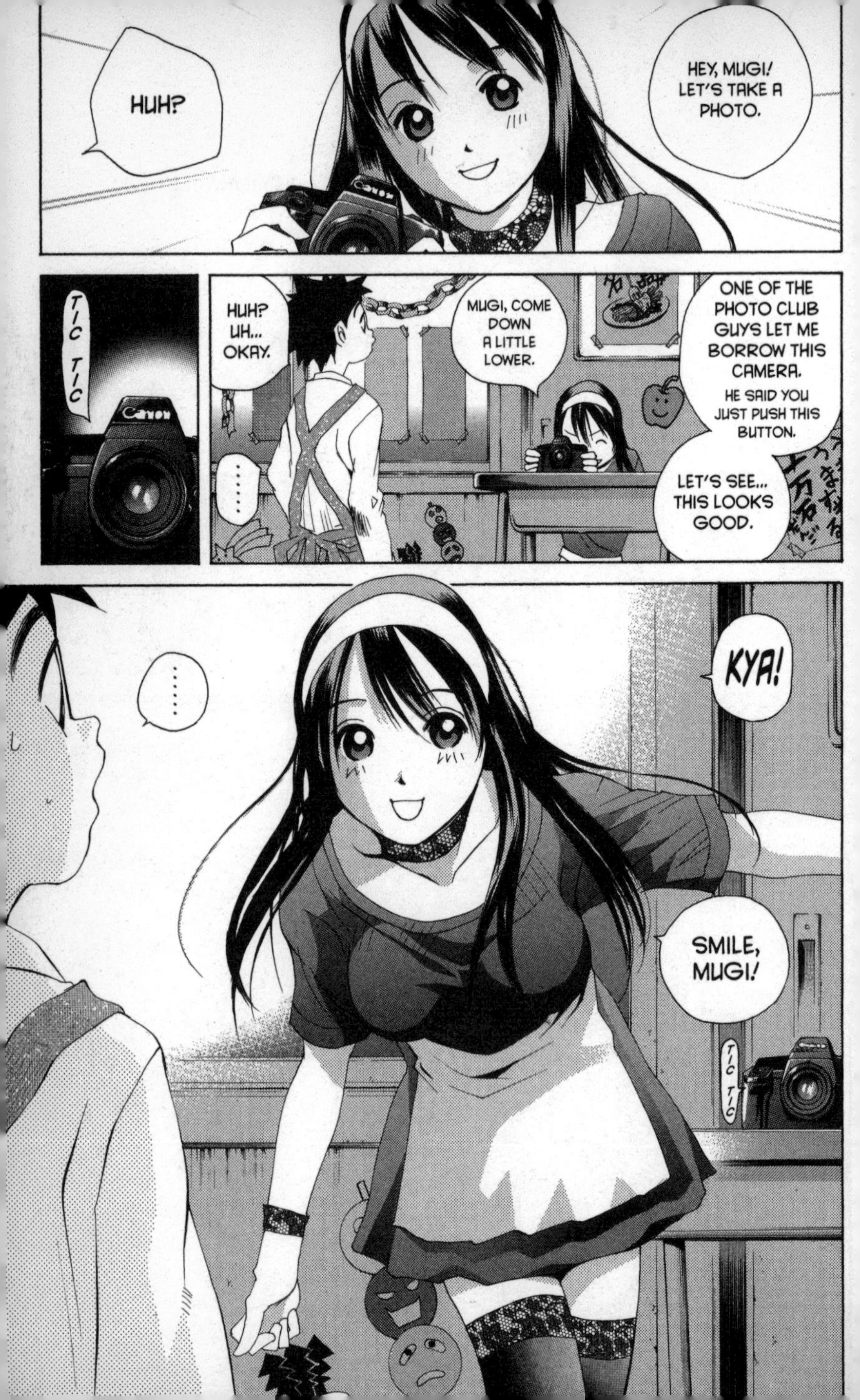
HEY, MUGI! LET'S TAKE A PHOTO.
HUH?
ONE OF THE PHOTO CLUB GUYS LET ME BORROW THIS CAMERA.
HE SAID YOU JUST PUSH THIS BUTTON.
LET'S SEE... THIS LOOKS GOOD.
MUGI, COME DOWN A LITTLE LOWER.
HUH? UH... OKAY.
......
TIC TIC
KYA!
SMILE, MUGI!
TIC TIC
......

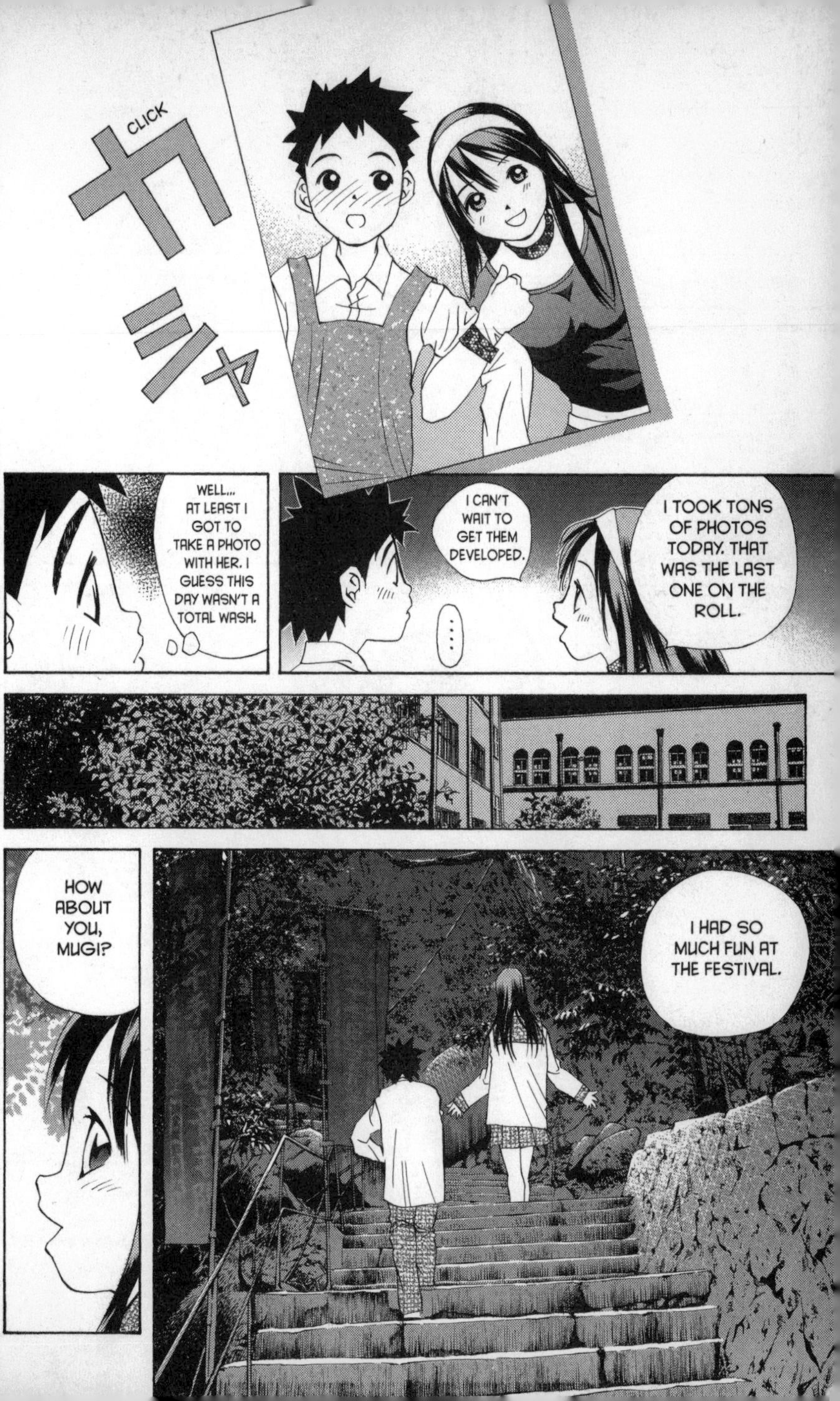
CLICK
カシャ
I TOOK TONS OF PHOTOS TODAY. THAT WAS THE LAST ONE ON THE ROLL.
I CAN'T WAIT TO GET THEM DEVELOPED.
....
WELL... AT LEAST I GOT TO TAKE A PHOTO WITH HER. I GUESS THIS DAY WASN'T A TOTAL WASH.
I HAD SO MUCH FUN AT THE FESTIVAL.
HOW ABOUT YOU, MUGI?

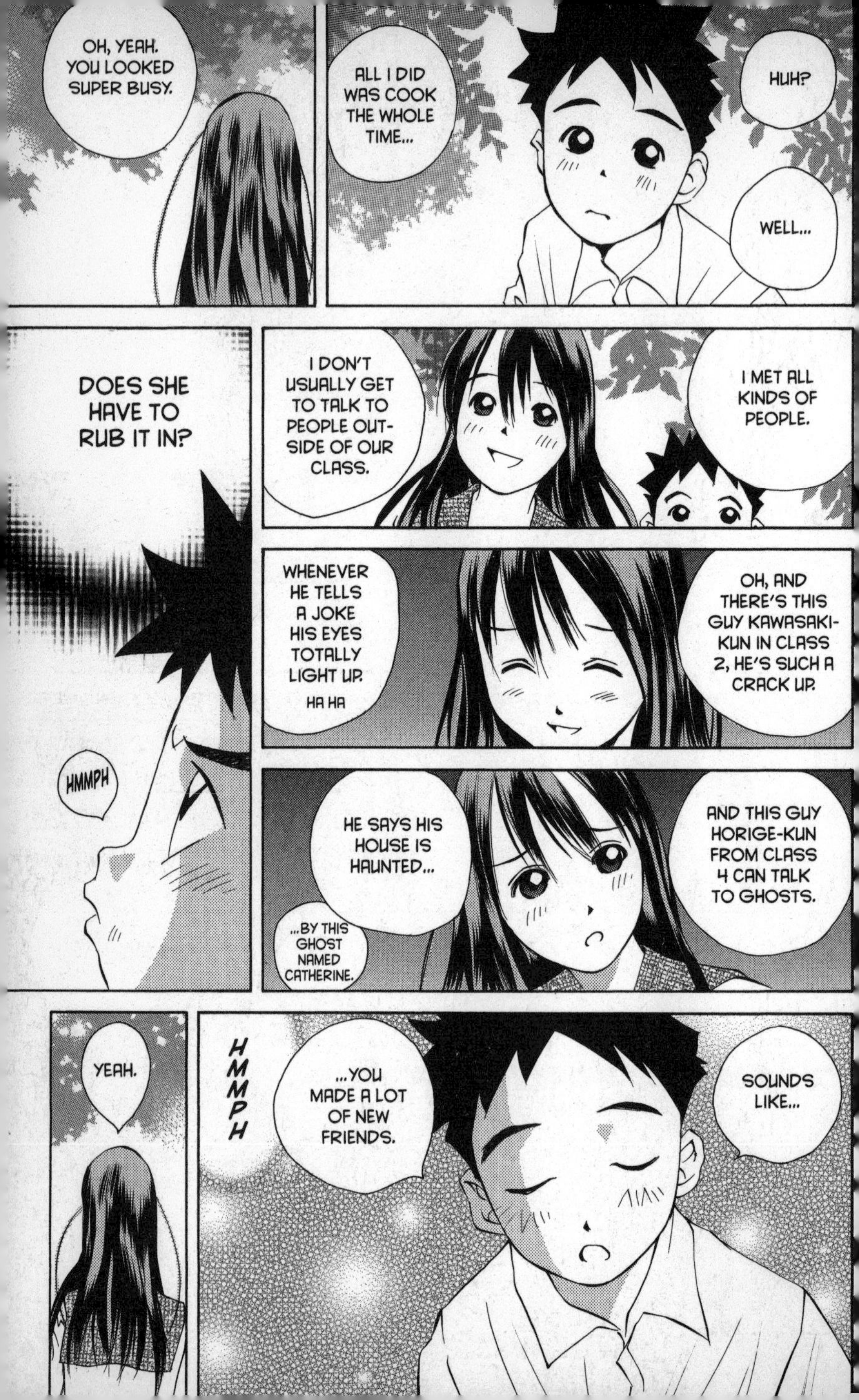
HUH?
WELL...
ALL I DID WAS COOK THE WHOLE TIME...
OH, YEAH. YOU LOOKED SUPER BUSY.
I MET ALL KINDS OF PEOPLE.
I DON'T USUALLY GET TO TALK TO PEOPLE OUT-SIDE OF OUR CLASS.
OH, AND THERE'S THIS GUY KAWASAKI-KUN IN CLASS 2, HE'S SUCH A CRACK UP.
WHENEVER HE TELLS A JOKE HIS EYES TOTALLY LIGHT UP.
HA HA
AND THIS GUY HORIGE-KUN FROM CLASS 4 CAN TALK TO GHOSTS.
HE SAYS HIS HOUSE IS HAUNTED...
...BY THIS GHOST NAMED CATHERINE.
DOES SHE HAVE TO RUB IT IN?
HMMPH
SOUNDS LIKE...
...YOU MADE A LOT OF NEW FRIENDS.
HMMPH
YEAH.

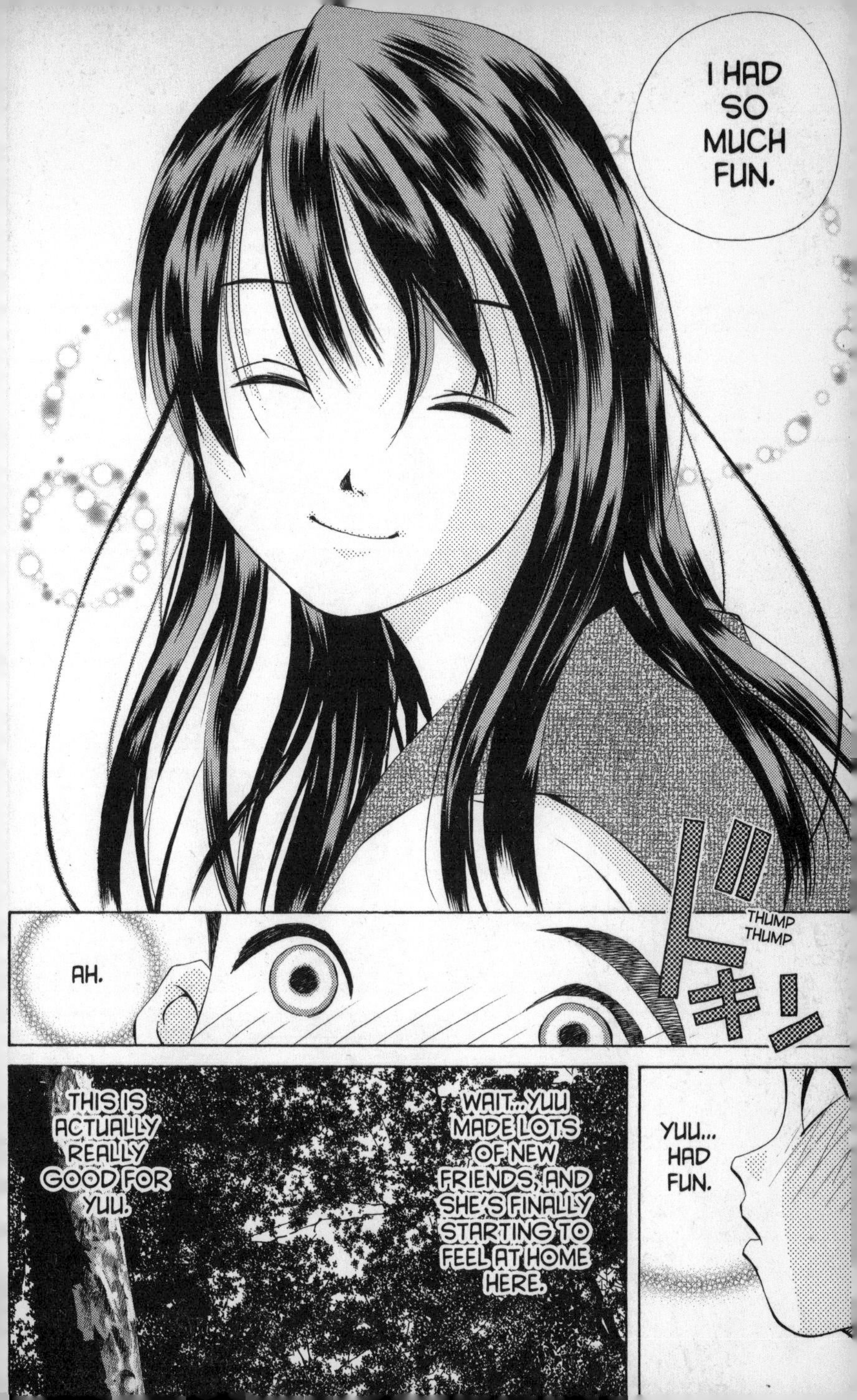
I HAD SO MUCH FUN.
ドキン
THUMP THUMP
AH.
YUU... HAD FUN.
WAIT... YUU MADE LOTS OF NEW FRIENDS, AND SHE'S FINALLY STARTING TO FEEL AT HOME HERE.
THIS IS ACTUALLY REALLY GOOD FOR YUU.

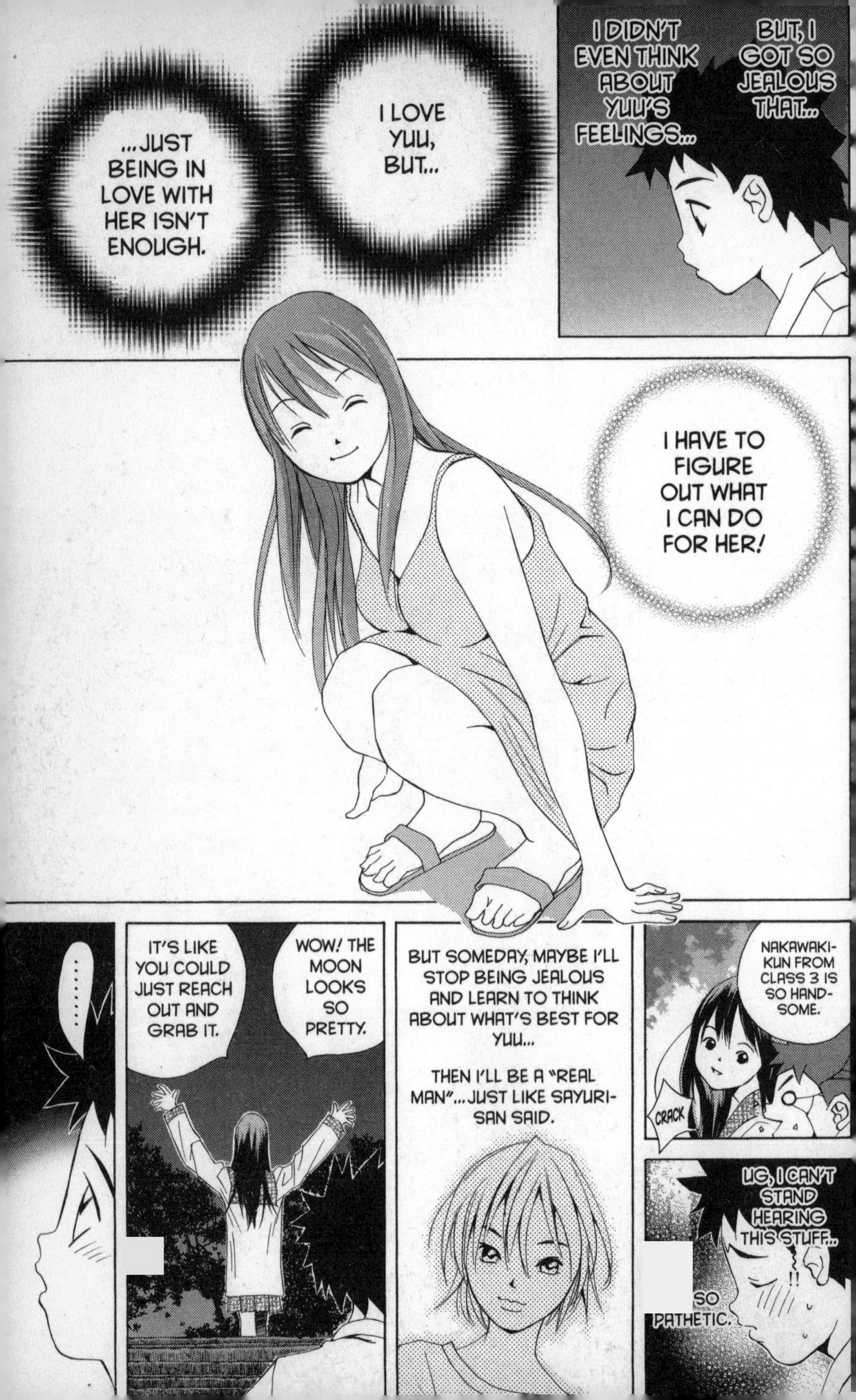
BUT, I GOT SO JEALOUS THAT...
I DIDN'T EVEN THINK ABOUT YUU'S FEELINGS...
I LOVE YUU, BUT...
...JUST BEING IN LOVE WITH HER ISN'T ENOUGH.
I HAVE TO FIGURE OUT WHAT I CAN DO FOR HER!
NAKAWAKI-KUN FROM CLASS 3 IS SO HAND-SOME.
CRACK
UG, I CAN'T STAND HEARING THIS STUFF...
!!
SO PATHETIC.
BUT SOMEDAY, MAYBE I'LL STOP BEING JEALOUS AND LEARN TO THINK ABOUT WHAT'S BEST FOR YUU...
THEN I'LL BE A "REAL MAN"... JUST LIKE SAYURI-SAN SAID.
WOW! THE MOON LOOKS SO PRETTY.
IT'S LIKE YOU COULD JUST REACH OUT AND GRAB IT.
......

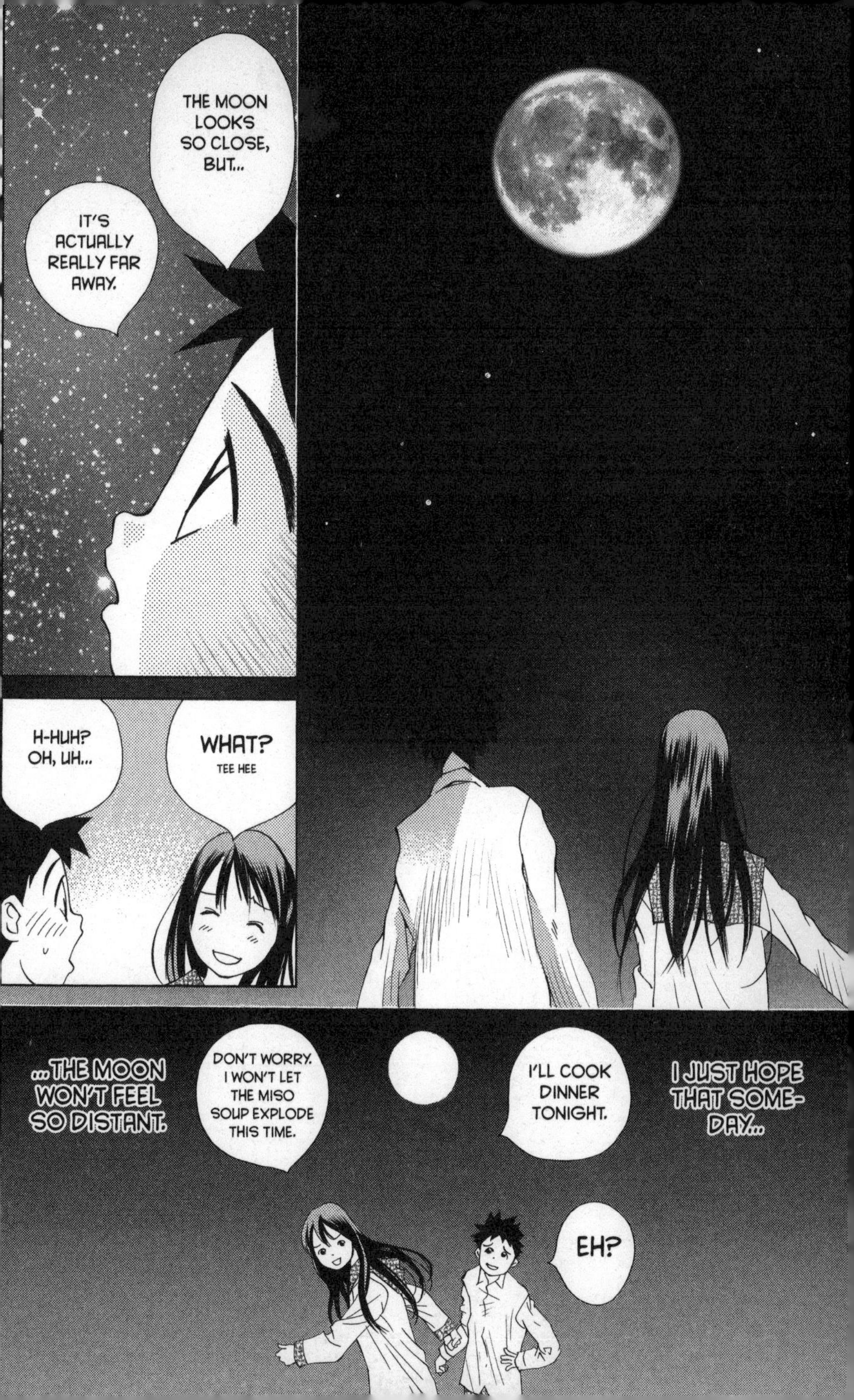
THE MOON LOOKS SO CLOSE, BUT...
IT'S ACTUALLY REALLY FAR AWAY.
WHAT?
TEE HEE
H-HUH? OH, UH...
I JUST HOPE THAT SOME-DAY...
I'LL COOK DINNER TONIGHT.
DON'T WORRY. I WON'T LET THE MISO SOUP EXPLODE THIS TIME.
...THE MOON WON'T FEEL SO DISTANT.
EH?

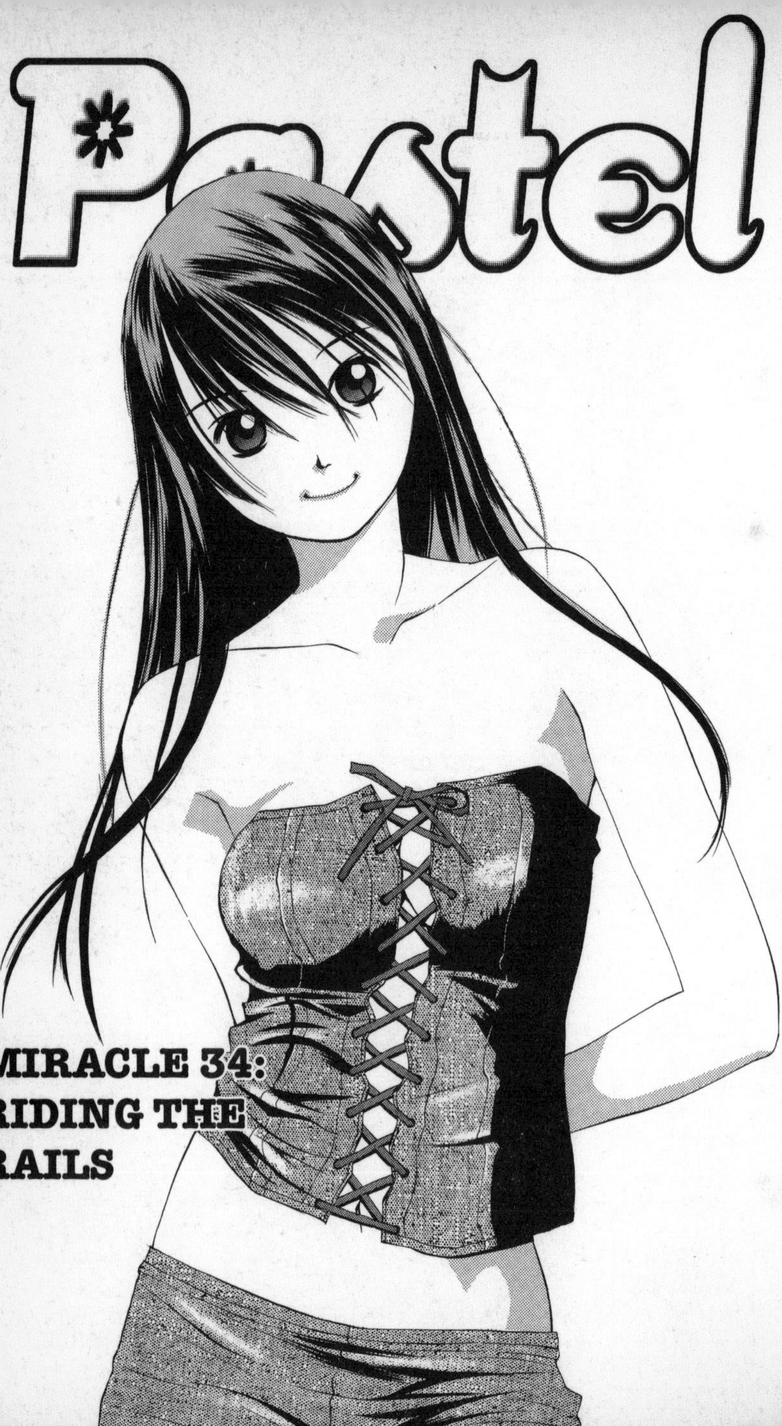
Pastel
MIRACLE 34:
RIDING THE
RAILS

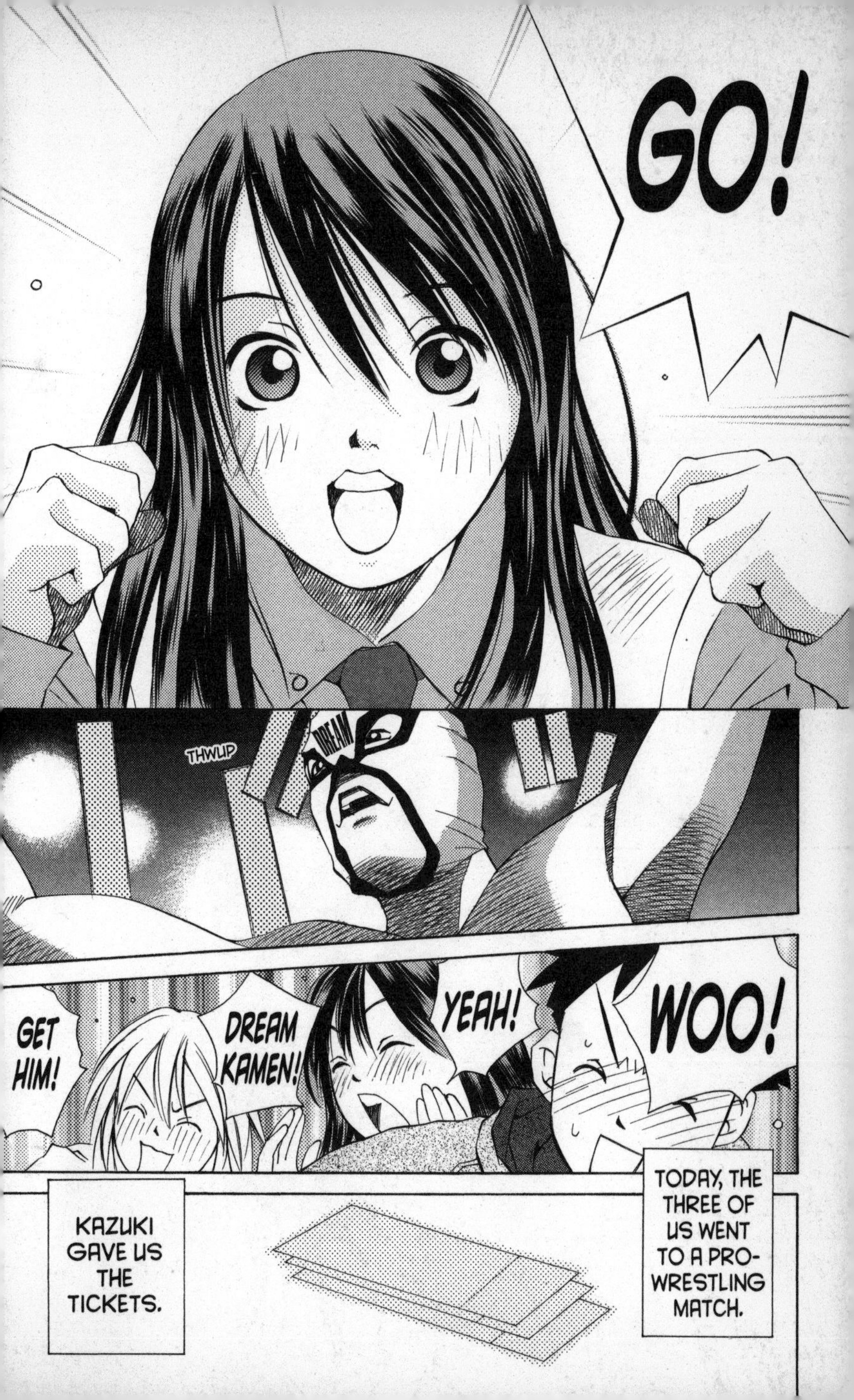
GO!
THWUP
DREAM
WOO!
YEAH!
DREAM KAMEN!
GET HIM!
TODAY, THE THREE OF US WENT TO A PRO-WRESTLING MATCH.
KAZUKI GAVE US THE TICKETS.

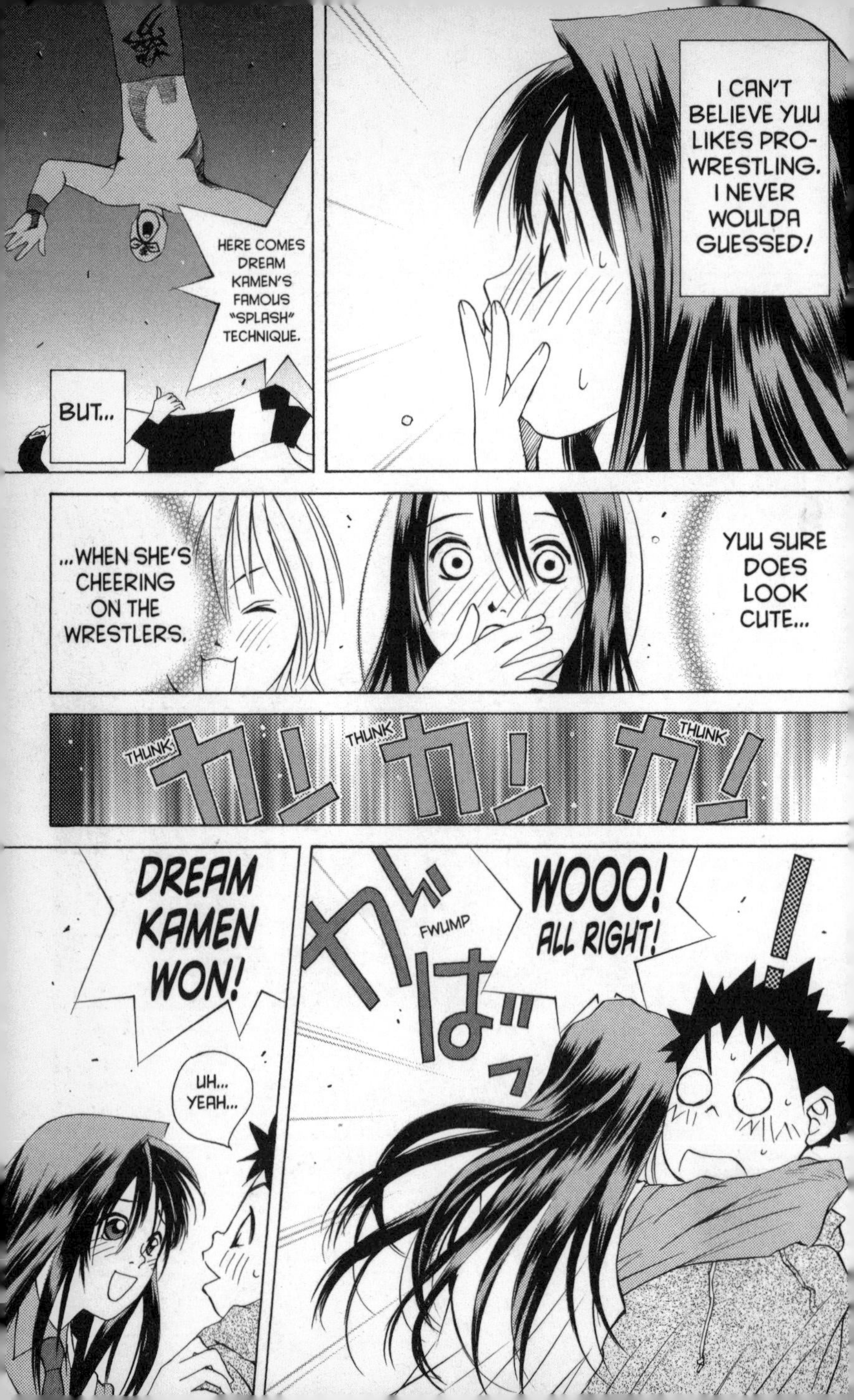

I CAN'T BELIEVE YUU LIKES PRO-WRESTLING. I NEVER WOULDA GUESSED!
HERE COMES DREAM KAMEN'S FAMOUS "SPLASH" TECHNIQUE.
BUT...
YUU SURE DOES LOOK CUTE...
...WHEN SHE'S CHEERING ON THE WRESTLERS.
THUNK
THUNK
THUNK
WOOO! ALL RIGHT!
FWUMP
!
DREAM KAMEN WON!
UH... YEAH...

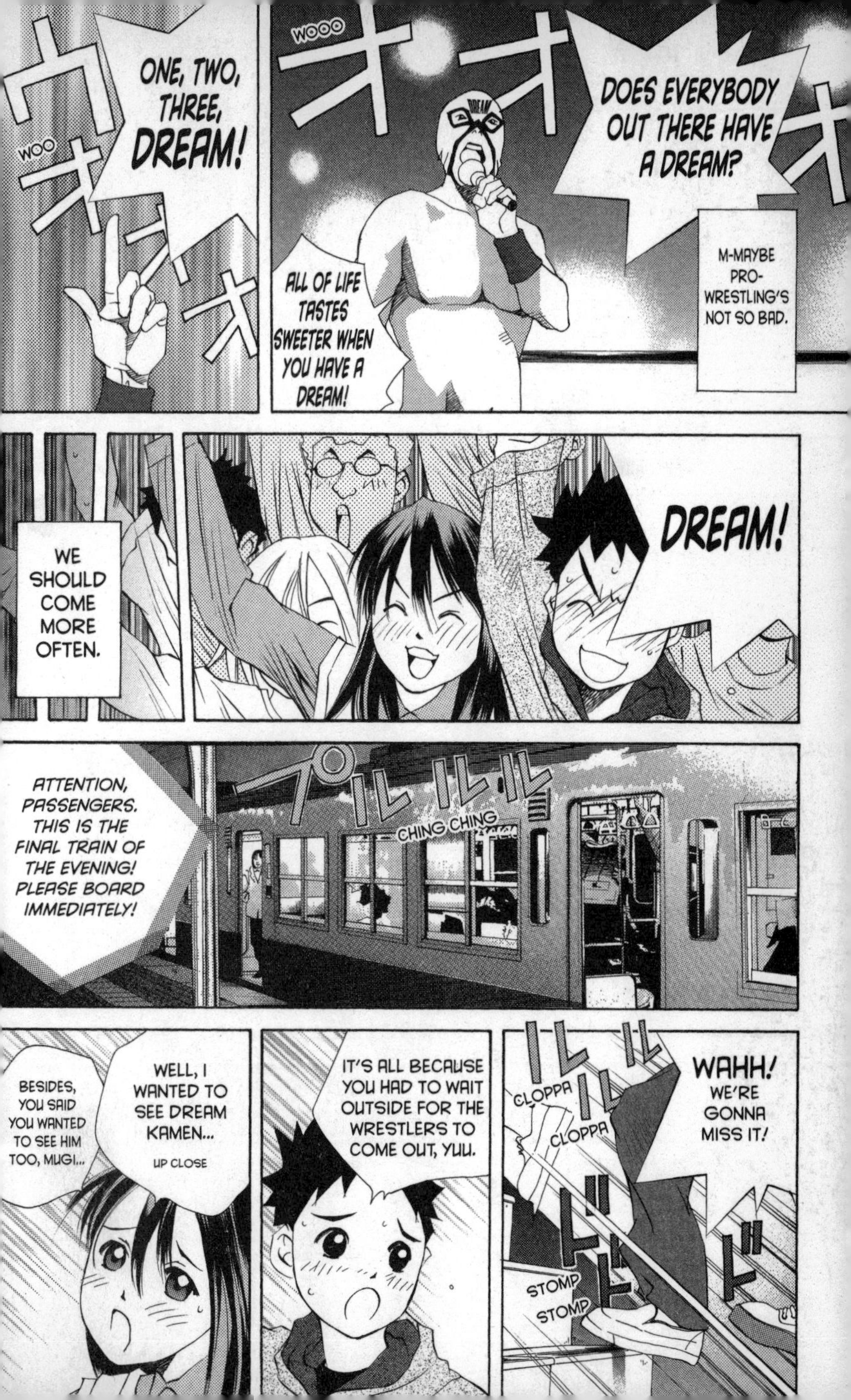
DOES EVERYBODY OUT THERE HAVE A DREAM?
WOOO
M-MAYBE PRO-WRESTLING'S NOT SO BAD.
ALL OF LIFE TASTES SWEETER WHEN YOU HAVE A DREAM!
ONE, TWO, THREE, DREAM!
WOO
DREAM!
WE SHOULD COME MORE OFTEN.
ATTENTION, PASSENGERS. THIS IS THE FINAL TRAIN OF THE EVENING! PLEASE BOARD IMMEDIATELY!
CHING CHING
WAHH! WE'RE GONNA MISS IT!
CLOPPA
CLOPPA
STOMP
STOMP
IT'S ALL BECAUSE YOU HAD TO WAIT OUTSIDE FOR THE WRESTLERS TO COME OUT, YUU.
WELL, I WANTED TO SEE DREAM KAMEN...
UP CLOSE
BESIDES, YOU SAID YOU WANTED TO SEE HIM TOO, MUGI...

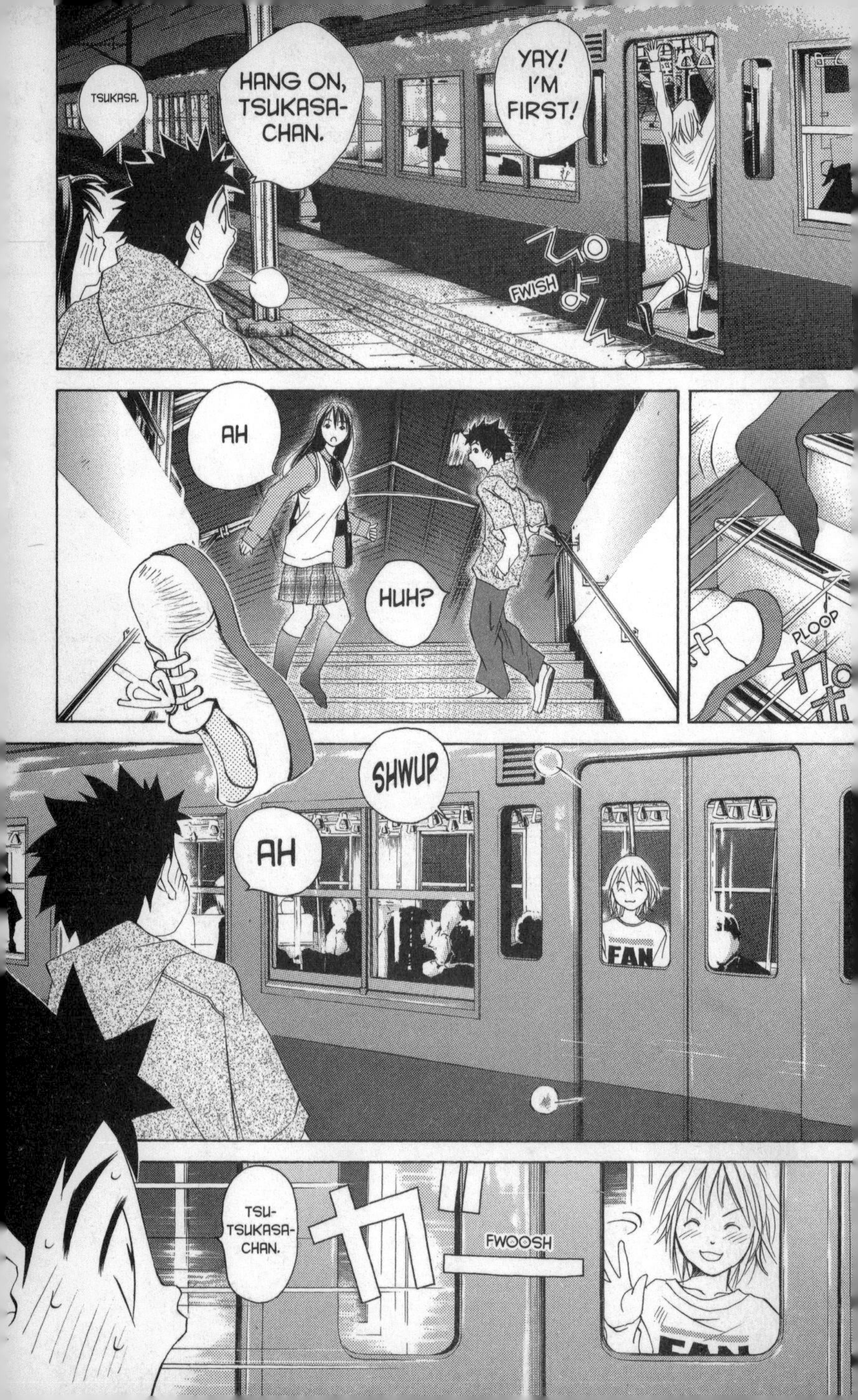
YAY! I'M FIRST!
FWISH
HANG ON, TSUKASA-CHAN.
TSUKASA.
PLOOP
AH
HUH?
SHWUP
AH
FWOOSH
TSU- TSUKASA-CHAN.

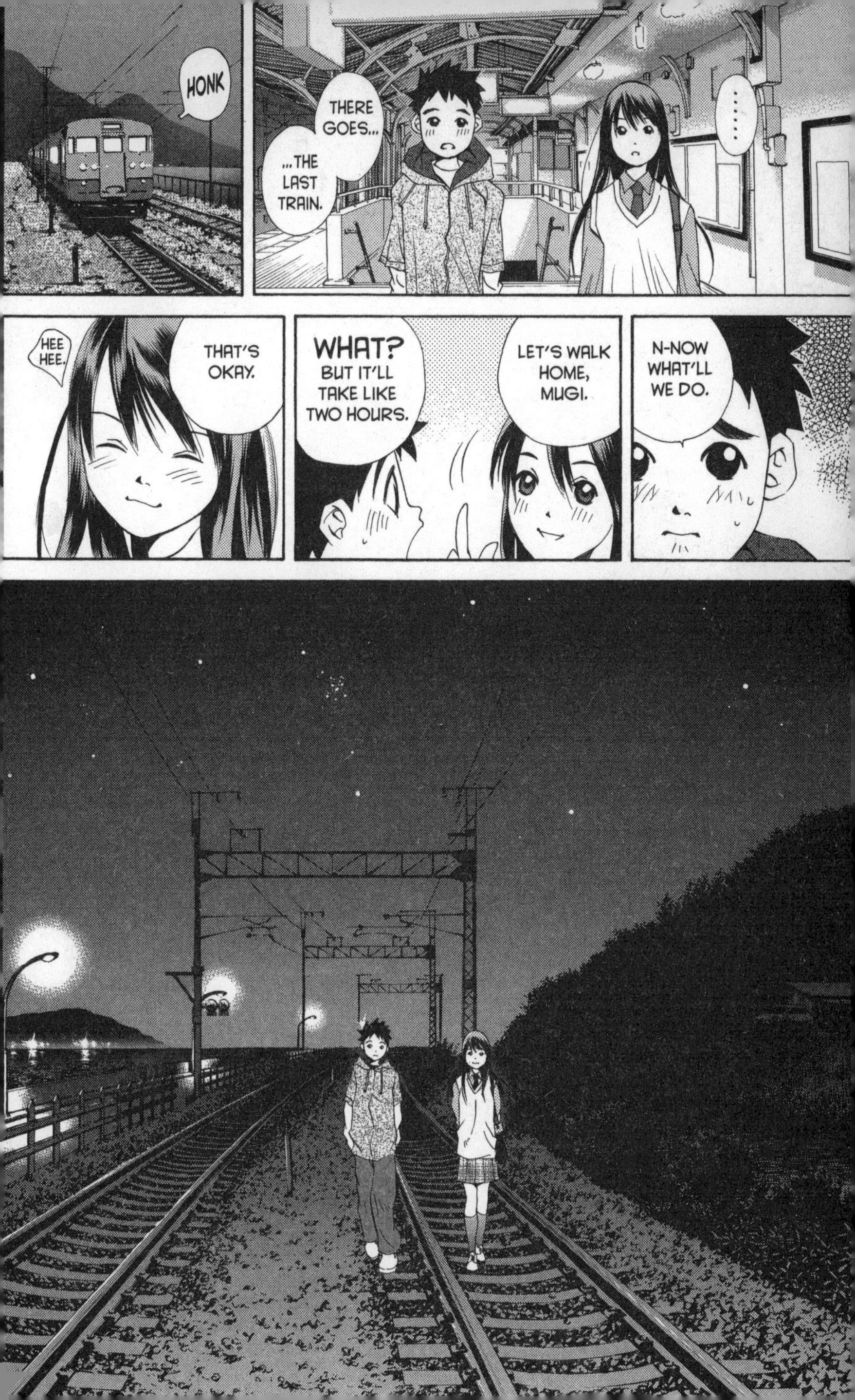
......
THERE GOES...
...THE LAST TRAIN.
HONK
N-NOW WHAT'LL WE DO.
LET'S WALK HOME, MUGI.
WHAT? BUT IT'LL TAKE LIKE TWO HOURS.
THAT'S OKAY.
HEE HEE.

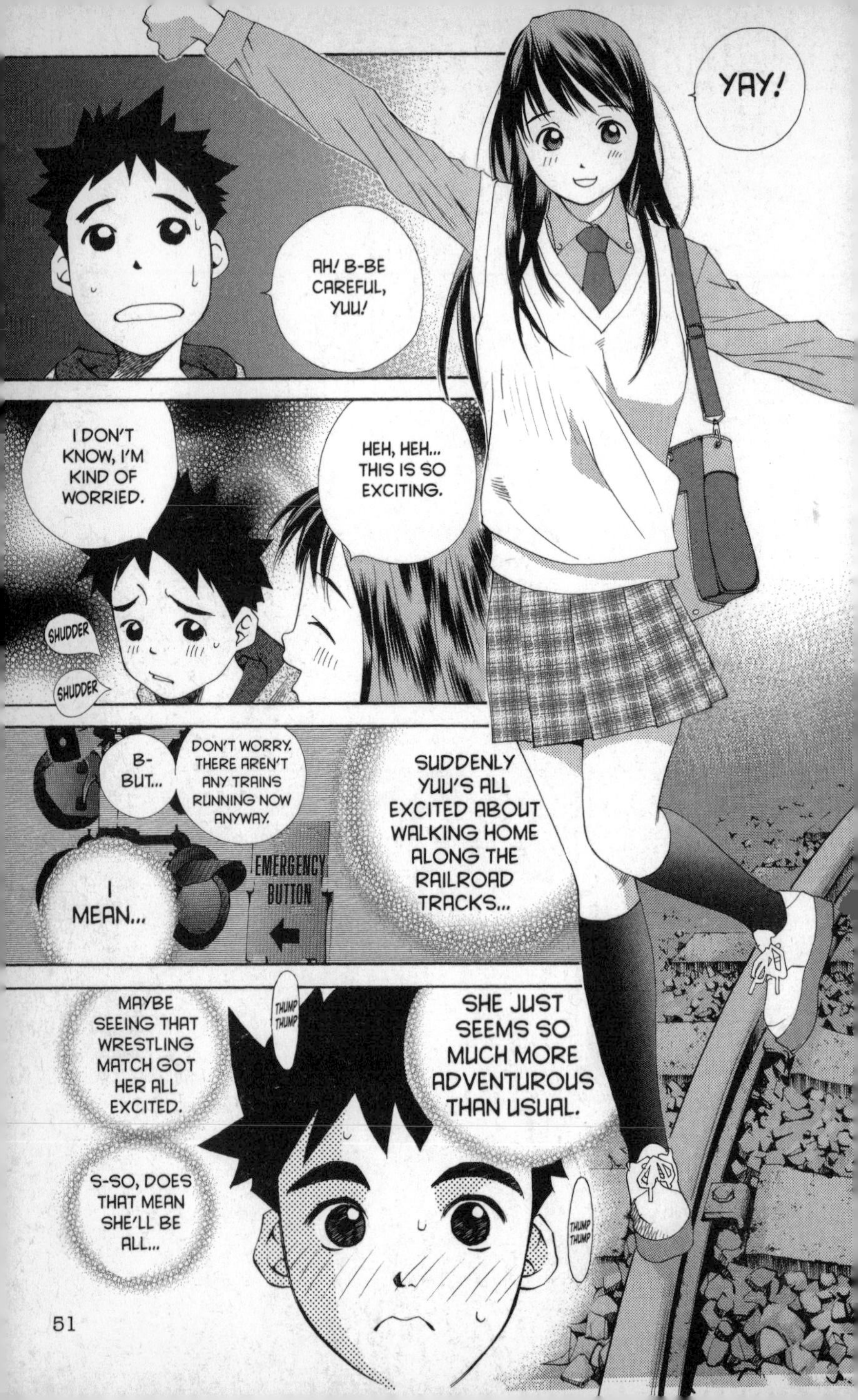
YAY!
AH! B-BE CAREFUL, YUU!
HEH, HEH... THIS IS SO EXCITING.
I DON'T KNOW, I'M KIND OF WORRIED.
SHUDDER
SHUDDER
SUDDENLY YUU'S ALL EXCITED ABOUT WALKING HOME ALONG THE RAILROAD TRACKS...
DON'T WORRY. THERE AREN'T ANY TRAINS RUNNING NOW ANYWAY.
B-BUT...
EMERGENCY BUTTON
I MEAN...
SHE JUST SEEMS SO MUCH MORE ADVENTUROUS THAN USUAL.
THUMP THUMP
MAYBE SEEING THAT WRESTLING MATCH GOT HER ALL EXCITED.
S-SO, DOES THAT MEAN SHE'LL BE ALL...
THUMP THUMP

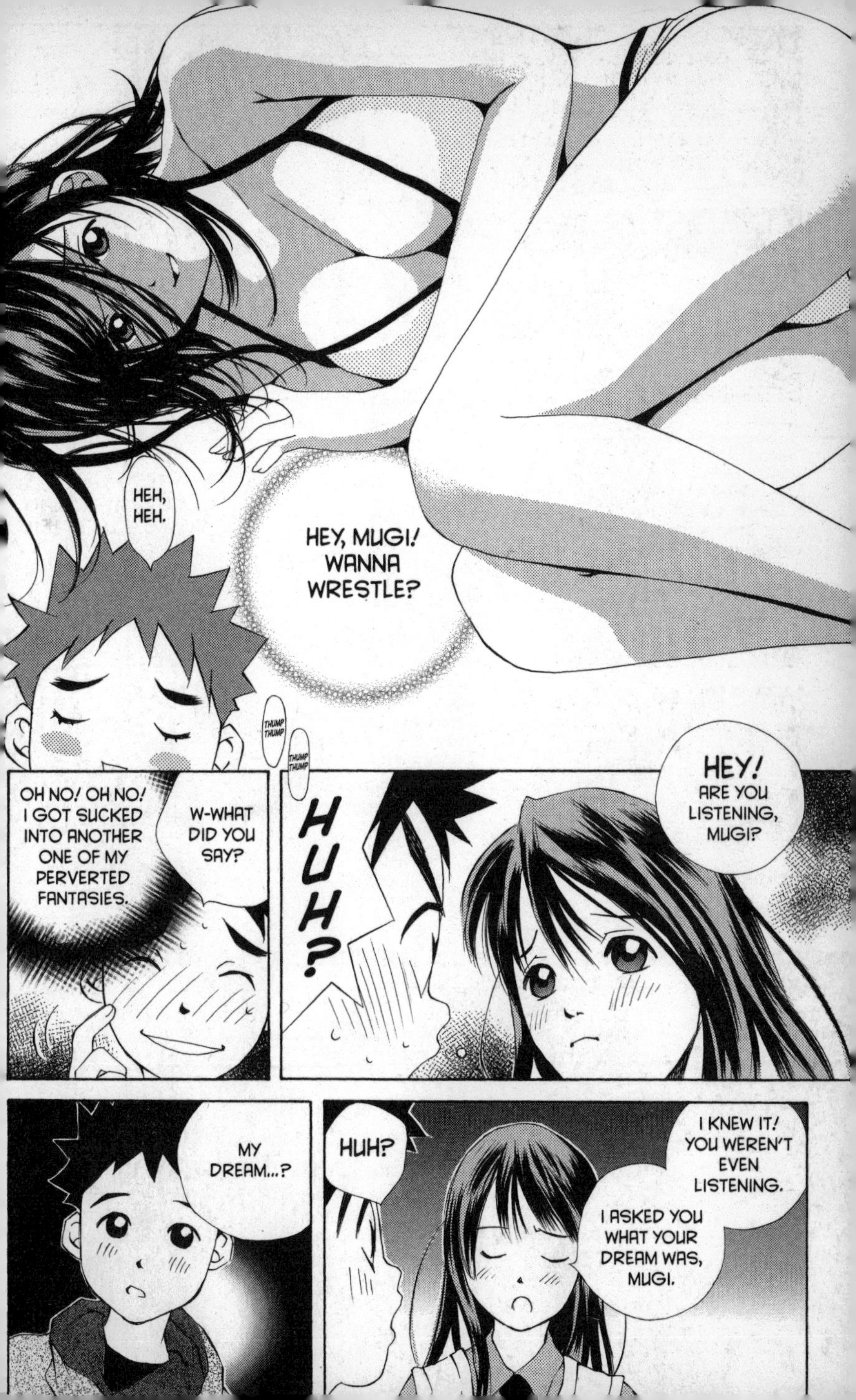
HEY, MUGI! WANNA WRESTLE?
HEH, HEH.
THUMP THUMP
THUMP THUMP
HEY! ARE YOU LISTENING, MUGI?
HUH?
W-WHAT DID YOU SAY?
OH NO! OH NO! I GOT SUCKED INTO ANOTHER ONE OF MY PERVERTED FANTASIES.
HUH?
I KNEW IT! YOU WEREN'T EVEN LISTENING.
I ASKED YOU WHAT YOUR DREAM WAS, MUGI.
MY DREAM...?

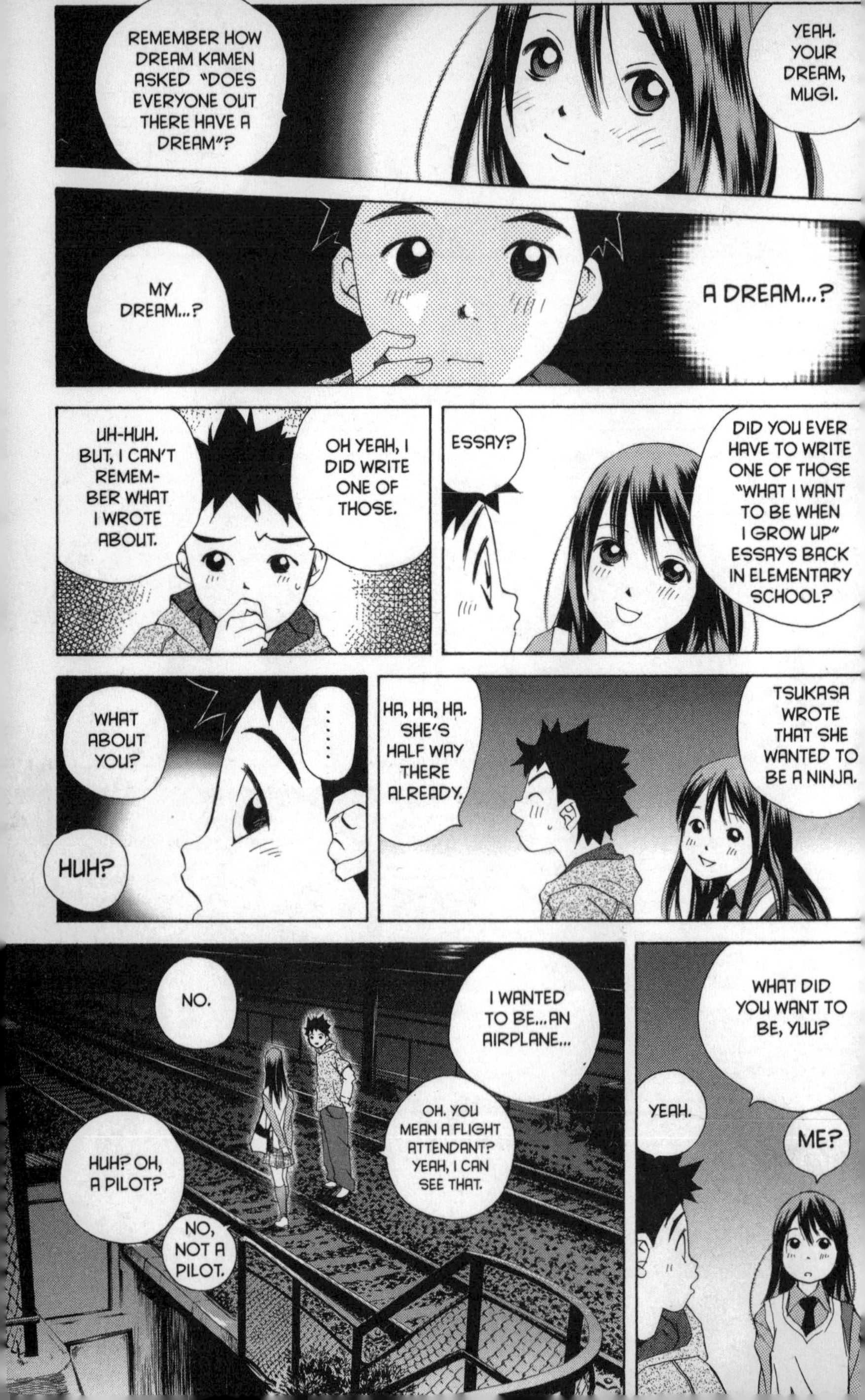
YEAH. YOUR DREAM, MUGI.
REMEMBER HOW DREAM KAMEN ASKED "DOES EVERYONE OUT THERE HAVE A DREAM"?
A DREAM...?
MY DREAM...?
DID YOU EVER HAVE TO WRITE ONE OF THOSE "WHAT I WANT TO BE WHEN I GROW UP" ESSAYS BACK IN ELEMENTARY SCHOOL?
ESSAY?
OH YEAH, I DID WRITE ONE OF THOSE.
UH-HUH. BUT, I CAN'T REMEMBER WHAT I WROTE ABOUT.
TSUKASA WROTE THAT SHE WANTED TO BE A NINJA.
HA, HA, HA. SHE'S HALF WAY THERE ALREADY.
......
WHAT ABOUT YOU?
HUH?
WHAT DID YOU WANT TO BE, YUU?
ME?
YEAH.
I WANTED TO BE...AN AIRPLANE...
OH. YOU MEAN A FLIGHT ATTENDANT? YEAH, I CAN SEE THAT.
NO.
HUH? OH, A PILOT?
NO, NOT A PILOT.

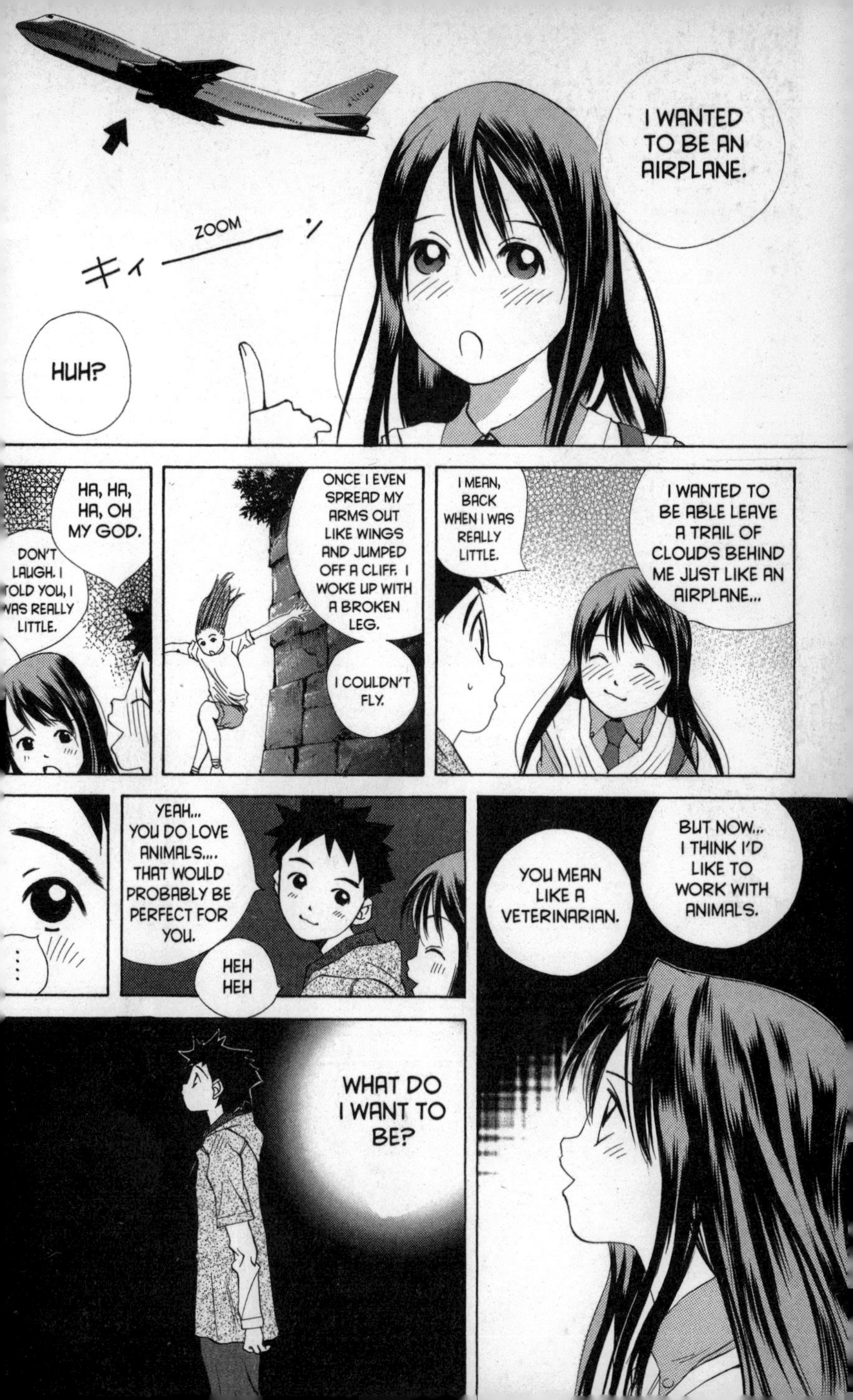
I WANTED TO BE AN AIRPLANE.
ZOOM
キィーーン
HUH?
I WANTED TO BE ABLE LEAVE A TRAIL OF CLOUDS BEHIND ME JUST LIKE AN AIRPLANE...
I MEAN, BACK WHEN I WAS REALLY LITTLE.
ONCE I EVEN SPREAD MY ARMS OUT LIKE WINGS AND JUMPED OFF A CLIFF. I WOKE UP WITH A BROKEN LEG.
I COULDN'T FLY.
HA, HA, HA, OH MY GOD.
DON'T LAUGH. I TOLD YOU, I WAS REALLY LITTLE.
BUT NOW... I THINK I'D LIKE TO WORK WITH ANIMALS.
YOU MEAN LIKE A VETERINARIAN.
YEAH... YOU DO LOVE ANIMALS.... THAT WOULD PROBABLY BE PERFECT FOR YOU.
HEH HEH
.....
WHAT DO I WANT TO BE?

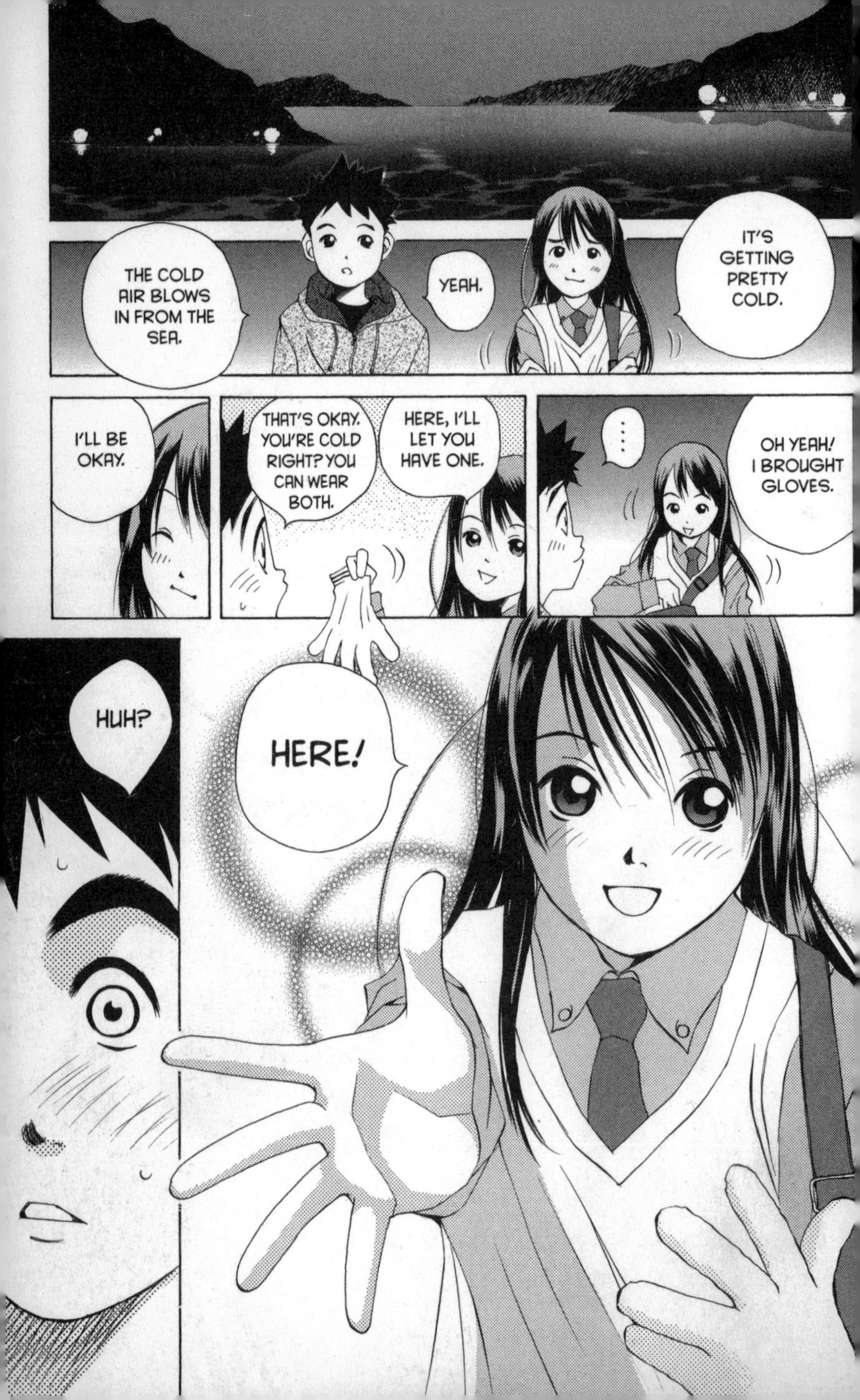
IT'S GETTING PRETTY COLD.
YEAH.
THE COLD AIR BLOWS IN FROM THE SEA.
OH YEAH! I BROUGHT GLOVES.
....
HERE, I'LL LET YOU HAVE ONE.
THAT'S OKAY. YOU'RE COLD RIGHT? YOU CAN WEAR BOTH.
I'LL BE OKAY.
HERE!
HUH?

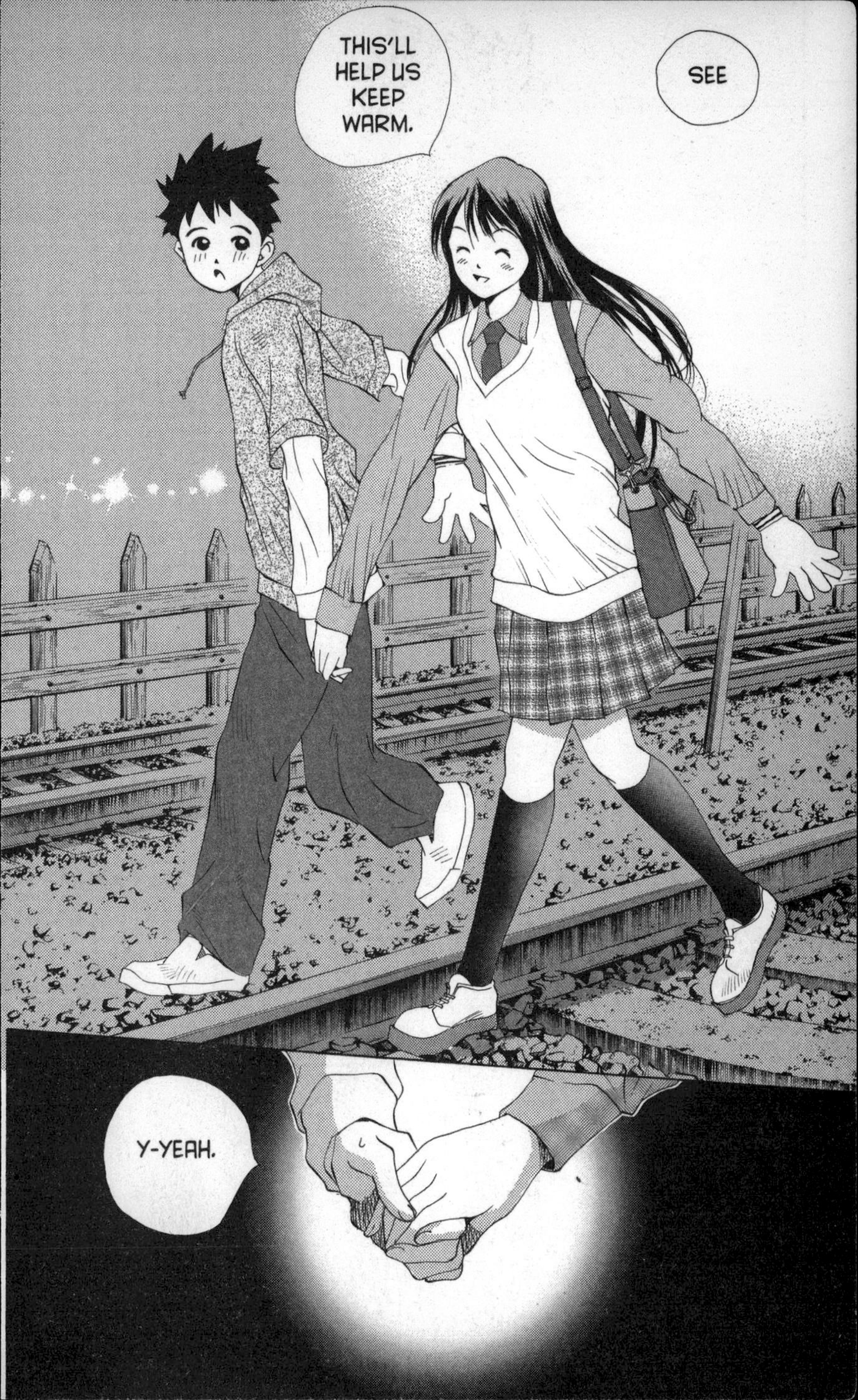
SEE
THIS'LL HELP US KEEP WARM.
Y-YEAH.

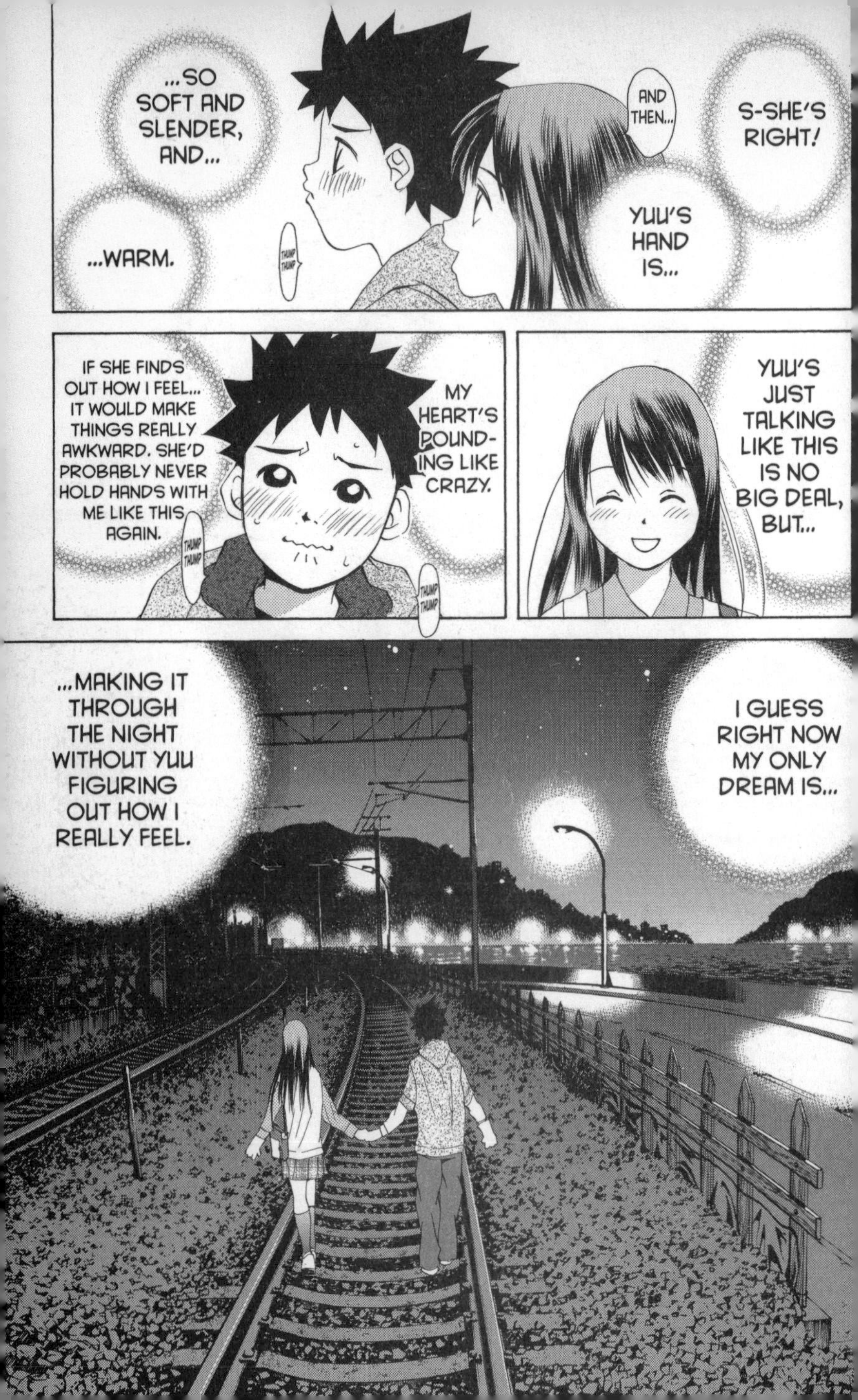
S-SHE'S RIGHT!
AND THEN...
YUU'S HAND IS...
...SO SOFT AND SLENDER, AND...
THUMP THUMP
...WARM.
YUU'S JUST TALKING LIKE THIS IS NO BIG DEAL, BUT...
MY HEART'S POUNDING LIKE CRAZY.
THUMP THUMP
IF SHE FINDS OUT HOW I FEEL... IT WOULD MAKE THINGS REALLY AWKWARD. SHE'D PROBABLY NEVER HOLD HANDS WITH ME LIKE THIS AGAIN.
THUMP THUMP
I GUESS RIGHT NOW MY ONLY DREAM IS...
...MAKING IT THROUGH THE NIGHT WITHOUT YUU FIGURING OUT HOW I REALLY FEEL.

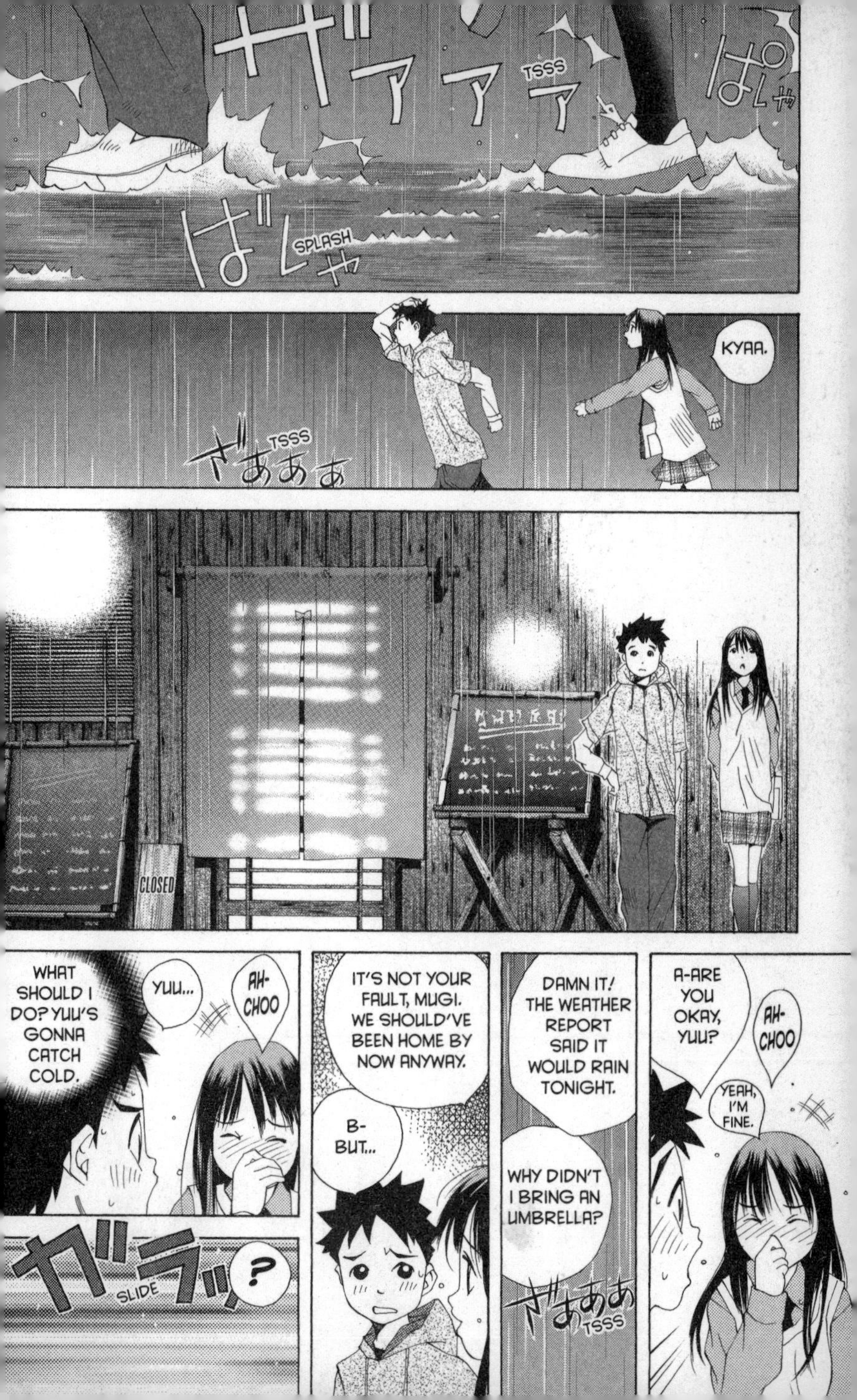
ぱしゃ
ザァァァ
TSSS
ばしゃ
SPLASH
KYAA.
ざあああ
TSSS
CLOSED
A-ARE YOU OKAY, YUU?
AH-CHOO
YEAH, I'M FINE.
DAMN IT! THE WEATHER REPORT SAID IT WOULD RAIN TONIGHT.
WHY DIDN'T I BRING AN UMBRELLA?
ざあああ
TSSS
IT'S NOT YOUR FAULT, MUGI. WE SHOULD'VE BEEN HOME BY NOW ANYWAY.
B-BUT...
AH-CHOO
YUU...
WHAT SHOULD I DO? YUU'S GONNA CATCH COLD.
ガラッ
SLIDE
?

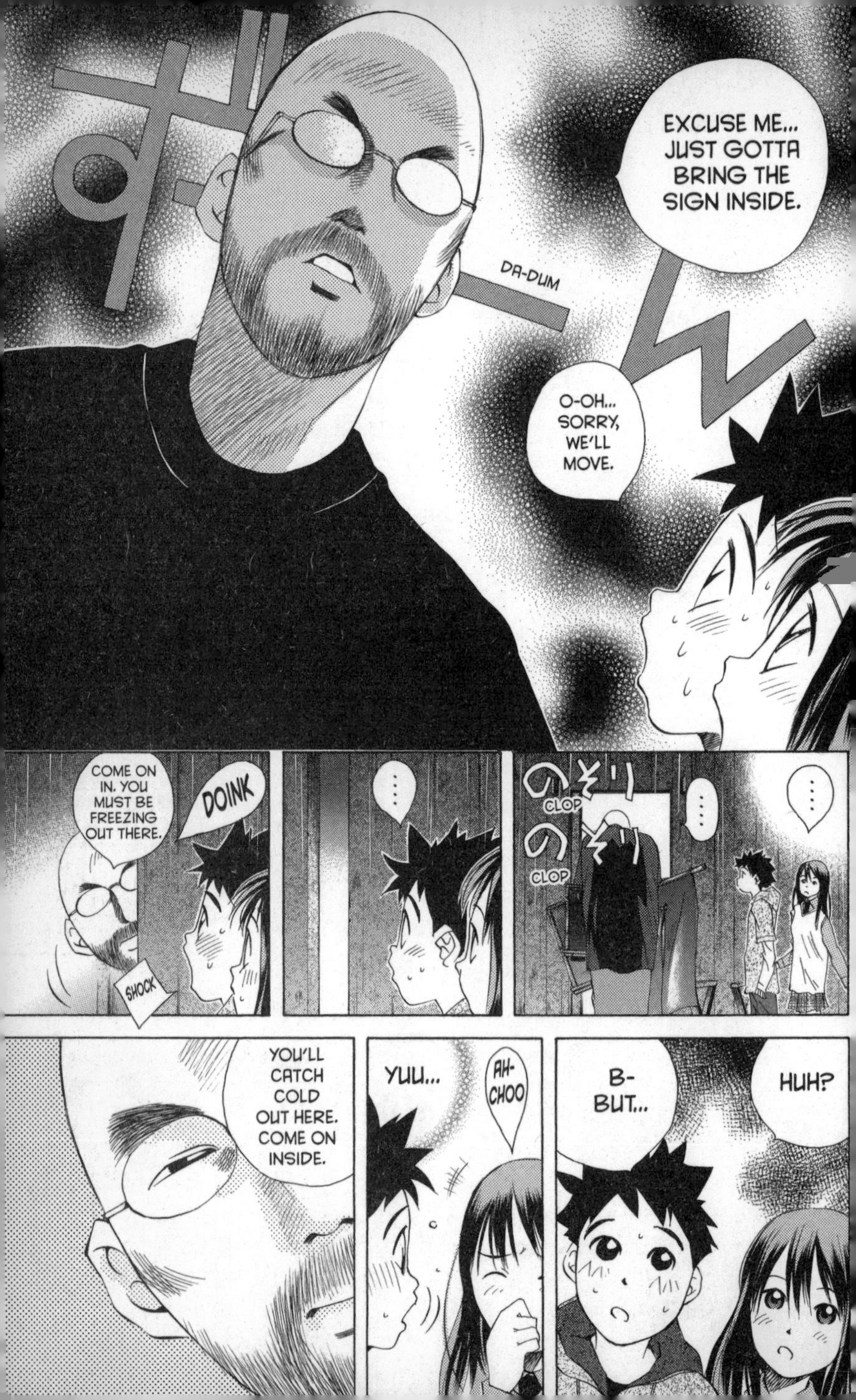
EXCUSE ME... JUST GOTTA BRING THE SIGN INSIDE.
DA-DUM
O-OH... SORRY, WE'LL MOVE.
....
....
CLOP
CLOP
....
DOINK
COME ON IN. YOU MUST BE FREEZING OUT THERE.
SHOCK
HUH?
B- BUT...
AH-CHOO
YUU...
YOU'LL CATCH COLD OUT HERE. COME ON INSIDE.

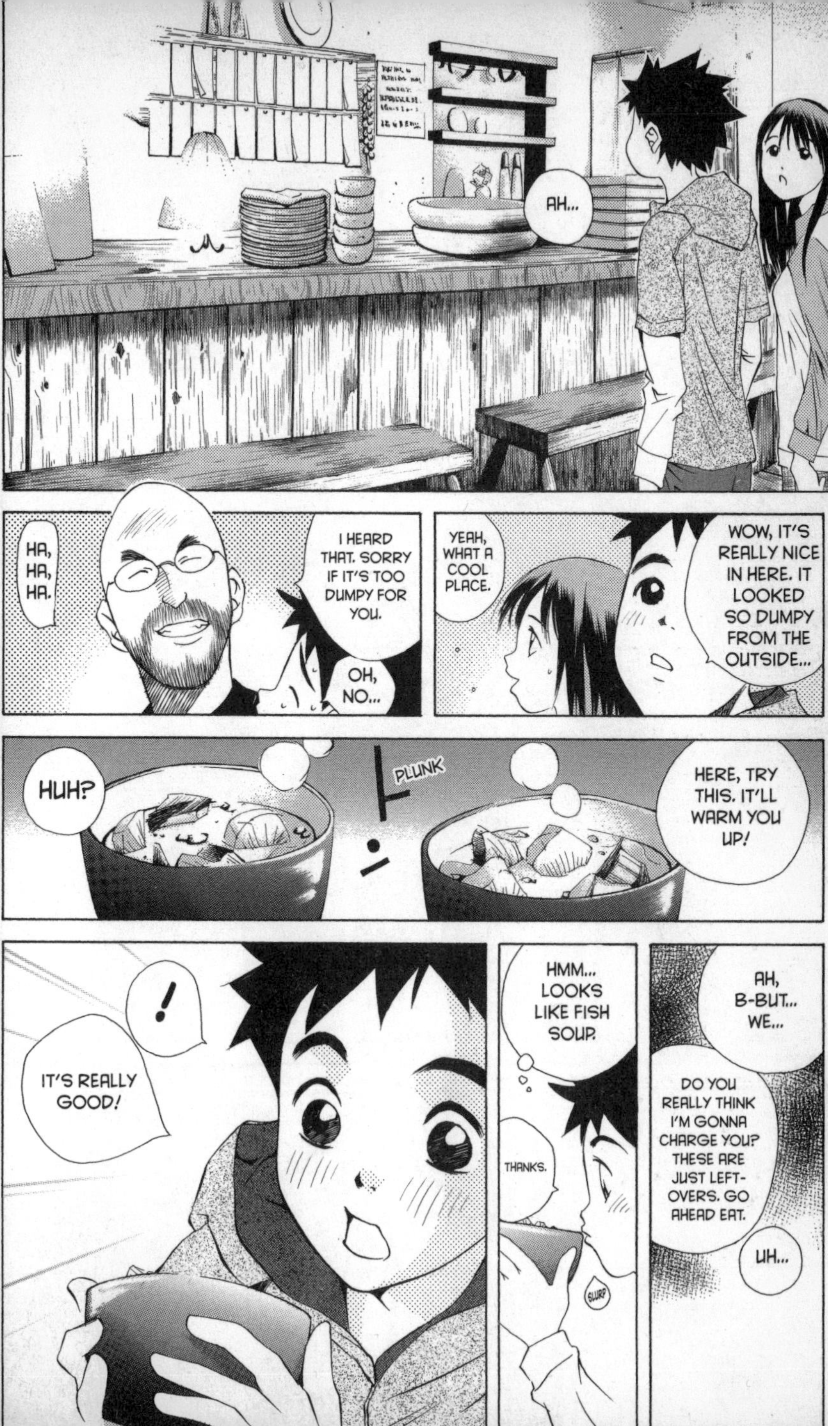
AH...
WOW, IT'S REALLY NICE IN HERE. IT LOOKED SO DUMPY FROM THE OUTSIDE...
YEAH, WHAT A COOL PLACE.
I HEARD THAT. SORRY IF IT'S TOO DUMPY FOR YOU.
HA, HA, HA.
OH, NO...
HERE, TRY THIS. IT'LL WARM YOU UP!
PLUNK
HUH?
AH, B-BUT... WE...
DO YOU REALLY THINK I'M GONNA CHARGE YOU? THESE ARE JUST LEFT-OVERS. GO AHEAD EAT.
UH...
HMM... LOOKS LIKE FISH SOUP.
THANKS.
SLURP
!
IT'S REALLY GOOD!

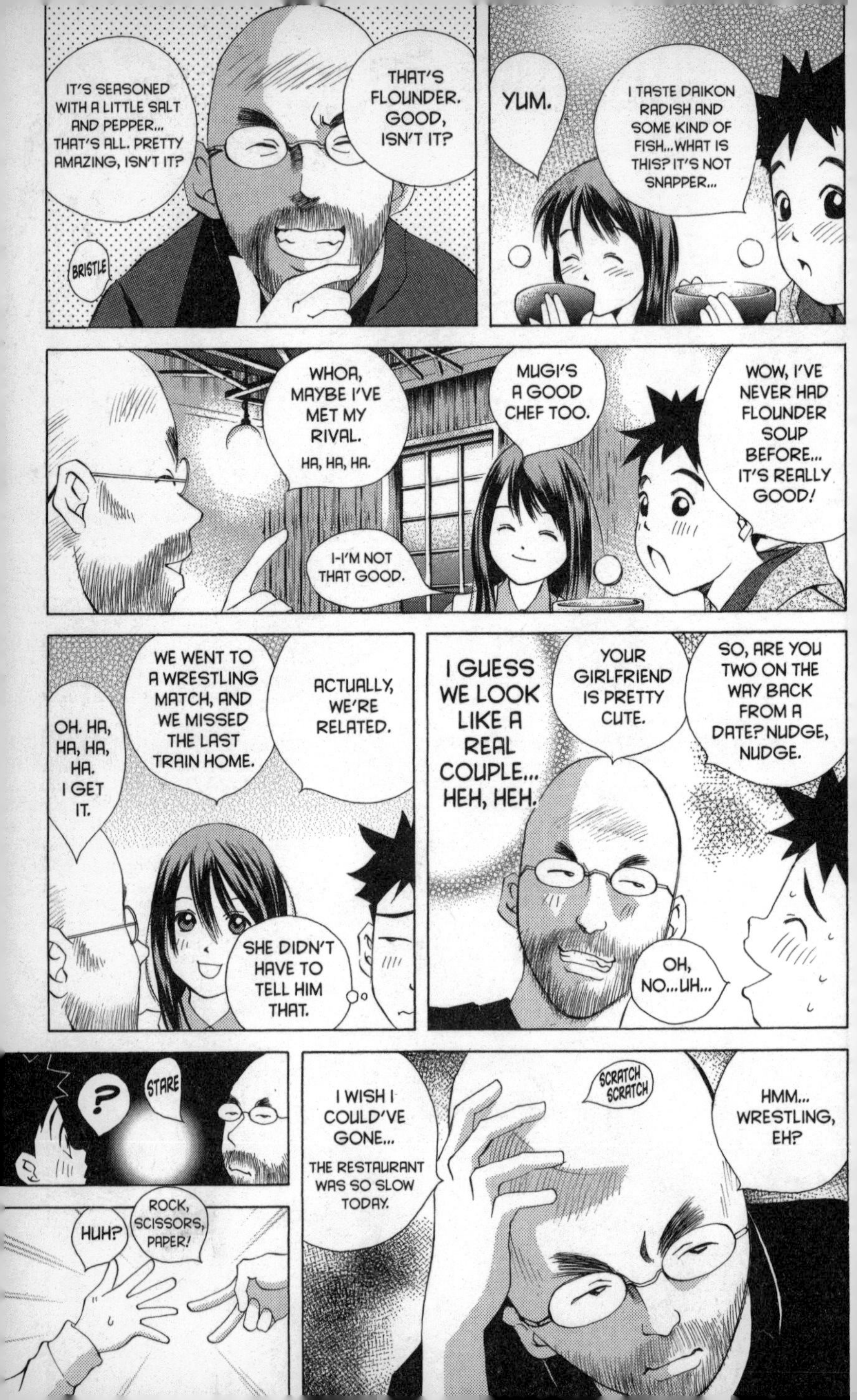
I TASTE DAIKON RADISH AND SOME KIND OF FISH...WHAT IS THIS? IT'S NOT SNAPPER...
YUM.
THAT'S FLOUNDER. GOOD, ISN'T IT?
IT'S SEASONED WITH A LITTLE SALT AND PEPPER... THAT'S ALL. PRETTY AMAZING, ISN'T IT?
BRISTLE
WOW, I'VE NEVER HAD FLOUNDER SOUP BEFORE... IT'S REALLY GOOD!
MUGI'S A GOOD CHEF TOO.
WHOA, MAYBE I'VE MET MY RIVAL. HA, HA, HA.
I-I'M NOT THAT GOOD.
SO, ARE YOU TWO ON THE WAY BACK FROM A DATE? NUDGE, NUDGE.
YOUR GIRLFRIEND IS PRETTY CUTE.
I GUESS WE LOOK LIKE A REAL COUPLE... HEH, HEH.
OH, NO...UH...
ACTUALLY, WE'RE RELATED.
WE WENT TO A WRESTLING MATCH, AND WE MISSED THE LAST TRAIN HOME.
OH. HA, HA, HA, HA. I GET IT.
SHE DIDN'T HAVE TO TELL HIM THAT.
HMM... WRESTLING, EH?
SCRATCH SCRATCH
I WISH I COULD'VE GONE... THE RESTAURANT WAS SO SLOW TODAY.
STARE
?
ROCK, SCISSORS, PAPER!
HUH?

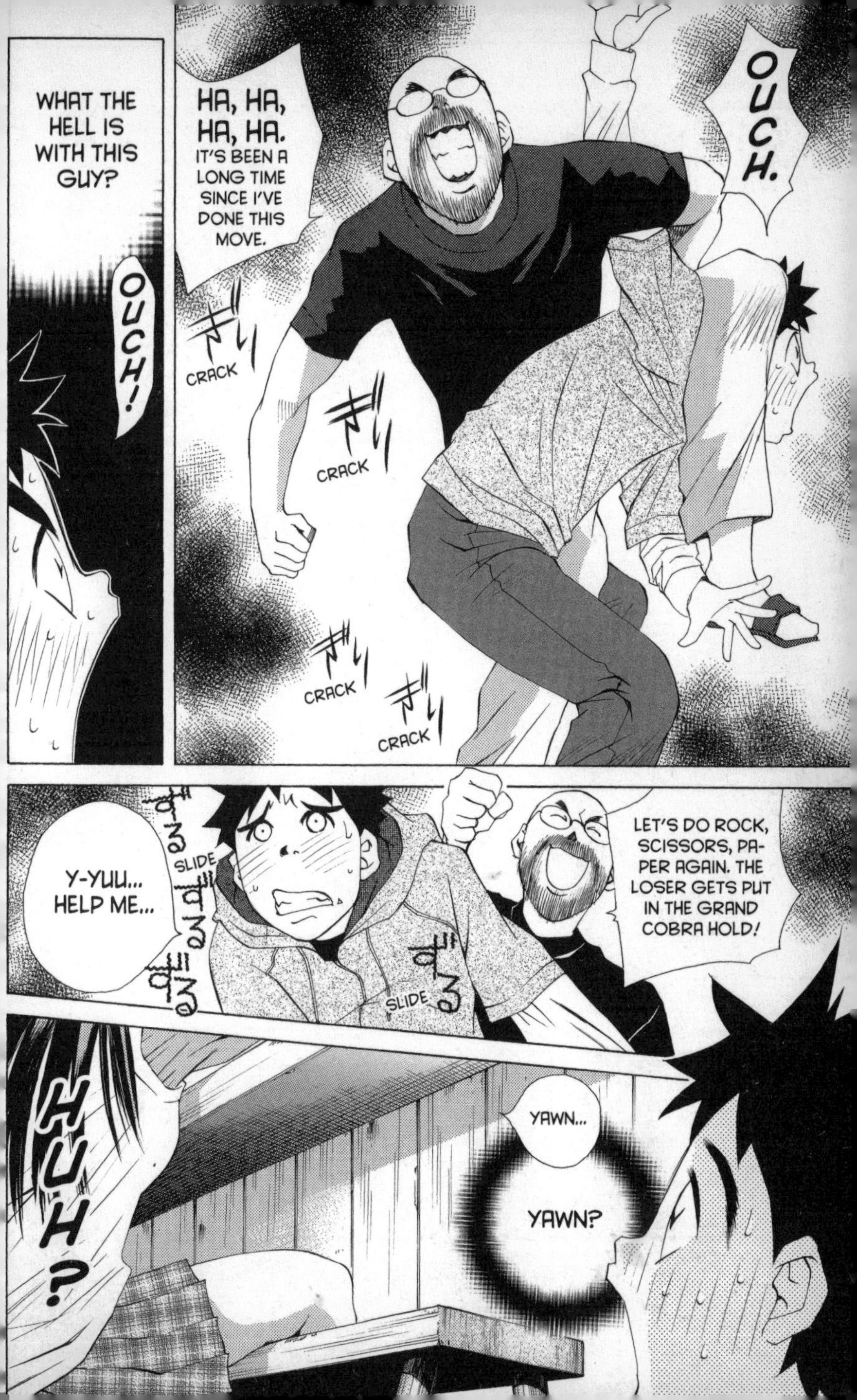
OUCH.
HA, HA, HA, HA. IT'S BEEN A LONG TIME SINCE I'VE DONE THIS MOVE.
CRACK
CRACK
CRACK
CRACK
WHAT THE HELL IS WITH THIS GUY?
OUCH!
LET'S DO ROCK, SCISSORS, PAPER AGAIN. THE LOSER GETS PUT IN THE GRAND COBRA HOLD!
SLIDE
SLIDE
Y-YUU... HELP ME...
YAWN...
YAWN?
HUH?

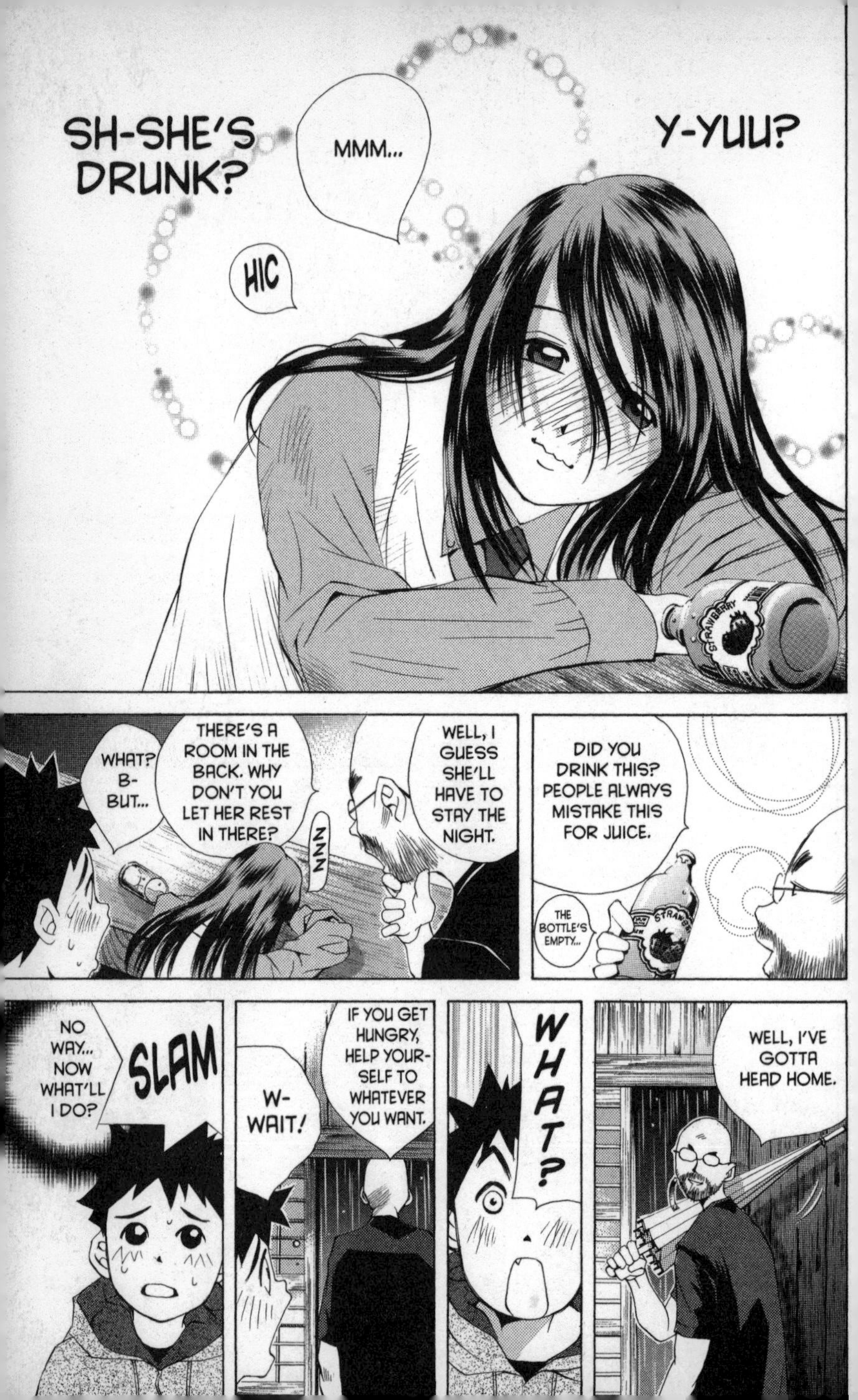
Y-YUU?
MMM...
SH-SHE'S DRUNK?
HIC
DID YOU DRINK THIS? PEOPLE ALWAYS MISTAKE THIS FOR JUICE.
THE BOTTLE'S EMPTY...
STRAWBERRY
WELL, I GUESS SHE'LL HAVE TO STAY THE NIGHT.
ZZZ
THERE'S A ROOM IN THE BACK. WHY DON'T YOU LET HER REST IN THERE?
WHAT? B-BUT...
WELL, I'VE GOTTA HEAD HOME.
WHAT?
IF YOU GET HUNGRY, HELP YOURSELF TO WHATEVER YOU WANT.
W-WAIT!
SLAM
NO WAY... NOW WHAT'LL I DO?

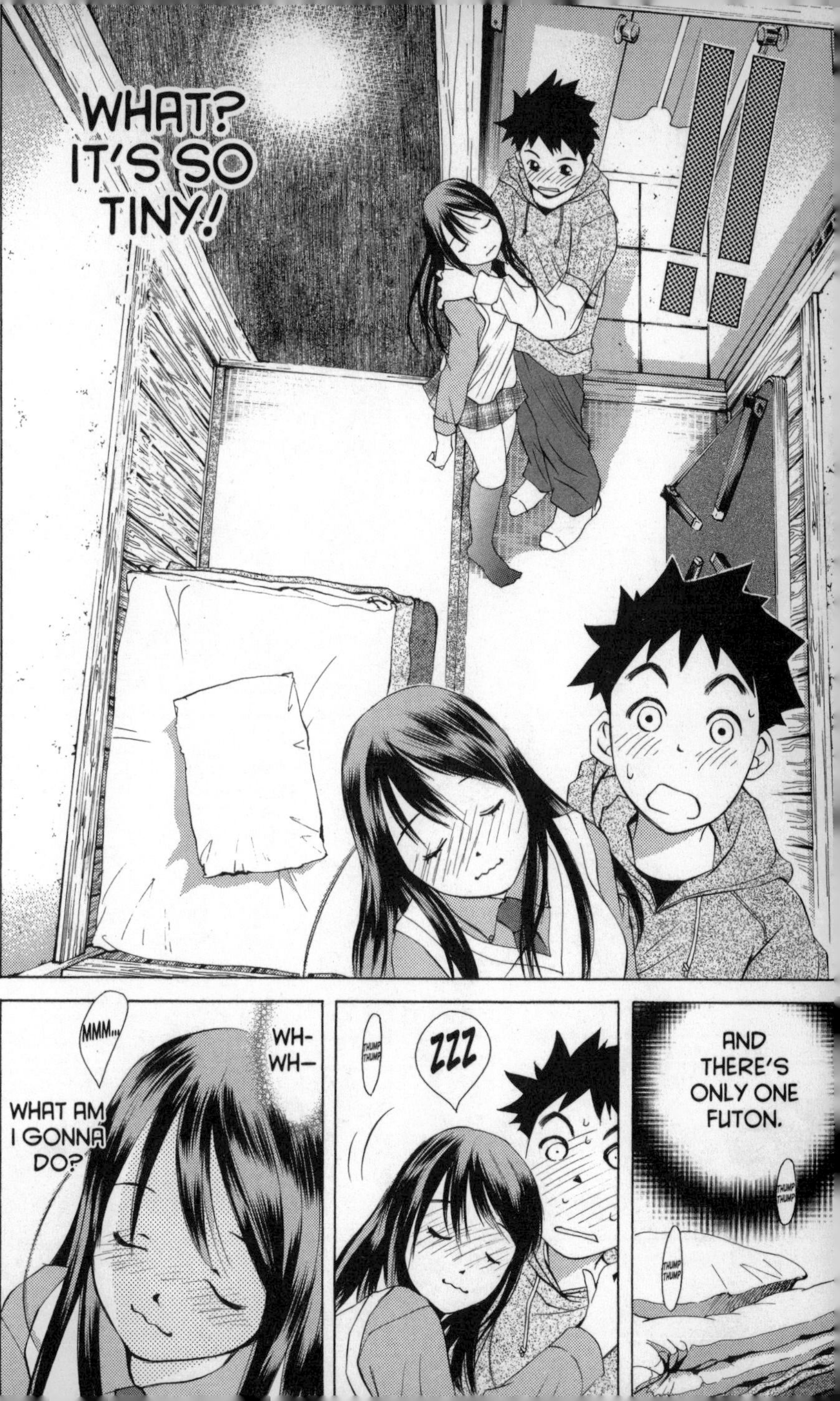
WHAT? IT'S SO TINY!
AND THERE'S ONLY ONE FUTON.
THUMP THUMP
THUMP THUMP
ZZZ
THUMP THUMP
WH- WH-
MMM...
WHAT AM I GONNA DO?

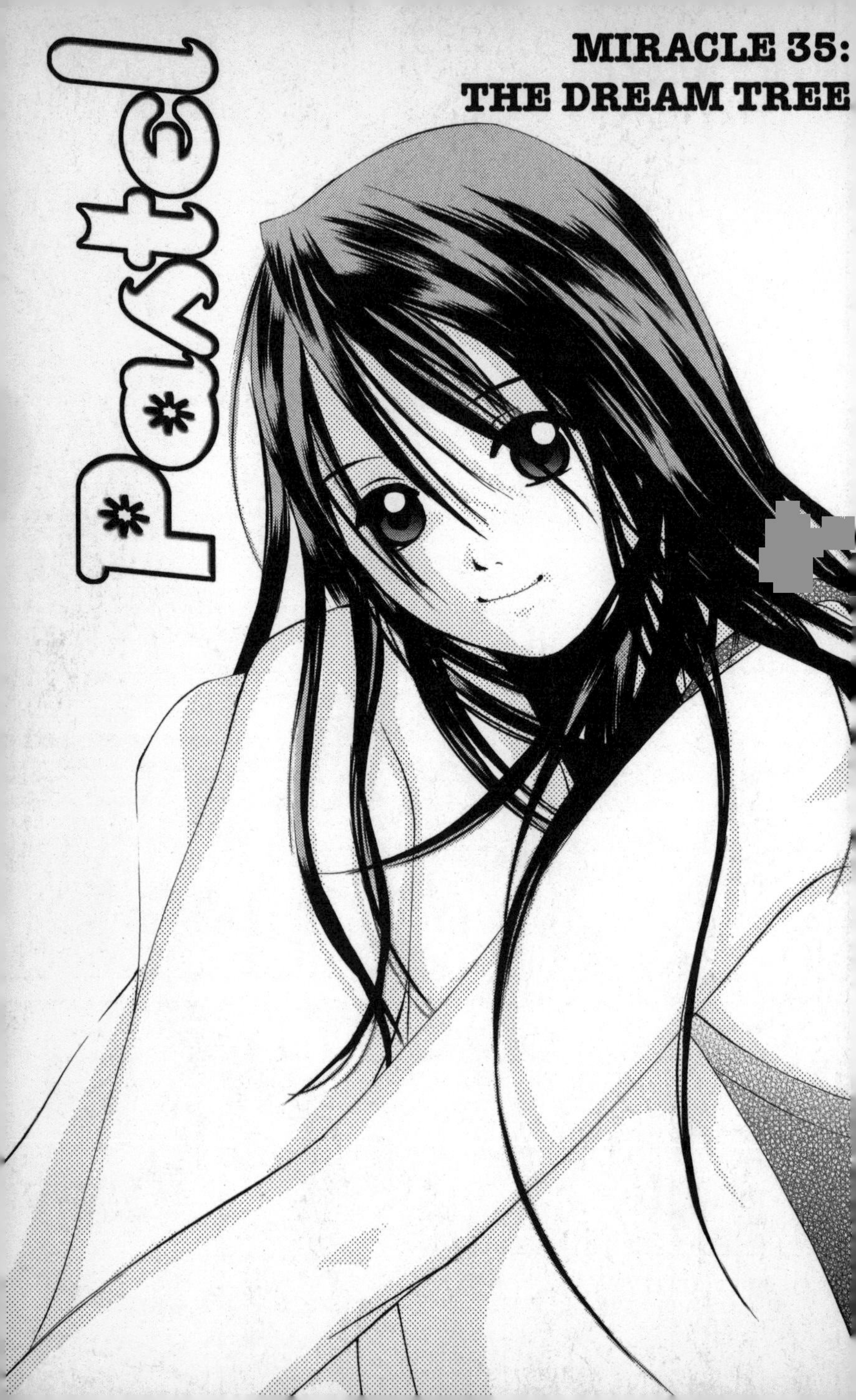
Pastel
MIRACLE 35:
THE DREAM TREE

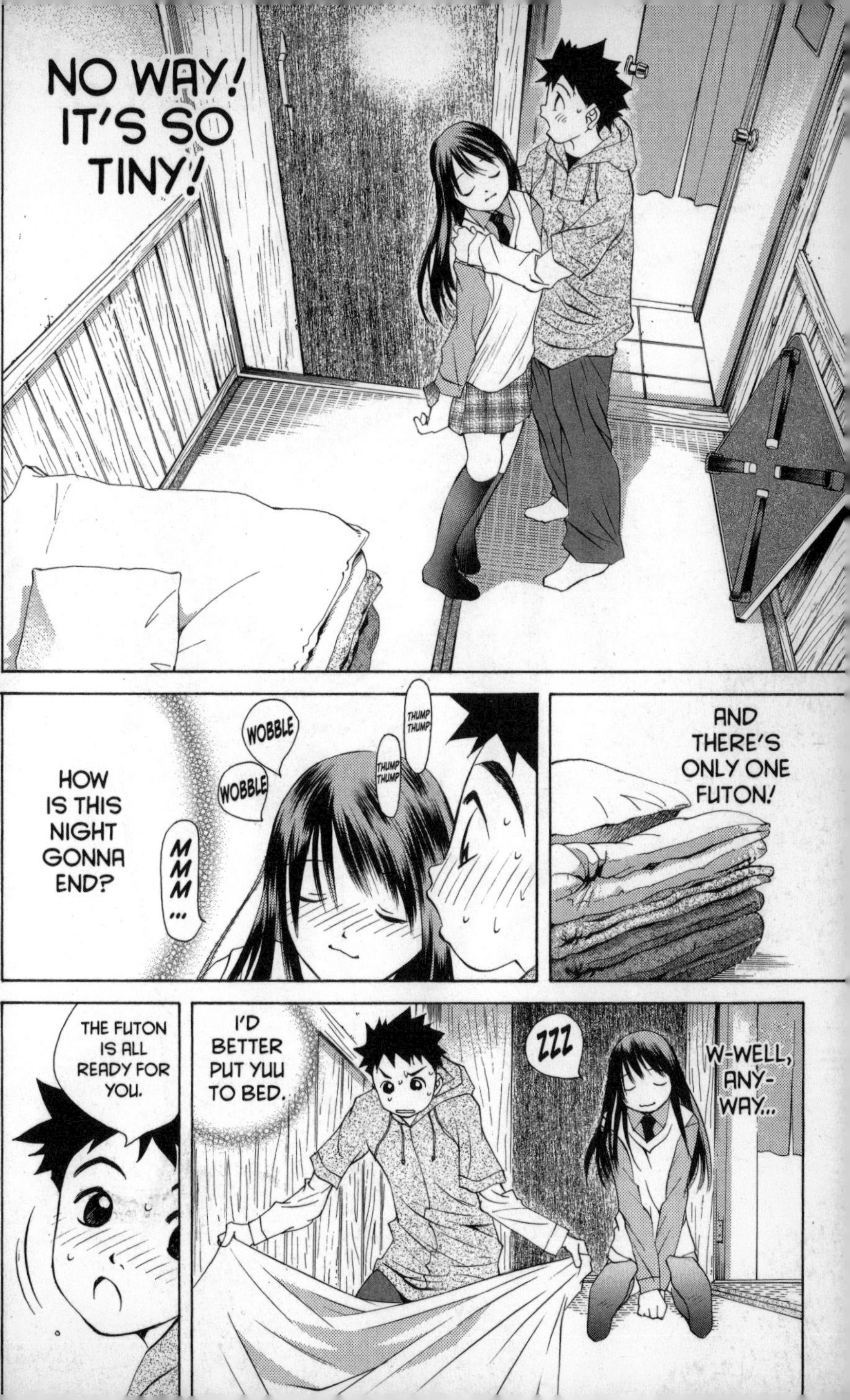
NO WAY! IT'S SO TINY!
AND THERE'S ONLY ONE FUTON!
THUMP THUMP
WOBBLE
THUMP THUMP
WOBBLE
MMM...
HOW IS THIS NIGHT GONNA END?
W-WELL, ANY-WAY...
ZZZ
I'D BETTER PUT YUU TO BED.
THE FUTON IS ALL READY FOR YOU.

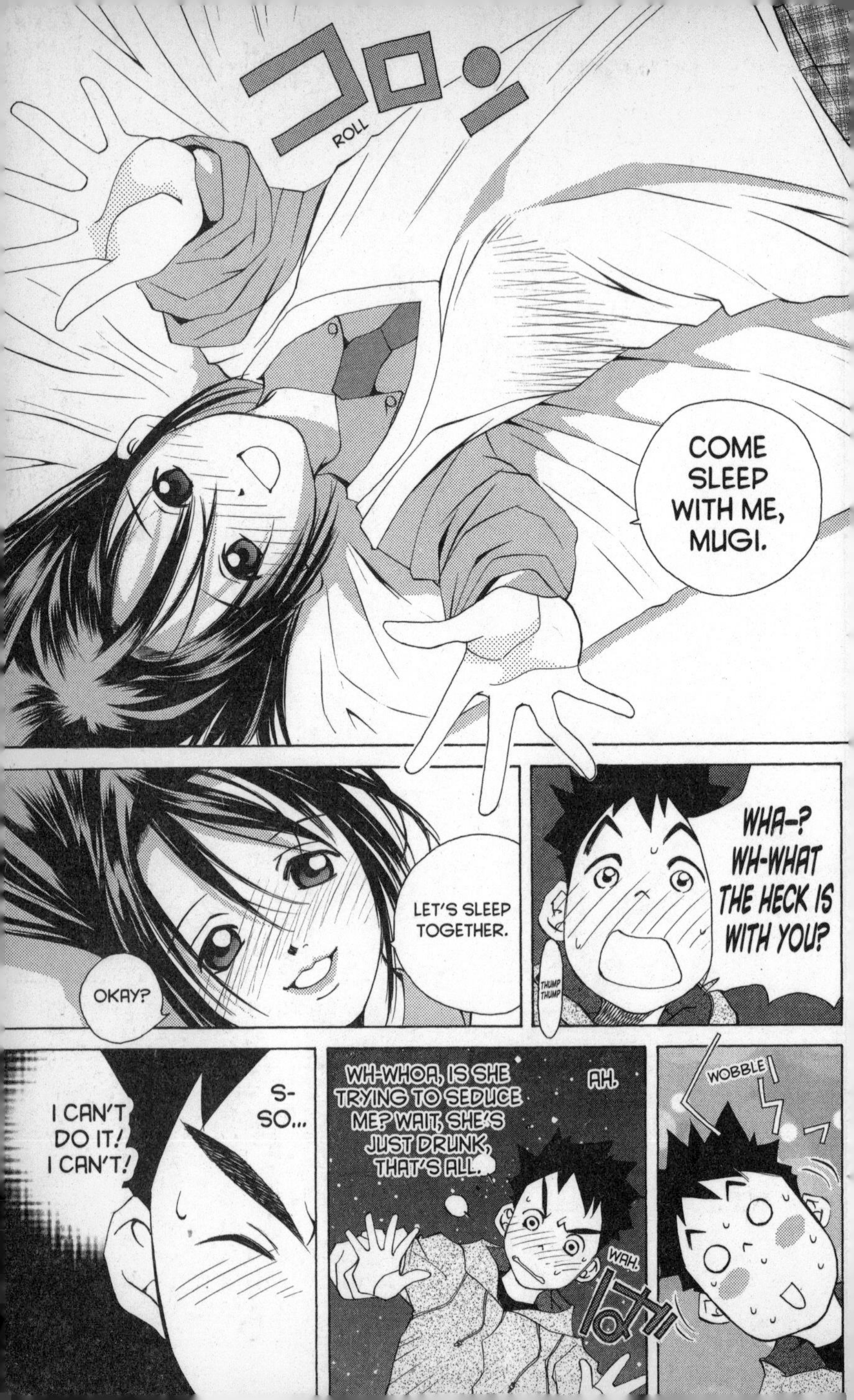
ROLL
COME SLEEP WITH ME, MUGI.
WHA-? WH-WHAT THE HECK IS WITH YOU?
THUMP THUMP
LET'S SLEEP TOGETHER.
OKAY?
WOBBLE
AH.
WH-WHOA, IS SHE TRYING TO SEDUCE ME? WAIT, SHE'S JUST DRUNK, THAT'S ALL.
WAH.
S-SO...
I CAN'T DO IT! I CAN'T!

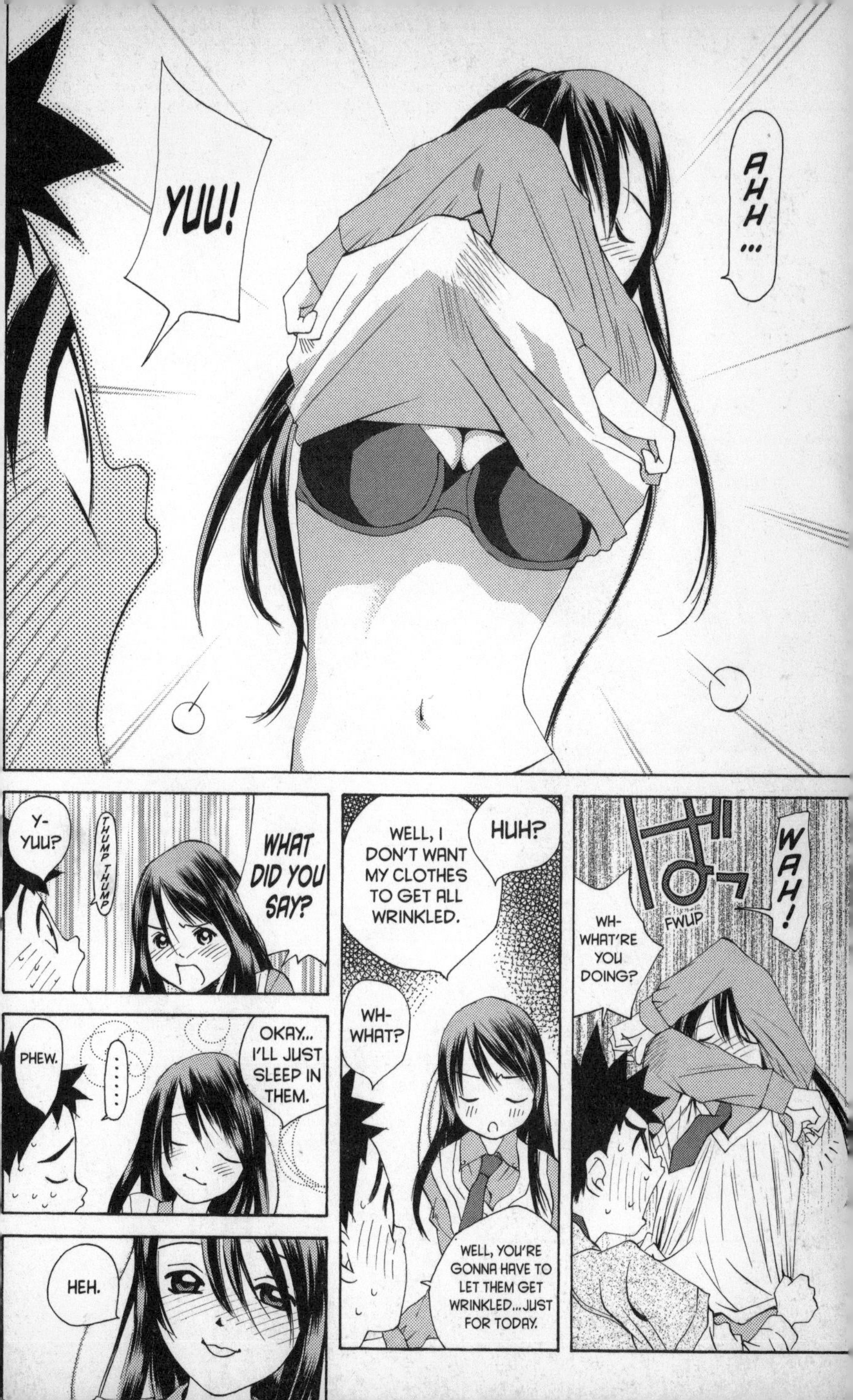
AHH...
YUU!
WAH!
FWUP
WH- WHAT'RE YOU DOING?
HUH?
WELL, I DON'T WANT MY CLOTHES TO GET ALL WRINKLED.
WH- WHAT?
WELL, YOU'RE GONNA HAVE TO LET THEM GET WRINKLED... JUST FOR TODAY.
WHAT DID YOU SAY?
THUMP THUMP
Y- YUU?
OKAY... I'LL JUST SLEEP IN THEM.
......
PHEW.
HEH.

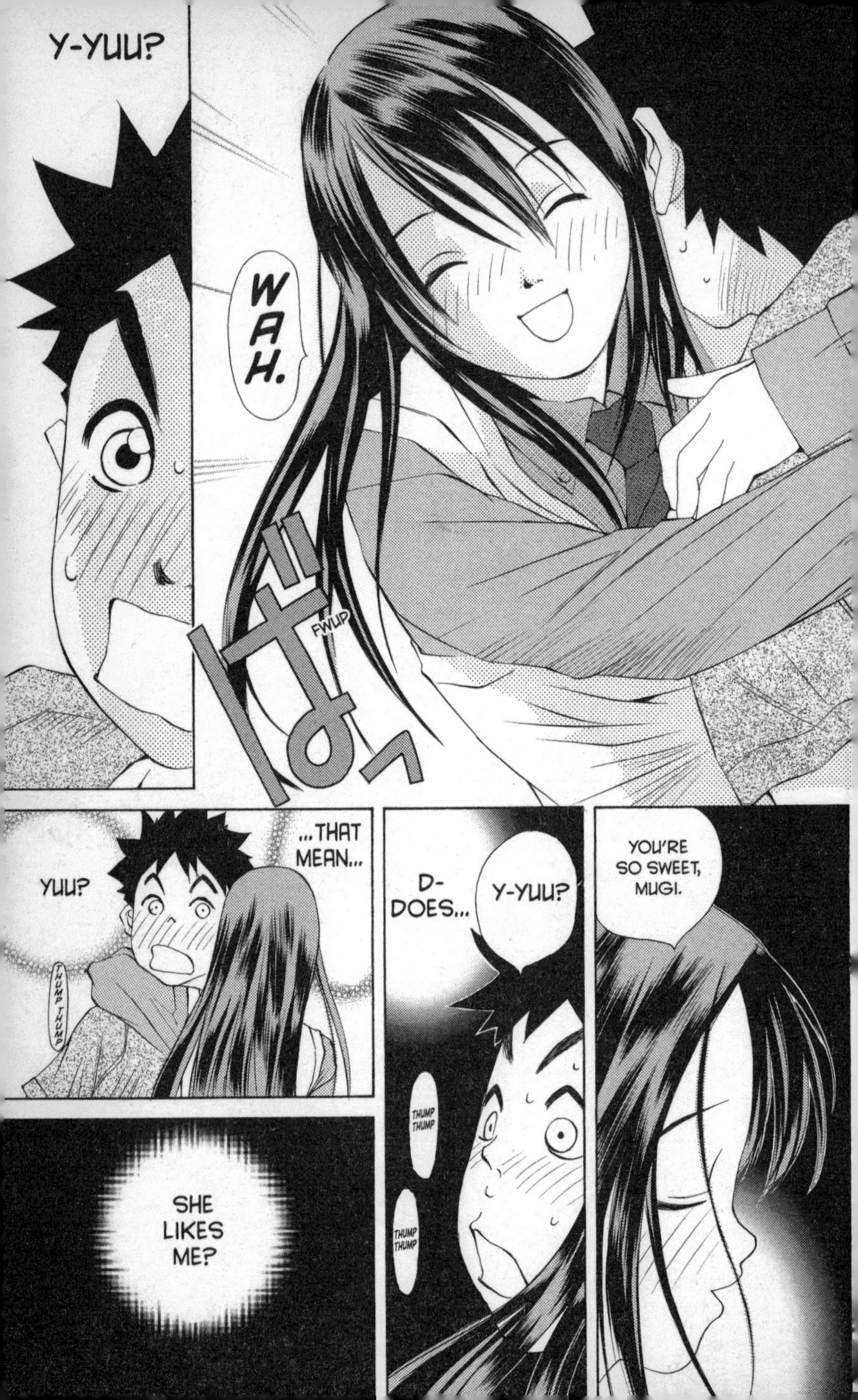

WAH.
FWUP
Y-YUU?
YOU'RE SO SWEET, MUGI.
Y-YUU?
D-DOES...
THUMP THUMP
THUMP THUMP
...THAT MEAN...
YUU?
THUMP THUMP
SHE LIKES ME?

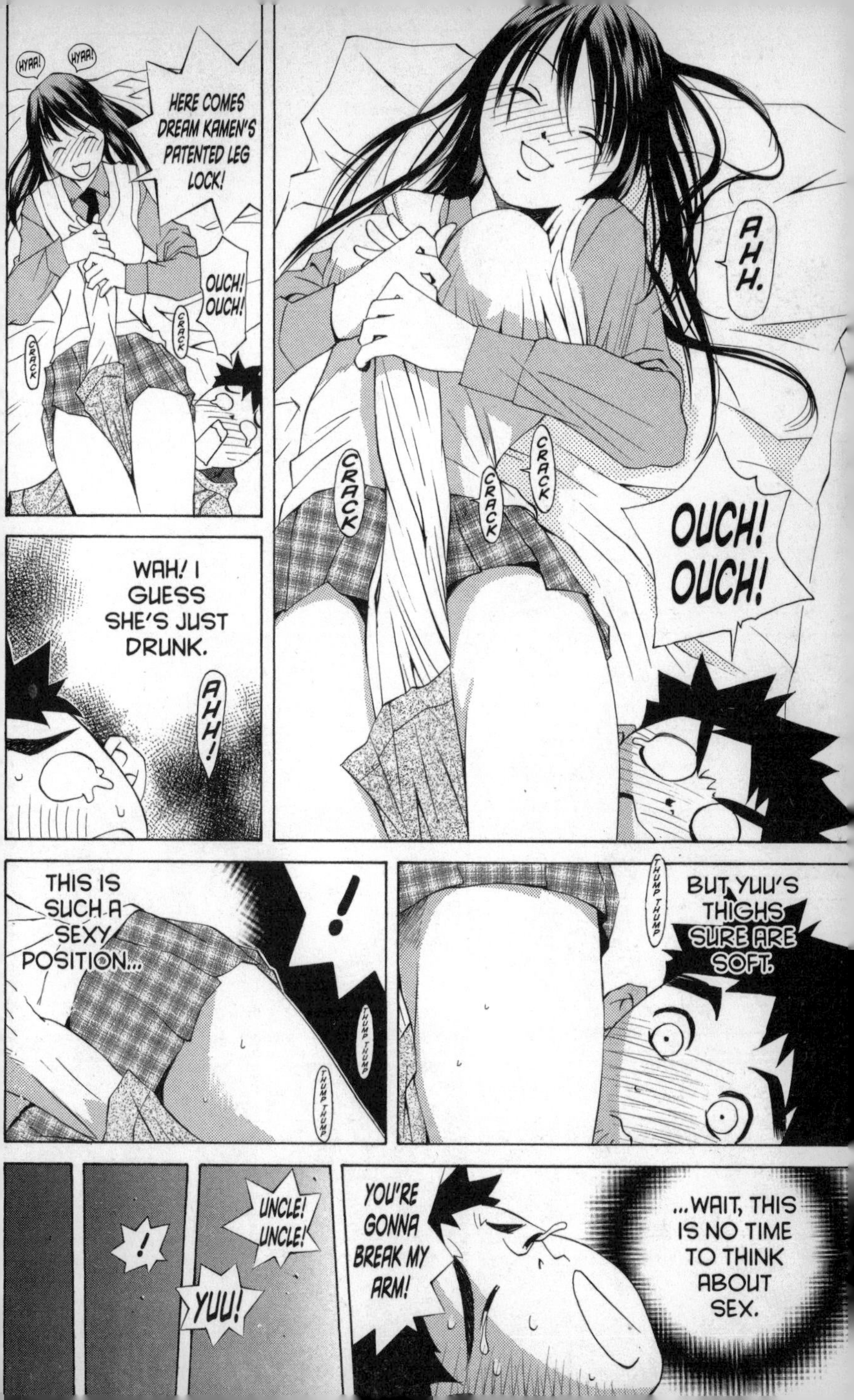
AHH.
CRACK
CRACK
CRACK
OUCH! OUCH!
HYAA!
HYAA!
HERE COMES DREAM KAMEN'S PATENTED LEG LOCK!
OUCH! OUCH!
CRACK
CRACK
WAH! I GUESS SHE'S JUST DRUNK.
AHH!
THUMP THUMP
BUT YUU'S THIGHS SURE ARE SOFT.
!
THIS IS SUCH A SEXY POSITION...
THUMP THUMP
THUMP THUMP
...WAIT, THIS IS NO TIME TO THINK ABOUT SEX.
YOU'RE GONNA BREAK MY ARM!
UNCLE! UNCLE!
!
YUU!

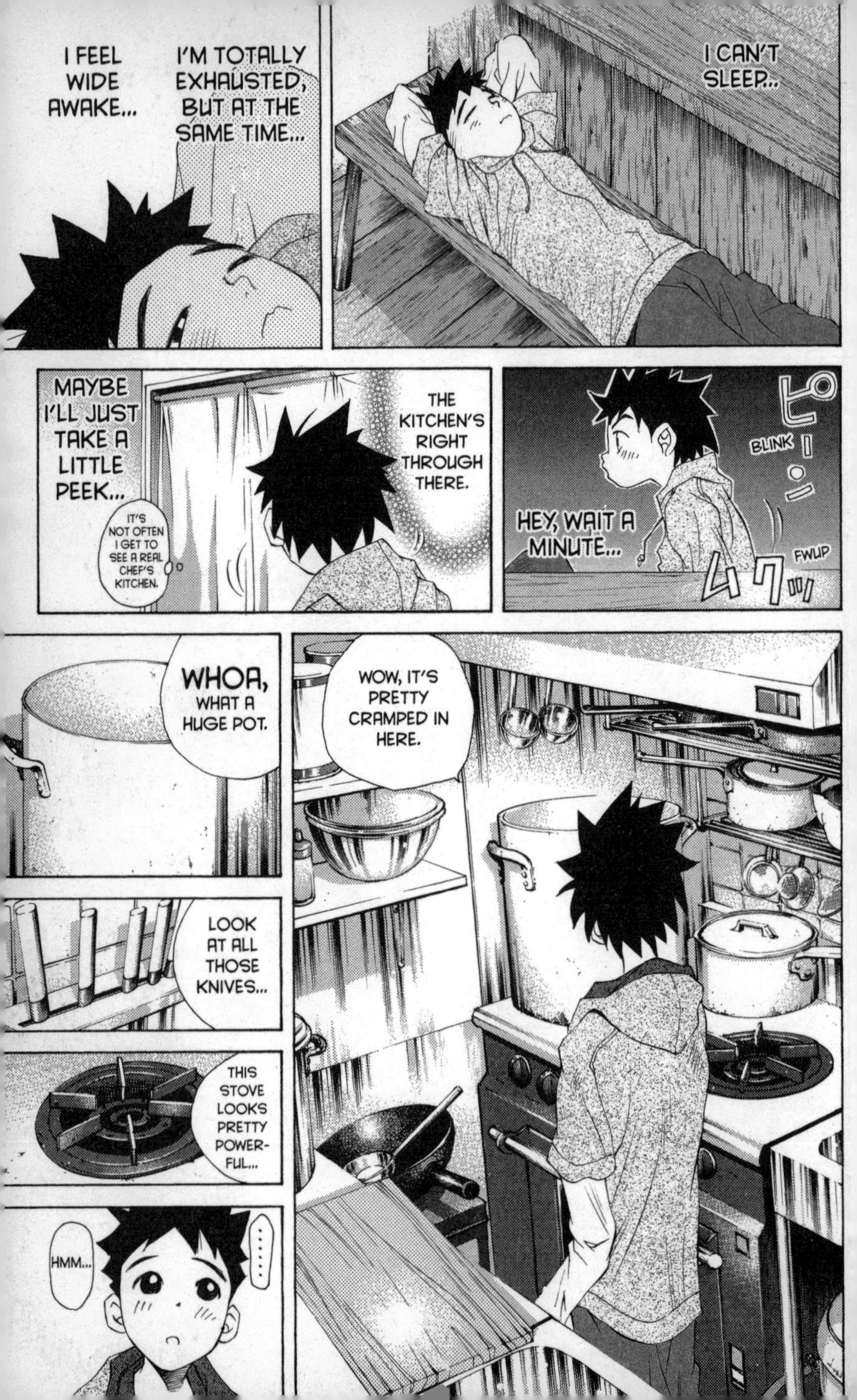
I CAN'T SLEEP...
I'M TOTALLY EXHAUSTED, BUT AT THE SAME TIME...
I FEEL WIDE AWAKE...
BLINK
HEY, WAIT A MINUTE...
FWUP
THE KITCHEN'S RIGHT THROUGH THERE.
MAYBE I'LL JUST TAKE A LITTLE PEEK...
IT'S NOT OFTEN I GET TO SEE A REAL CHEF'S KITCHEN.
WOW, IT'S PRETTY CRAMPED IN HERE.
WHOA, WHAT A HUGE POT.
LOOK AT ALL THOSE KNIVES...
THIS STOVE LOOKS PRETTY POWER-FUL...
......
HMM...

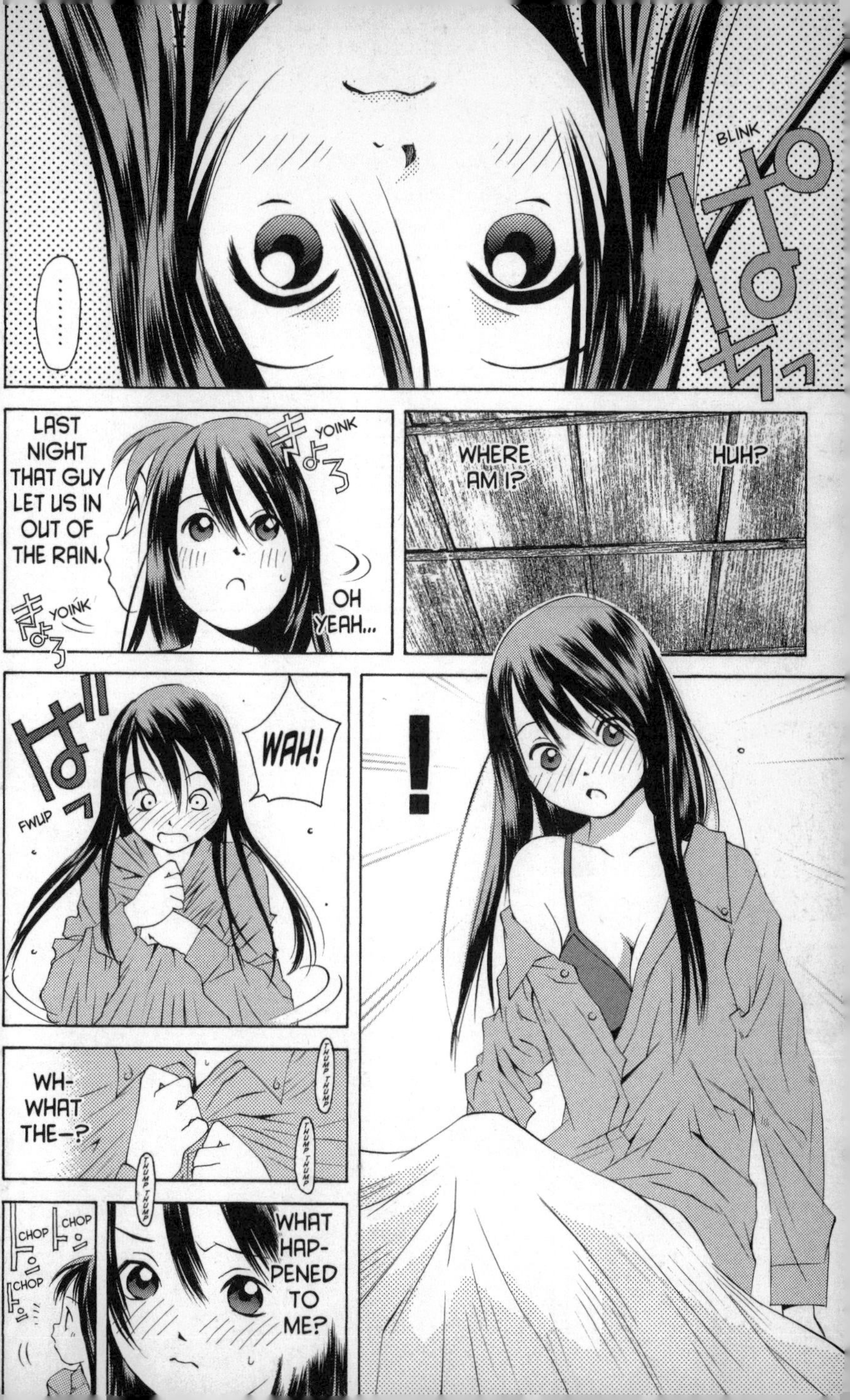
BLINK
......
HUH?
WHERE AM I?
OH YEAH...
YOINK
LAST NIGHT THAT GUY LET US IN OUT OF THE RAIN.
YOINK
!
WAH!
FWUP
THUMP THUMP
THUMP THUMP
WH- WHAT THE-?
THUMP THUMP
WHAT HAP-PENED TO ME?
CHOP
CHOP

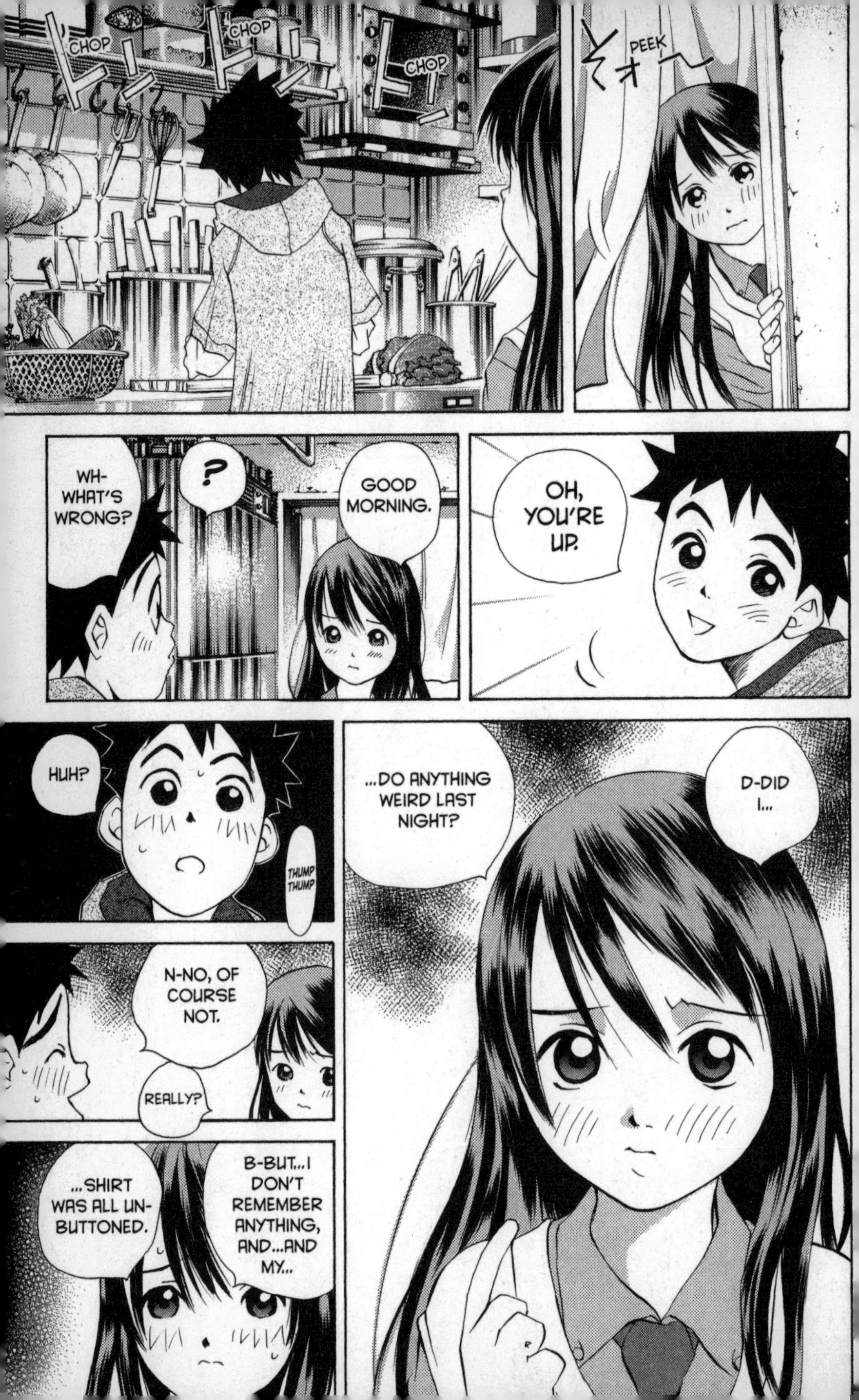
PEEK
CHOP
CHOP
CHOP
OH, YOU'RE UP.
GOOD MORNING.
?
WH- WHAT'S WRONG?
D-DID I...
...DO ANYTHING WEIRD LAST NIGHT?
HUH?
THUMP THUMP
N-NO, OF COURSE NOT.
REALLY?
B-BUT...I DON'T REMEMBER ANYTHING, AND...AND MY...
...SHIRT WAS ALL UN-BUTTONED.

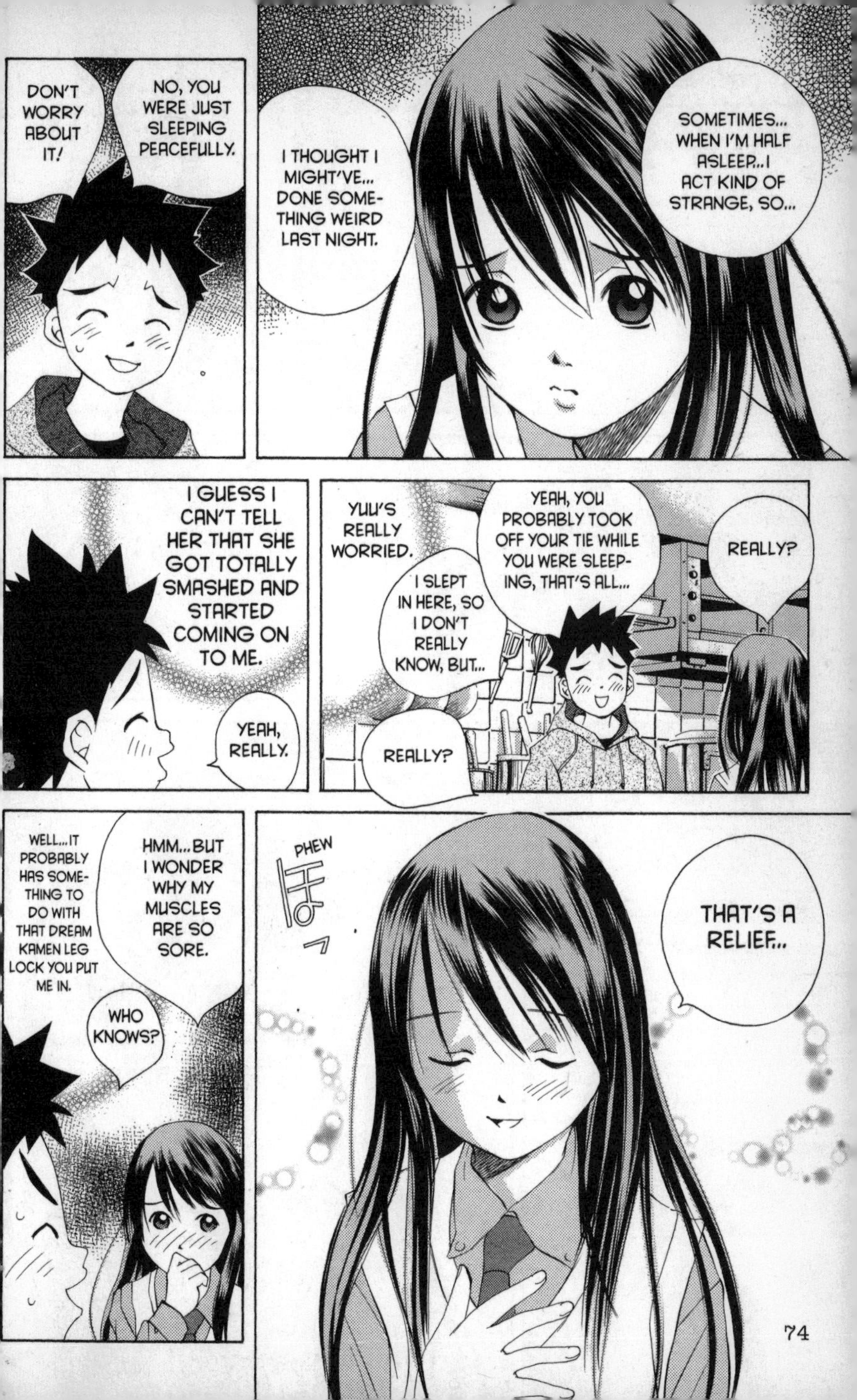
SOMETIMES... WHEN I'M HALF ASLEEP...I ACT KIND OF STRANGE, SO...
I THOUGHT I MIGHT'VE... DONE SOMETHING WEIRD LAST NIGHT.
NO, YOU WERE JUST SLEEPING PEACEFULLY.
DON'T WORRY ABOUT IT!
REALLY?
YEAH, YOU PROBABLY TOOK OFF YOUR TIE WHILE YOU WERE SLEEPING, THAT'S ALL...
I SLEPT IN HERE, SO I DON'T REALLY KNOW, BUT...
YUU'S REALLY WORRIED.
REALLY?
I GUESS I CAN'T TELL HER THAT SHE GOT TOTALLY SMASHED AND STARTED COMING ON TO ME.
YEAH, REALLY.
THAT'S A RELIEF...
PHEW
HMM...BUT I WONDER WHY MY MUSCLES ARE SO SORE.
WELL...IT PROBABLY HAS SOMETHING TO DO WITH THAT DREAM KAMEN LEG LOCK YOU PUT ME IN.
WHO KNOWS?

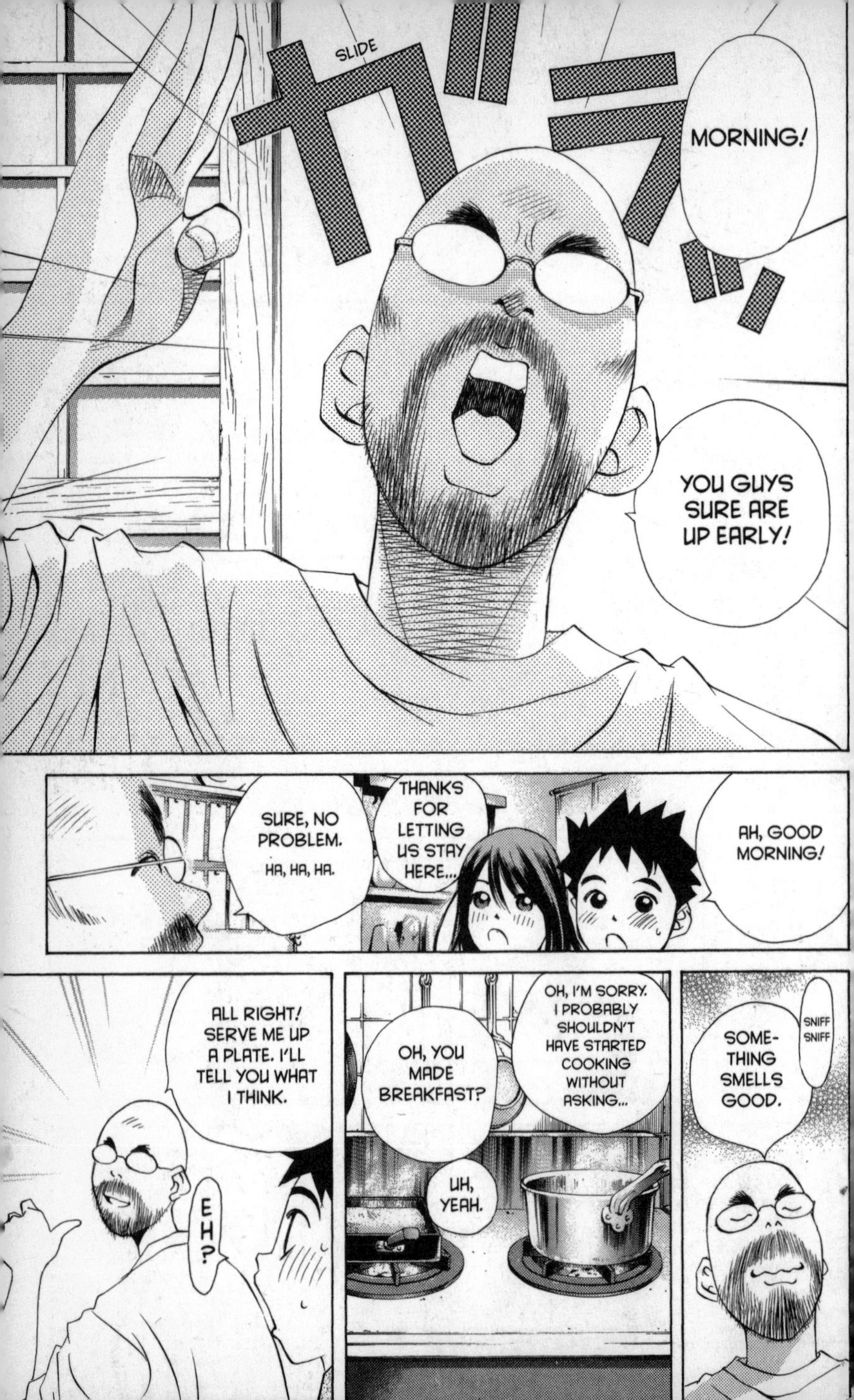
SLIDE
MORNING!
YOU GUYS SURE ARE UP EARLY!
AH, GOOD MORNING!
THANKS FOR LETTING US STAY HERE...
SURE, NO PROBLEM.
HA, HA, HA.
SNIFF SNIFF
SOME-THING SMELLS GOOD.
OH, I'M SORRY. I PROBABLY SHOULDN'T HAVE STARTED COOKING WITHOUT ASKING...
OH, YOU MADE BREAKFAST?
UH, YEAH.
ALL RIGHT! SERVE ME UP A PLATE. I'LL TELL YOU WHAT I THINK.
EH?

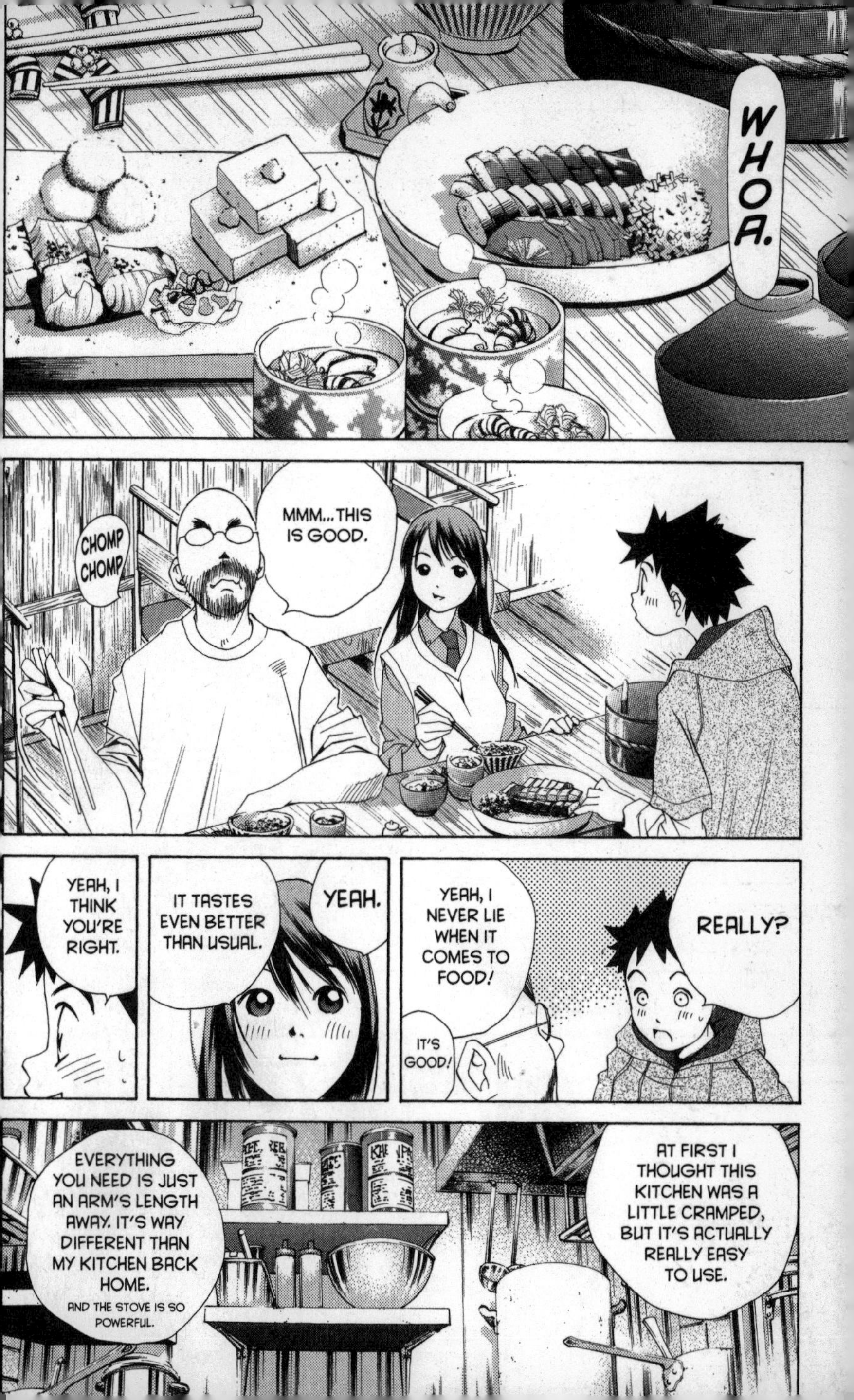
WHOA.
MMM...THIS IS GOOD.
CHOMP CHOMP
REALLY?
YEAH, I NEVER LIE WHEN IT COMES TO FOOD!
IT'S GOOD!
YEAH.
IT TASTES EVEN BETTER THAN USUAL.
YEAH, I THINK YOU'RE RIGHT.
AT FIRST I THOUGHT THIS KITCHEN WAS A LITTLE CRAMPED, BUT IT'S ACTUALLY REALLY EASY TO USE.
EVERYTHING YOU NEED IS JUST AN ARM'S LENGTH AWAY. IT'S WAY DIFFERENT THAN MY KITCHEN BACK HOME.
AND THE STOVE IS SO POWERFUL.

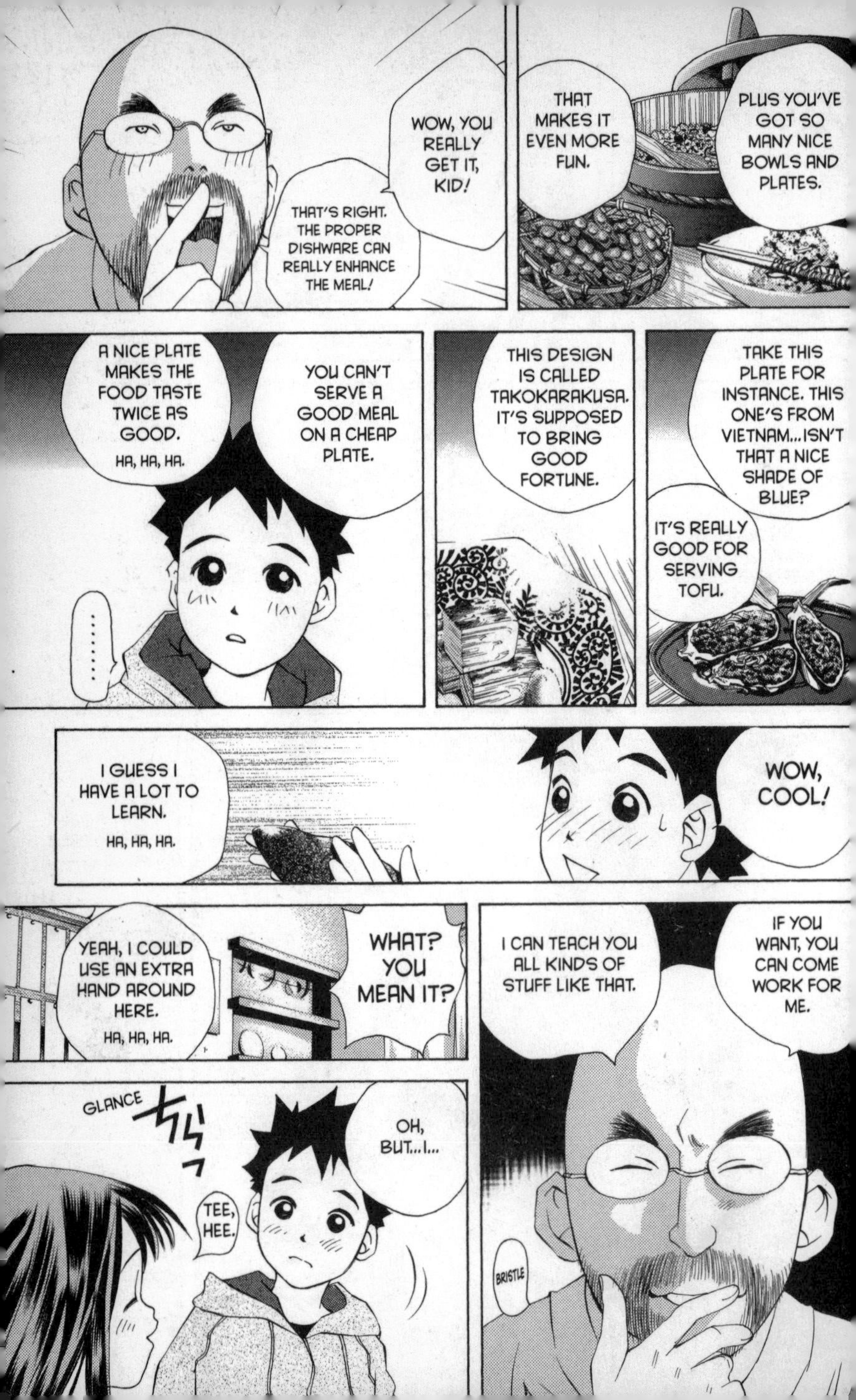
PLUS YOU'VE GOT SO MANY NICE BOWLS AND PLATES.
THAT MAKES IT EVEN MORE FUN.
WOW, YOU REALLY GET IT, KID!
THAT'S RIGHT. THE PROPER DISHWARE CAN REALLY ENHANCE THE MEAL!
TAKE THIS PLATE FOR INSTANCE. THIS ONE'S FROM VIETNAM...ISN'T THAT A NICE SHADE OF BLUE?
IT'S REALLY GOOD FOR SERVING TOFU.
THIS DESIGN IS CALLED TAKOKARAKUSA. IT'S SUPPOSED TO BRING GOOD FORTUNE.
YOU CAN'T SERVE A GOOD MEAL ON A CHEAP PLATE.
A NICE PLATE MAKES THE FOOD TASTE TWICE AS GOOD.
HA, HA, HA.
......
WOW, COOL!
I GUESS I HAVE A LOT TO LEARN.
HA, HA, HA.
IF YOU WANT, YOU CAN COME WORK FOR ME.
I CAN TEACH YOU ALL KINDS OF STUFF LIKE THAT.
BRISTLE
WHAT? YOU MEAN IT?
YEAH, I COULD USE AN EXTRA HAND AROUND HERE.
HA, HA, HA.
OH, BUT...I...
GLANCE
TEE, HEE.

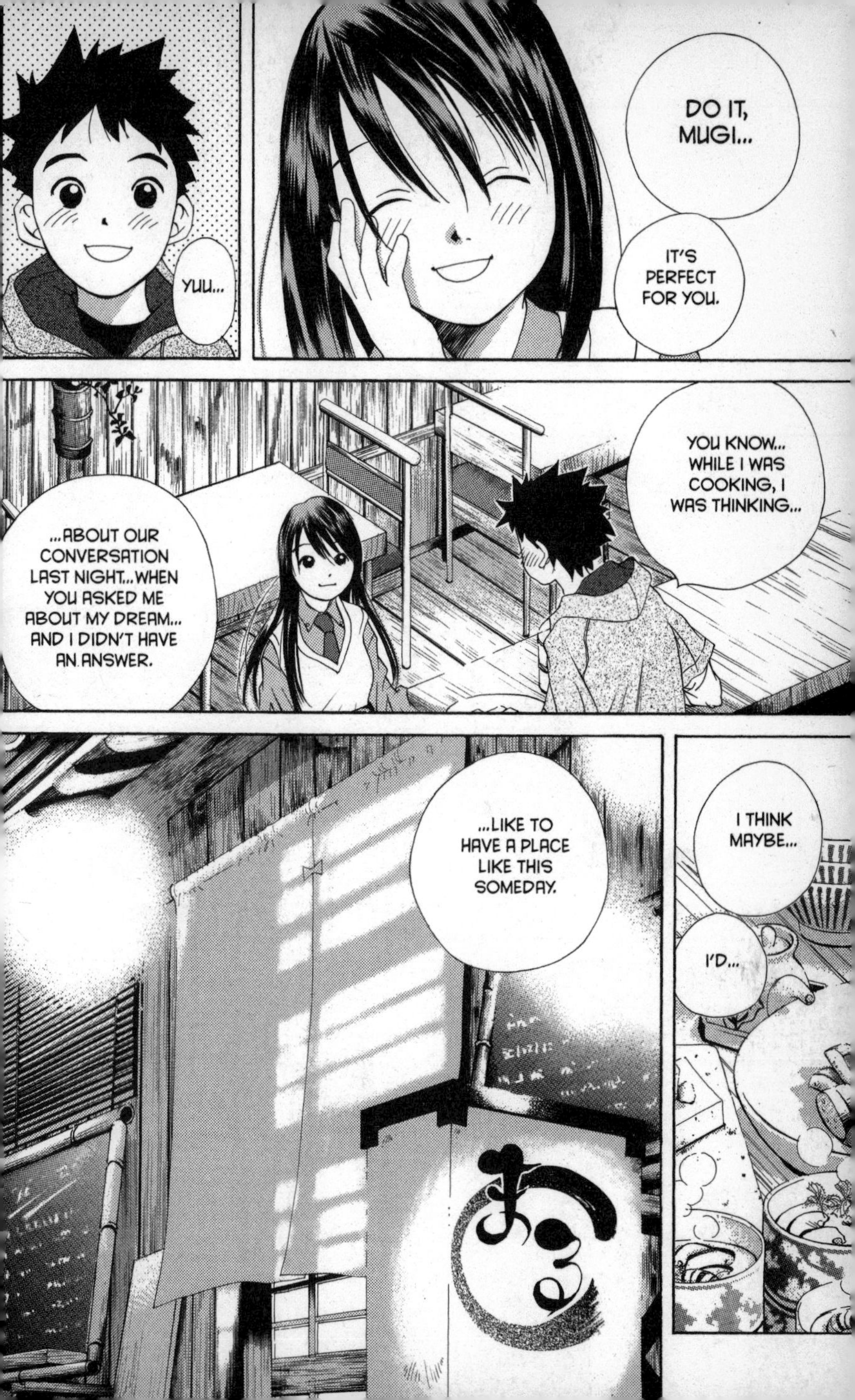
DO IT, MUGI...
IT'S PERFECT FOR YOU.
YUU...
YOU KNOW... WHILE I WAS COOKING, I WAS THINKING...
...ABOUT OUR CONVERSATION LAST NIGHT...WHEN YOU ASKED ME ABOUT MY DREAM... AND I DIDN'T HAVE AN ANSWER.
I THINK MAYBE...
I'D...
...LIKE TO HAVE A PLACE LIKE THIS SOMEDAY.

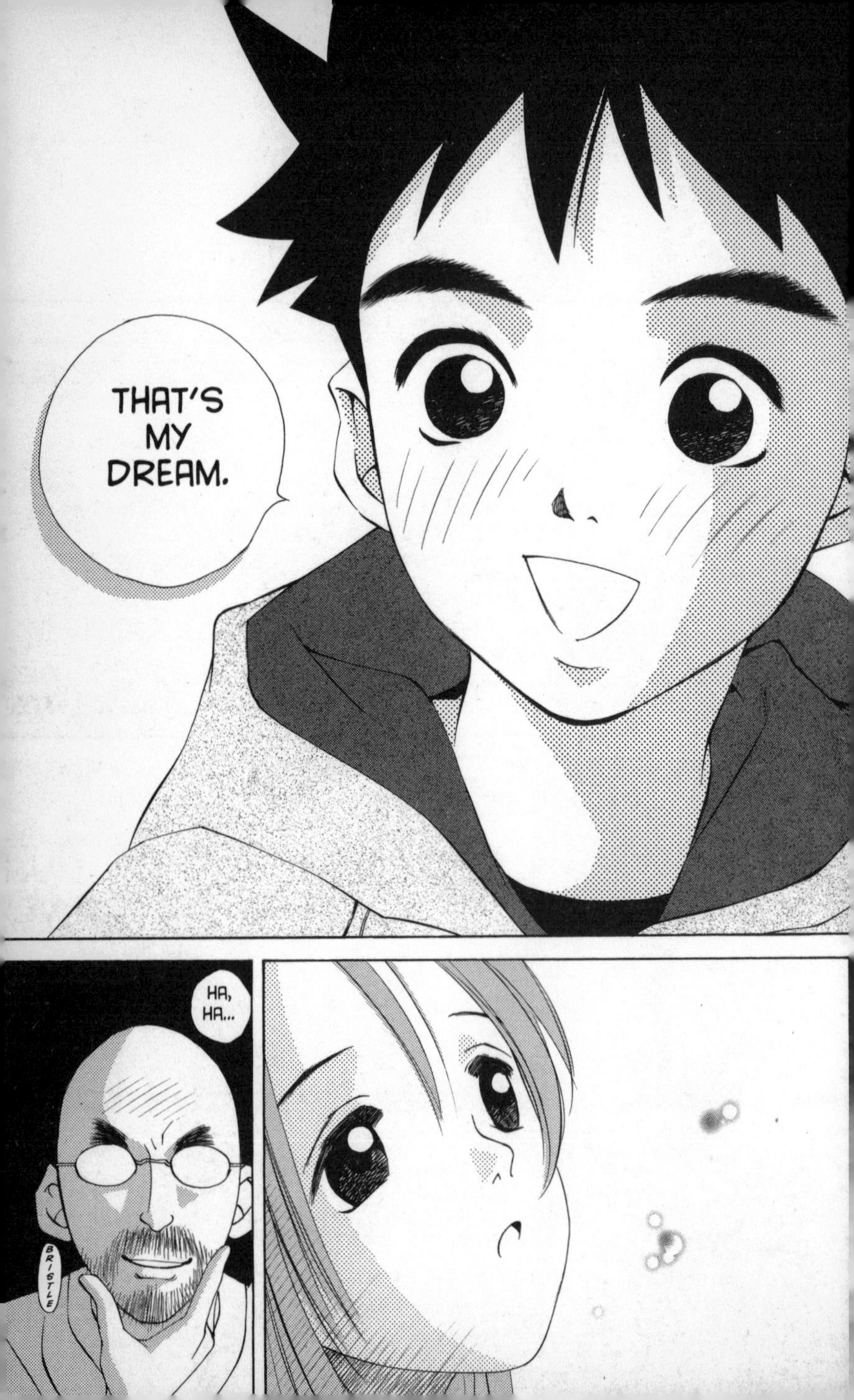
THAT'S MY DREAM.
HA, HA...
BRISTLE

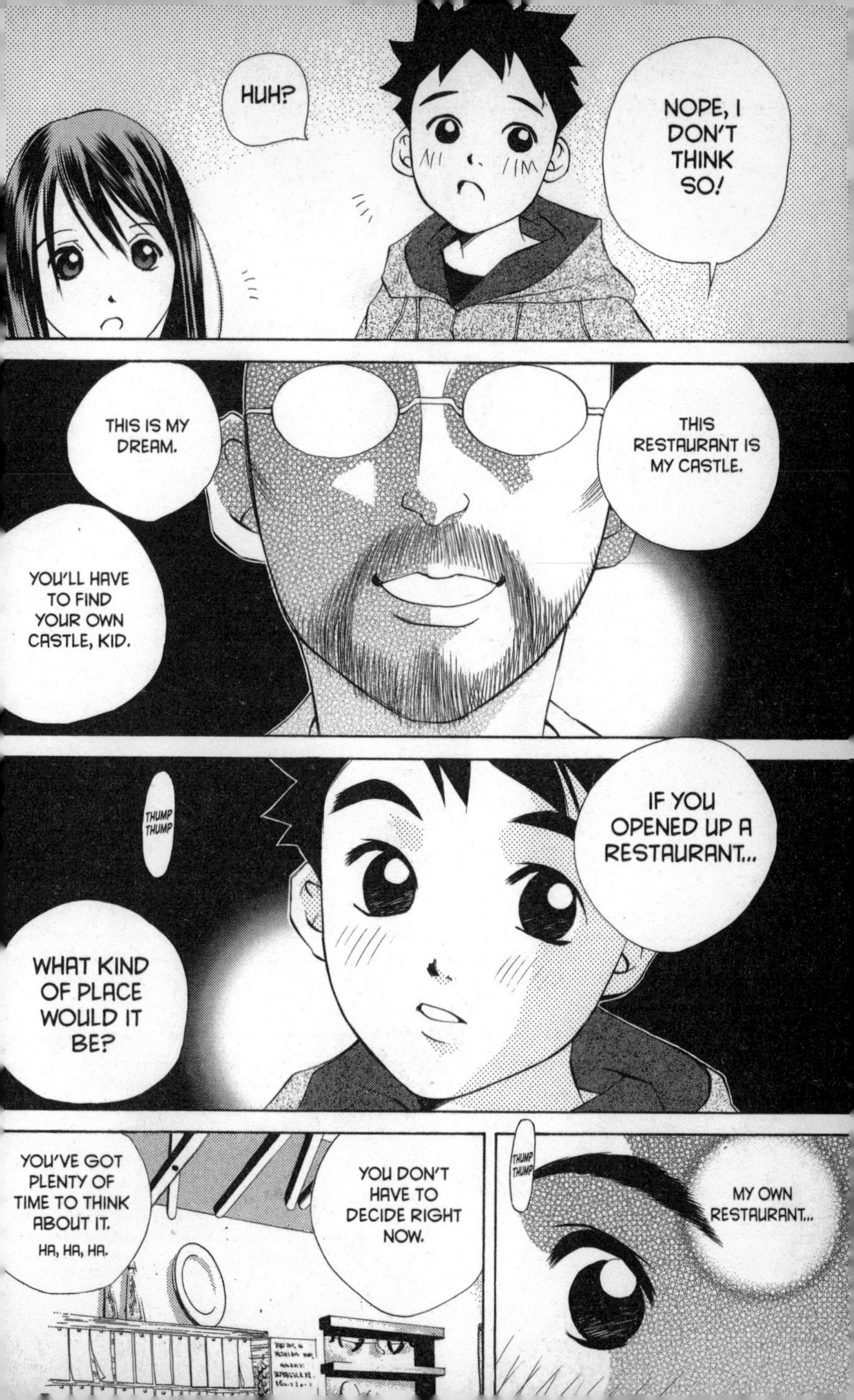
NOPE, I DON'T THINK SO!
HUH?
THIS RESTAURANT IS MY CASTLE.
THIS IS MY DREAM.
YOU'LL HAVE TO FIND YOUR OWN CASTLE, KID.
IF YOU OPENED UP A RESTAURANT...
THUMP THUMP
WHAT KIND OF PLACE WOULD IT BE?
MY OWN RESTAURANT...
THUMP THUMP
YOU DON'T HAVE TO DECIDE RIGHT NOW.
YOU'VE GOT PLENTY OF TIME TO THINK ABOUT IT.
HA, HA, HA.

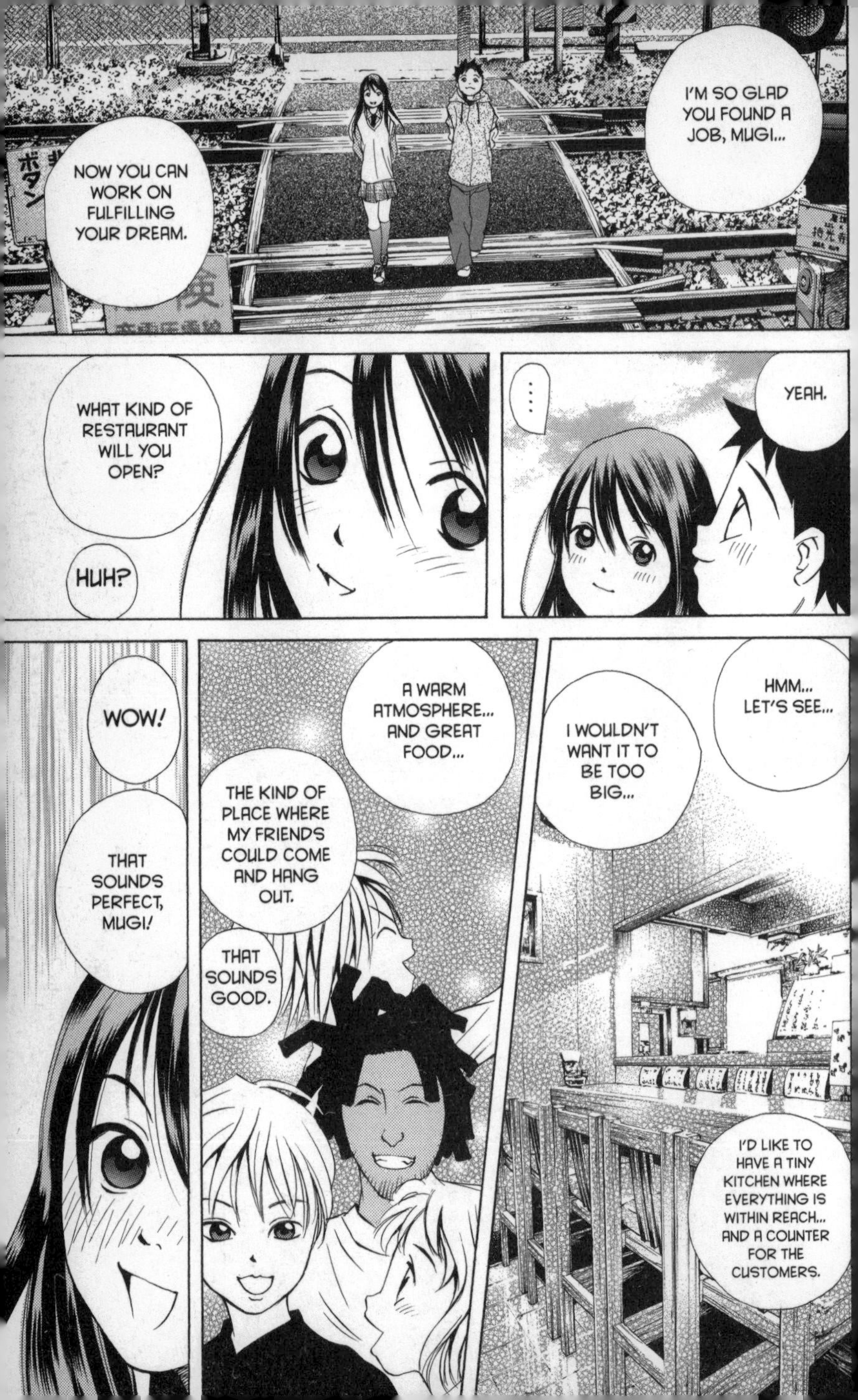
I'M SO GLAD YOU FOUND A JOB, MUGI...
NOW YOU CAN WORK ON FULFILLING YOUR DREAM.
YEAH.
...
WHAT KIND OF RESTAURANT WILL YOU OPEN?
HUH?
HMM... LET'S SEE...
I WOULDN'T WANT IT TO BE TOO BIG...
I'D LIKE TO HAVE A TINY KITCHEN WHERE EVERYTHING IS WITHIN REACH... AND A COUNTER FOR THE CUSTOMERS.
A WARM ATMOSPHERE... AND GREAT FOOD...
THE KIND OF PLACE WHERE MY FRIENDS COULD COME AND HANG OUT.
THAT SOUNDS GOOD.
WOW!
THAT SOUNDS PERFECT, MUGI!

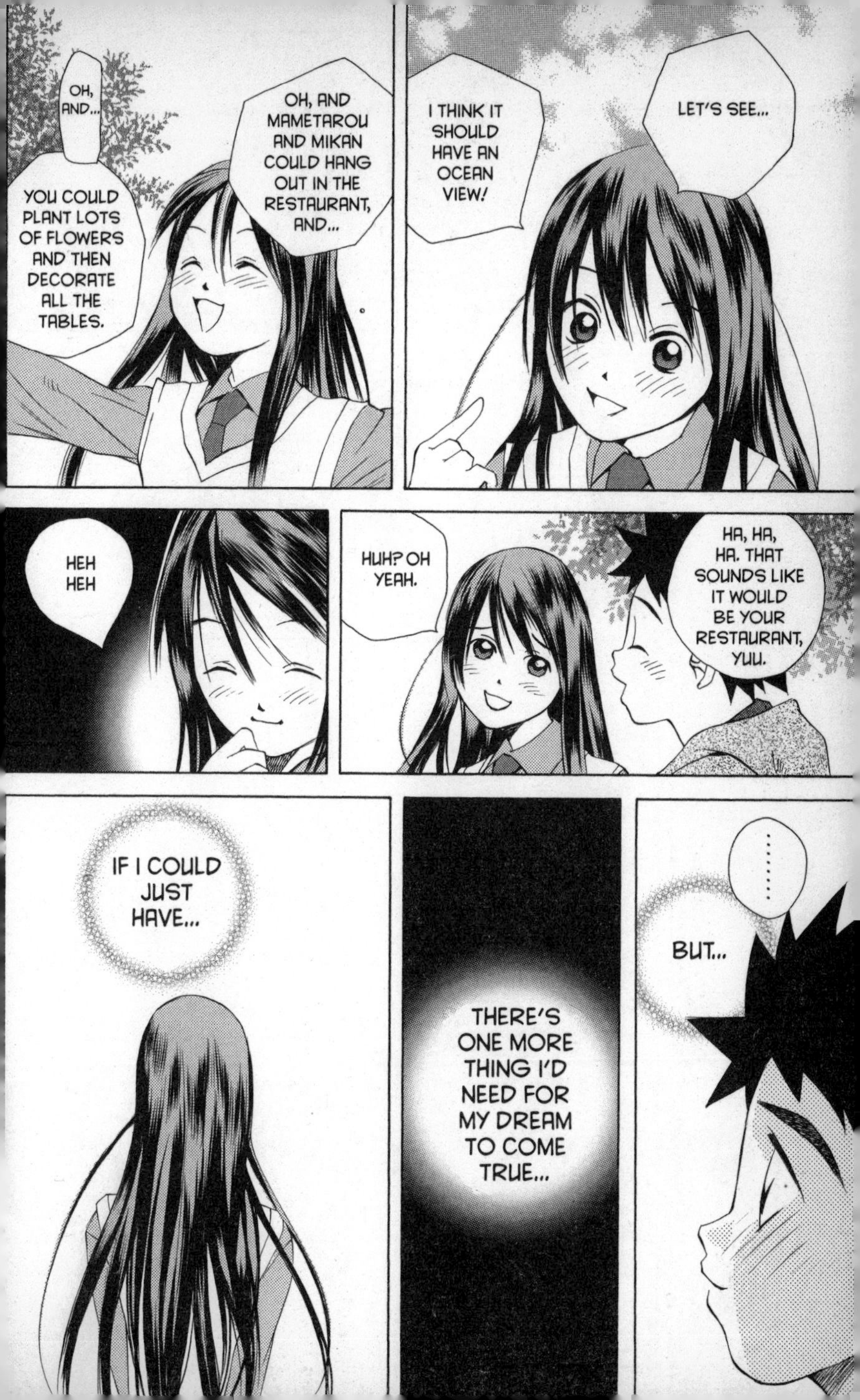
LET'S SEE...
I THINK IT SHOULD HAVE AN OCEAN VIEW!
OH, AND MAMETAROU AND MIKAN COULD HANG OUT IN THE RESTAURANT, AND...
OH, AND...
YOU COULD PLANT LOTS OF FLOWERS AND THEN DECORATE ALL THE TABLES.
HA, HA, HA. THAT SOUNDS LIKE IT WOULD BE YOUR RESTAURANT, YUU.
HUH? OH YEAH.
HEH HEH
....
BUT...
THERE'S ONE MORE THING I'D NEED FOR MY DREAM TO COME TRUE...
IF I COULD JUST HAVE...

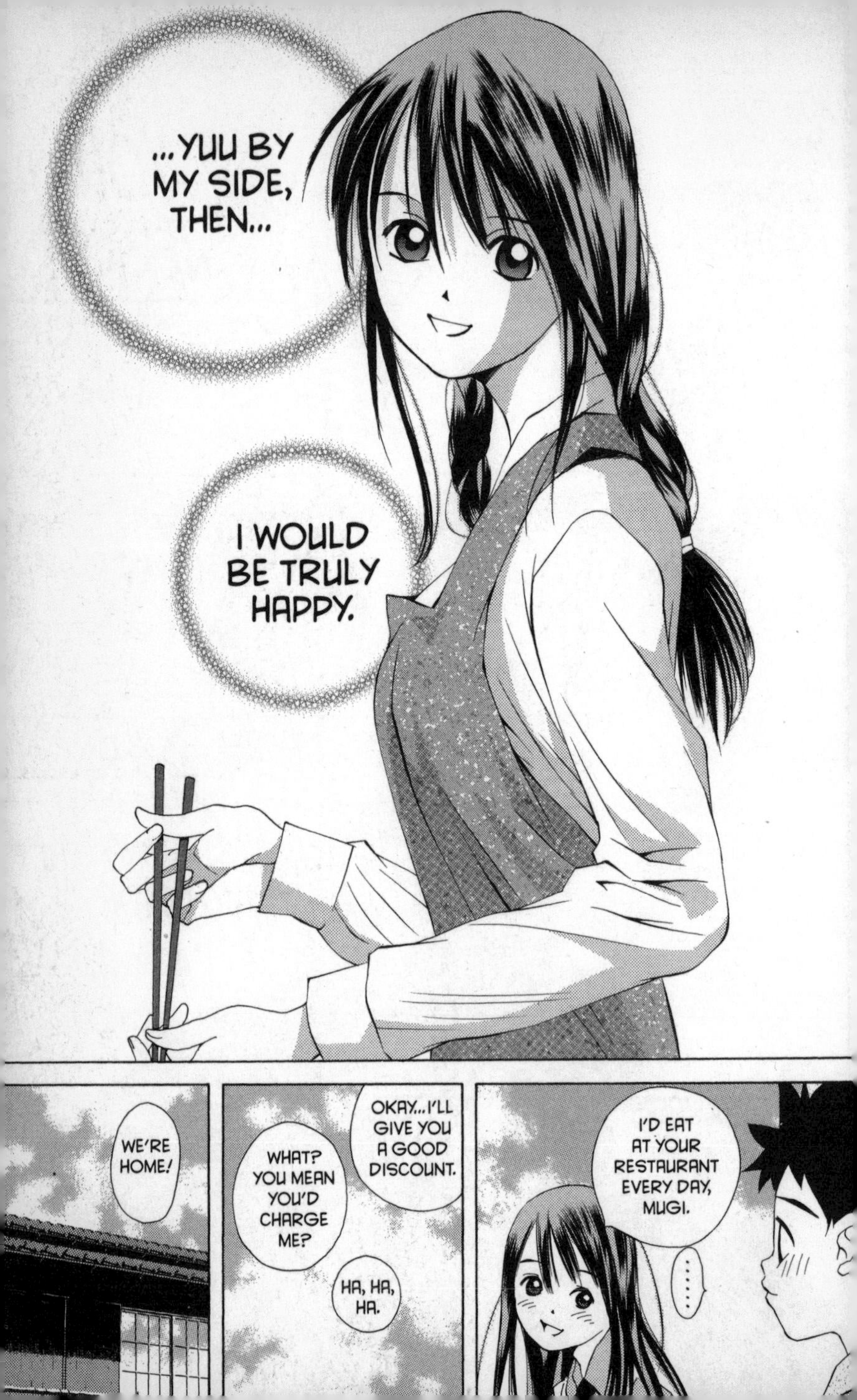
...YUU BY MY SIDE, THEN...
I WOULD BE TRULY HAPPY.
I'D EAT AT YOUR RESTAURANT EVERY DAY, MUGI.
......
OKAY...I'LL GIVE YOU A GOOD DISCOUNT.
WHAT? YOU MEAN YOU'D CHARGE ME?
HA, HA, HA.
WE'RE HOME!

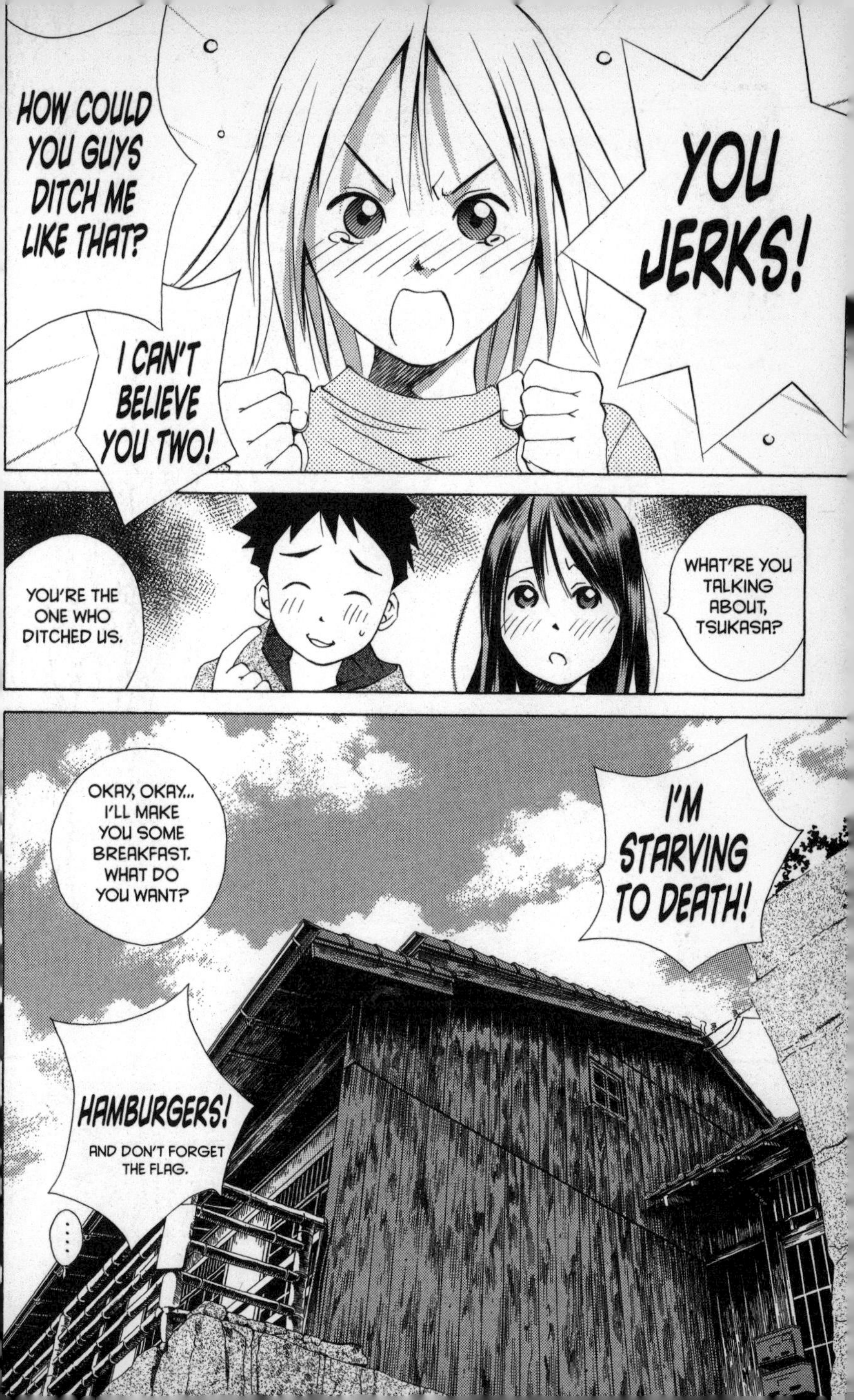
YOU JERKS!
HOW COULD YOU GUYS DITCH ME LIKE THAT?
I CAN'T BELIEVE YOU TWO!
WHAT'RE YOU TALKING ABOUT, TSUKASA?
YOU'RE THE ONE WHO DITCHED US.
I'M STARVING TO DEATH!
OKAY, OKAY... I'LL MAKE YOU SOME BREAKFAST. WHAT DO YOU WANT?
HAMBURGERS!
AND DON'T FORGET THE FLAG.
.....

Pastel

MIRACLE 36: A PLEASANT SHOWER

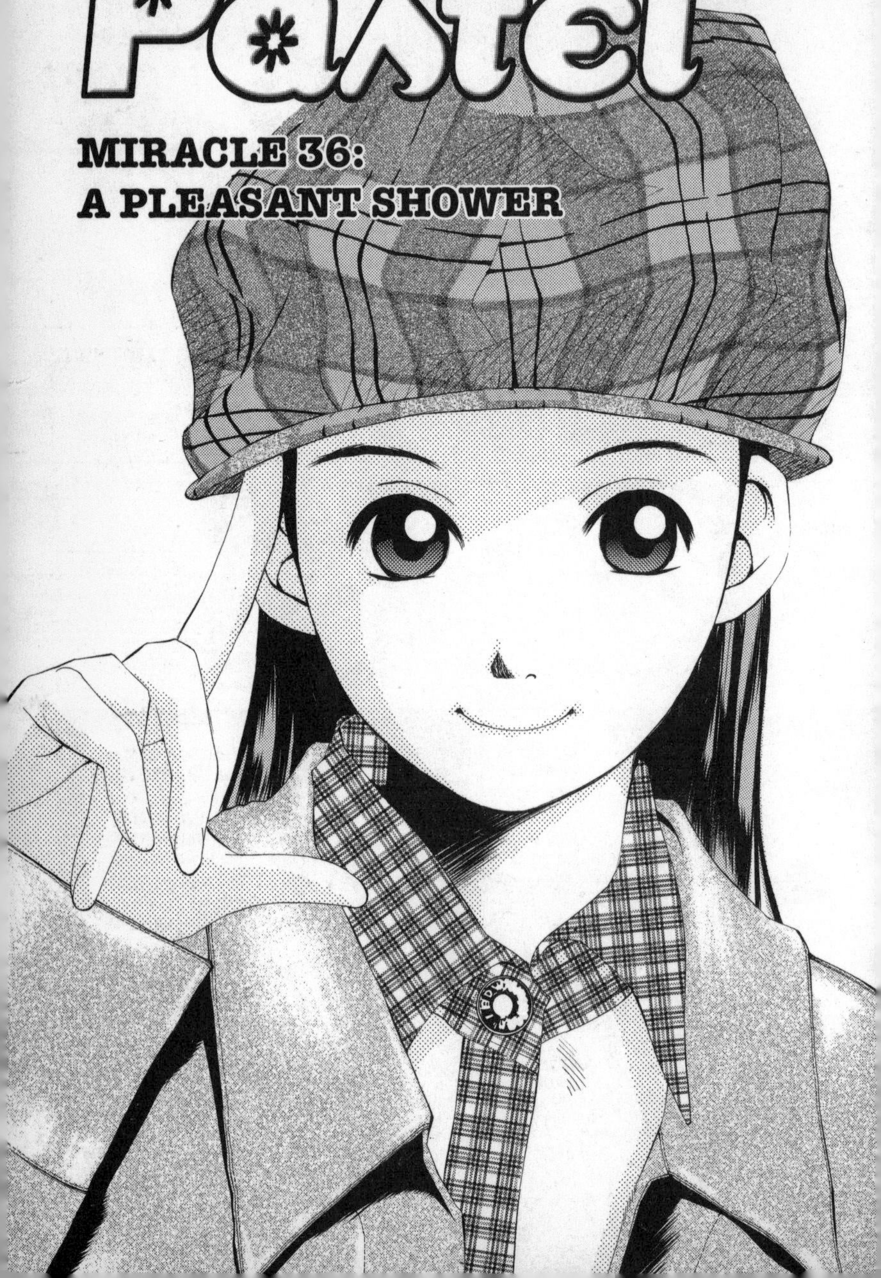

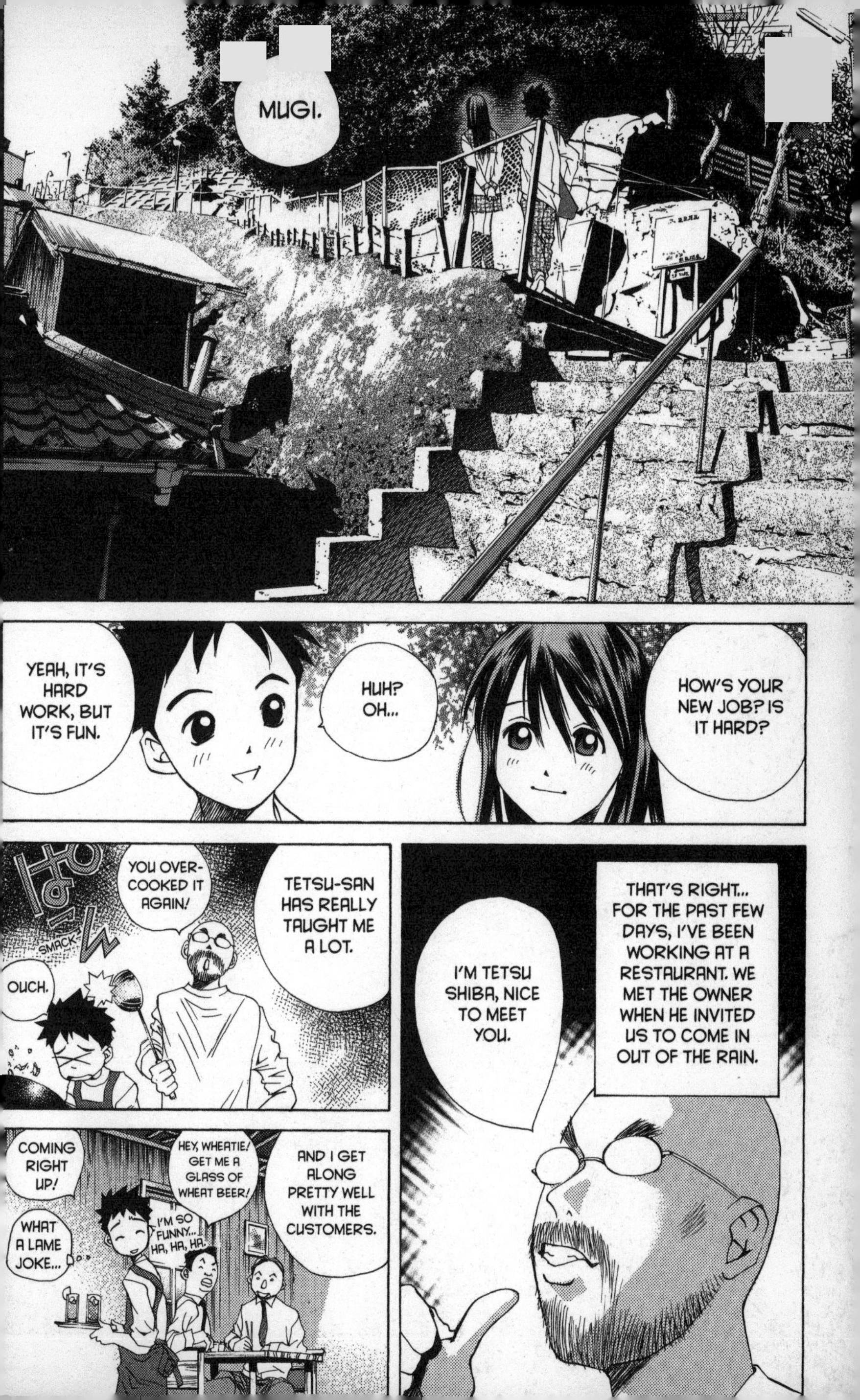
MUGI.
HOW'S YOUR NEW JOB? IS IT HARD?
HUH? OH...
YEAH, IT'S HARD WORK, BUT IT'S FUN.
THAT'S RIGHT... FOR THE PAST FEW DAYS, I'VE BEEN WORKING AT A RESTAURANT. WE MET THE OWNER WHEN HE INVITED US TO COME IN OUT OF THE RAIN.
I'M TETSU SHIBA, NICE TO MEET YOU.
TETSU-SAN HAS REALLY TAUGHT ME A LOT.
YOU OVER-COOKED IT AGAIN!
SMACK
OUCH.
AND I GET ALONG PRETTY WELL WITH THE CUSTOMERS.
HEY, WHEATIE! GET ME A GLASS OF WHEAT BEER!
I'M SO FUNNY... HA, HA, HA.
COMING RIGHT UP!
WHAT A LAME JOKE...

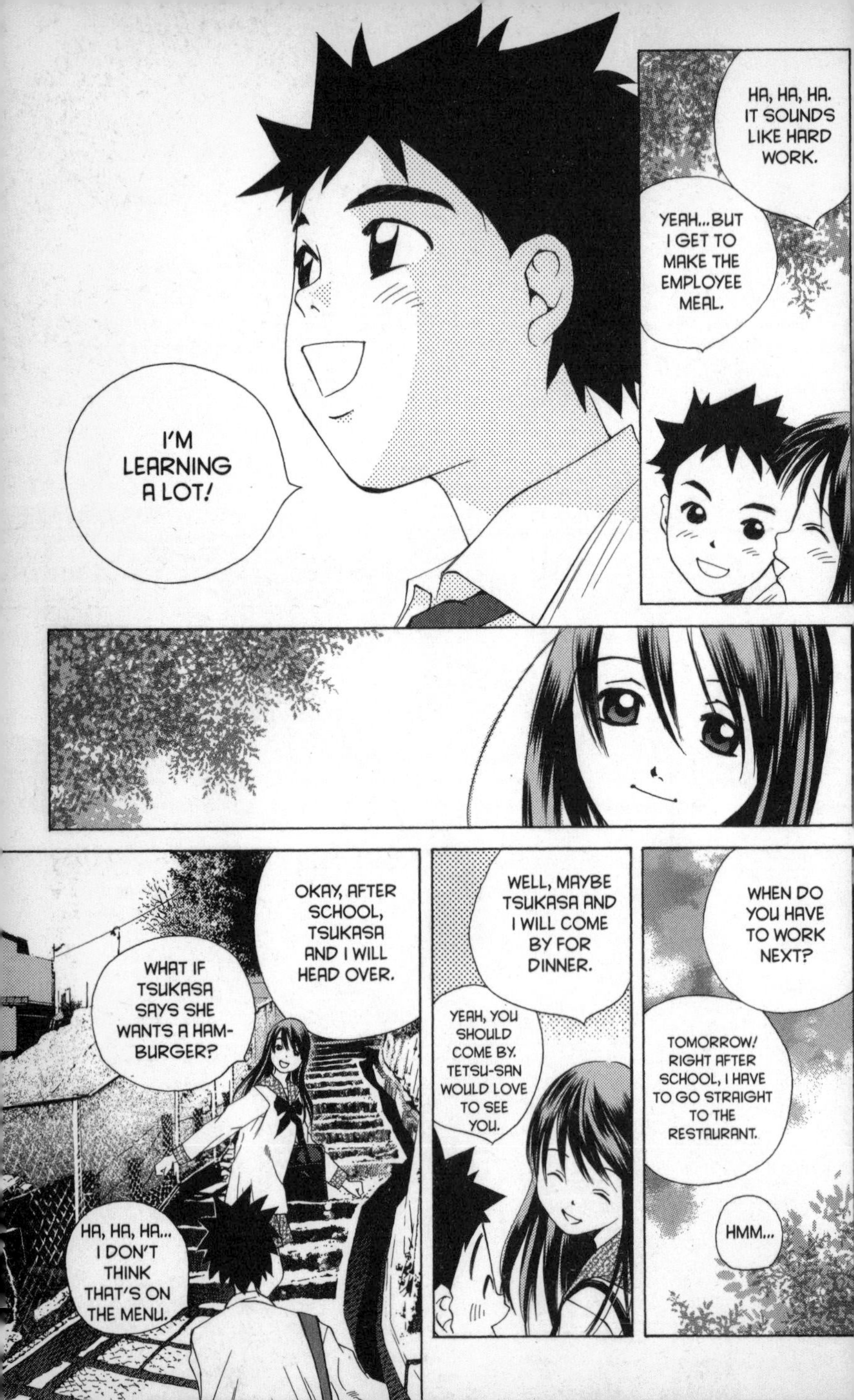
HA, HA, HA. IT SOUNDS LIKE HARD WORK.
YEAH...BUT I GET TO MAKE THE EMPLOYEE MEAL.
I'M LEARNING A LOT!
WHEN DO YOU HAVE TO WORK NEXT?
TOMORROW! RIGHT AFTER SCHOOL, I HAVE TO GO STRAIGHT TO THE RESTAURANT.
HMM...
WELL, MAYBE TSUKASA AND I WILL COME BY FOR DINNER.
YEAH, YOU SHOULD COME BY. TETSU-SAN WOULD LOVE TO SEE YOU.
OKAY, AFTER SCHOOL, TSUKASA AND I WILL HEAD OVER.
WHAT IF TSUKASA SAYS SHE WANTS A HAM-BURGER?
HA, HA, HA... I DON'T THINK THAT'S ON THE MENU.

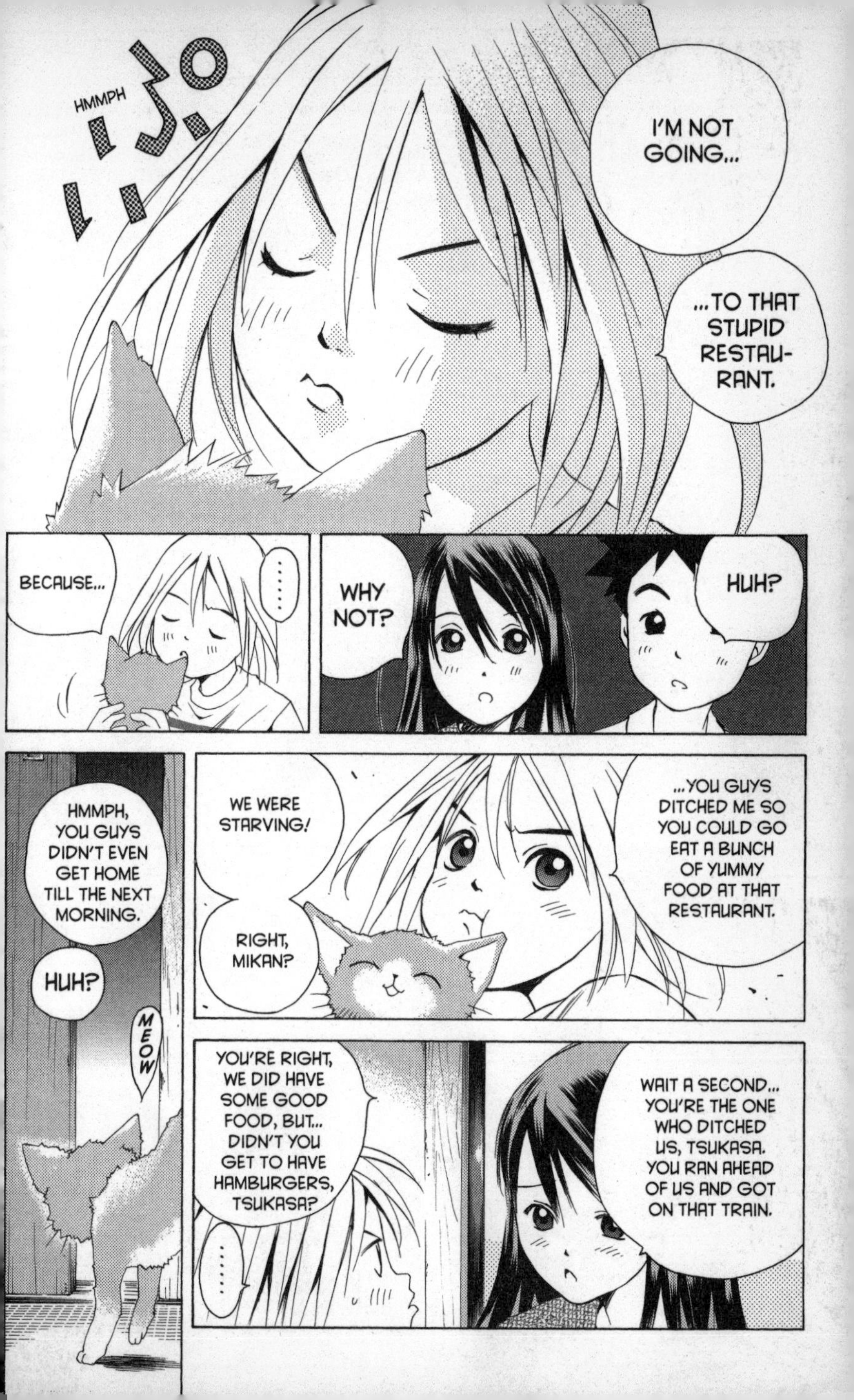
I'M NOT GOING...
...TO THAT STUPID RESTAURANT.
HMMPH
HUH?
WHY NOT?
......
BECAUSE...
...YOU GUYS DITCHED ME SO YOU COULD GO EAT A BUNCH OF YUMMY FOOD AT THAT RESTAURANT.
WE WERE STARVING!
RIGHT, MIKAN?
WAIT A SECOND... YOU'RE THE ONE WHO DITCHED US, TSUKASA. YOU RAN AHEAD OF US AND GOT ON THAT TRAIN.
YOU'RE RIGHT, WE DID HAVE SOME GOOD FOOD, BUT... DIDN'T YOU GET TO HAVE HAMBURGERS, TSUKASA?
......
HMMPH, YOU GUYS DIDN'T EVEN GET HOME TILL THE NEXT MORNING.
HUH?
MEOW

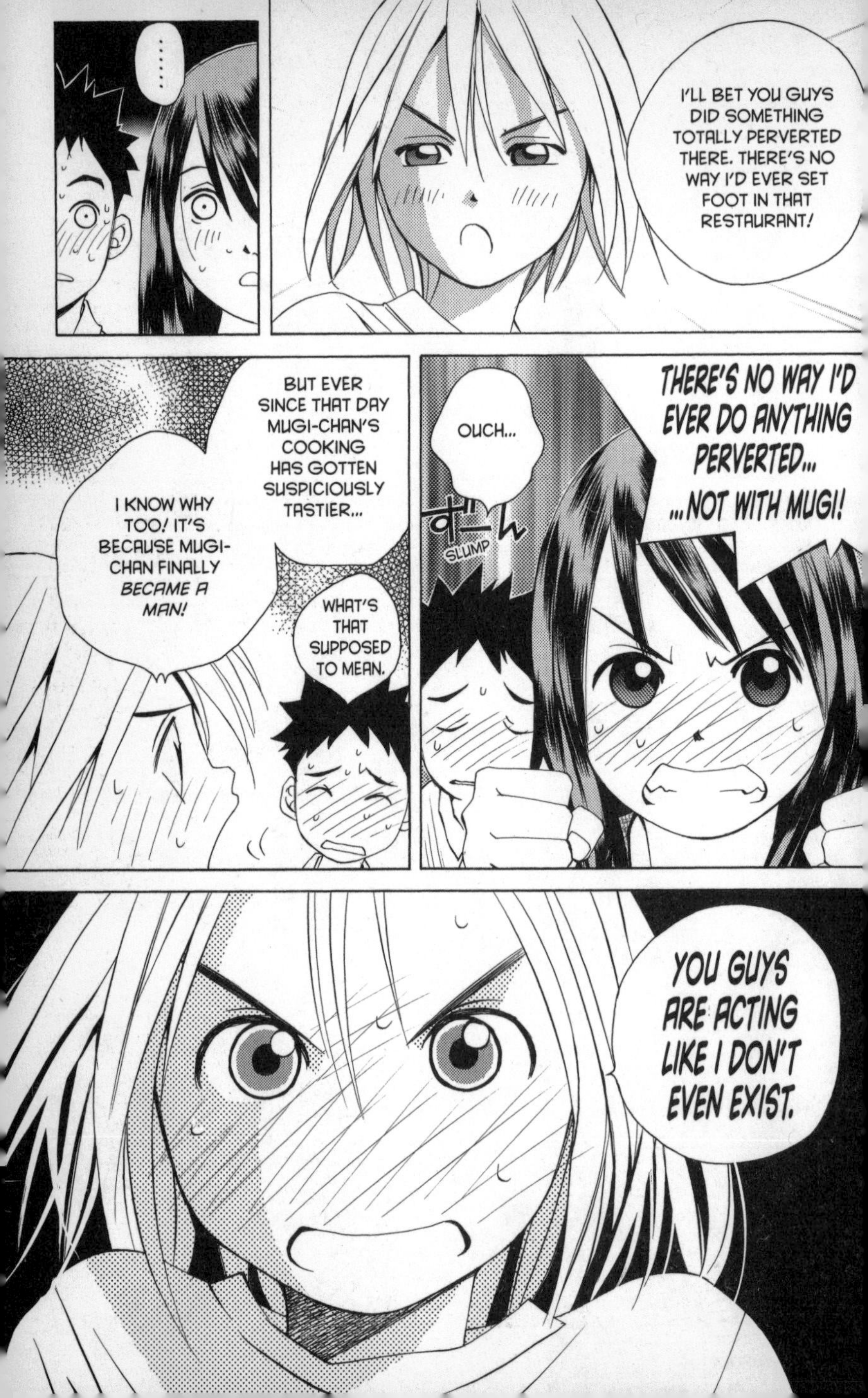
I'LL BET YOU GUYS DID SOMETHING TOTALLY PERVERTED THERE. THERE'S NO WAY I'D EVER SET FOOT IN THAT RESTAURANT!
......
THERE'S NO WAY I'D EVER DO ANYTHING PERVERTED... ...NOT WITH MUGI!
OUCH...
ずーん
SLUMP
BUT EVER SINCE THAT DAY MUGI-CHAN'S COOKING HAS GOTTEN SUSPICIOUSLY TASTIER...
I KNOW WHY TOO! IT'S BECAUSE MUGI-CHAN FINALLY *BECAME A MAN!*
WHAT'S THAT SUPPOSED TO MEAN.
YOU GUYS ARE ACTING LIKE I DON'T EVEN EXIST.

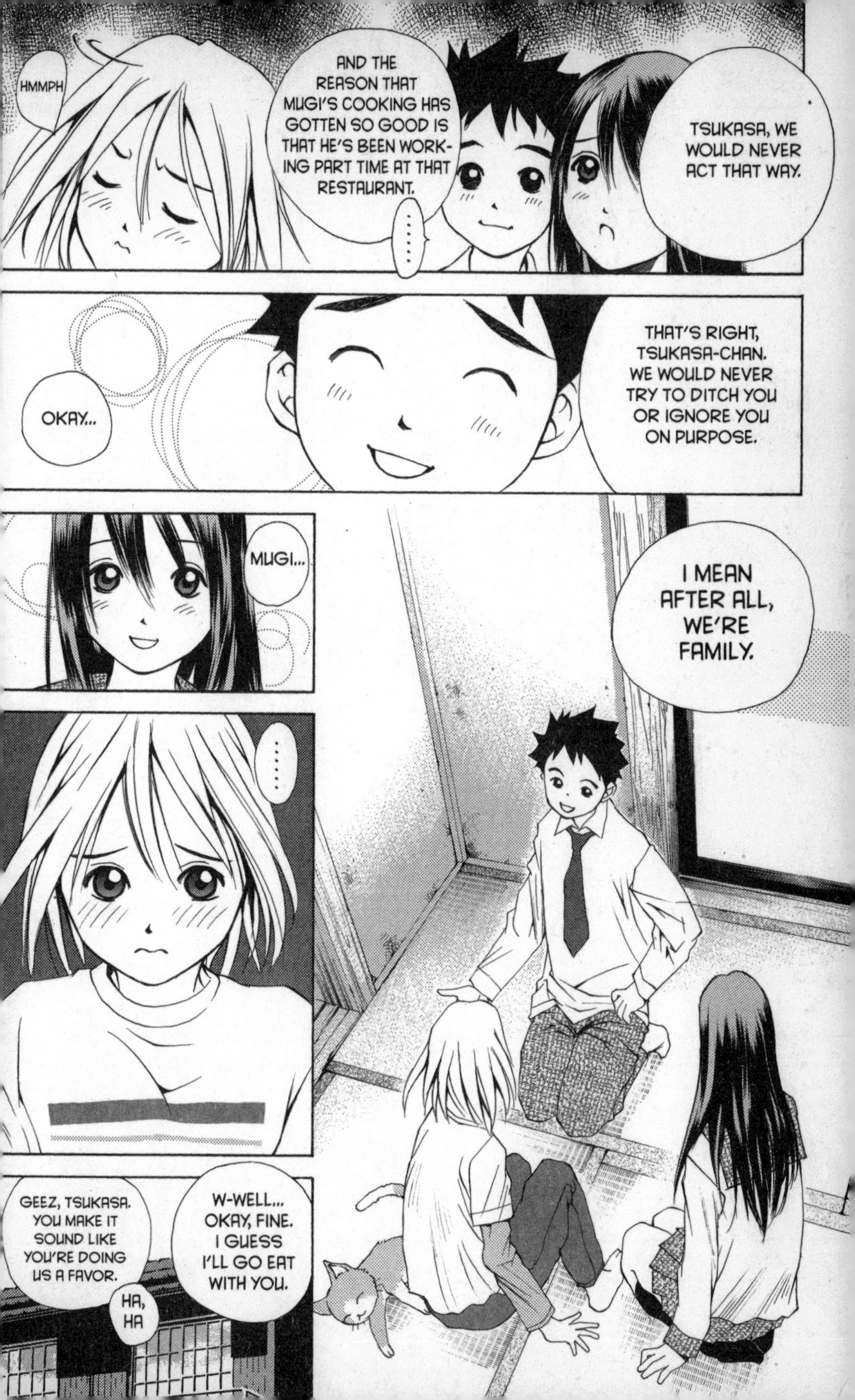
TSUKASA, WE WOULD NEVER ACT THAT WAY.
AND THE REASON THAT MUGI'S COOKING HAS GOTTEN SO GOOD IS THAT HE'S BEEN WORKING PART TIME AT THAT RESTAURANT.
......
HMMPH
THAT'S RIGHT, TSUKASA-CHAN. WE WOULD NEVER TRY TO DITCH YOU OR IGNORE YOU ON PURPOSE.
OKAY...
I MEAN AFTER ALL, WE'RE FAMILY.
MUGI...
......
W-WELL... OKAY, FINE. I GUESS I'LL GO EAT WITH YOU.
GEEZ, TSUKASA. YOU MAKE IT SOUND LIKE YOU'RE DOING US A FAVOR.
HA, HA

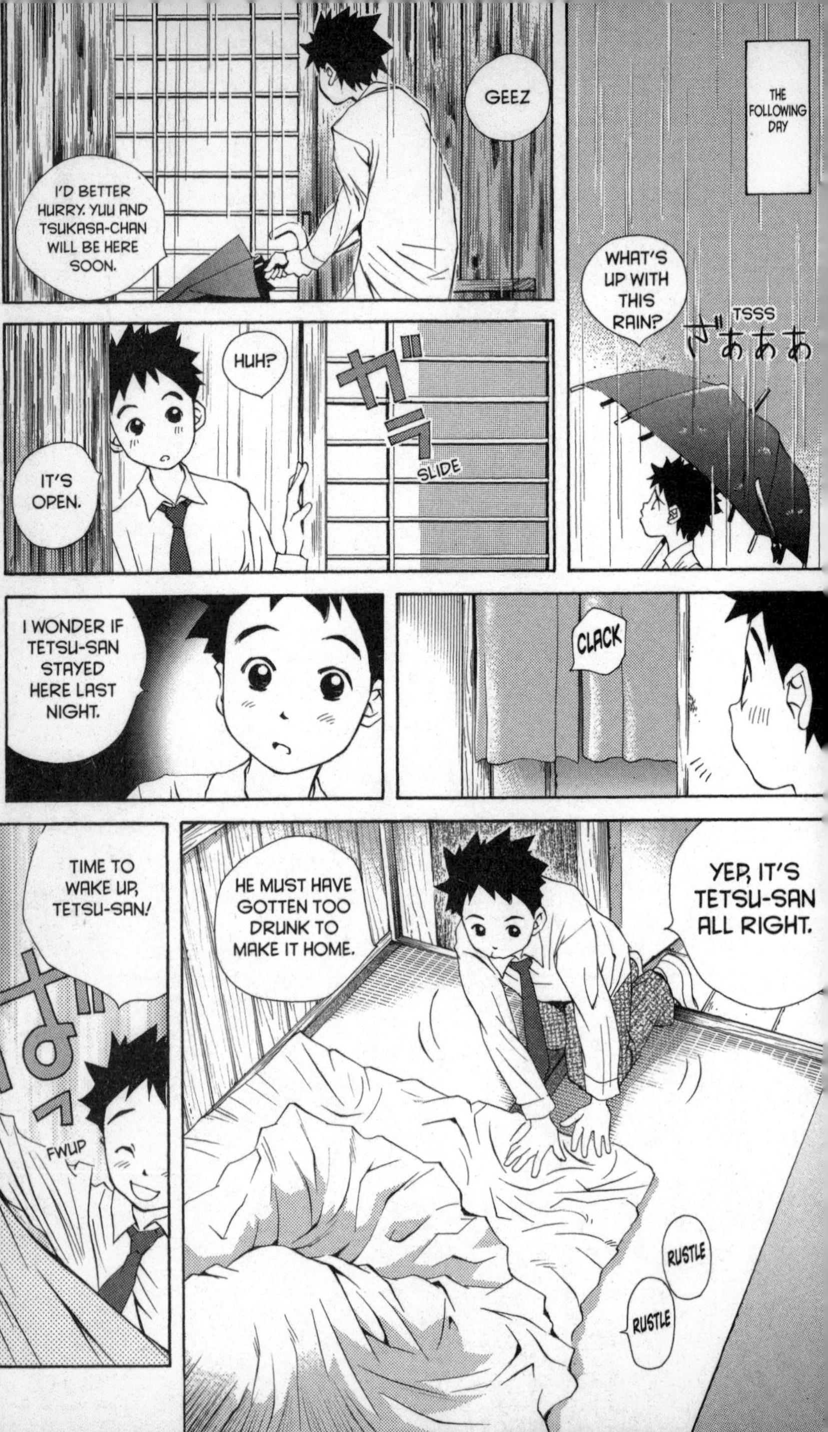
THE FOLLOWING DAY
WHAT'S UP WITH THIS RAIN?
ざあああ
TSSS
GEEZ
I'D BETTER HURRY. YUU AND TSUKASA-CHAN WILL BE HERE SOON.
HUH?
ガラ
SLIDE
IT'S OPEN.
CLACK
I WONDER IF TETSU-SAN STAYED HERE LAST NIGHT.
YEP, IT'S TETSU-SAN ALL RIGHT.
HE MUST HAVE GOTTEN TOO DRUNK TO MAKE IT HOME.
RUSTLE
RUSTLE
TIME TO WAKE UP, TETSU-SAN!
ばっ
FWUP

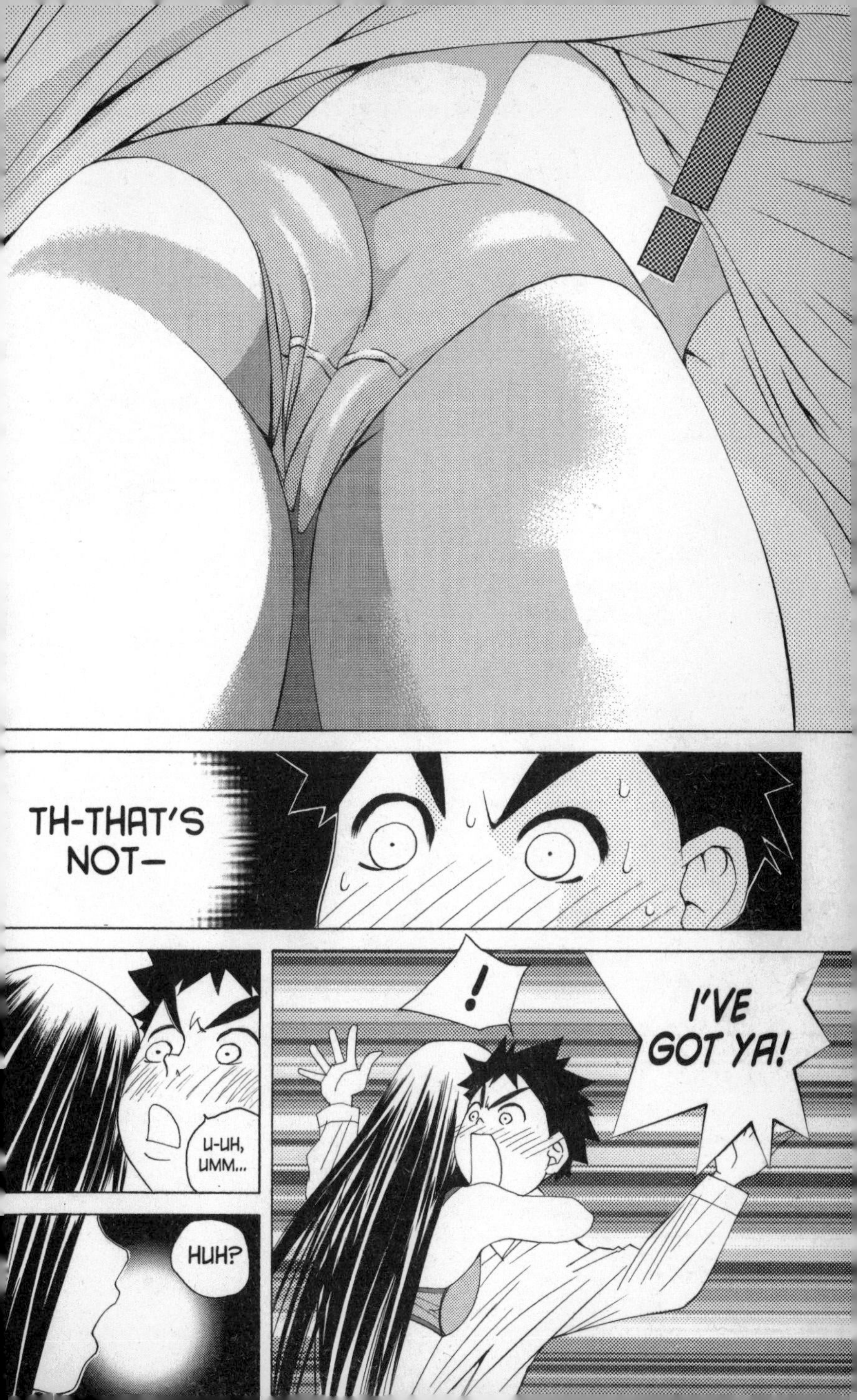
TH-THAT'S NOT-
!
I'VE GOT YA!
U-UH, UMM...
HUH?

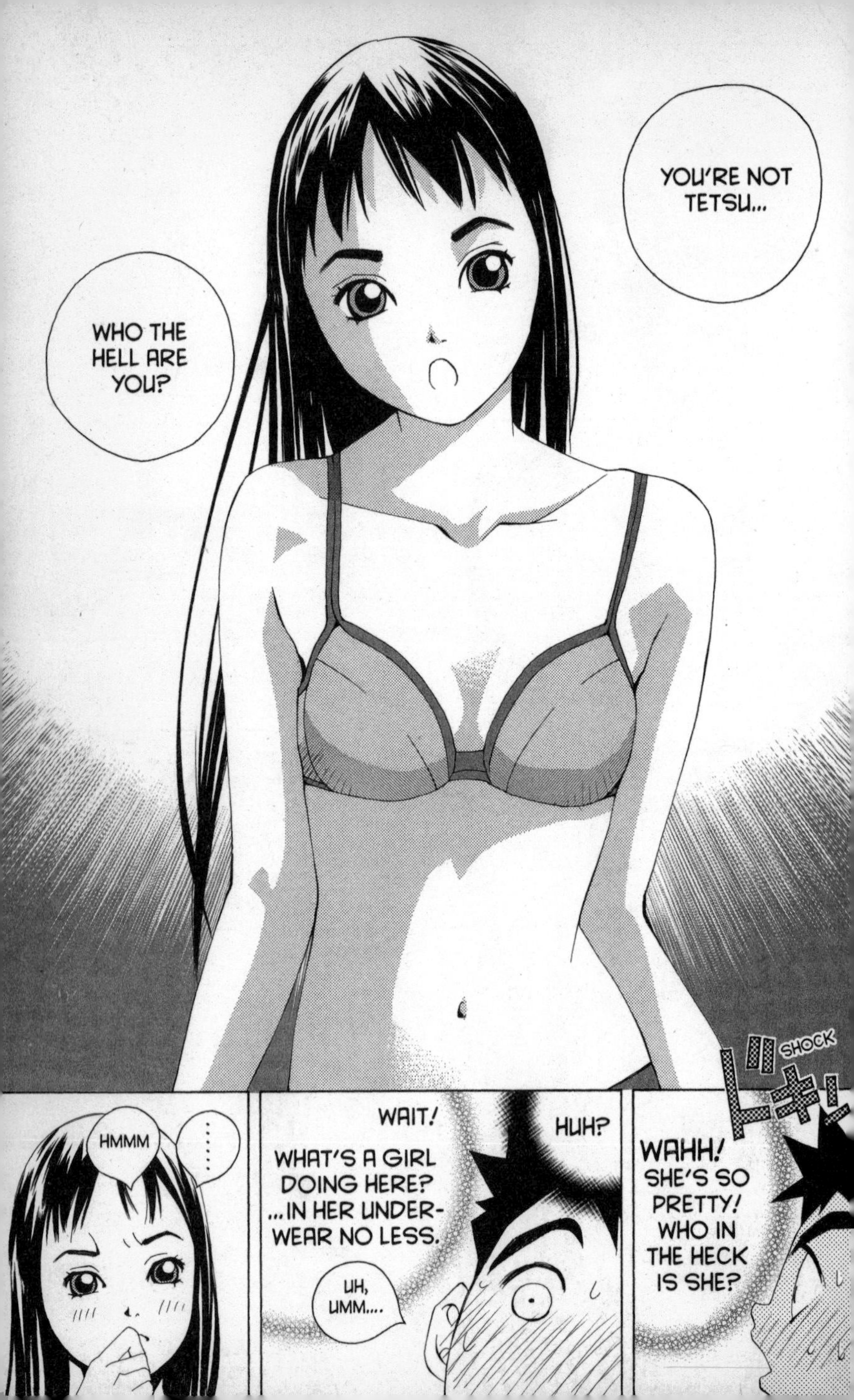
YOU'RE NOT TETSU...
WHO THE HELL ARE YOU?
SHOCK
WAHH! SHE'S SO PRETTY! WHO IN THE HECK IS SHE?
HUH?
WAIT!
WHAT'S A GIRL DOING HERE? ...IN HER UNDER-WEAR NO LESS.
UH, UMM....
......
HMMM

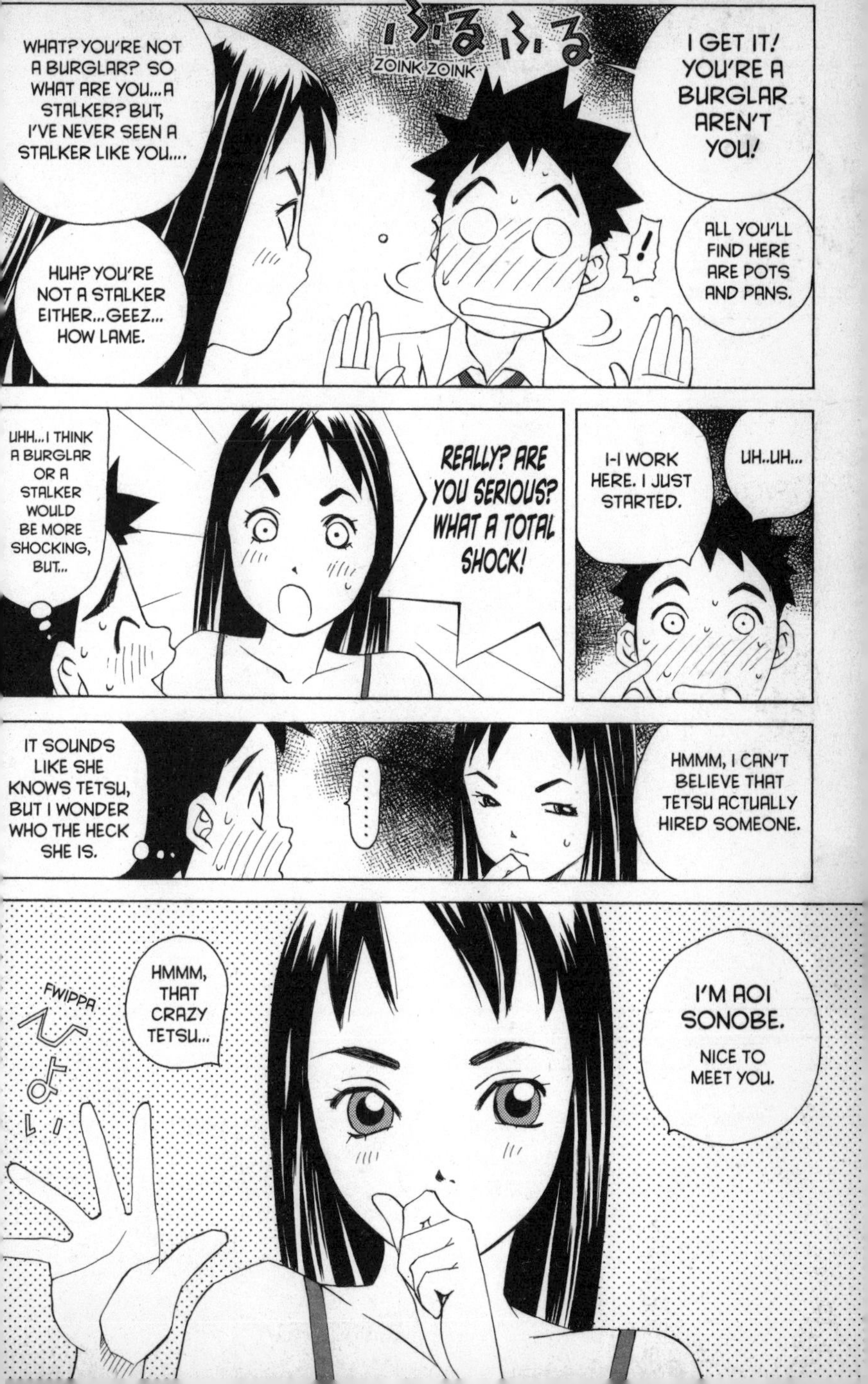
I GET IT! YOU'RE A BURGLAR AREN'T YOU!
ふるふる
ZOINK ZOINK
WHAT? YOU'RE NOT A BURGLAR? SO WHAT ARE YOU...A STALKER? BUT, I'VE NEVER SEEN A STALKER LIKE YOU....
ALL YOU'LL FIND HERE ARE POTS AND PANS.
!
HUH? YOU'RE NOT A STALKER EITHER...GEEZ... HOW LAME.
UH..UH...
I-I WORK HERE. I JUST STARTED.
REALLY? ARE YOU SERIOUS? WHAT A TOTAL SHOCK!
UHH...I THINK A BURGLAR OR A STALKER WOULD BE MORE SHOCKING, BUT...
HMMM, I CAN'T BELIEVE THAT TETSU ACTUALLY HIRED SOMEONE.
......
IT SOUNDS LIKE SHE KNOWS TETSU, BUT I WONDER WHO THE HECK SHE IS.
I'M AOI SONOBE.
NICE TO MEET YOU.
HMMM, THAT CRAZY TETSU...
FWIPPA

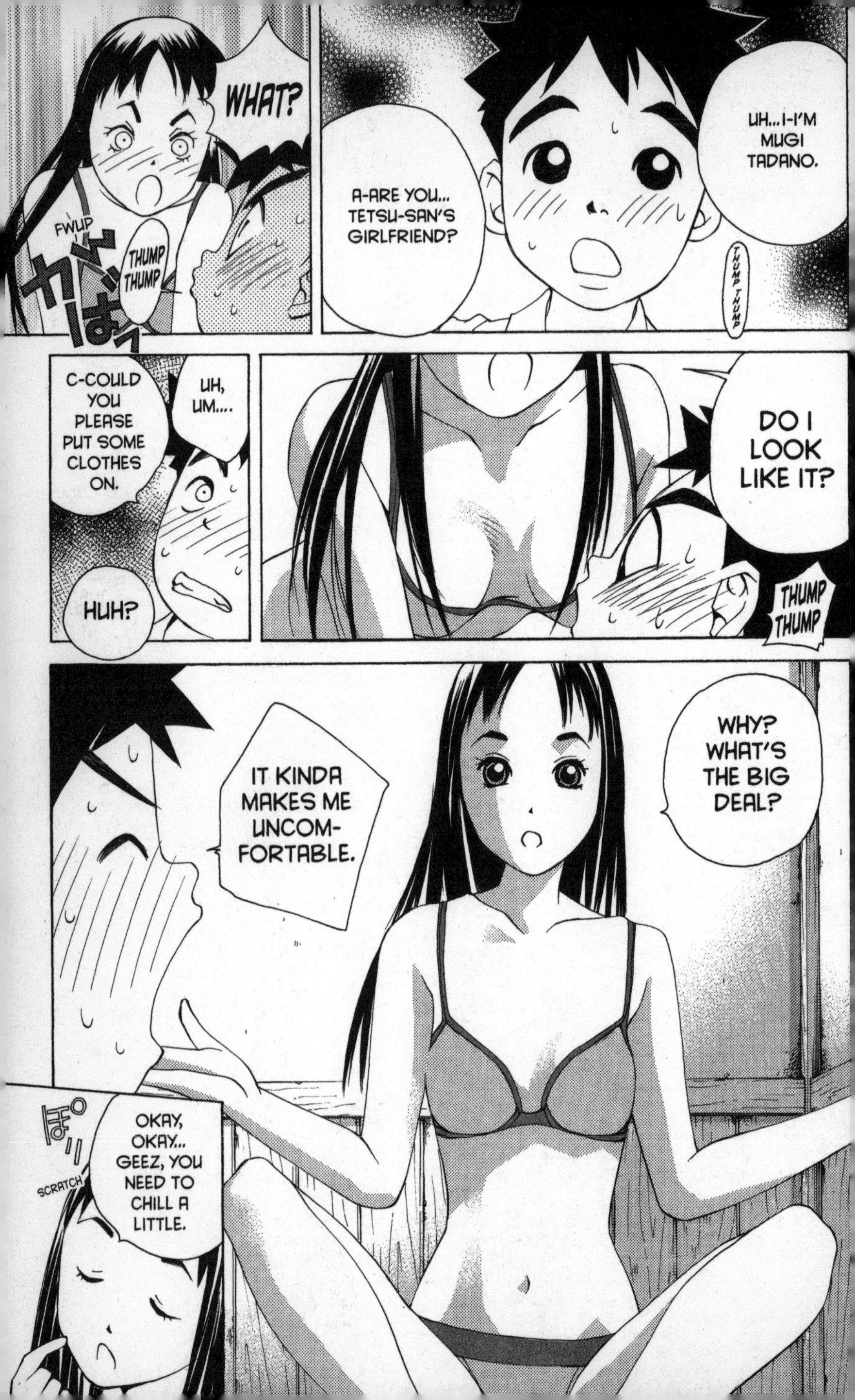
UH...I-I'M MUGI TADANO.
A-ARE YOU... TETSU-SAN'S GIRLFRIEND?
THUMP THUMP
WHAT?
FWUP
THUMP THUMP
DO I LOOK LIKE IT?
THUMP THUMP
UH, UM....
C-COULD YOU PLEASE PUT SOME CLOTHES ON.
HUH?
WHY? WHAT'S THE BIG DEAL?
IT KINDA MAKES ME UNCOM-FORTABLE.
OKAY, OKAY... GEEZ, YOU NEED TO CHILL A LITTLE.
SCRATCH

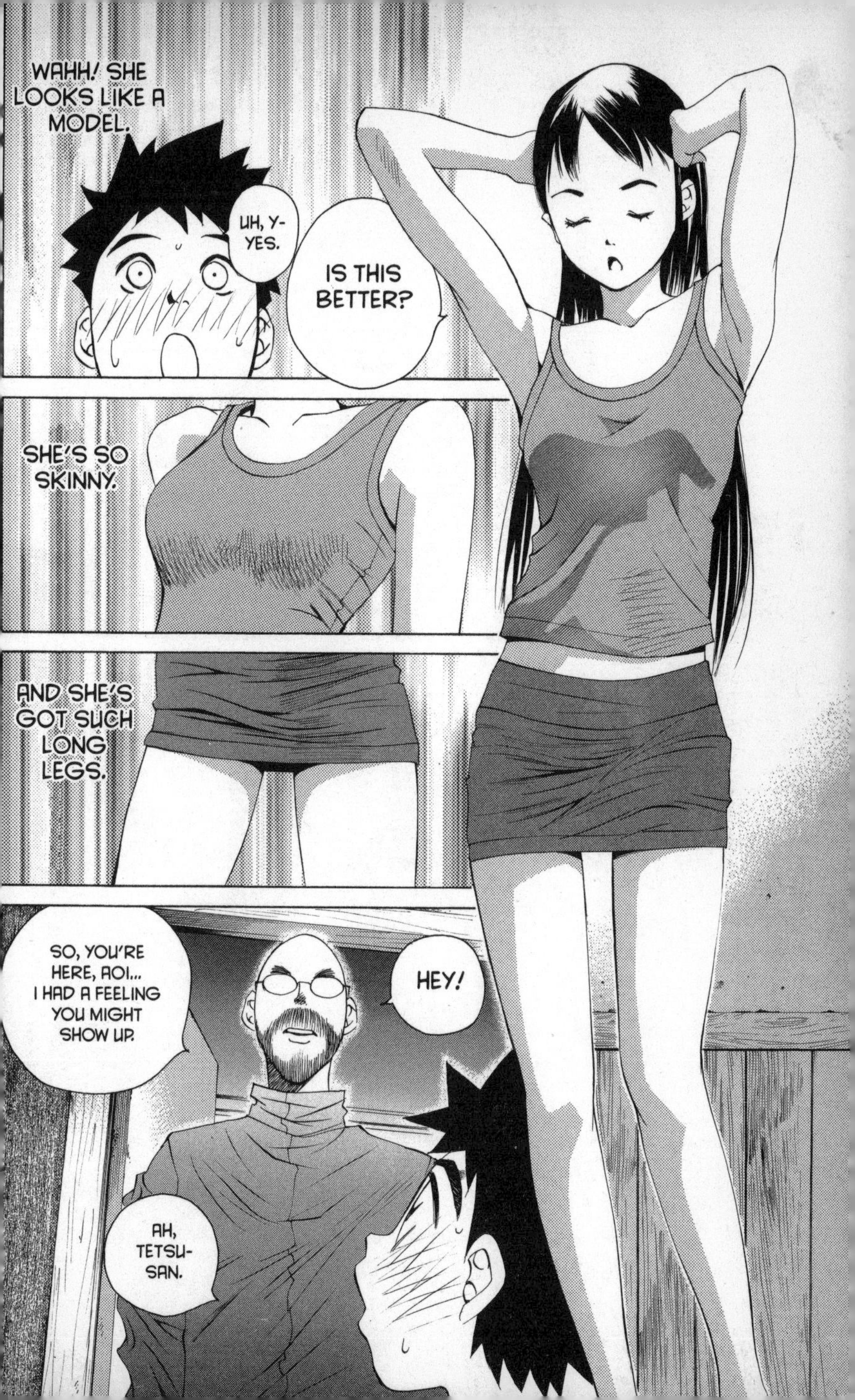

IS THIS BETTER?
UH, Y-YES.
WAHH! SHE LOOKS LIKE A MODEL.
SHE'S SO SKINNY.
AND SHE'S GOT SUCH LONG LEGS.
HEY!
SO, YOU'RE HERE, AOI... I HAD A FEELING YOU MIGHT SHOW UP.
AH, TETSU-SAN.

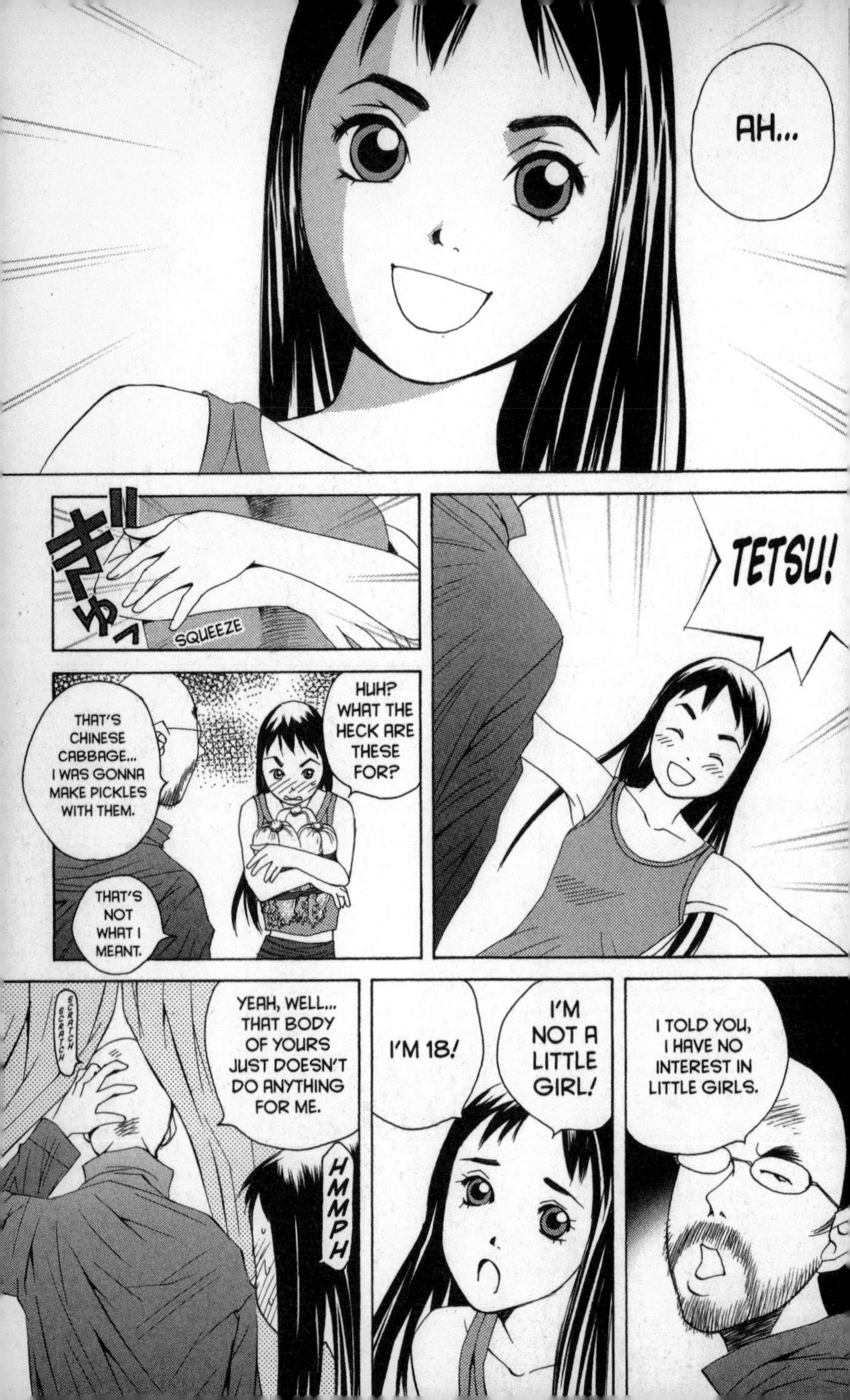
AH...
TETSU!
ぎゅっ
SQUEEZE
HUH? WHAT THE HECK ARE THESE FOR?
THAT'S CHINESE CABBAGE... I WAS GONNA MAKE PICKLES WITH THEM.
THAT'S NOT WHAT I MEANT.
I TOLD YOU, I HAVE NO INTEREST IN LITTLE GIRLS.
I'M NOT A LITTLE GIRL!
I'M 18!
YEAH, WELL... THAT BODY OF YOURS JUST DOESN'T DO ANYTHING FOR ME.
HMMPH
SCRATCH SCRATCH

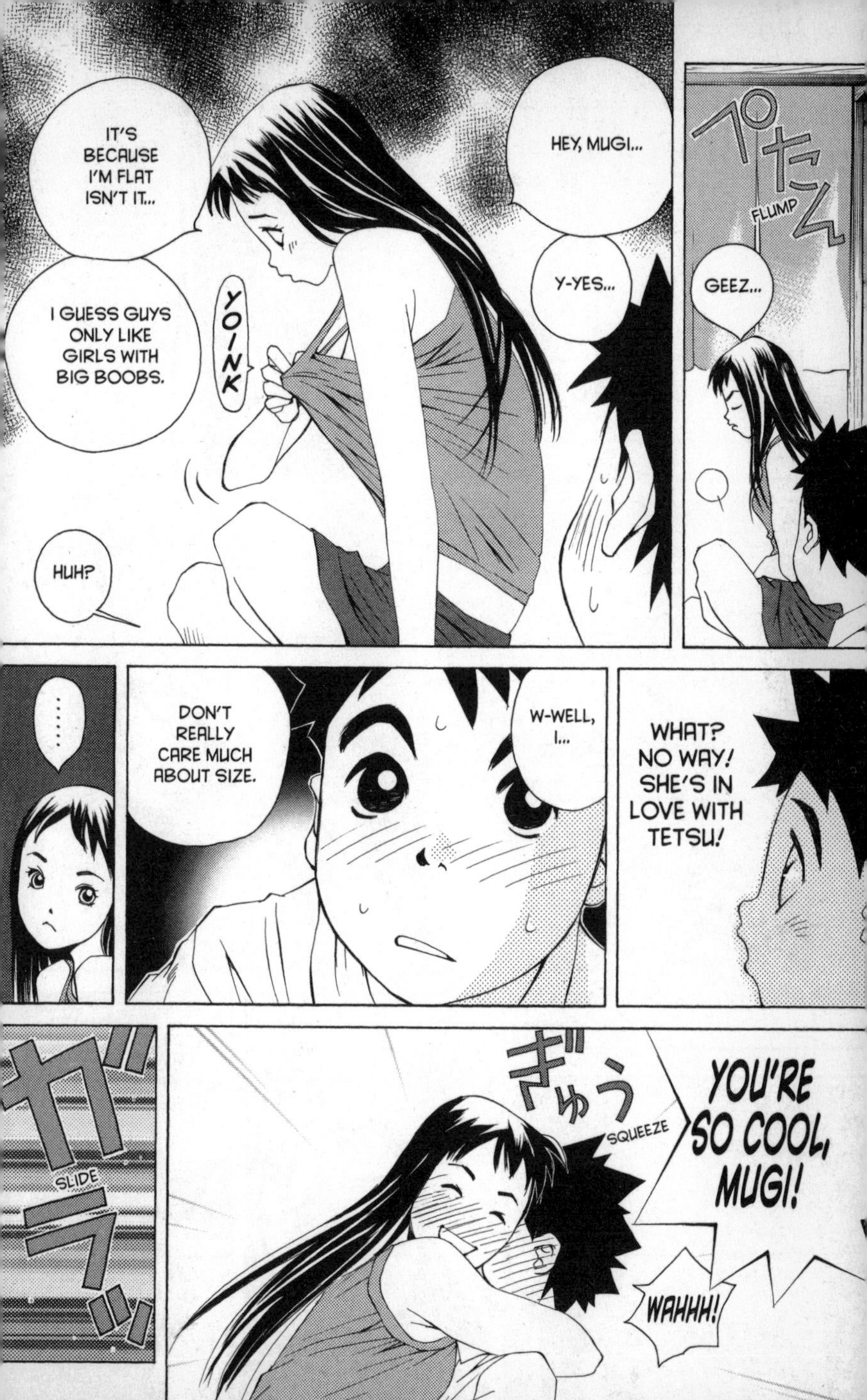
ぺたん
FLUMP
GEEZ...
HEY, MUGI...
Y-YES...
IT'S BECAUSE I'M FLAT ISN'T IT...
YOINK
I GUESS GUYS ONLY LIKE GIRLS WITH BIG BOOBS.
HUH?
WHAT? NO WAY! SHE'S IN LOVE WITH TETSU!
W-WELL, I...
DON'T REALLY CARE MUCH ABOUT SIZE.
......
ぎゅう
SQUEEZE
YOU'RE SO COOL, MUGI!
WAHHH!
ガラッ
SLIDE

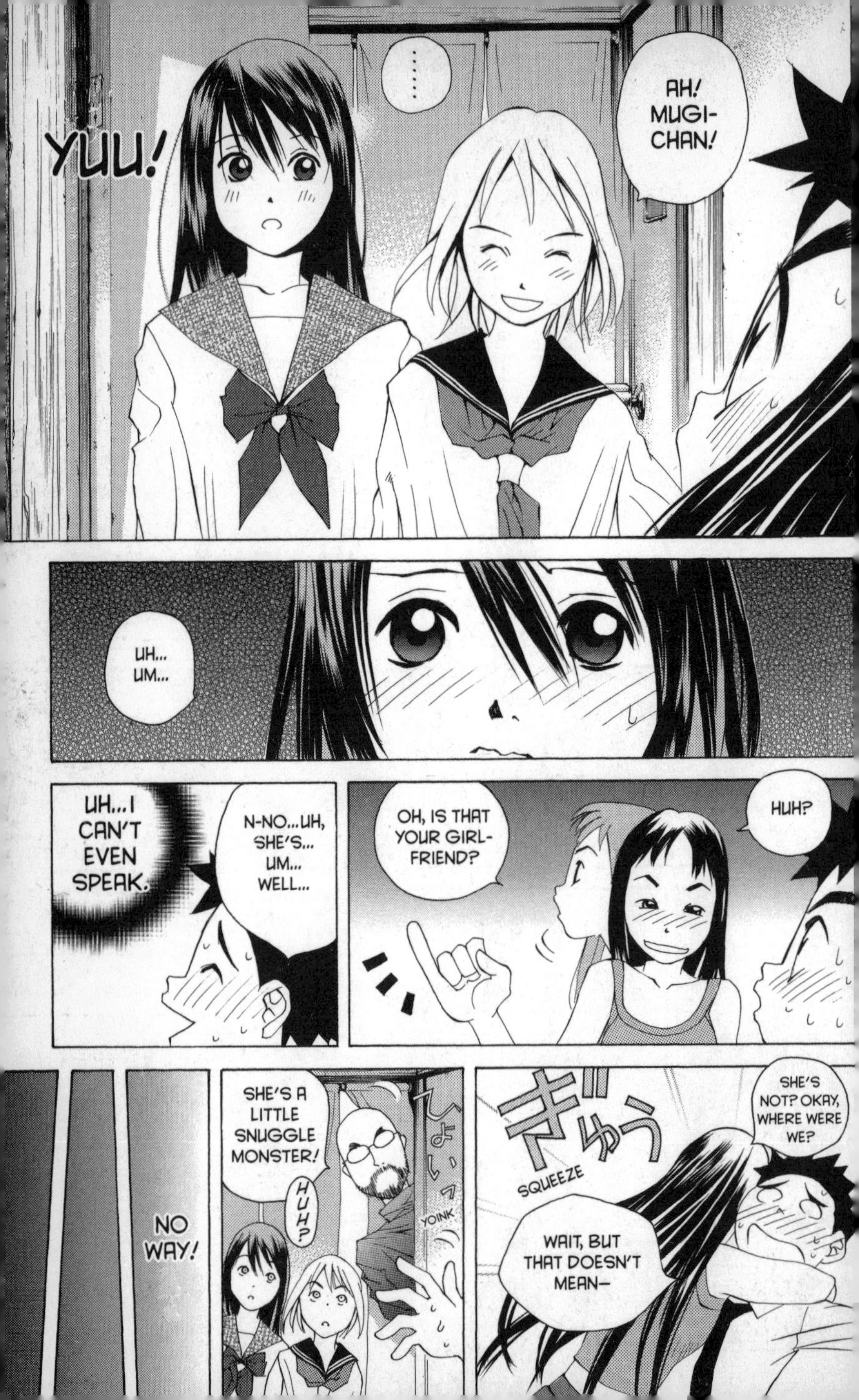

AH! MUGI-CHAN!
......
YUU!
UH... UM...
HUH?
OH, IS THAT YOUR GIRL-FRIEND?
N-NO...UH, SHE'S... UM... WELL...
UH...I CAN'T EVEN SPEAK.
SHE'S NOT? OKAY, WHERE WERE WE?
きゅう
SQUEEZE
WAIT, BUT THAT DOESN'T MEAN—
ひょいっ
YOINK
SHE'S A LITTLE SNUGGLE MONSTER!
HUH?
NO WAY!

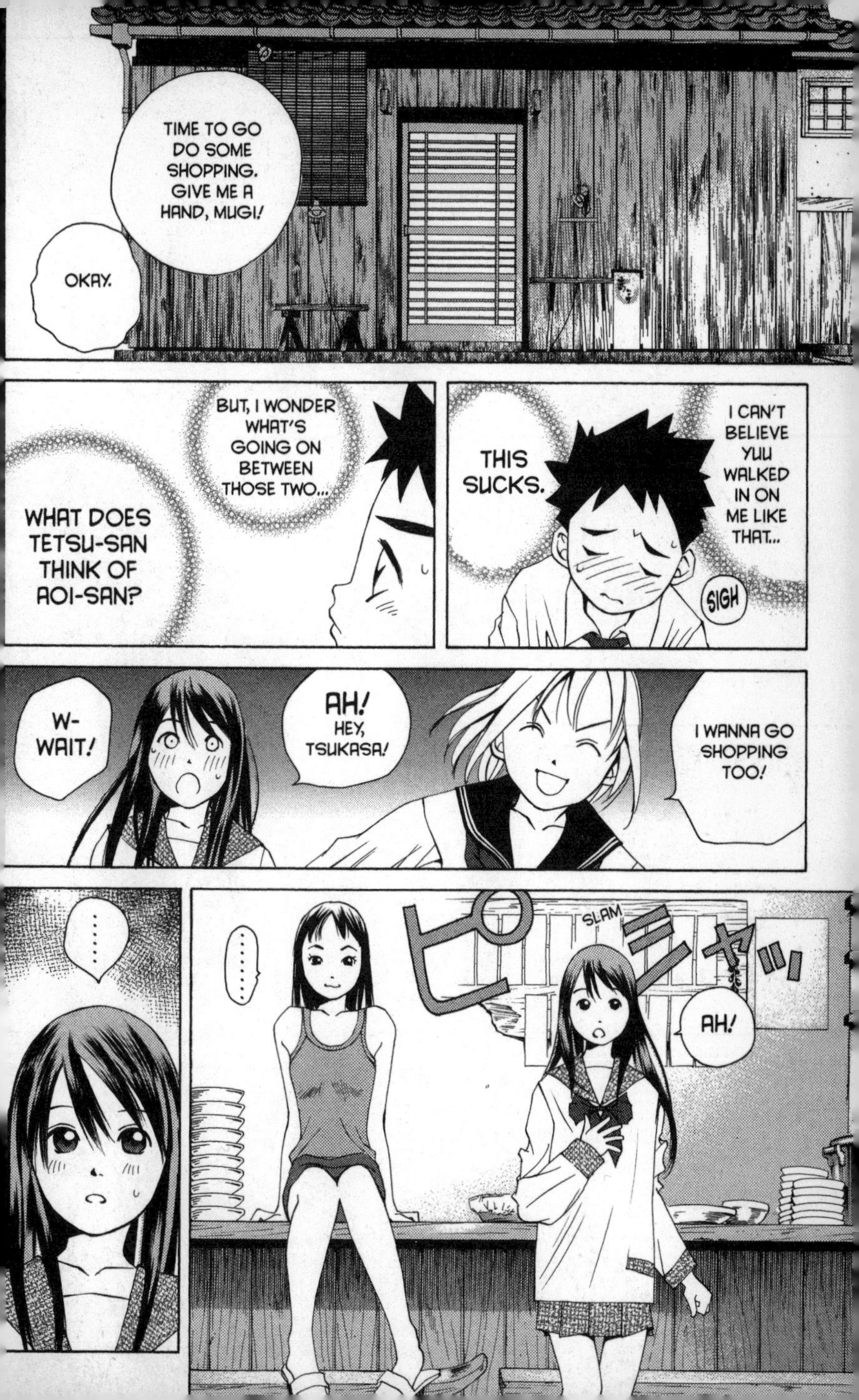
TIME TO GO DO SOME SHOPPING. GIVE ME A HAND, MUGI!
OKAY.
I CAN'T BELIEVE YUU WALKED IN ON ME LIKE THAT...
THIS SUCKS.
SIGH
BUT, I WONDER WHAT'S GOING ON BETWEEN THOSE TWO...
WHAT DOES TETSU-SAN THINK OF AOI-SAN?
I WANNA GO SHOPPING TOO!
AH! HEY, TSUKASA!
W-WAIT!
ピシャッ
SLAM
AH!
......
...

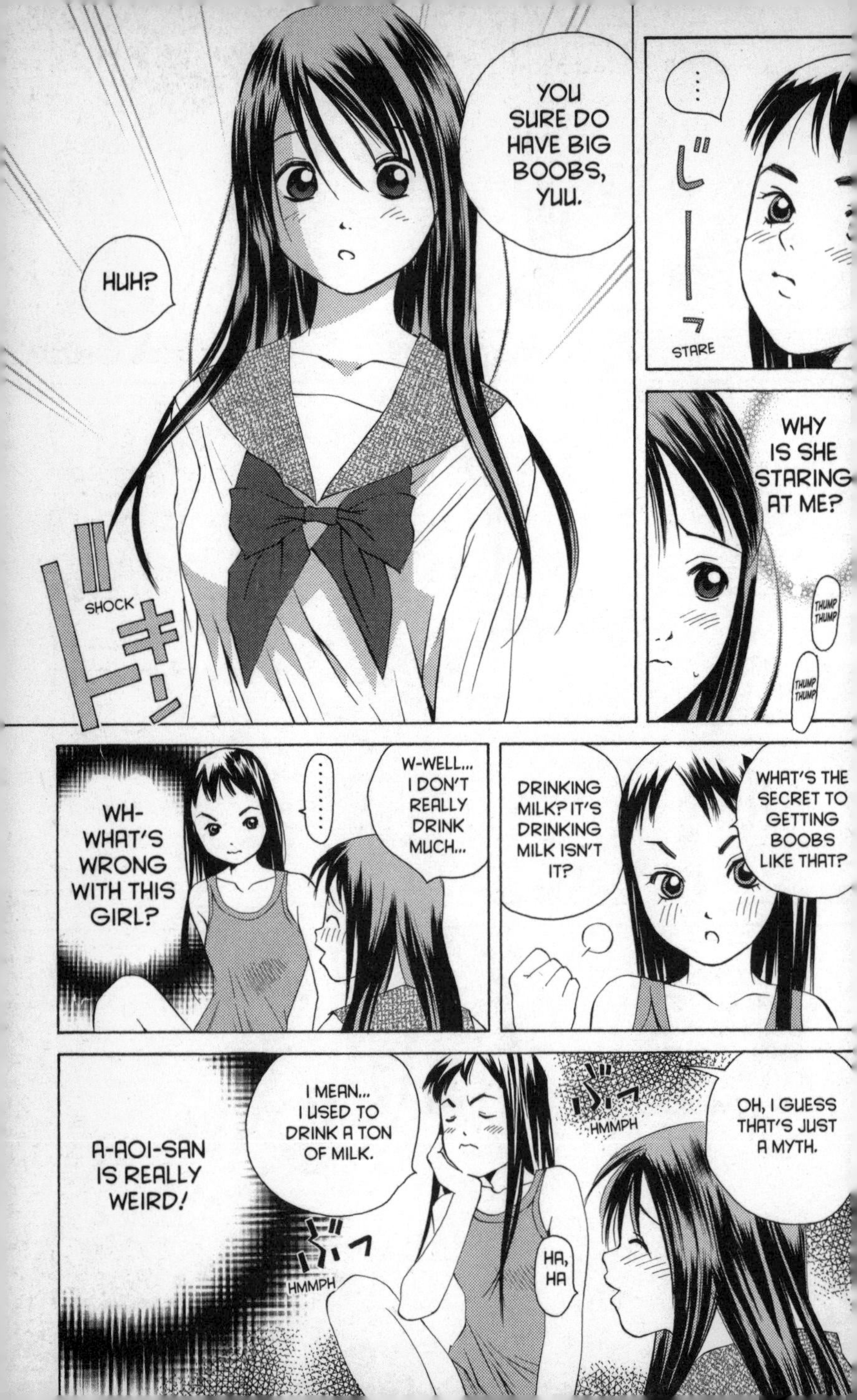
……
じーっ
STARE
WHY IS SHE STARING AT ME?
THUMP THUMP
THUMP THUMP
YOU SURE DO HAVE BIG BOOBS, YUU.
HUH?
ドキン
SHOCK
WHAT'S THE SECRET TO GETTING BOOBS LIKE THAT?
DRINKING MILK? IT'S DRINKING MILK ISN'T IT?
W-WELL... I DON'T REALLY DRINK MUCH...
....
WH- WHAT'S WRONG WITH THIS GIRL?
OH, I GUESS THAT'S JUST A MYTH.
HMMPH
HA, HA
I MEAN... I USED TO DRINK A TON OF MILK.
ぶっ
HMMPH
A-AOI-SAN IS REALLY WEIRD!

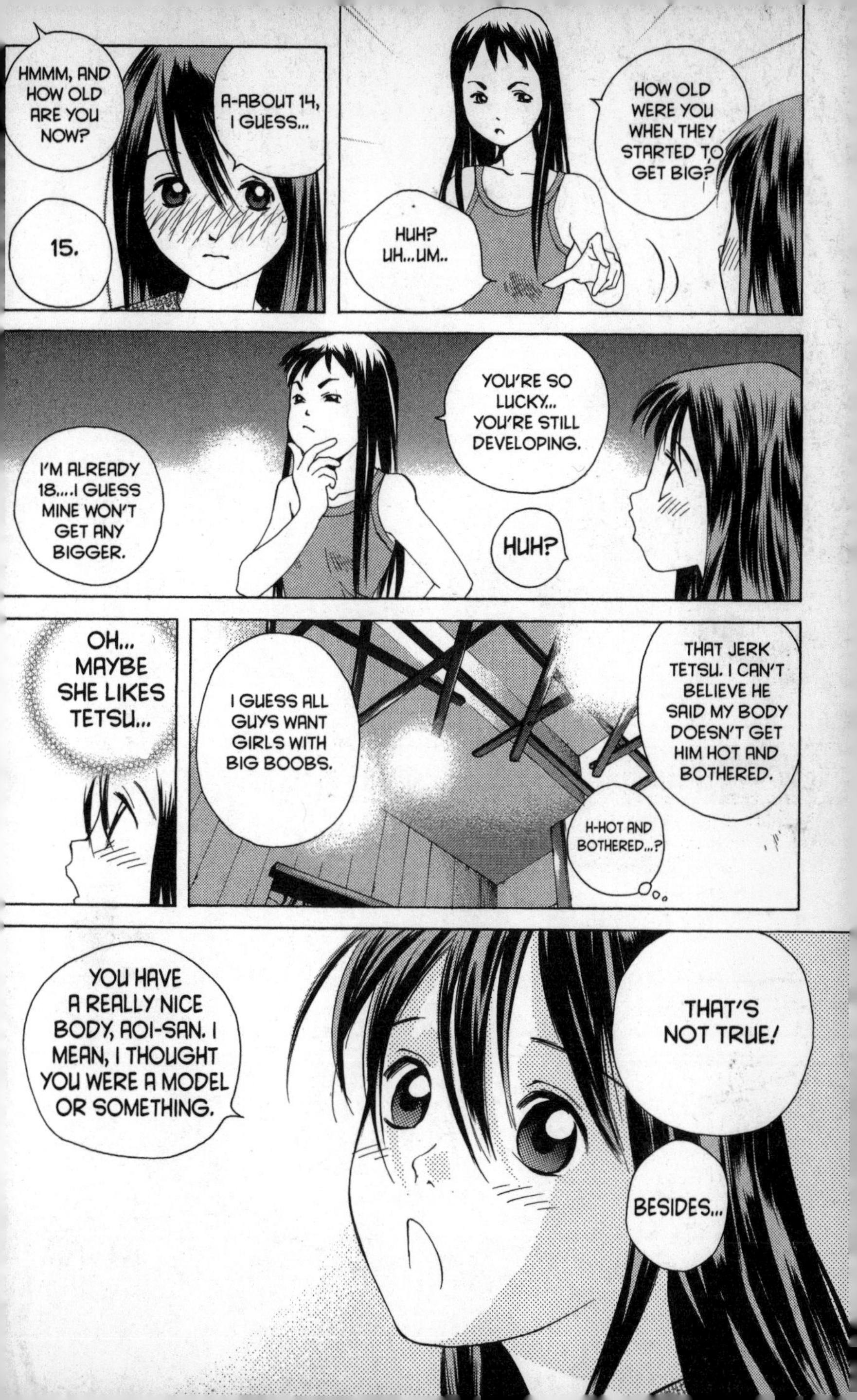

HOW OLD WERE YOU WHEN THEY STARTED TO GET BIG?
HUH? UH...UM..
A-ABOUT 14, I GUESS...
HMMM, AND HOW OLD ARE YOU NOW?
15.
YOU'RE SO LUCKY... YOU'RE STILL DEVELOPING.
HUH?
I'M ALREADY 18....I GUESS MINE WON'T GET ANY BIGGER.
THAT JERK TETSU. I CAN'T BELIEVE HE SAID MY BODY DOESN'T GET HIM HOT AND BOTHERED.
H-HOT AND BOTHERED...?
I GUESS ALL GUYS WANT GIRLS WITH BIG BOOBS.
OH... MAYBE SHE LIKES TETSU...
THAT'S NOT TRUE!
BESIDES...
YOU HAVE A REALLY NICE BODY, AOI-SAN. I MEAN, I THOUGHT YOU WERE A MODEL OR SOMETHING.

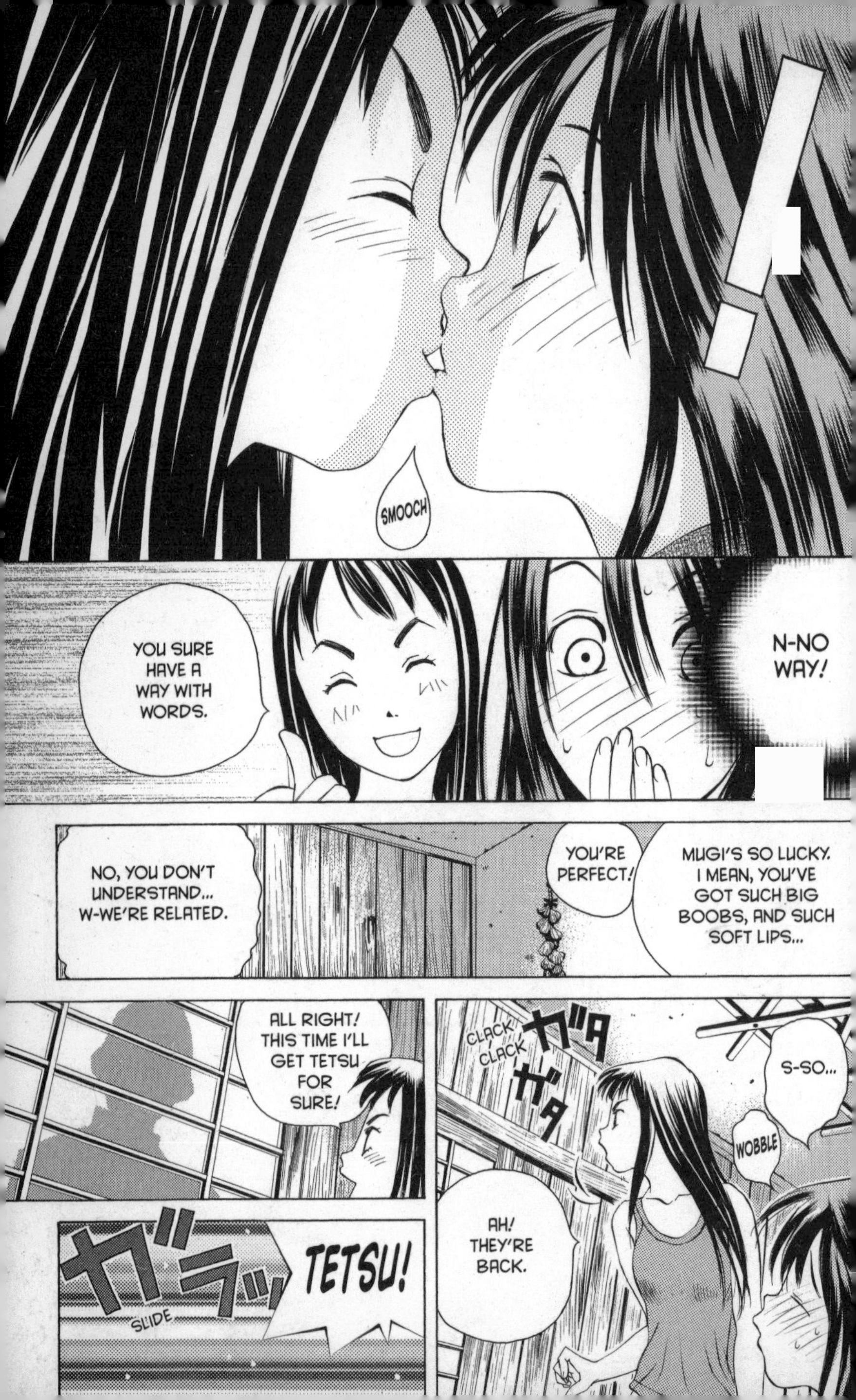
SMOOCH
N-NO WAY!
YOU SURE HAVE A WAY WITH WORDS.
MUGI'S SO LUCKY. I MEAN, YOU'VE GOT SUCH BIG BOOBS, AND SUCH SOFT LIPS...
YOU'RE PERFECT!
NO, YOU DON'T UNDERSTAND... W-WE'RE RELATED.
S-SO...
CLACK CLACK
WOBBLE
AH! THEY'RE BACK.
ALL RIGHT! THIS TIME I'LL GET TETSU FOR SURE!
TETSU!
SLIDE

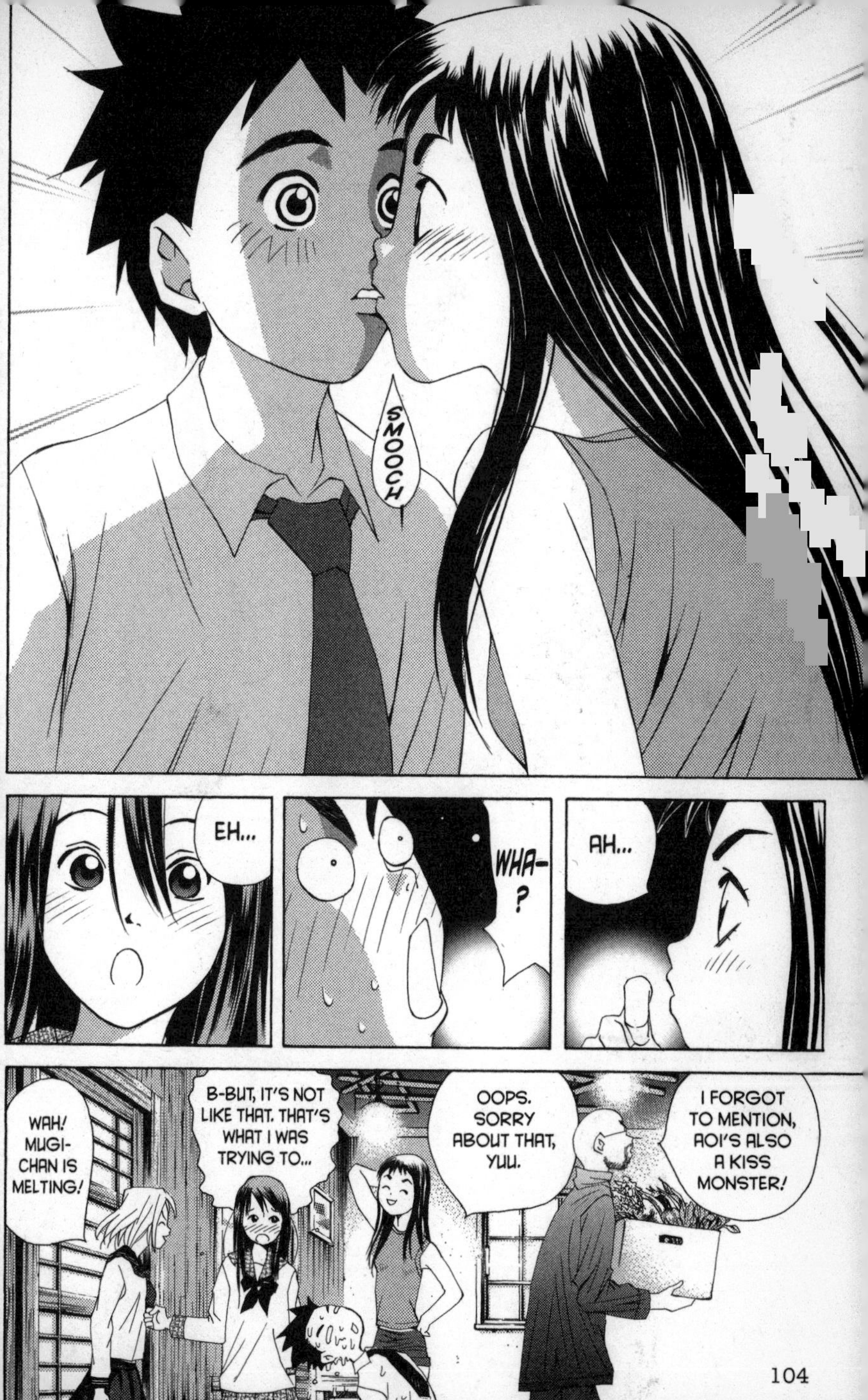
SMOOCH
AH...
WHA-?
EH...
I FORGOT TO MENTION, AOI'S ALSO A KISS MONSTER!
OOPS. SORRY ABOUT THAT, YUU.
B-BUT, IT'S NOT LIKE THAT. THAT'S WHAT I WAS TRYING TO...
WAH! MUGI-CHAN IS MELTING!

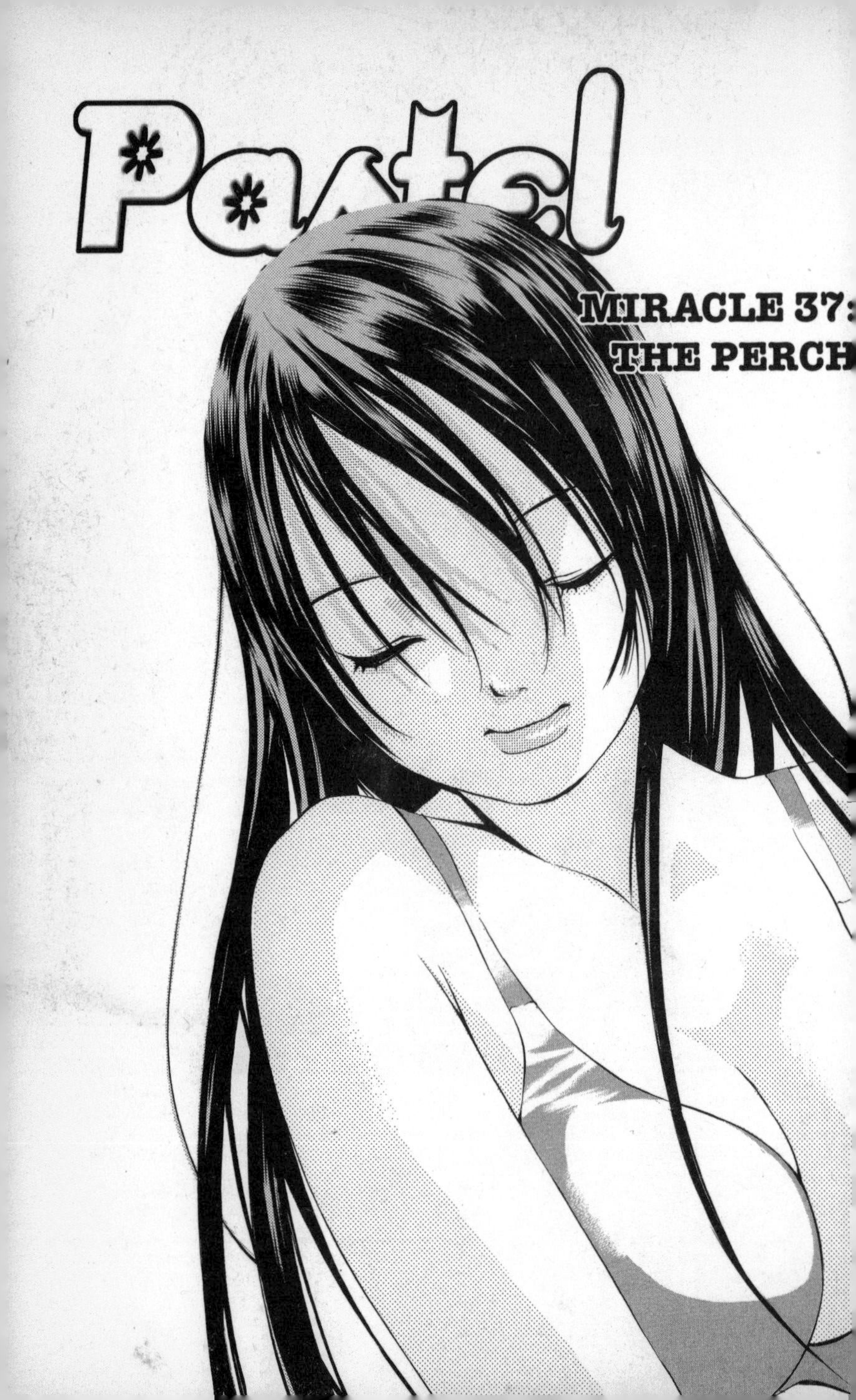
Pastel
MIRACLE 37:
THE PERCH

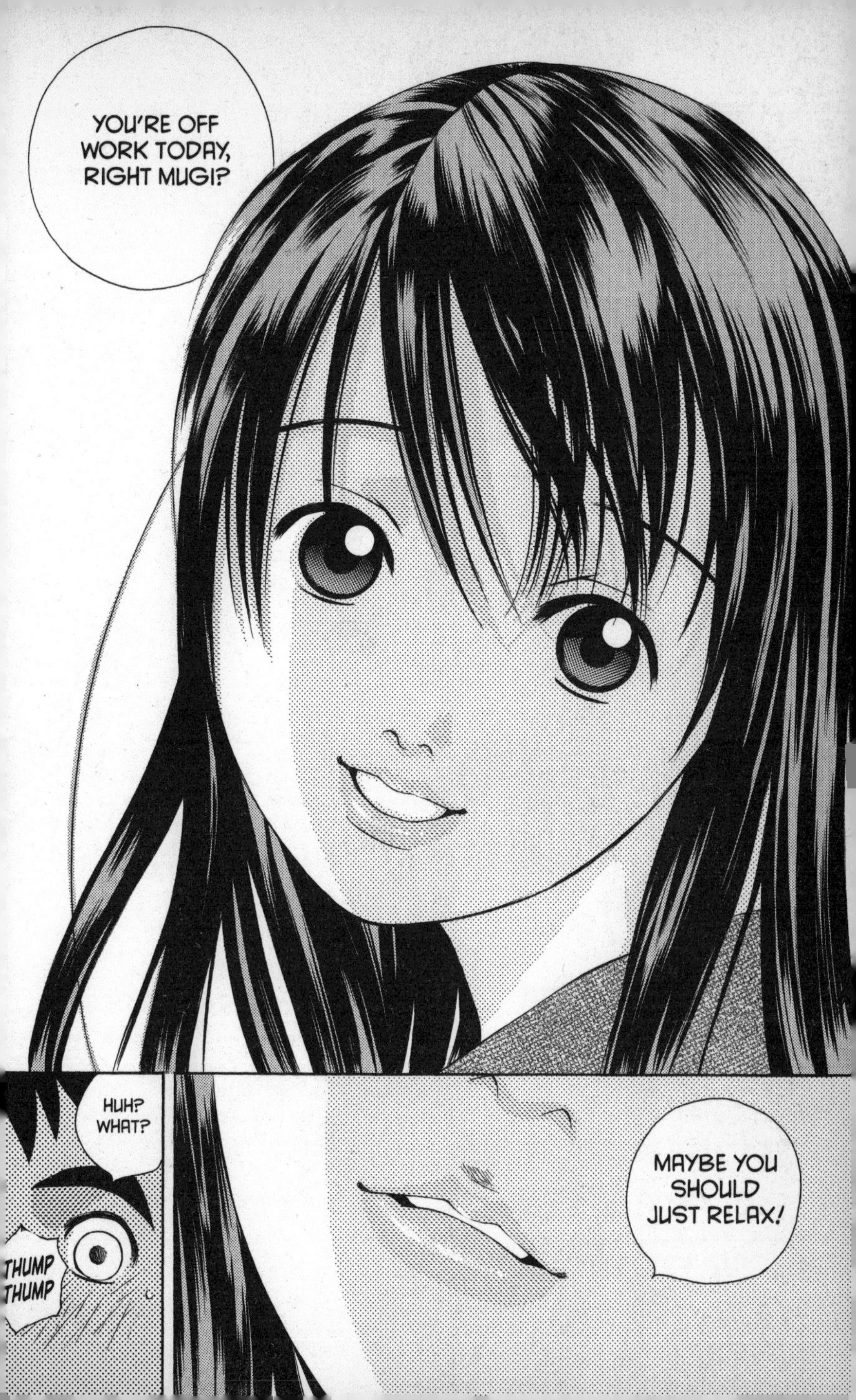
YOU'RE OFF WORK TODAY, RIGHT MUGI?
MAYBE YOU SHOULD JUST RELAX!
HUH? WHAT?
THUMP THUMP

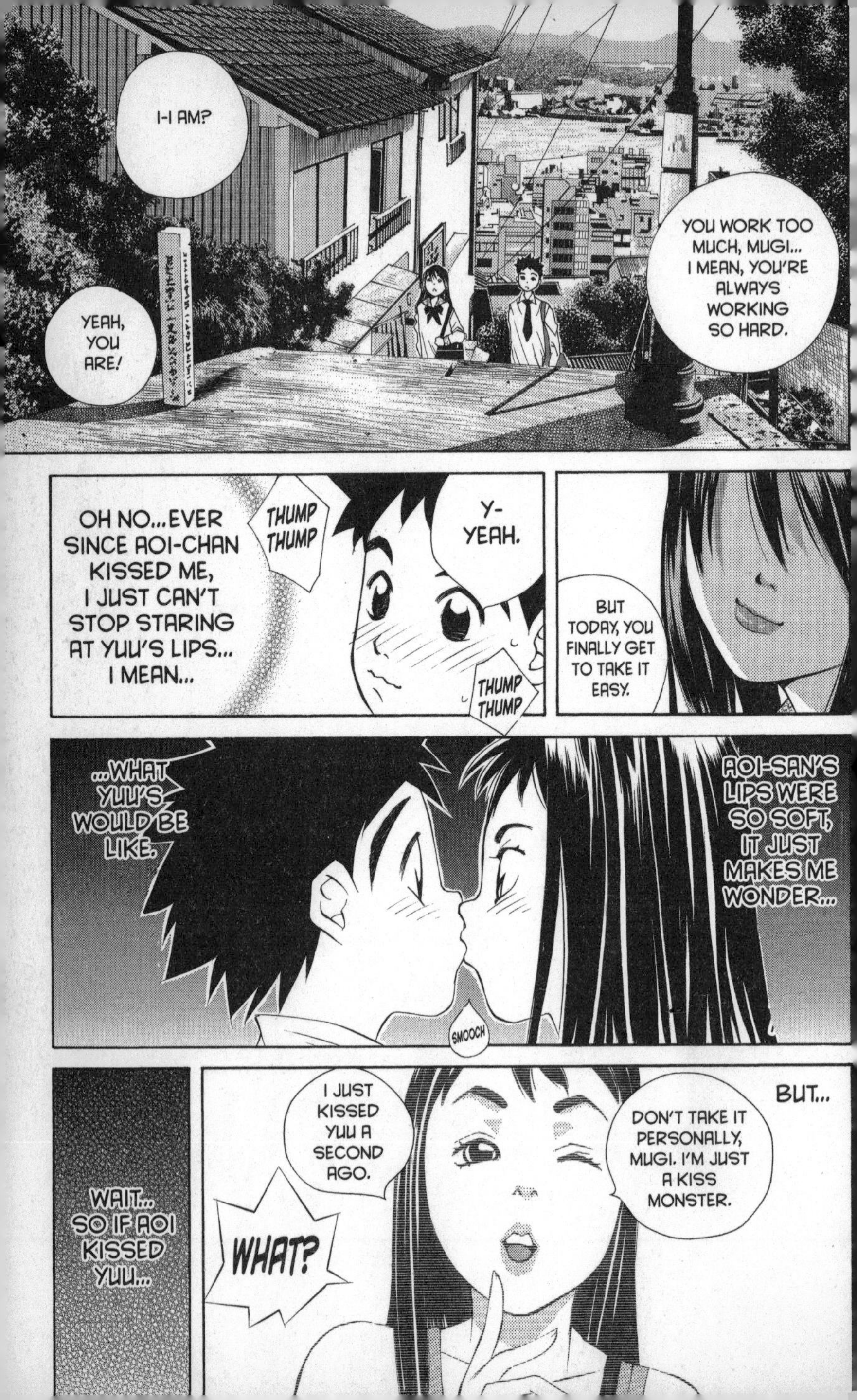
YOU WORK TOO MUCH, MUGI... I MEAN, YOU'RE ALWAYS WORKING SO HARD.
I-I AM?
YEAH, YOU ARE!
BUT TODAY, YOU FINALLY GET TO TAKE IT EASY.
Y-YEAH.
THUMP THUMP
OH NO...EVER SINCE AOI-CHAN KISSED ME, I JUST CAN'T STOP STARING AT YUU'S LIPS... I MEAN...
THUMP THUMP
AOI-SAN'S LIPS WERE SO SOFT, IT JUST MAKES ME WONDER...
...WHAT YUU'S WOULD BE LIKE.
SMOOCH
BUT...
DON'T TAKE IT PERSONALLY, MUGI. I'M JUST A KISS MONSTER.
I JUST KISSED YUU A SECOND AGO.
WHAT?
WAIT... SO IF AOI KISSED YUU...

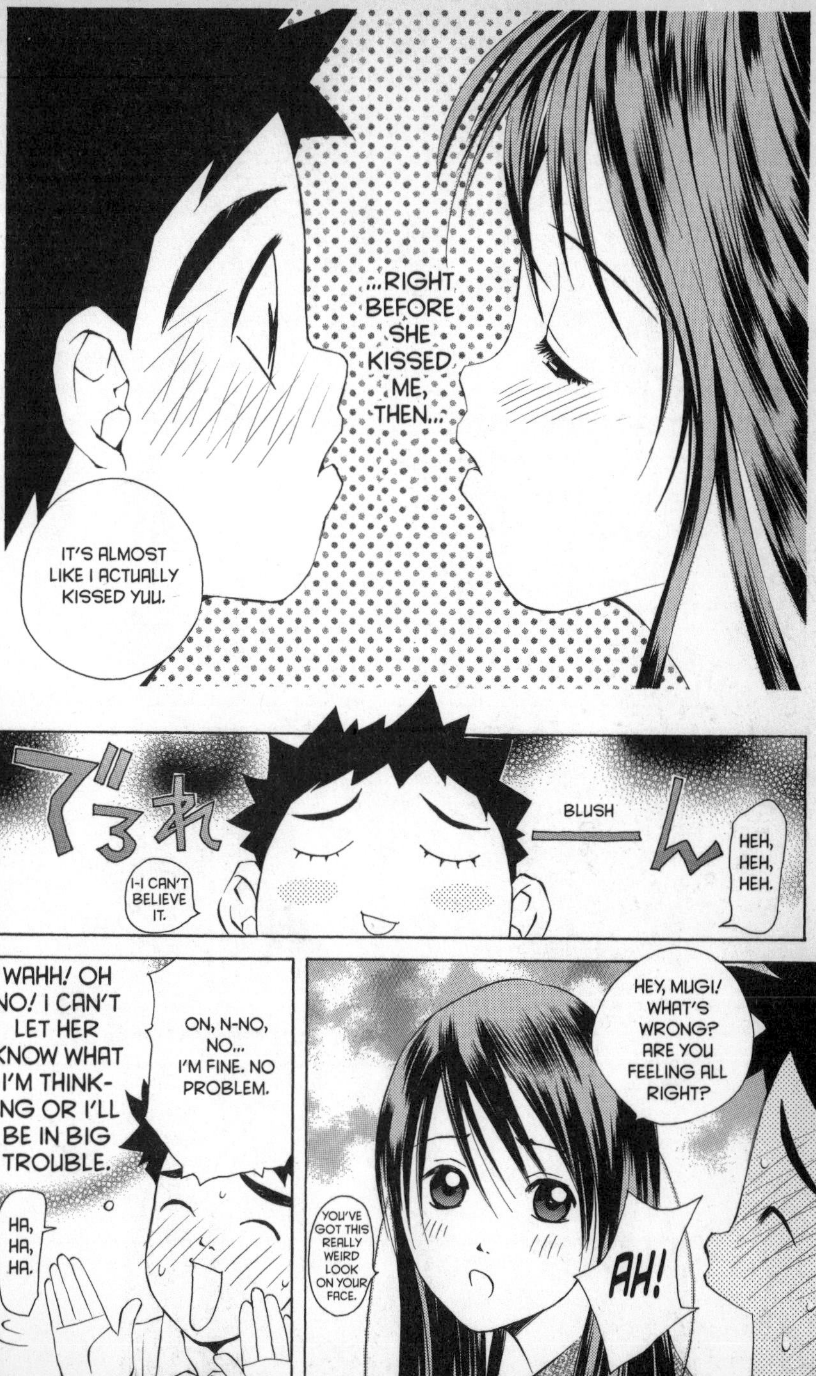
...RIGHT BEFORE SHE KISSED ME, THEN...
IT'S ALMOST LIKE I ACTUALLY KISSED YUU.
HEH, HEH, HEH.
BLUSH
でろれーん
I-I CAN'T BELIEVE IT.
HEY, MUGI! WHAT'S WRONG? ARE YOU FEELING ALL RIGHT?
AH!
YOU'VE GOT THIS REALLY WEIRD LOOK ON YOUR FACE.
WAHH! OH NO! I CAN'T LET HER KNOW WHAT I'M THINK-ING OR I'LL BE IN BIG TROUBLE.
ON, N-NO, NO... I'M FINE. NO PROBLEM.
HA, HA, HA.

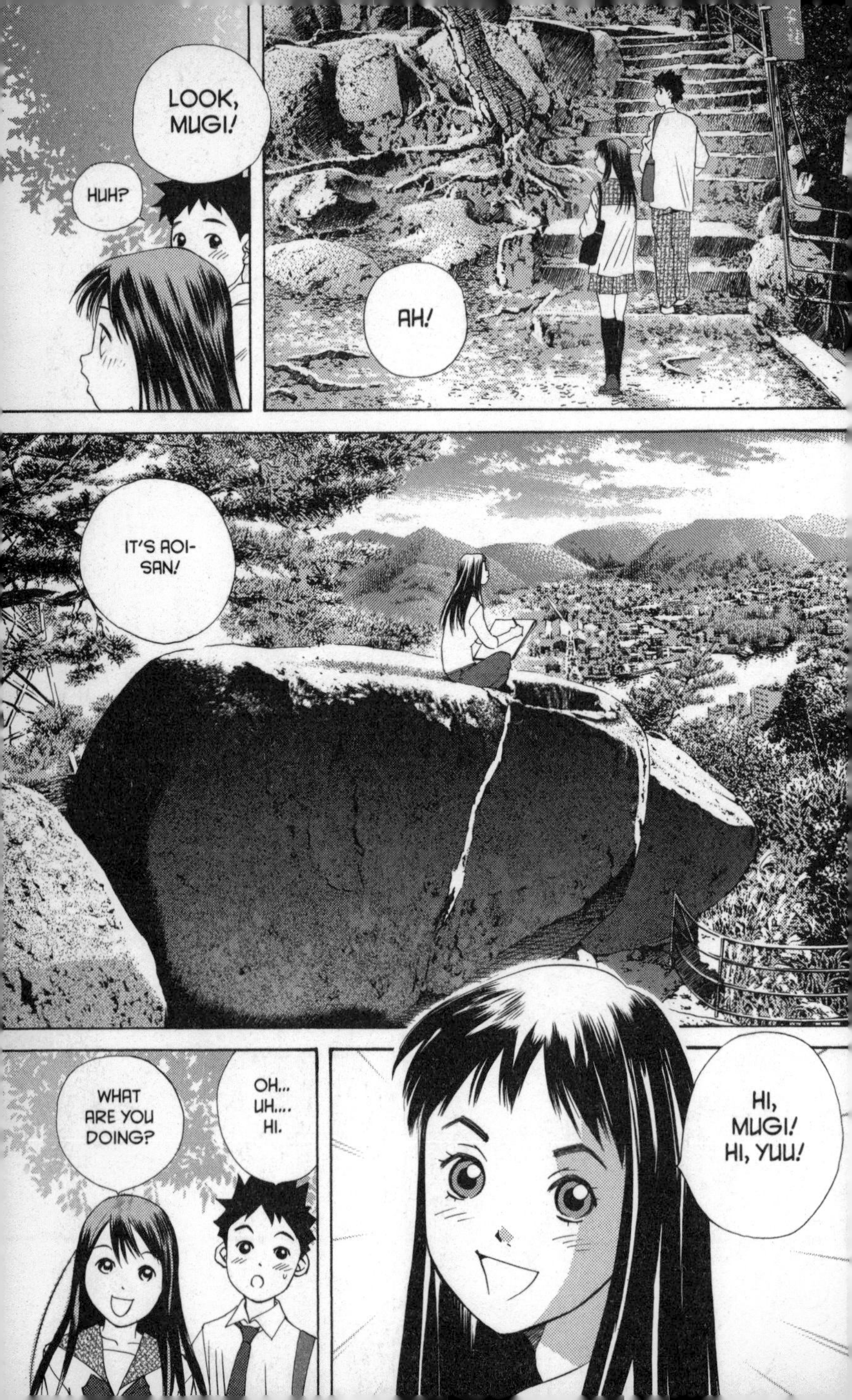
AH!
LOOK, MUGI!
HUH?
IT'S AOI-SAN!
HI, MUGI! HI, YUU!
OH... UH.... HI.
WHAT ARE YOU DOING?

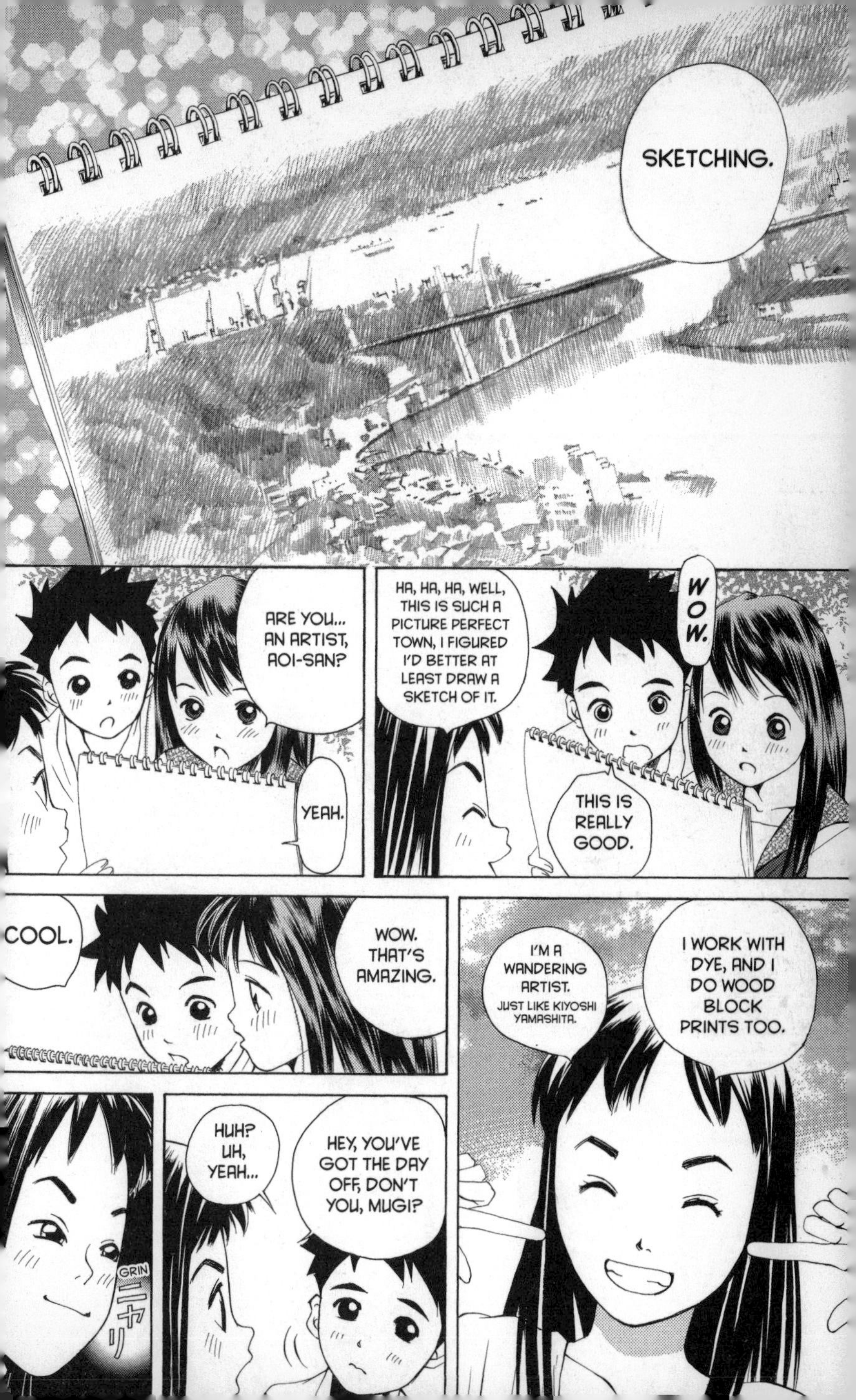

SKETCHING.
WOW.
HA, HA, HA, WELL, THIS IS SUCH A PICTURE PERFECT TOWN, I FIGURED I'D BETTER AT LEAST DRAW A SKETCH OF IT.
THIS IS REALLY GOOD.
ARE YOU... AN ARTIST, AOI-SAN?
YEAH.
I WORK WITH DYE, AND I DO WOOD BLOCK PRINTS TOO.
I'M A WANDERING ARTIST.
JUST LIKE KIYOSHI YAMASHITA.
WOW. THAT'S AMAZING.
COOL.
HEY, YOU'VE GOT THE DAY OFF, DON'T YOU, MUGI?
HUH? UH, YEAH...
GRIN
ニヤリ

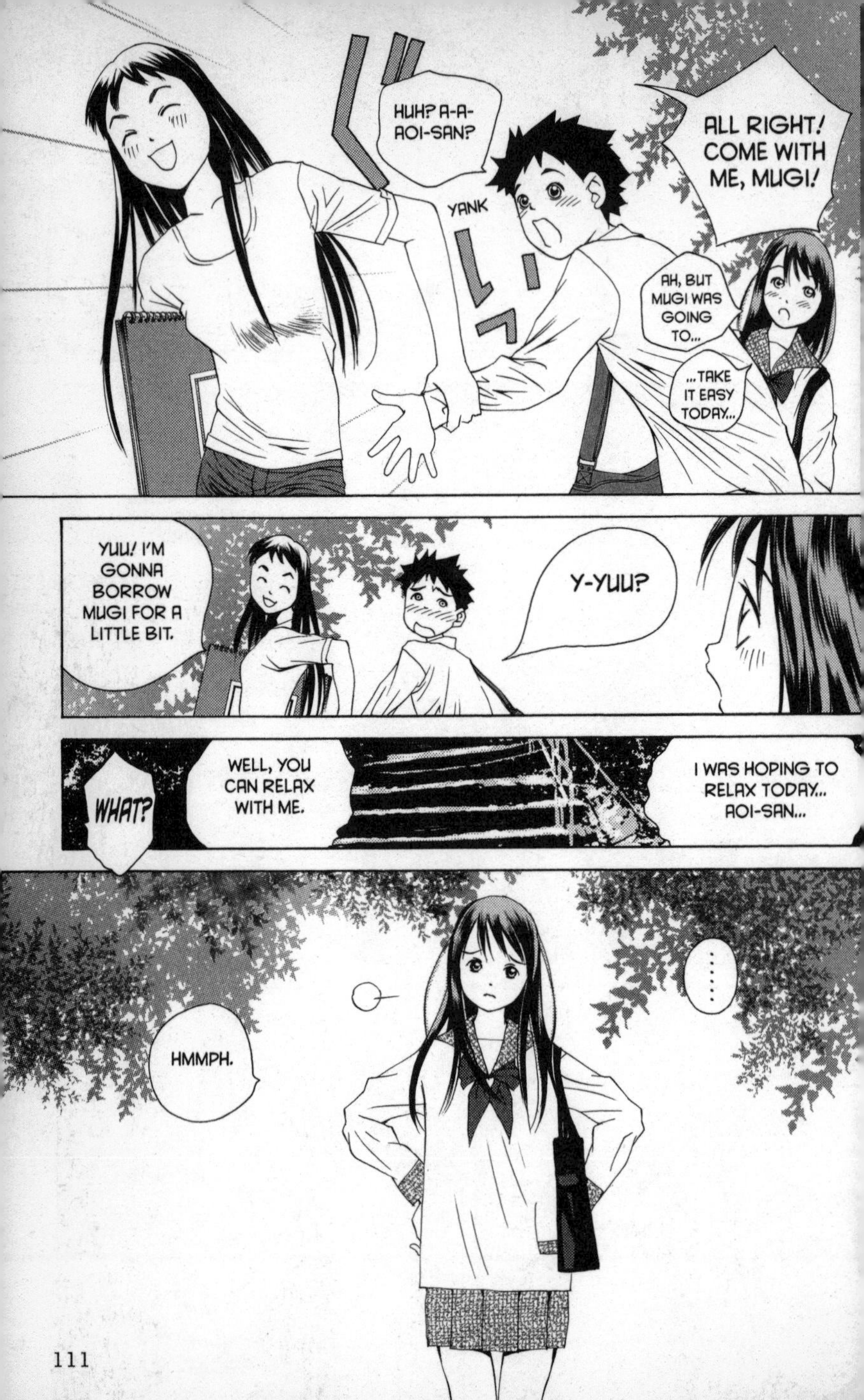

ALL RIGHT! COME WITH ME, MUGI!
HUH? A-A-AOI-SAN?
YANK
AH, BUT MUGI WAS GOING TO...
...TAKE IT EASY TODAY...
Y-YUU?
YUU! I'M GONNA BORROW MUGI FOR A LITTLE BIT.
I WAS HOPING TO RELAX TODAY... AOI-SAN...
WELL, YOU CAN RELAX WITH ME.
WHAT?
......
HMMPH.

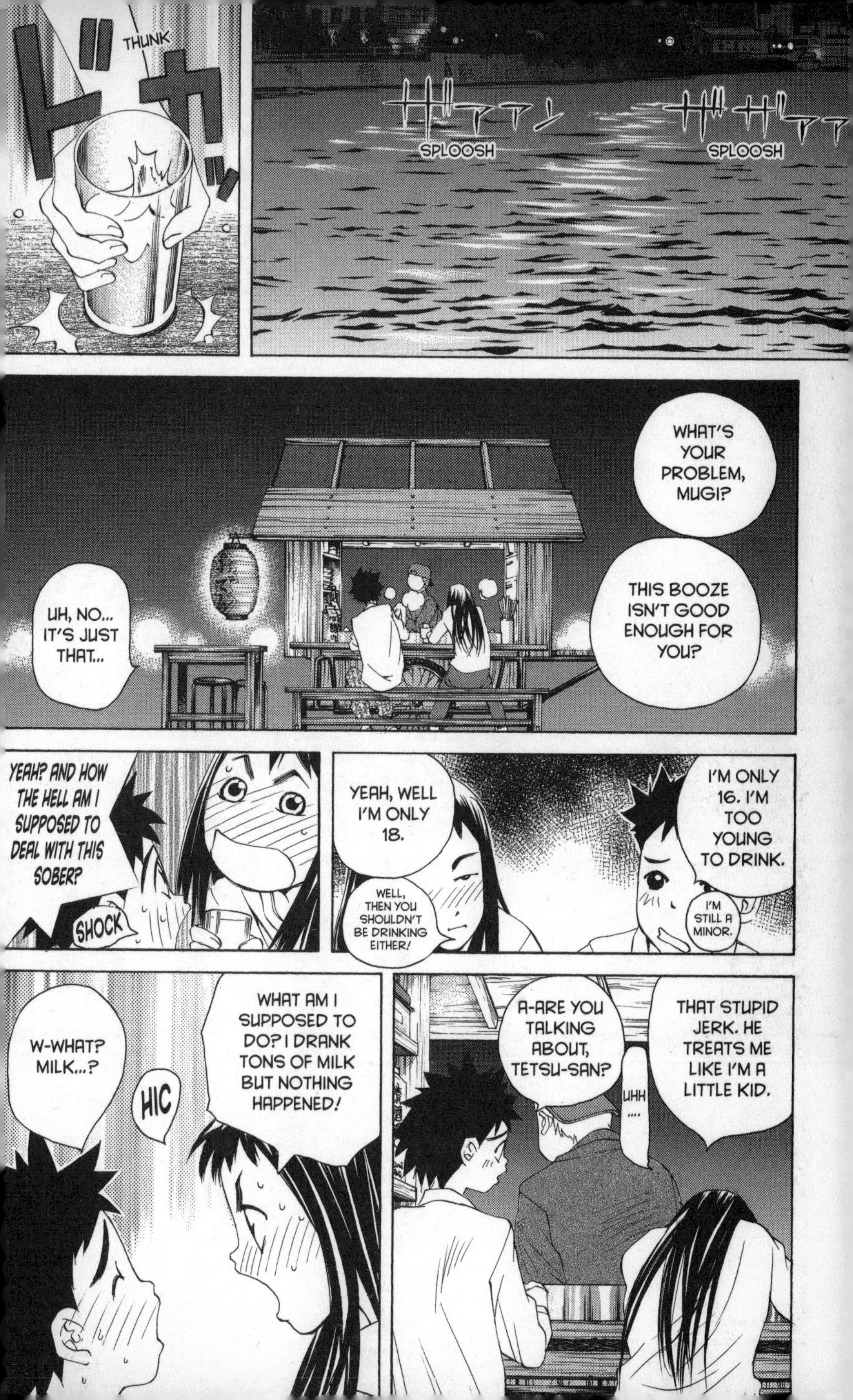
SPLOOSH
SPLOOSH
THUNK
WHAT'S YOUR PROBLEM, MUGI?
THIS BOOZE ISN'T GOOD ENOUGH FOR YOU?
UH, NO... IT'S JUST THAT...
I'M ONLY 16. I'M TOO YOUNG TO DRINK.
I'M STILL A MINOR.
YEAH, WELL I'M ONLY 18.
WELL, THEN YOU SHOULDN'T BE DRINKING EITHER!
YEAH? AND HOW THE HELL AM I SUPPOSED TO DEAL WITH THIS SOBER?
SHOCK
THAT STUPID JERK. HE TREATS ME LIKE I'M A LITTLE KID.
UHH....
A-ARE YOU TALKING ABOUT, TETSU-SAN?
WHAT AM I SUPPOSED TO DO? I DRANK TONS OF MILK BUT NOTHING HAPPENED!
HIC
W-WHAT? MILK...?

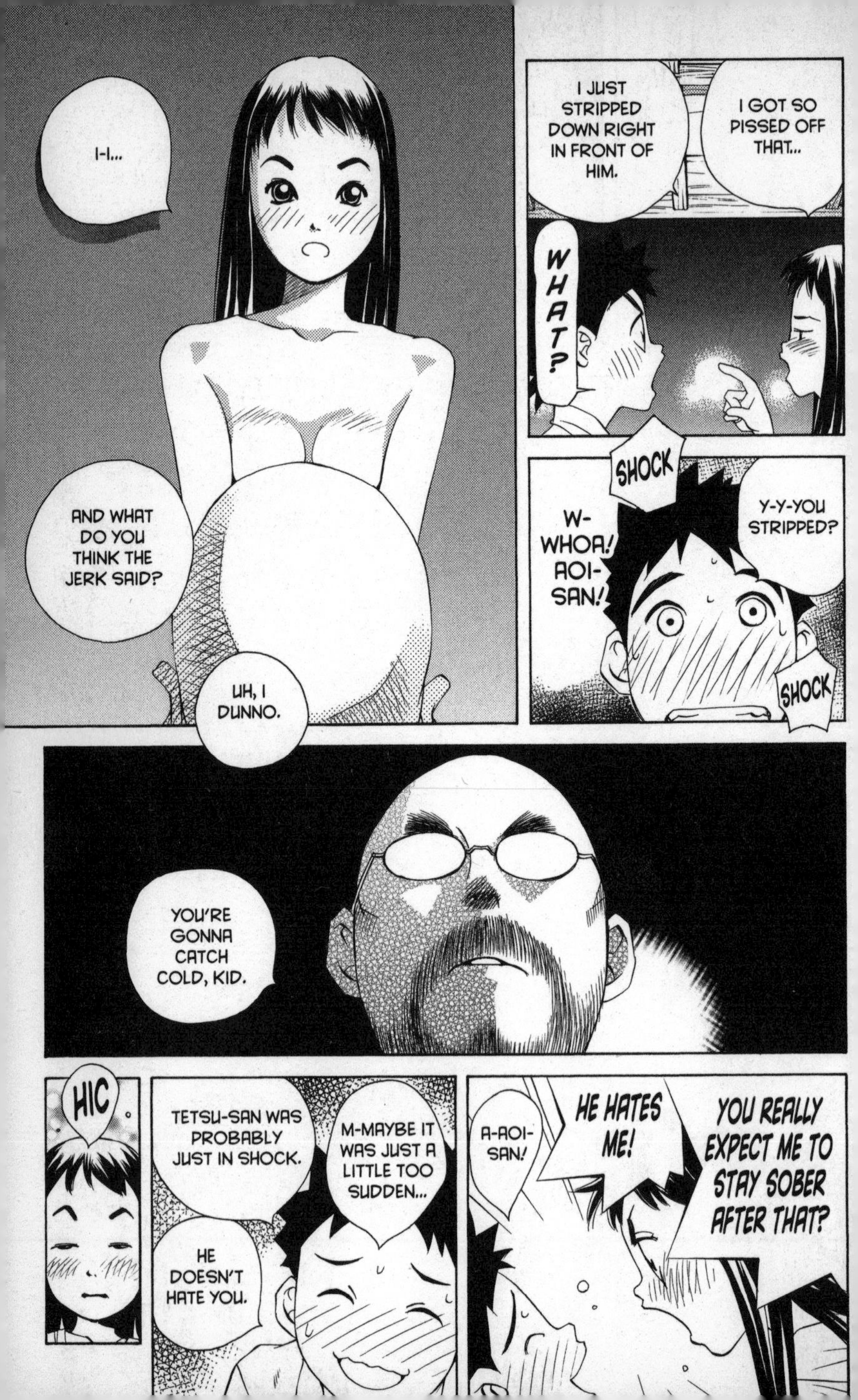
I GOT SO PISSED OFF THAT...
I JUST STRIPPED DOWN RIGHT IN FRONT OF HIM.
WHAT?
SHOCK
Y-Y-YOU STRIPPED?
W-WHOA! AOI-SAN!
SHOCK
I-I...
AND WHAT DO YOU THINK THE JERK SAID?
UH, I DUNNO.
YOU'RE GONNA CATCH COLD, KID.
YOU REALLY EXPECT ME TO STAY SOBER AFTER THAT?
HE HATES ME!
A-AOI-SAN!
M-MAYBE IT WAS JUST A LITTLE TOO SUDDEN...
TETSU-SAN WAS PROBABLY JUST IN SHOCK.
HE DOESN'T HATE YOU.
HIC

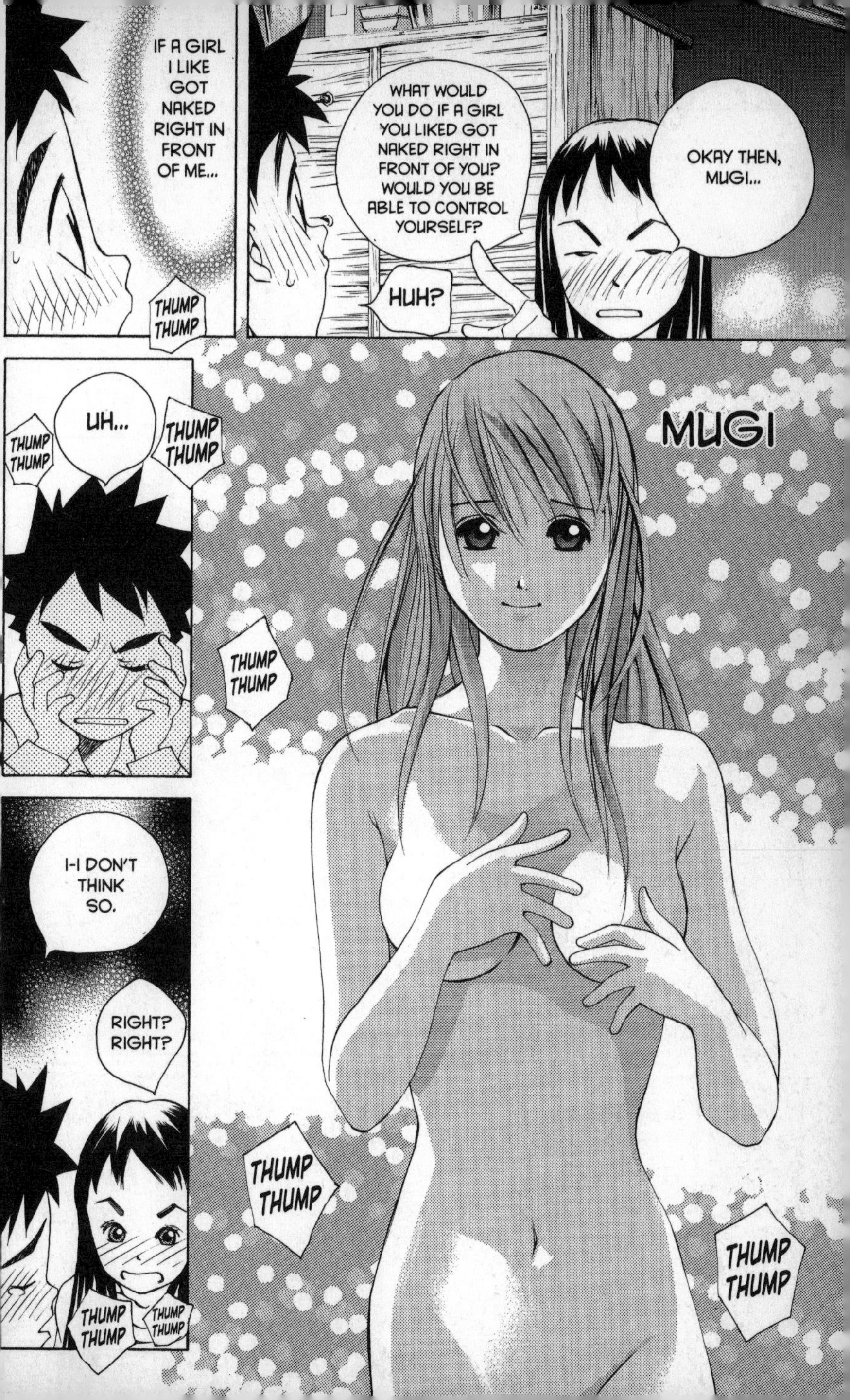
OKAY THEN, MUGI...
WHAT WOULD YOU DO IF A GIRL YOU LIKED GOT NAKED RIGHT IN FRONT OF YOU? WOULD YOU BE ABLE TO CONTROL YOURSELF?
HUH?
IF A GIRL I LIKE GOT NAKED RIGHT IN FRONT OF ME...
THUMP THUMP
MUGI
THUMP THUMP
THUMP THUMP
THUMP THUMP
THUMP THUMP
UH...
THUMP THUMP
I-I DON'T THINK SO.
RIGHT? RIGHT?
THUMP THUMP
THUMP THUMP

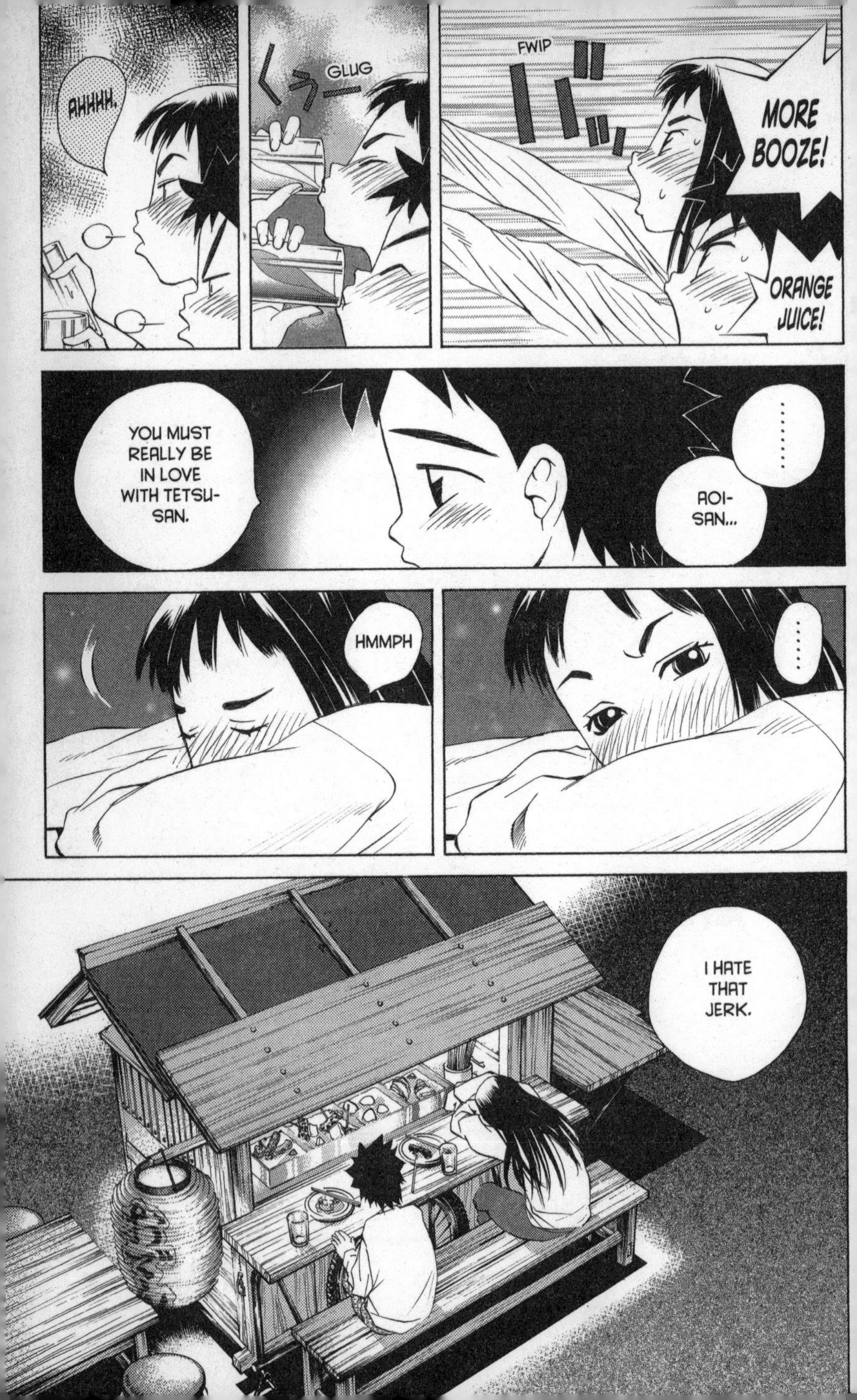
FWIP
MORE BOOZE!
ORANGE JUICE!
GLUG
AHHHH.
......
AOI-SAN...
YOU MUST REALLY BE IN LOVE WITH TETSU-SAN.
......
HMMPH
I HATE THAT JERK.

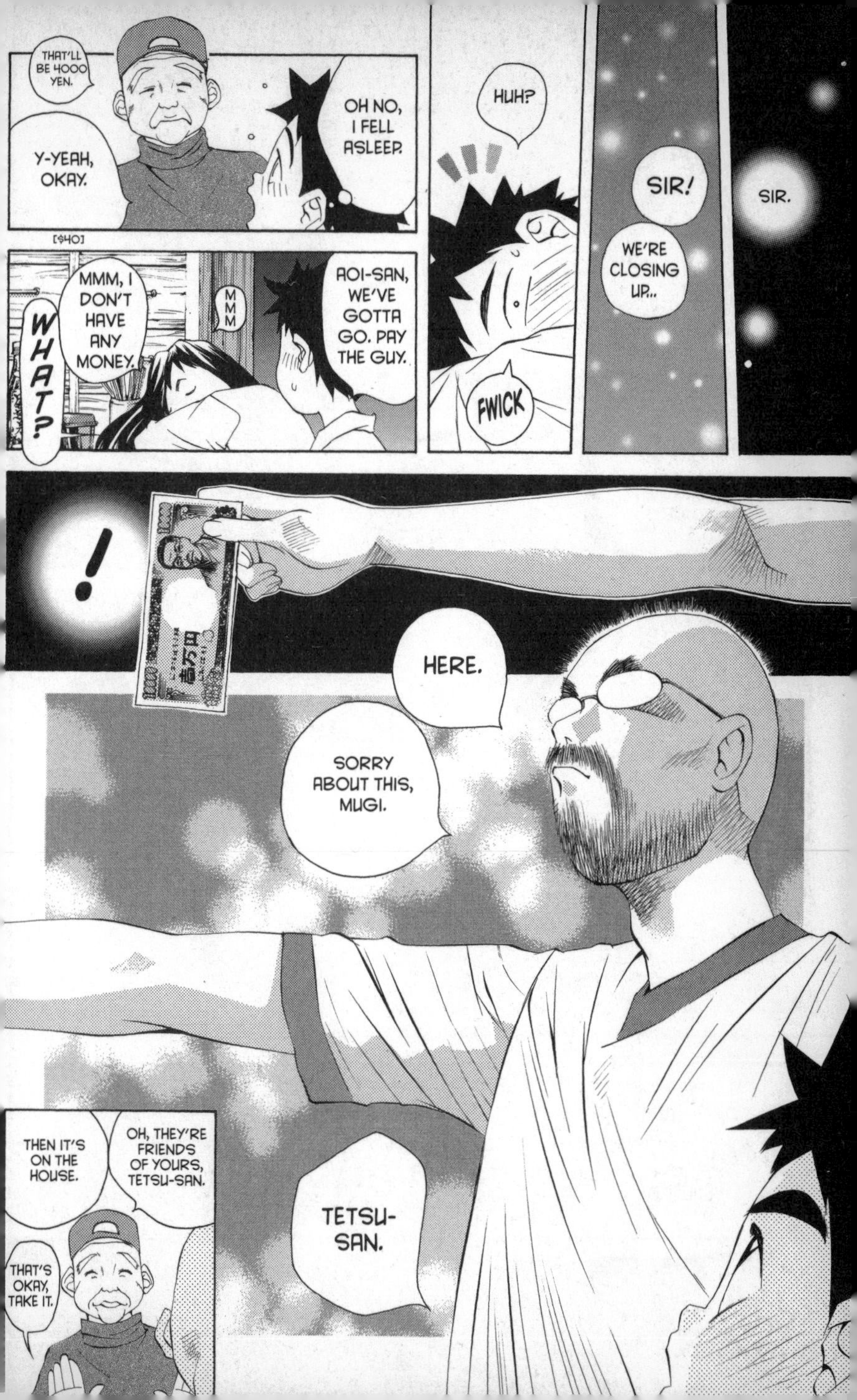
SIR.
SIR!
WE'RE CLOSING UP...
HUH?
FWICK
OH NO, I FELL ASLEEP.
THAT'LL BE 4000 YEN.
Y-YEAH, OKAY.
[$40]
AOI-SAN, WE'VE GOTTA GO. PAY THE GUY.
MMM
MMM, I DON'T HAVE ANY MONEY.
WHAT?
!
HERE.
SORRY ABOUT THIS, MUGI.
TETSU-SAN.
OH, THEY'RE FRIENDS OF YOURS, TETSU-SAN.
THEN IT'S ON THE HOUSE.
THAT'S OKAY, TAKE IT.

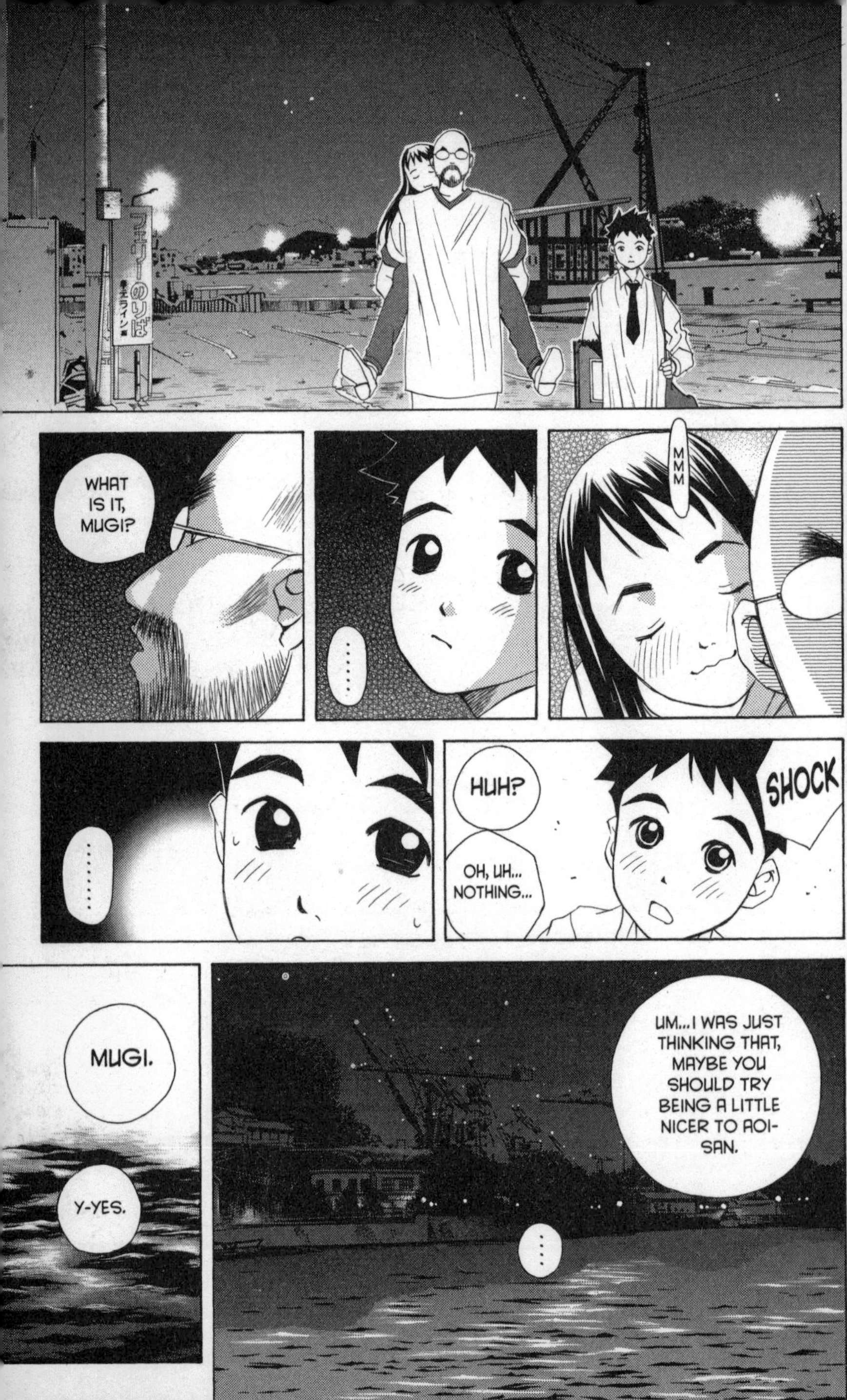
フェリーのりば
MMM
......
WHAT IS IT, MUGI?
HUH?
OH, UH... NOTHING...
SHOCK
......
UM...I WAS JUST THINKING THAT, MAYBE YOU SHOULD TRY BEING A LITTLE NICER TO AOI-SAN.
....
MUGI.
Y-YES.

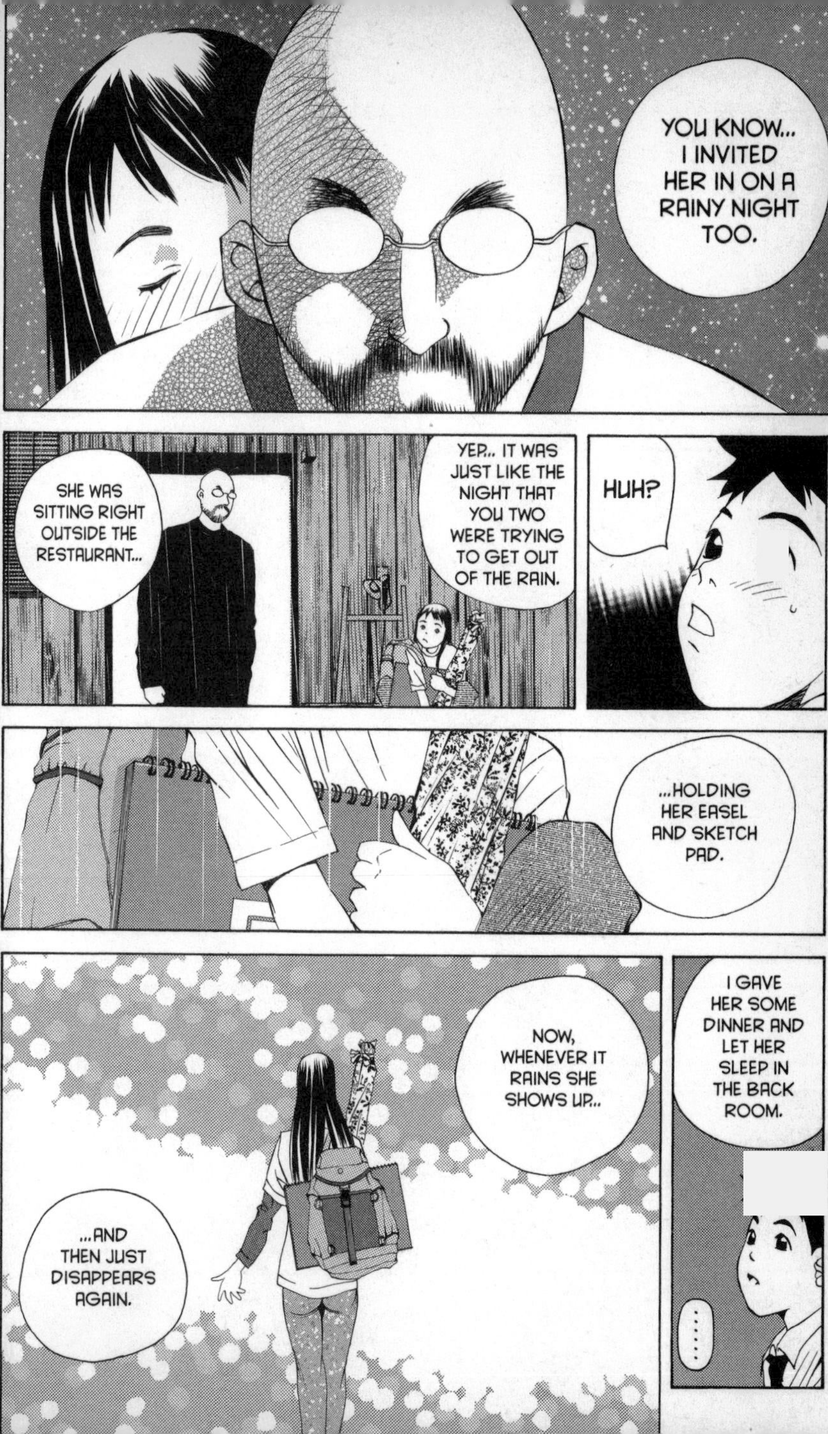
YOU KNOW... I INVITED HER IN ON A RAINY NIGHT TOO.
HUH?
YEP... IT WAS JUST LIKE THE NIGHT THAT YOU TWO WERE TRYING TO GET OUT OF THE RAIN.
SHE WAS SITTING RIGHT OUTSIDE THE RESTAURANT...
...HOLDING HER EASEL AND SKETCH PAD.
I GAVE HER SOME DINNER AND LET HER SLEEP IN THE BACK ROOM.
......
NOW, WHENEVER IT RAINS SHE SHOWS UP...
...AND THEN JUST DISAPPEARS AGAIN.

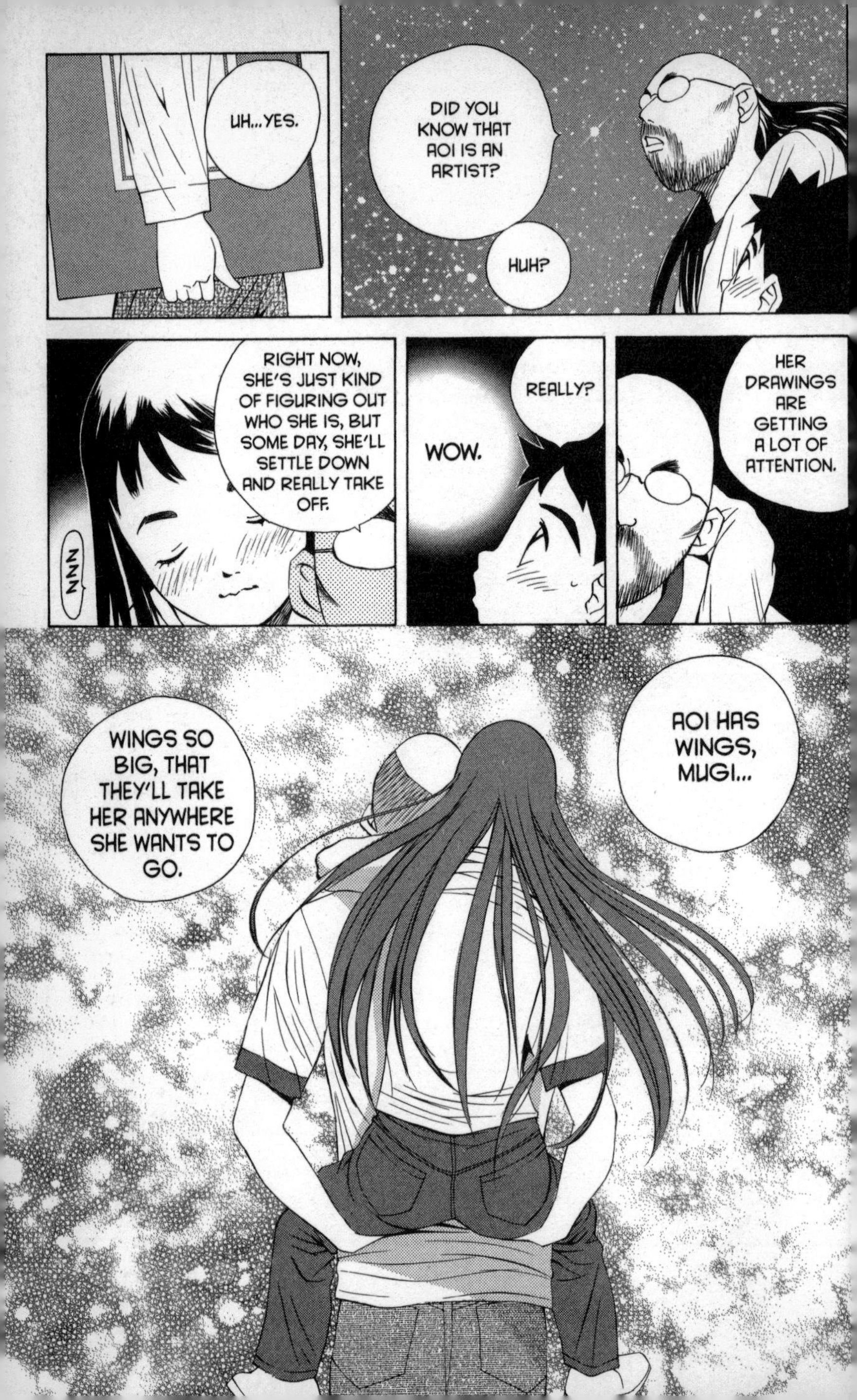
DID YOU KNOW THAT AOI IS AN ARTIST?
HUH?
UH...YES.
HER DRAWINGS ARE GETTING A LOT OF ATTENTION.
REALLY?
WOW.
RIGHT NOW, SHE'S JUST KIND OF FIGURING OUT WHO SHE IS, BUT SOME DAY, SHE'LL SETTLE DOWN AND REALLY TAKE OFF.
NNN
AOI HAS WINGS, MUGI...
WINGS SO BIG, THAT THEY'LL TAKE HER ANYWHERE SHE WANTS TO GO.

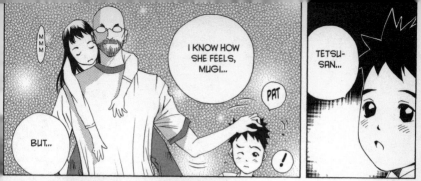

MMM

I KNOW HOW SHE FEELS, MUGI...

PAT

BUT...

TETSU-SAN...

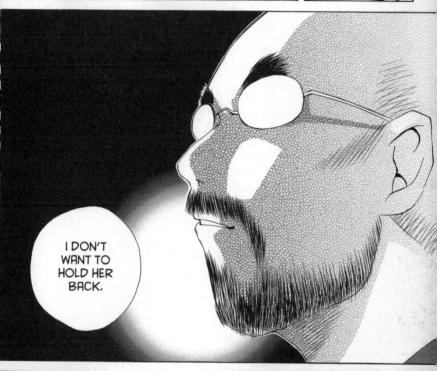

I DON'T WANT TO HOLD HER BACK.

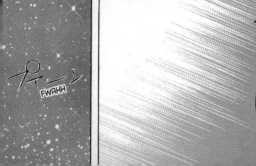

FWAHH

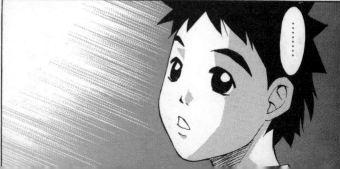

......

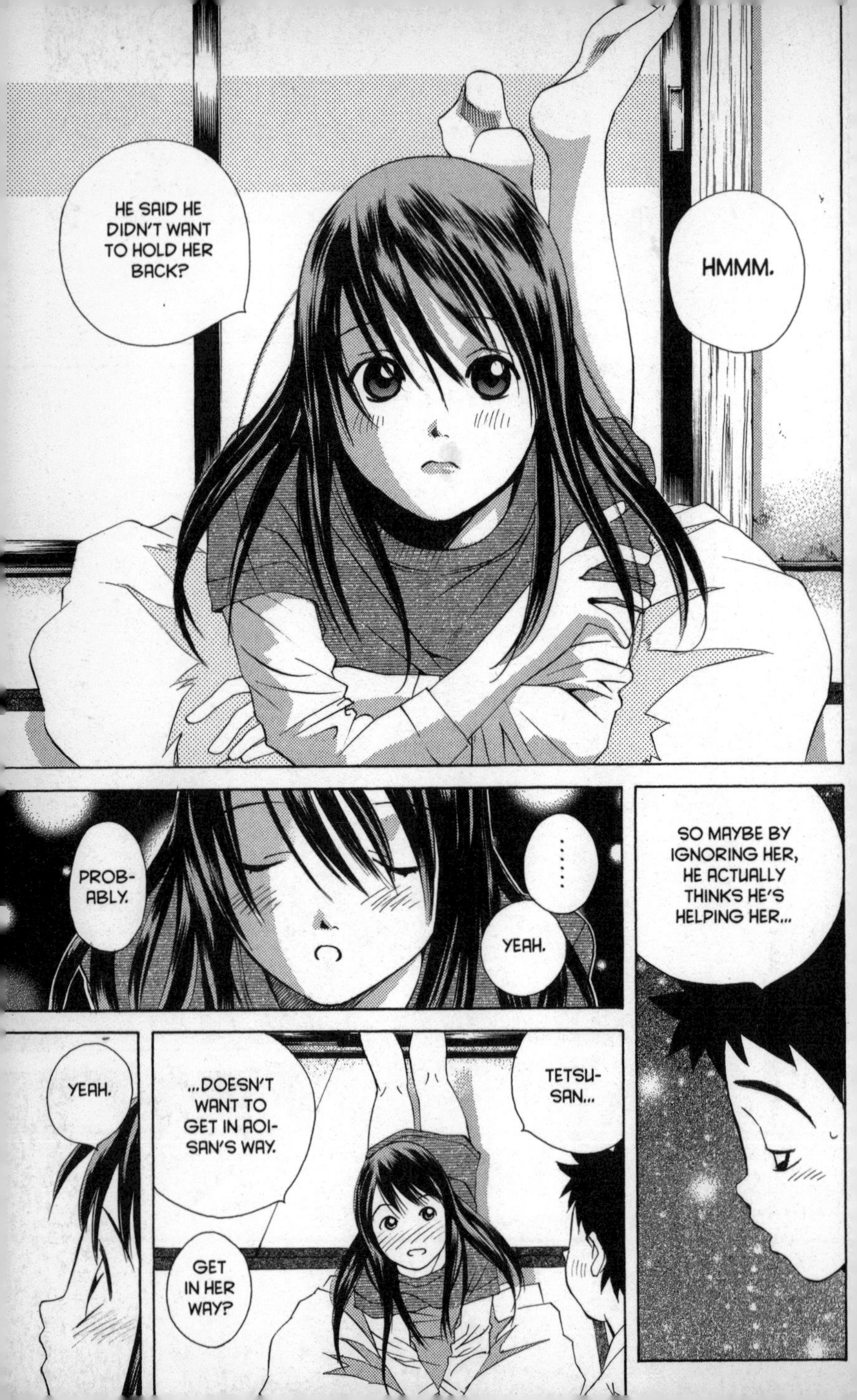

HMMM.
HE SAID HE DIDN'T WANT TO HOLD HER BACK?
SO MAYBE BY IGNORING HER, HE ACTUALLY THINKS HE'S HELPING HER...
......
YEAH.
PROBABLY.
TETSU-SAN...
...DOESN'T WANT TO GET IN AOI-SAN'S WAY.
GET IN HER WAY?
YEAH.

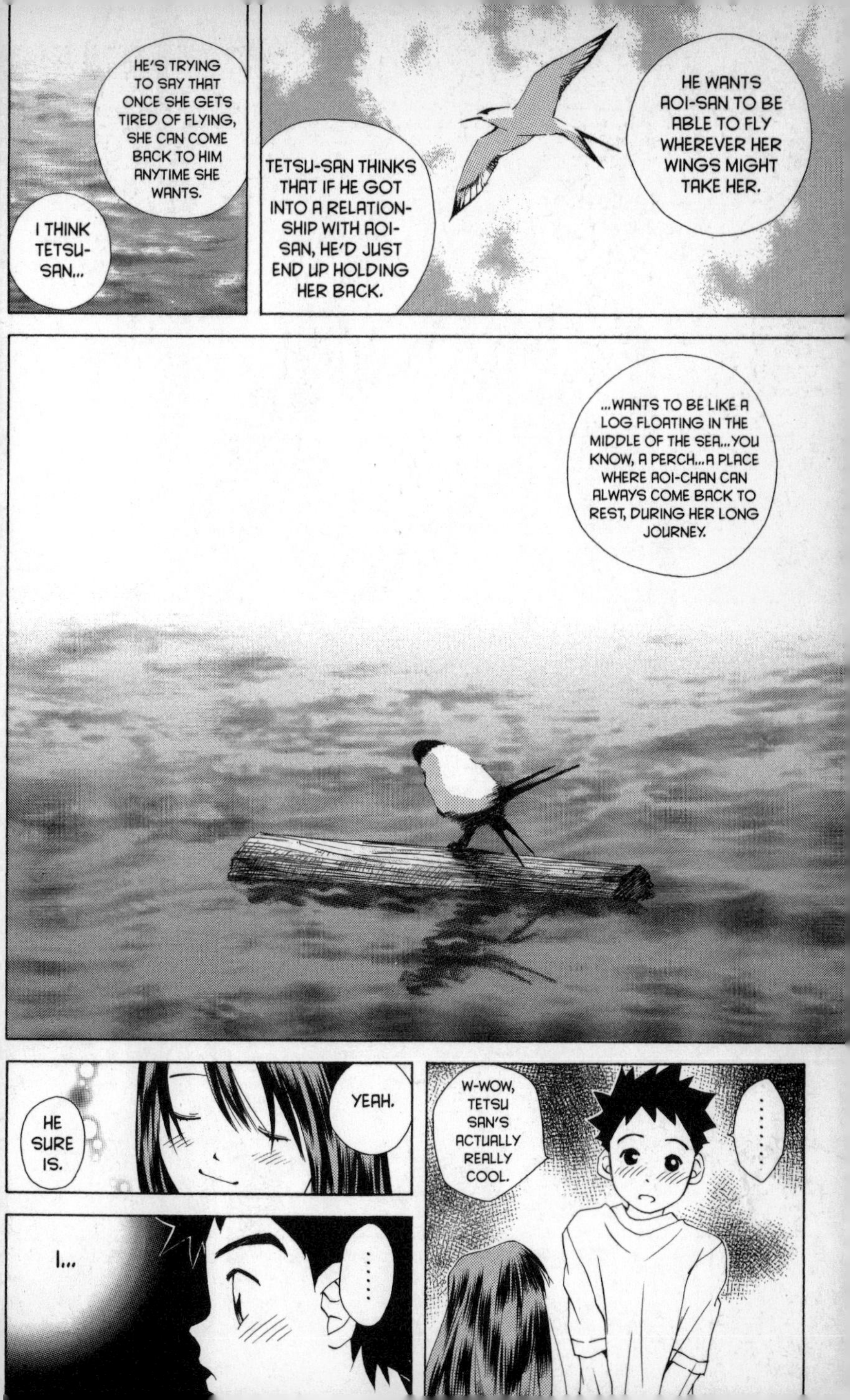
HE WANTS AOI-SAN TO BE ABLE TO FLY WHEREVER HER WINGS MIGHT TAKE HER.
TETSU-SAN THINKS THAT IF HE GOT INTO A RELATION-SHIP WITH AOI-SAN, HE'D JUST END UP HOLDING HER BACK.
HE'S TRYING TO SAY THAT ONCE SHE GETS TIRED OF FLYING, SHE CAN COME BACK TO HIM ANYTIME SHE WANTS.
I THINK TETSU-SAN...
...WANTS TO BE LIKE A LOG FLOATING IN THE MIDDLE OF THE SEA...YOU KNOW, A PERCH...A PLACE WHERE AOI-CHAN CAN ALWAYS COME BACK TO REST, DURING HER LONG JOURNEY.
......
W-WOW, TETSU SAN'S ACTUALLY REALLY COOL.
YEAH.
HE SURE IS.
......
I...

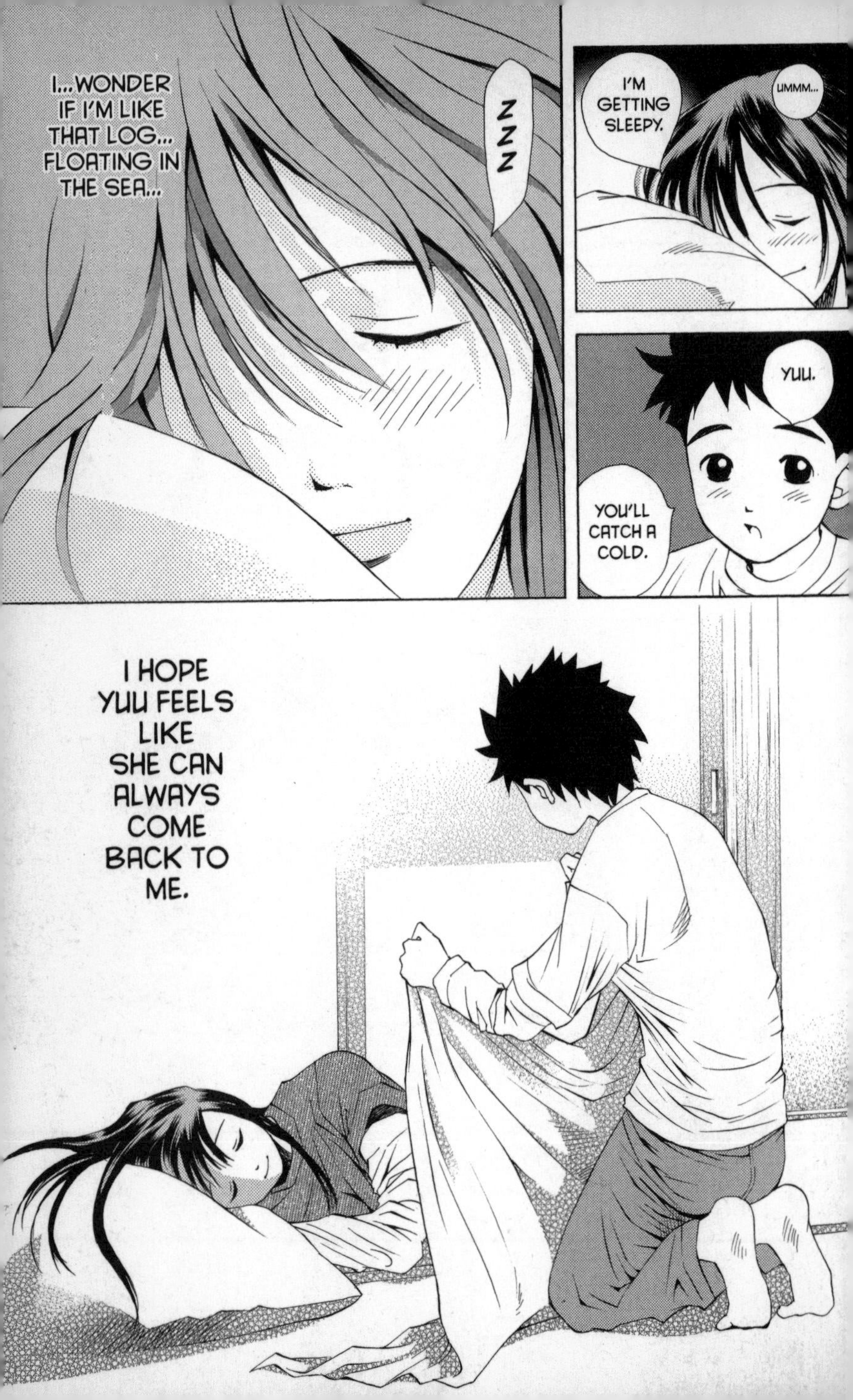
UMMM...
I'M GETTING SLEEPY.
YUU.
YOU'LL CATCH A COLD.
ZZZ
I...WONDER IF I'M LIKE THAT LOG... FLOATING IN THE SEA...
I HOPE YUU FEELS LIKE SHE CAN ALWAYS COME BACK TO ME.

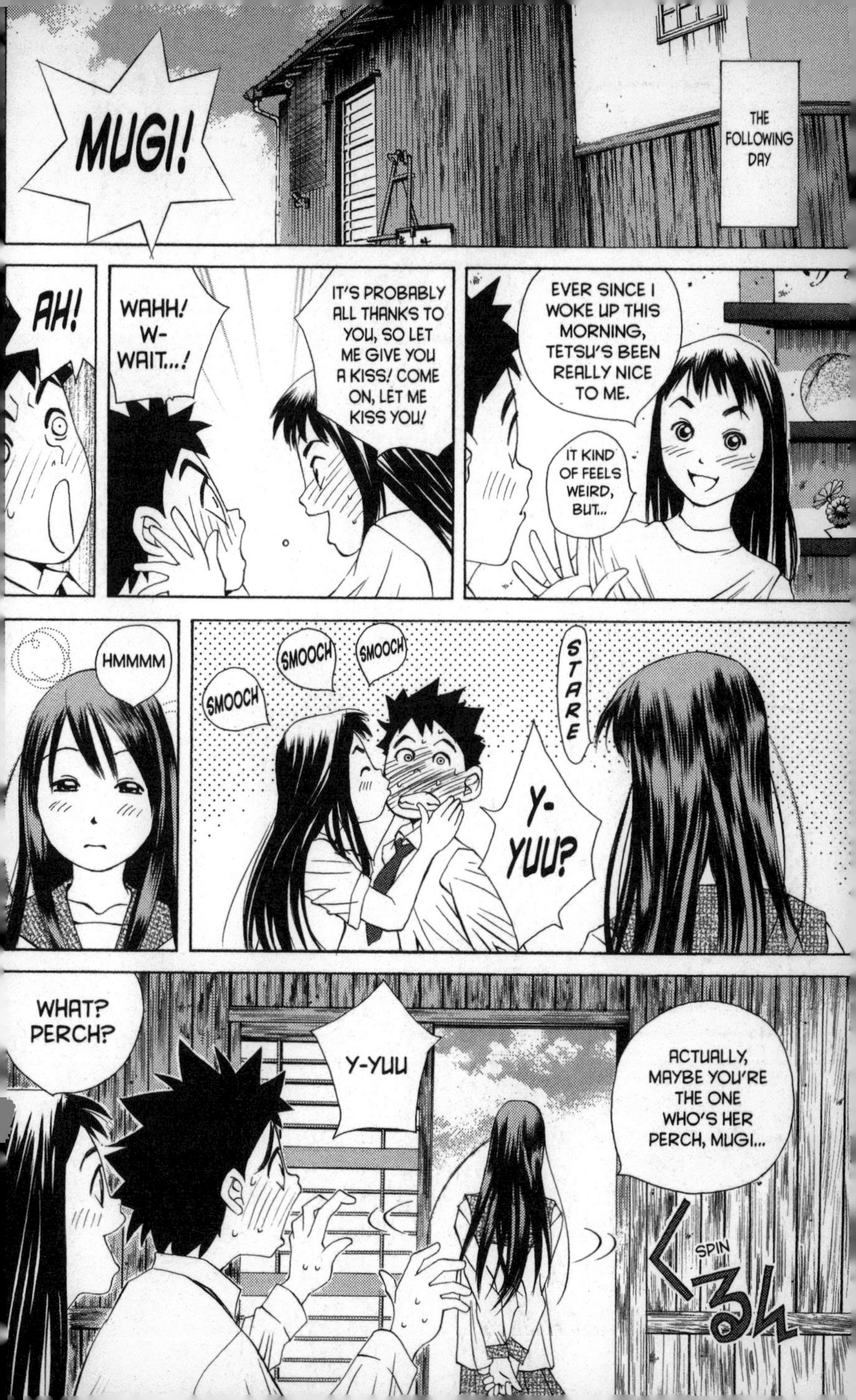
THE FOLLOWING DAY
MUGI!
EVER SINCE I WOKE UP THIS MORNING, TETSU'S BEEN REALLY NICE TO ME.
IT KIND OF FEELS WEIRD, BUT...
IT'S PROBABLY ALL THANKS TO YOU, SO LET ME GIVE YOU A KISS! COME ON, LET ME KISS YOU!
WAHH! W-WAIT...!
AH!
STARE
Y-YUU?
SMOOCH
SMOOCH
SMOOCH
HMMMM
ACTUALLY, MAYBE YOU'RE THE ONE WHO'S HER PERCH, MUGI...
SPIN
Y-YUU
WHAT? PERCH?

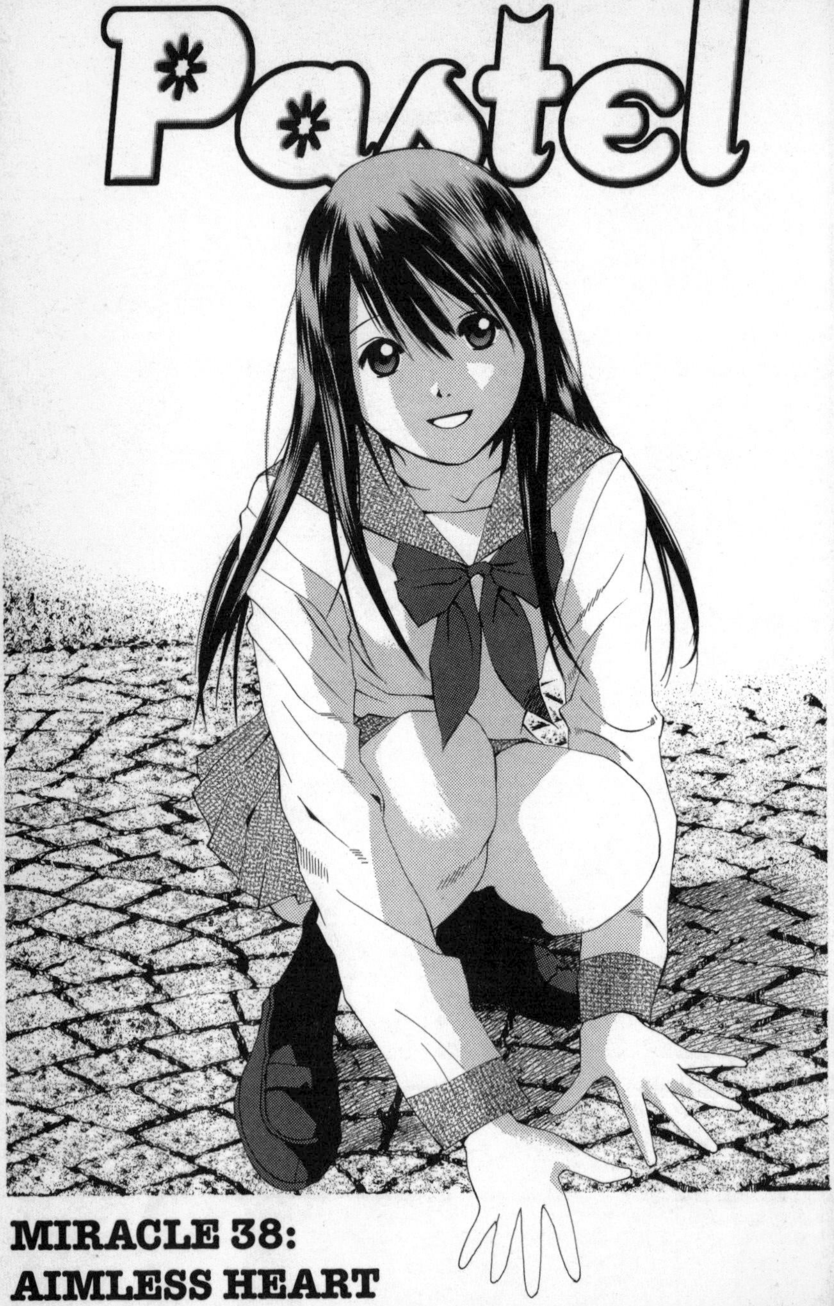
Pastel

MIRACLE 38: AIMLESS HEART

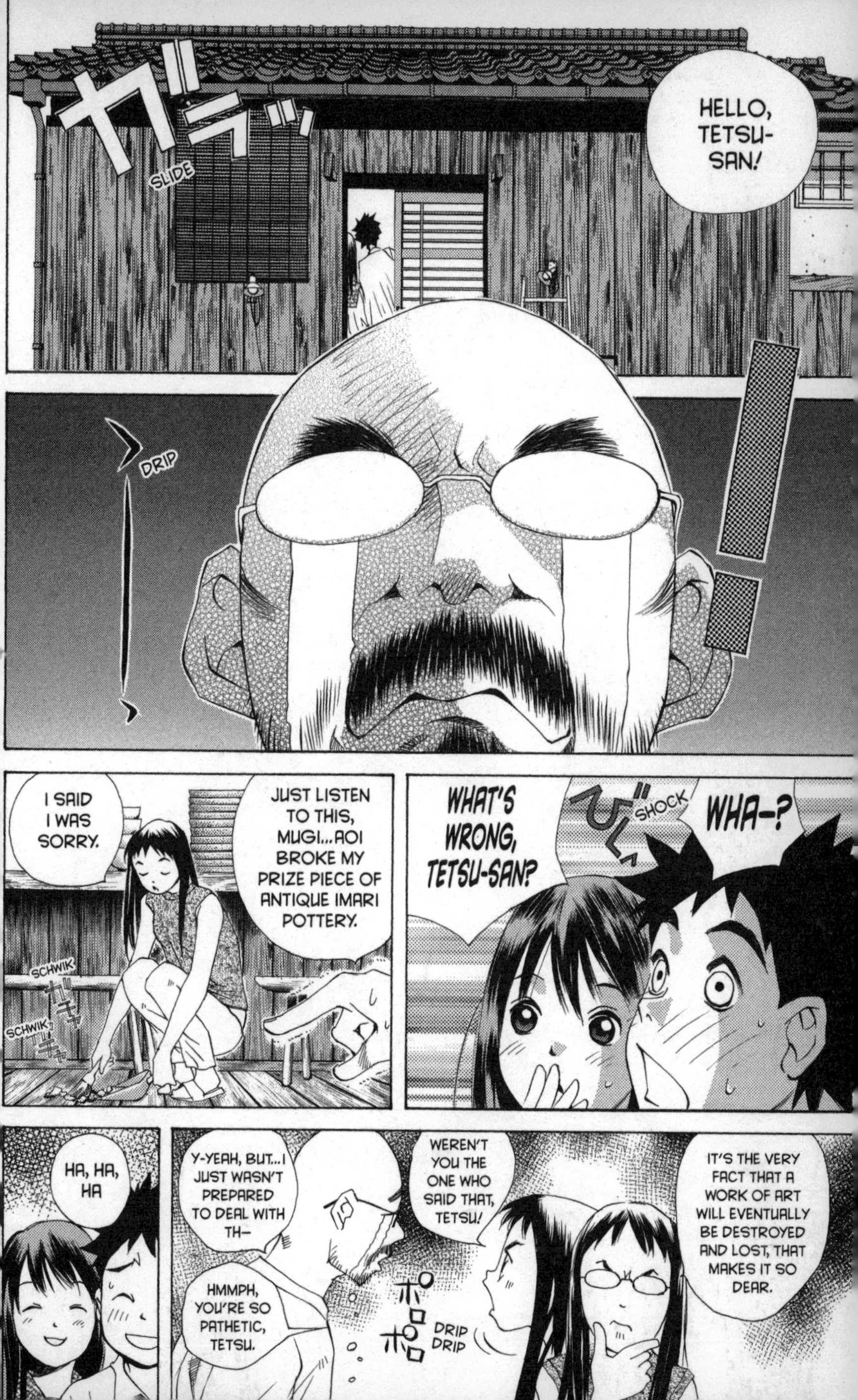

HELLO, TETSU-SAN!
SLIDE
!
DRIP
WHA-?
SHOCK
WHAT'S WRONG, TETSU-SAN?
JUST LISTEN TO THIS, MUGI...AOI BROKE MY PRIZE PIECE OF ANTIQUE IMARI POTTERY.
I SAID I WAS SORRY.
SCHWIK
SCHWIK
IT'S THE VERY FACT THAT A WORK OF ART WILL EVENTUALLY BE DESTROYED AND LOST, THAT MAKES IT SO DEAR.
WEREN'T YOU THE ONE WHO SAID THAT, TETSU!
Y-YEAH, BUT...I JUST WASN'T PREPARED TO DEAL WITH TH–
HMMPH, YOU'RE SO PATHETIC, TETSU.
DRIP DRIP
HA, HA, HA

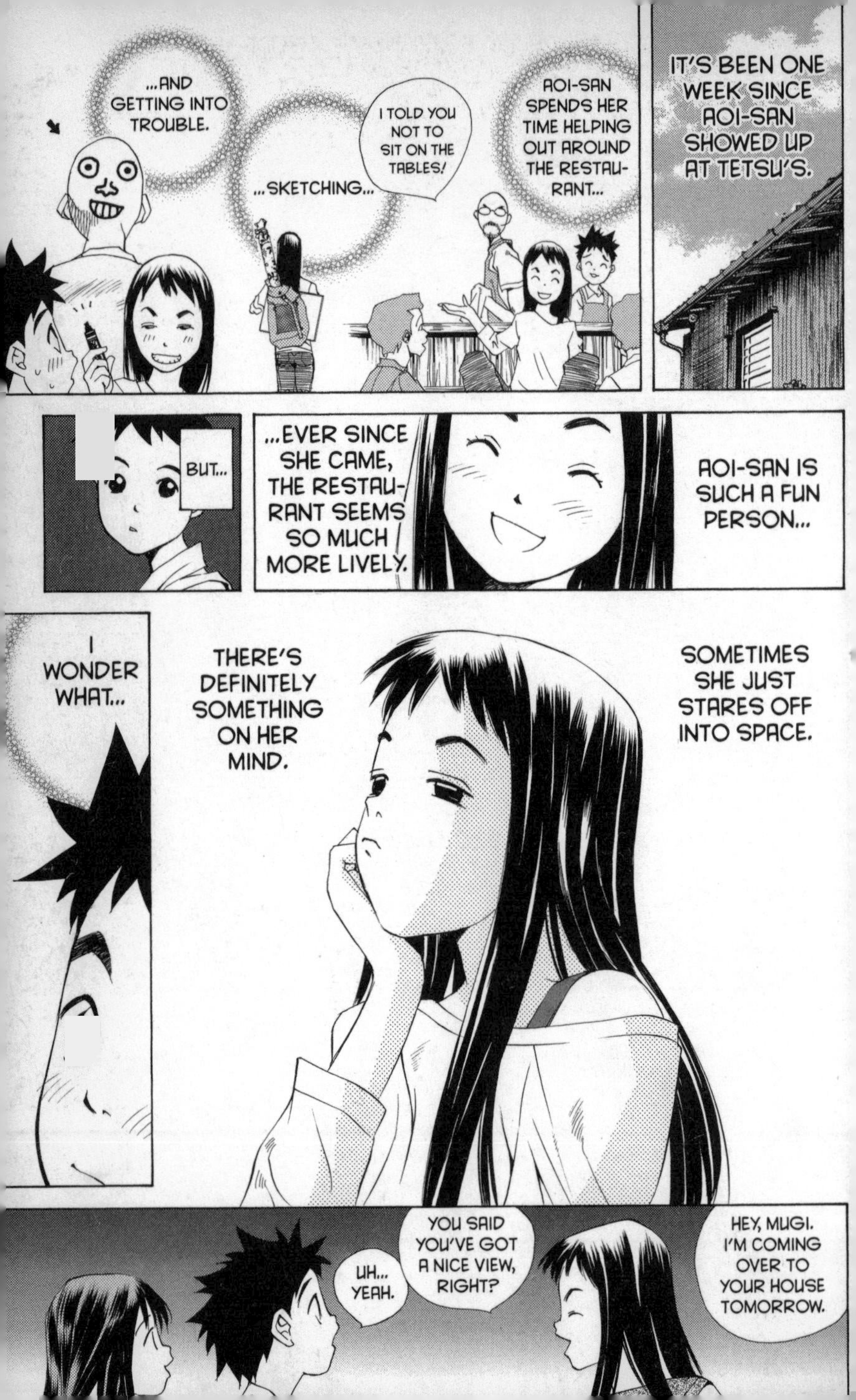
IT'S BEEN ONE WEEK SINCE AOI-SAN SHOWED UP AT TETSU'S.
AOI-SAN SPENDS HER TIME HELPING OUT AROUND THE RESTAU-RANT...
I TOLD YOU NOT TO SIT ON THE TABLES!
...SKETCHING...
...AND GETTING INTO TROUBLE.
AOI-SAN IS SUCH A FUN PERSON...
...EVER SINCE SHE CAME, THE RESTAU-RANT SEEMS SO MUCH MORE LIVELY.
BUT...
SOMETIMES SHE JUST STARES OFF INTO SPACE.
THERE'S DEFINITELY SOMETHING ON HER MIND.
I WONDER WHAT...
HEY, MUGI. I'M COMING OVER TO YOUR HOUSE TOMORROW.
YOU SAID YOU'VE GOT A NICE VIEW, RIGHT?
UH... YEAH.

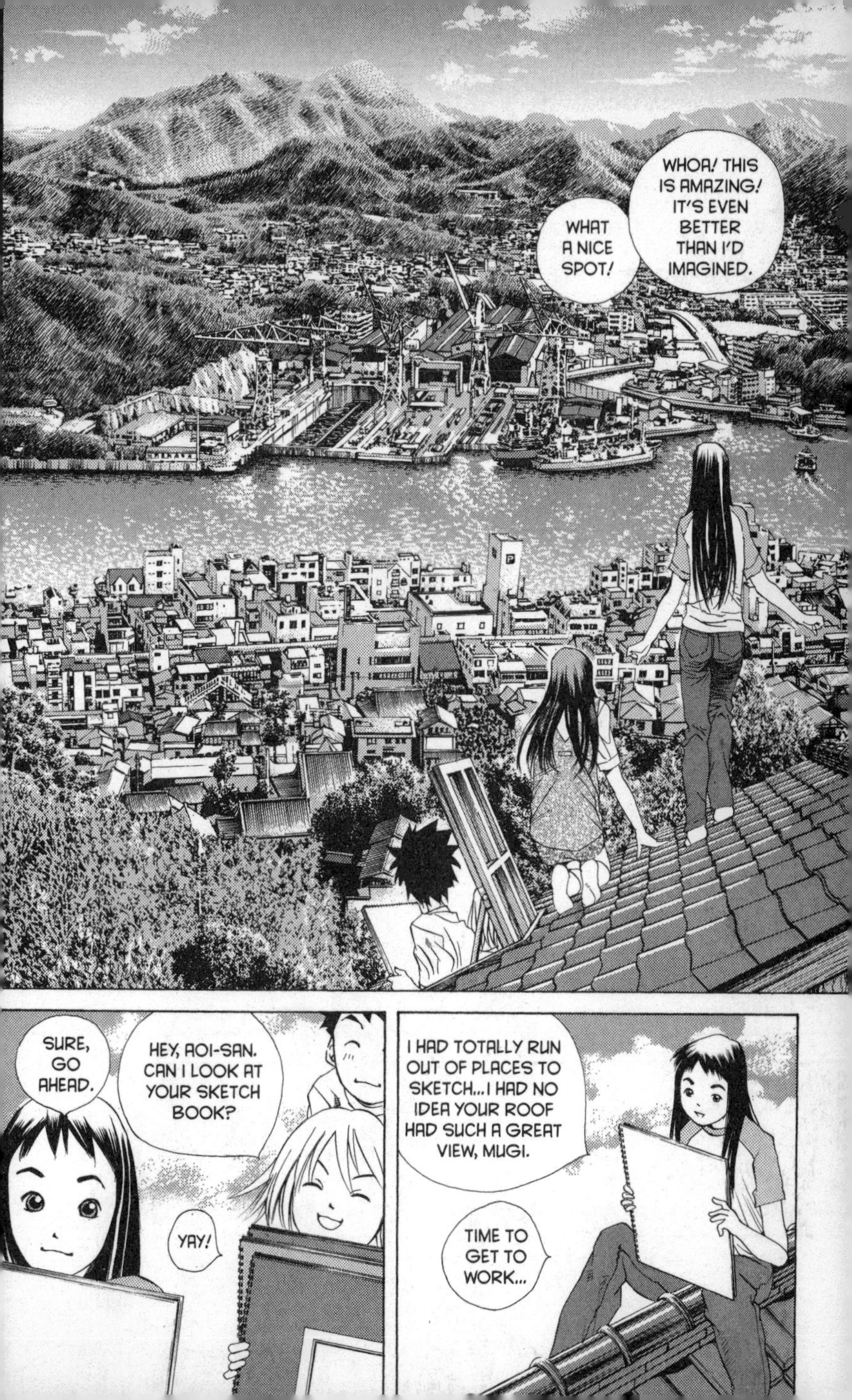
WHOA! THIS IS AMAZING! IT'S EVEN BETTER THAN I'D IMAGINED.
WHAT A NICE SPOT!
I HAD TOTALLY RUN OUT OF PLACES TO SKETCH...I HAD NO IDEA YOUR ROOF HAD SUCH A GREAT VIEW, MUGI.
TIME TO GET TO WORK...
HEY, AOI-SAN. CAN I LOOK AT YOUR SKETCH BOOK?
SURE, GO AHEAD.
YAY!

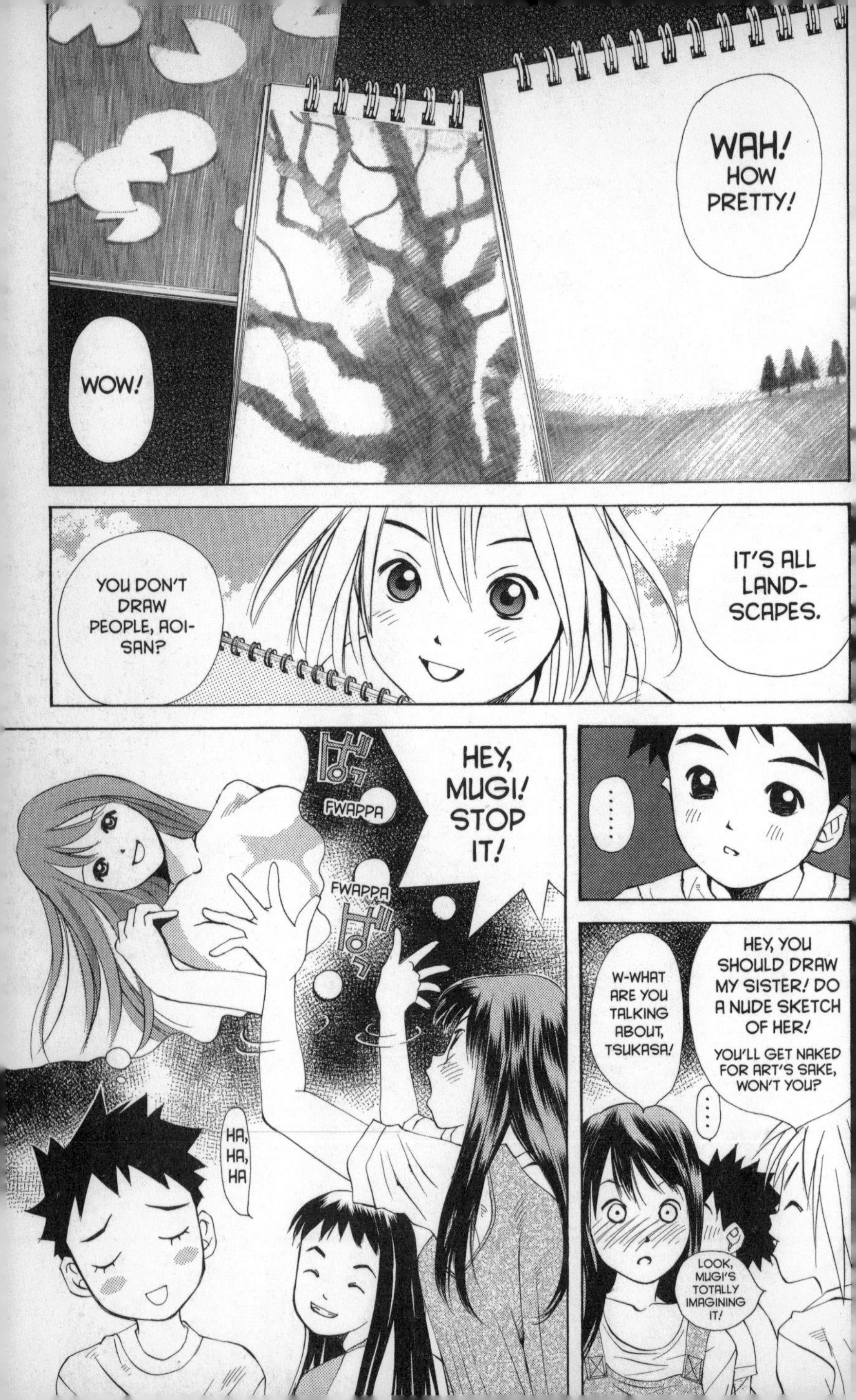
WAH! HOW PRETTY!
WOW!
IT'S ALL LAND-SCAPES.
YOU DON'T DRAW PEOPLE, AOI-SAN?
......
HEY, MUGI! STOP IT!
FWAPPA
FWAPPA
HA, HA, HA
HEY, YOU SHOULD DRAW MY SISTER! DO A NUDE SKETCH OF HER!
YOU'LL GET NAKED FOR ART'S SAKE, WON'T YOU?
W-WHAT ARE YOU TALKING ABOUT, TSUKASA!
...
LOOK, MUGI'S TOTALLY IMAGINING IT!

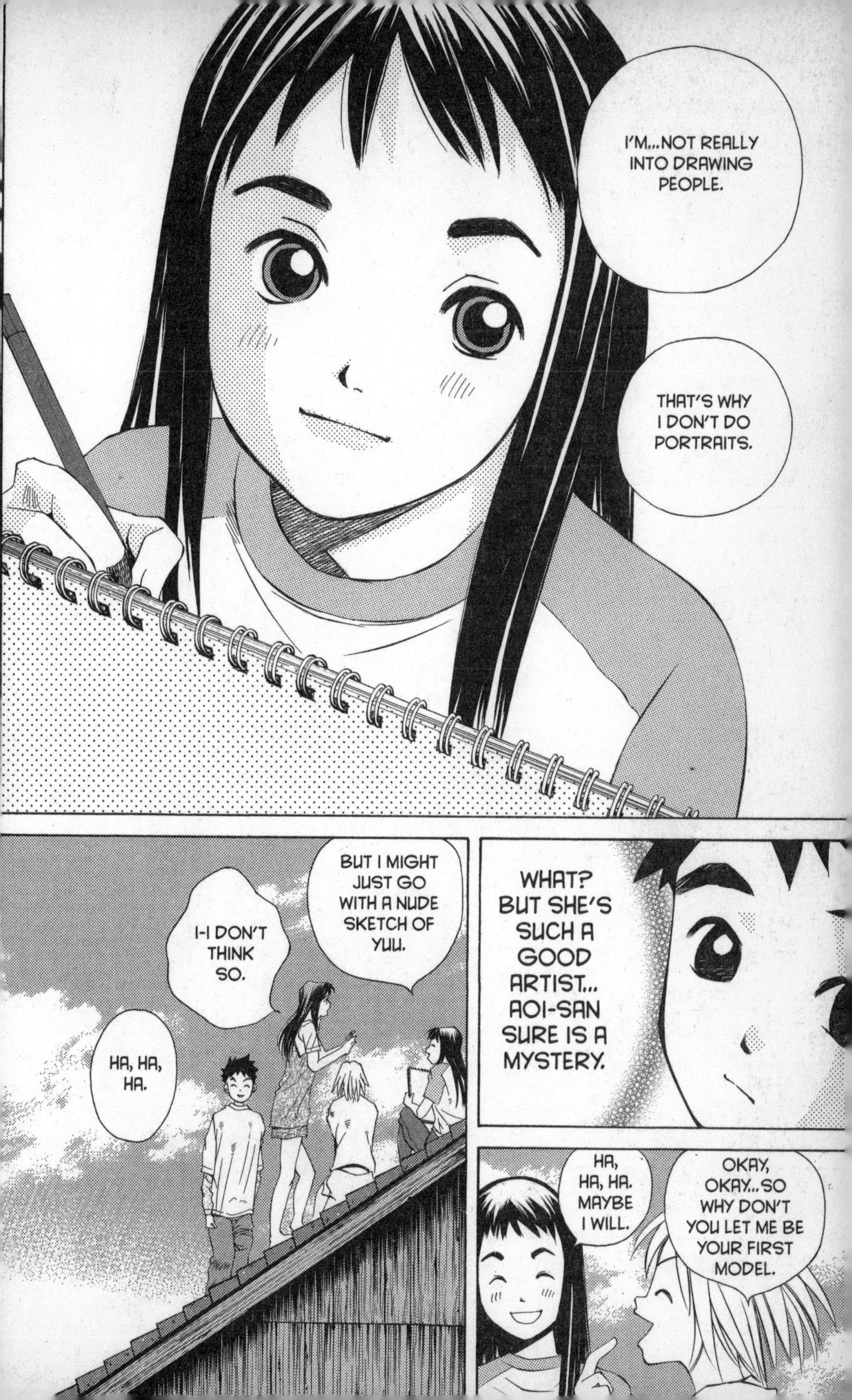
I'M...NOT REALLY INTO DRAWING PEOPLE.
THAT'S WHY I DON'T DO PORTRAITS.
WHAT? BUT SHE'S SUCH A GOOD ARTIST... AOI-SAN SURE IS A MYSTERY.
OKAY, OKAY...SO WHY DON'T YOU LET ME BE YOUR FIRST MODEL.
HA, HA, HA. MAYBE I WILL.
BUT I MIGHT JUST GO WITH A NUDE SKETCH OF YUU.
I-I DON'T THINK SO.
HA, HA, HA.

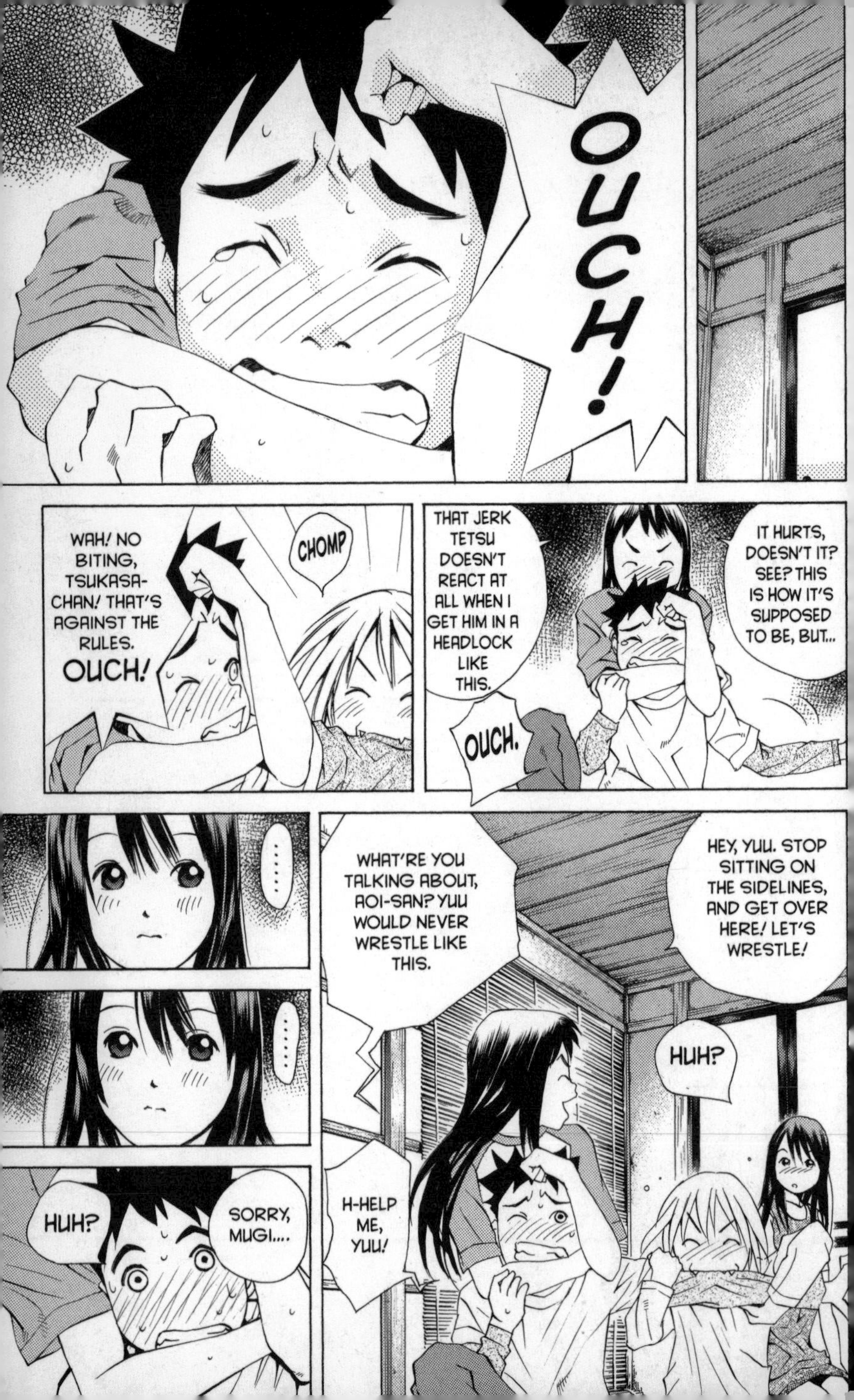
OUCH!
IT HURTS, DOESN'T IT? SEE? THIS IS HOW IT'S SUPPOSED TO BE, BUT...
THAT JERK TETSU DOESN'T REACT AT ALL WHEN I GET HIM IN A HEADLOCK LIKE THIS.
OUCH.
CHOMP
WAH! NO BITING, TSUKASA-CHAN! THAT'S AGAINST THE RULES.
OUCH!
HEY, YUU. STOP SITTING ON THE SIDELINES, AND GET OVER HERE! LET'S WRESTLE!
WHAT'RE YOU TALKING ABOUT, AOI-SAN? YUU WOULD NEVER WRESTLE LIKE THIS.
HUH?
H-HELP ME, YUU!
......
......
SORRY, MUGI....
HUH?

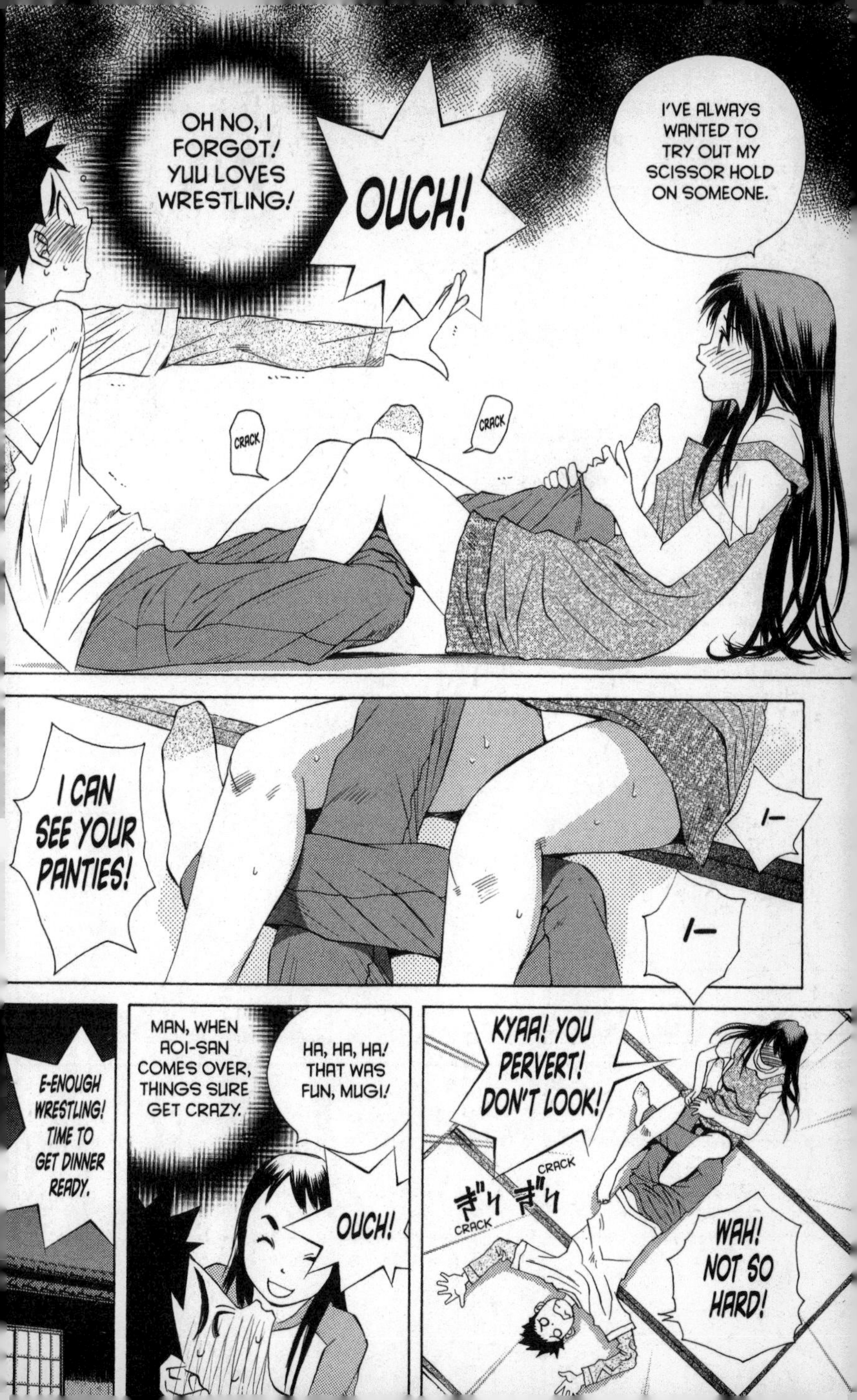
I'VE ALWAYS WANTED TO TRY OUT MY SCISSOR HOLD ON SOMEONE.
OUCH!
OH NO, I FORGOT! YUU LOVES WRESTLING!
CRACK
CRACK
!–
!–
I CAN SEE YOUR PANTIES!
KYAA! YOU PERVERT! DON'T LOOK!
ぎり ぎり
CRACK
CRACK
WAH! NOT SO HARD!
HA, HA, HA! THAT WAS FUN, MUGI!
MAN, WHEN AOI-SAN COMES OVER, THINGS SURE GET CRAZY.
OUCH!
E-ENOUGH WRESTLING! TIME TO GET DINNER READY.

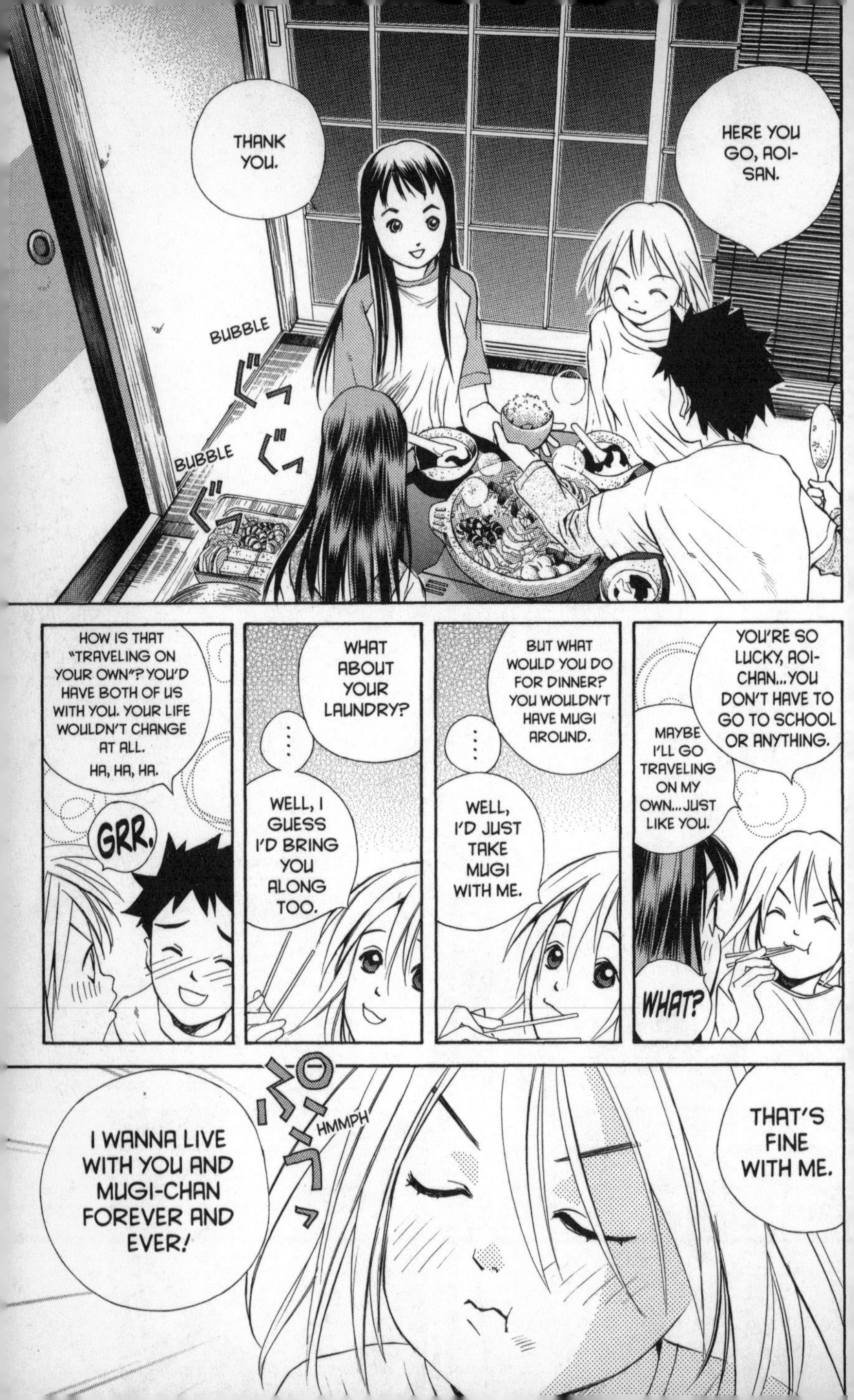
HERE YOU GO, AOI-SAN.
THANK YOU.
BUBBLE
BUBBLE
YOU'RE SO LUCKY, AOI-CHAN...YOU DON'T HAVE TO GO TO SCHOOL OR ANYTHING.
MAYBE I'LL GO TRAVELING ON MY OWN...JUST LIKE YOU.
WHAT?
BUT WHAT WOULD YOU DO FOR DINNER? YOU WOULDN'T HAVE MUGI AROUND.
.....
WELL, I'D JUST TAKE MUGI WITH ME.
WHAT ABOUT YOUR LAUNDRY?
.....
WELL, I GUESS I'D BRING YOU ALONG TOO.
HOW IS THAT "TRAVELING ON YOUR OWN"? YOU'D HAVE BOTH OF US WITH YOU. YOUR LIFE WOULDN'T CHANGE AT ALL.
HA, HA, HA.
GRR.
THAT'S FINE WITH ME.
HMMPH
I WANNA LIVE WITH YOU AND MUGI-CHAN FOREVER AND EVER!

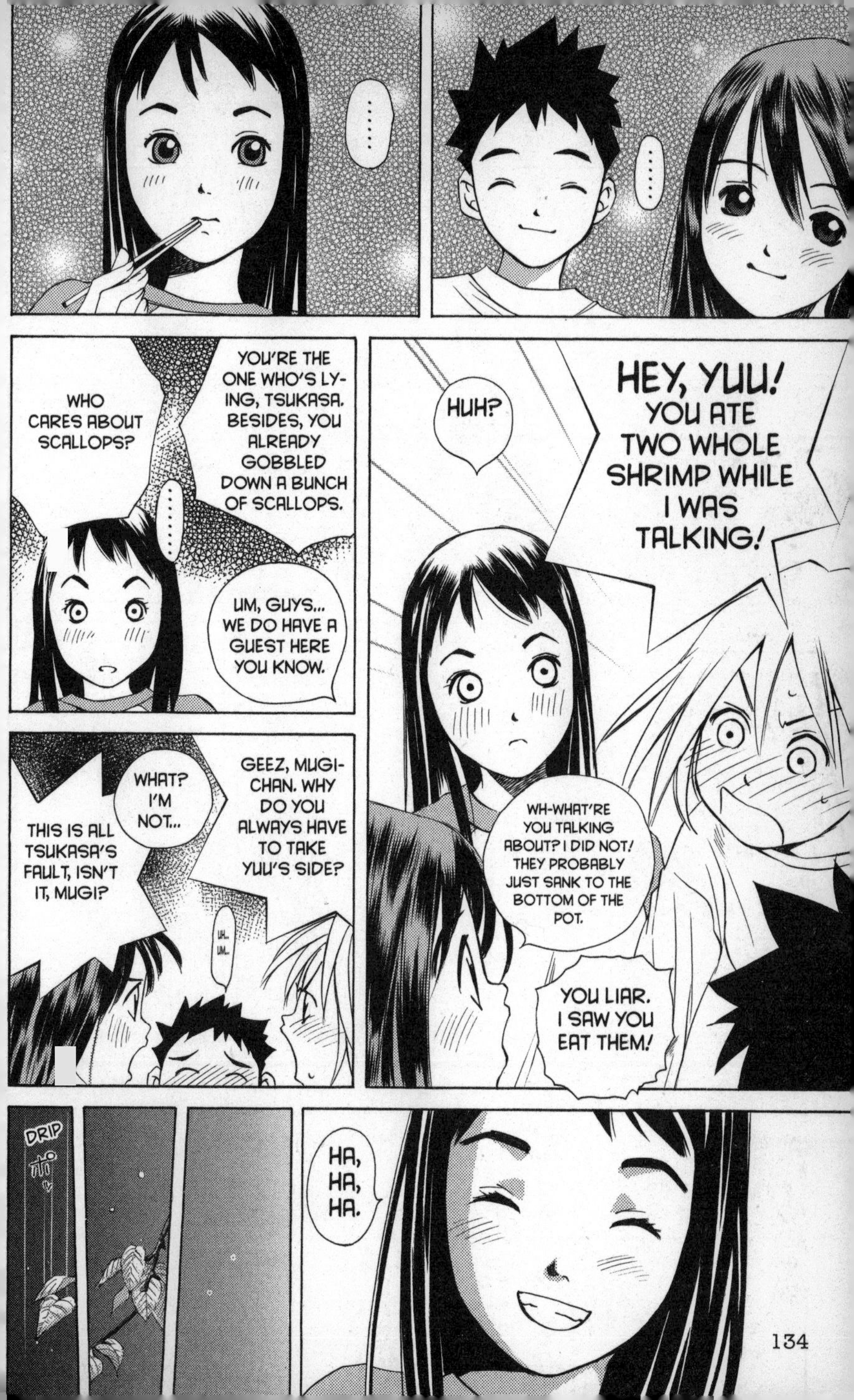
......
......
HEY, YUU! YOU ATE TWO WHOLE SHRIMP WHILE I WAS TALKING!
HUH?
WH-WHAT'RE YOU TALKING ABOUT? I DID NOT! THEY PROBABLY JUST SANK TO THE BOTTOM OF THE POT.
YOU LIAR. I SAW YOU EAT THEM!
YOU'RE THE ONE WHO'S LY-ING, TSUKASA. BESIDES, YOU ALREADY GOBBLED DOWN A BUNCH OF SCALLOPS.
WHO CARES ABOUT SCALLOPS?
......
UM, GUYS... WE DO HAVE A GUEST HERE YOU KNOW.
GEEZ, MUGI-CHAN. WHY DO YOU ALWAYS HAVE TO TAKE YUU'S SIDE?
WHAT? I'M NOT...
THIS IS ALL TSUKASA'S FAULT, ISN'T IT, MUGI?
UH... UM...
HA, HA, HA.
DRIP

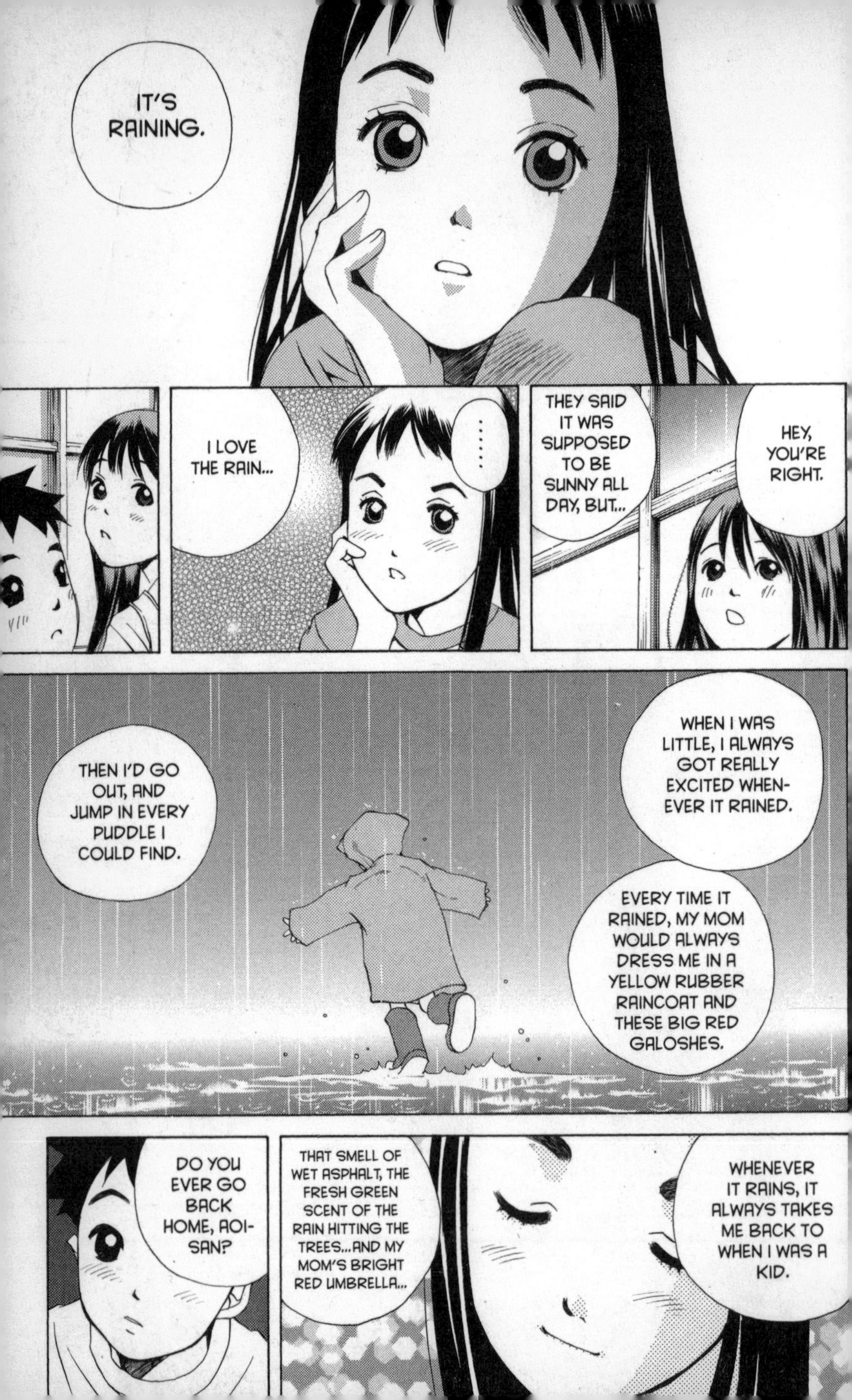
IT'S RAINING.
HEY, YOU'RE RIGHT.
THEY SAID IT WAS SUPPOSED TO BE SUNNY ALL DAY, BUT...
......
I LOVE THE RAIN...
WHEN I WAS LITTLE, I ALWAYS GOT REALLY EXCITED WHEN-EVER IT RAINED.
EVERY TIME IT RAINED, MY MOM WOULD ALWAYS DRESS ME IN A YELLOW RUBBER RAINCOAT AND THESE BIG RED GALOSHES.
THEN I'D GO OUT, AND JUMP IN EVERY PUDDLE I COULD FIND.
WHENEVER IT RAINS, IT ALWAYS TAKES ME BACK TO WHEN I WAS A KID.
THAT SMELL OF WET ASPHALT, THE FRESH GREEN SCENT OF THE RAIN HITTING THE TREES...AND MY MOM'S BRIGHT RED UMBRELLA...
DO YOU EVER GO BACK HOME, AOI-SAN?

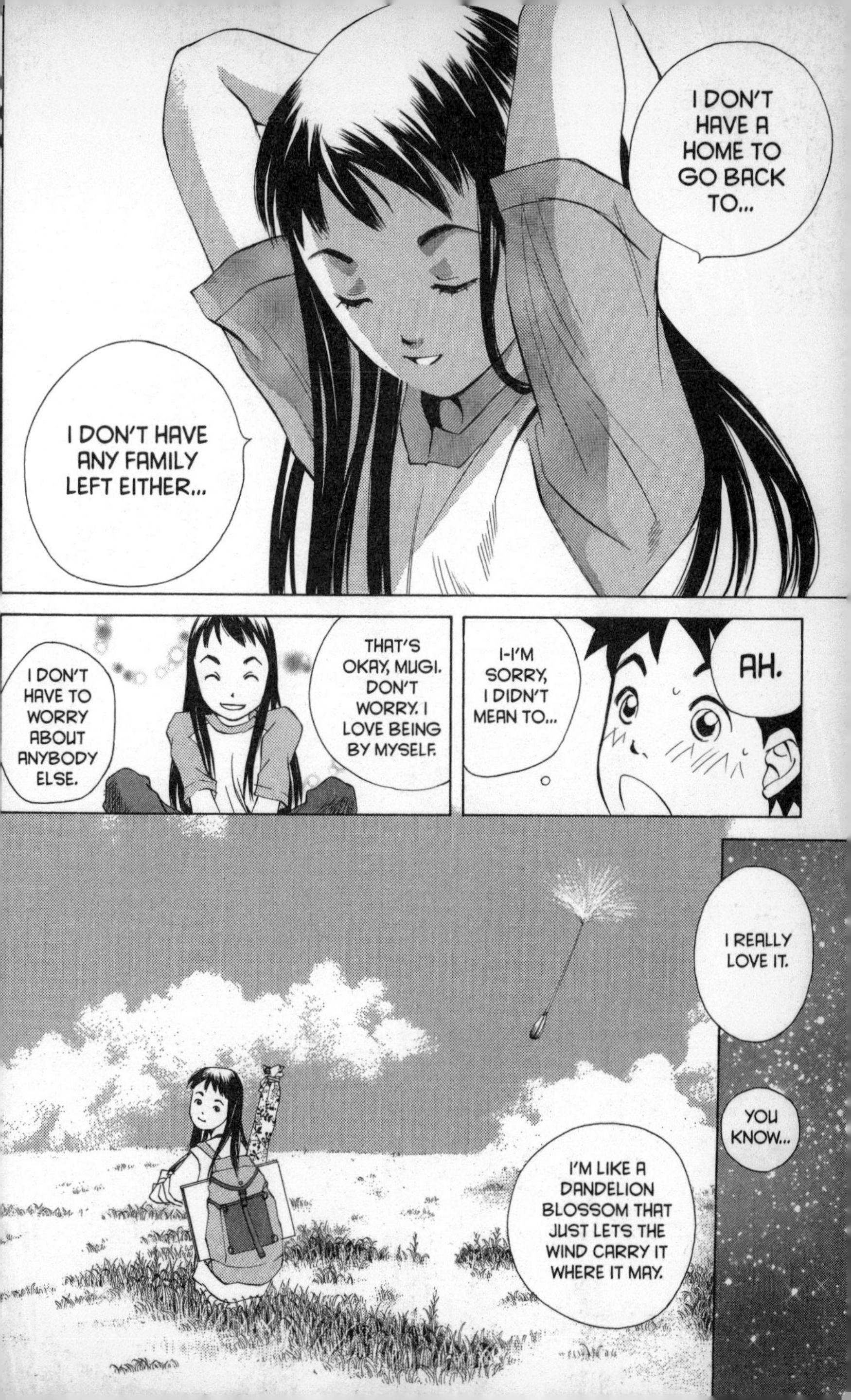
I DON'T HAVE A HOME TO GO BACK TO...
I DON'T HAVE ANY FAMILY LEFT EITHER...
AH.
I-I'M SORRY, I DIDN'T MEAN TO...
THAT'S OKAY, MUGI. DON'T WORRY. I LOVE BEING BY MYSELF.
I DON'T HAVE TO WORRY ABOUT ANYBODY ELSE.
I REALLY LOVE IT.
YOU KNOW...
I'M LIKE A DANDELION BLOSSOM THAT JUST LETS THE WIND CARRY IT WHERE IT MAY.

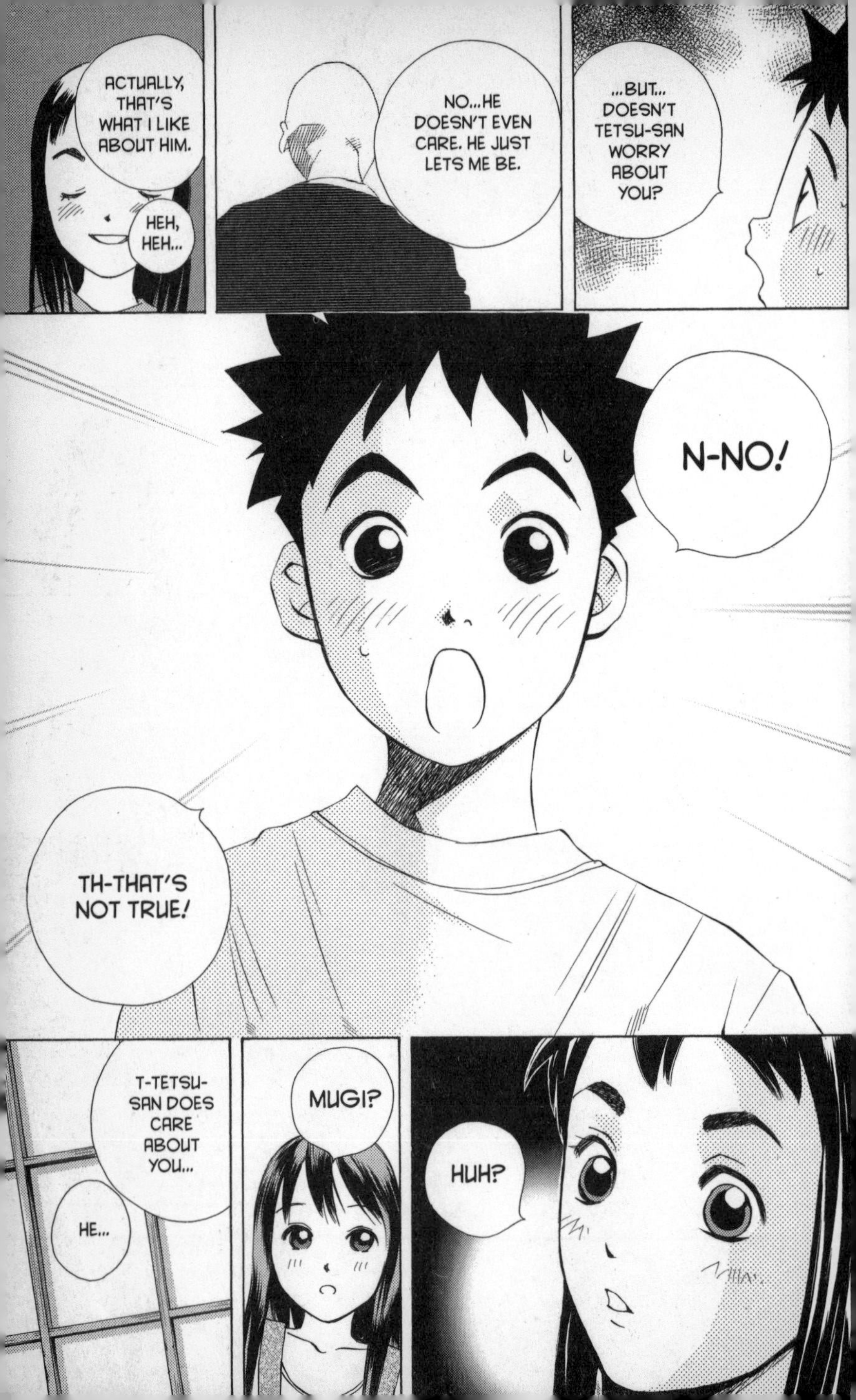
...BUT... DOESN'T TETSU-SAN WORRY ABOUT YOU?
NO...HE DOESN'T EVEN CARE. HE JUST LETS ME BE.
ACTUALLY, THAT'S WHAT I LIKE ABOUT HIM.
HEH, HEH...
N-NO!
TH-THAT'S NOT TRUE!
HUH?
MUGI?
T-TETSU-SAN DOES CARE ABOUT YOU...
HE...

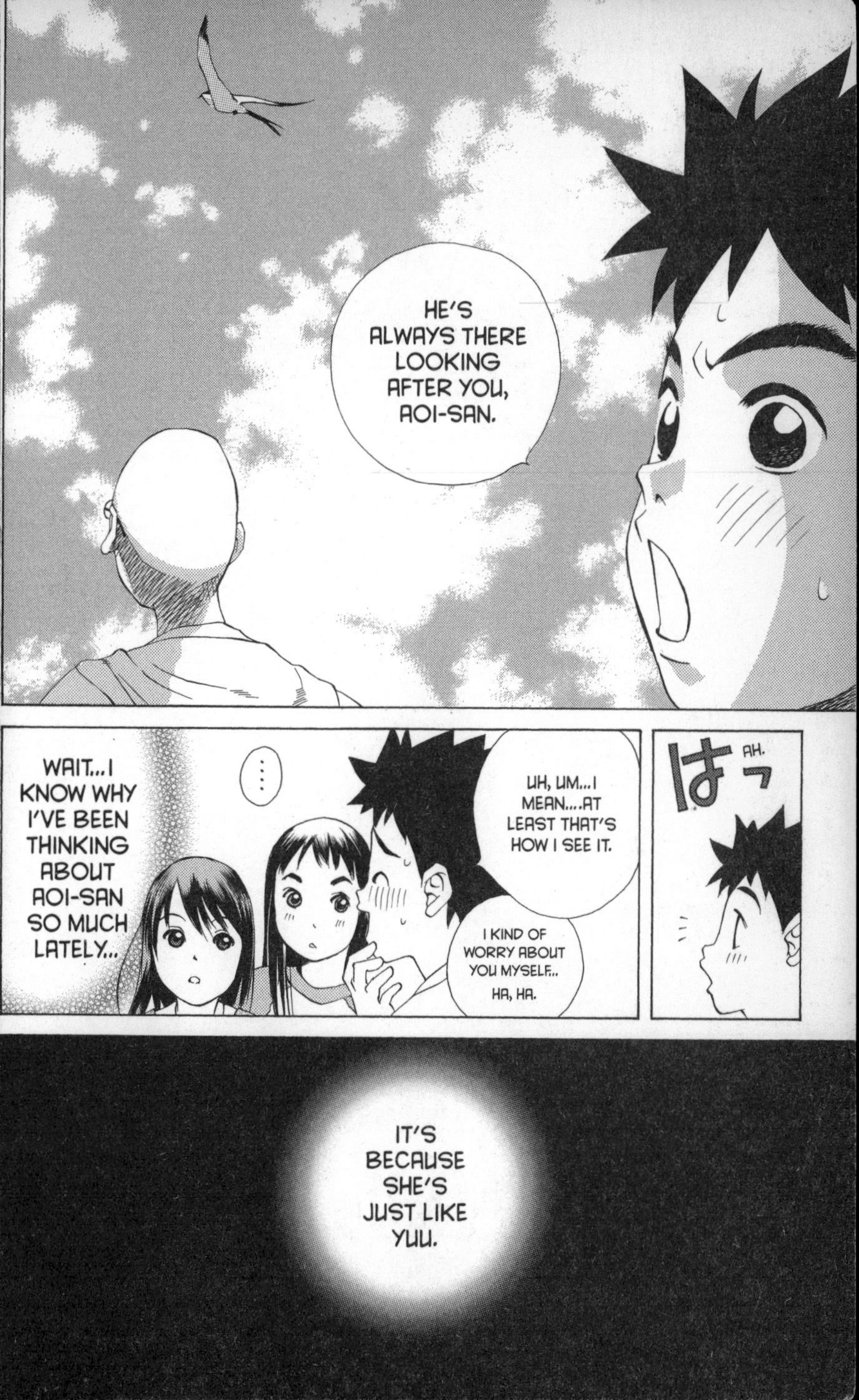
HE'S ALWAYS THERE LOOKING AFTER YOU, AOI-SAN.
はっ
AH.
UH, UM...I MEAN....AT LEAST THAT'S HOW I SEE IT.
I KIND OF WORRY ABOUT YOU MYSELF... HA, HA.
...
WAIT...I KNOW WHY I'VE BEEN THINKING ABOUT AOI-SAN SO MUCH LATELY...
IT'S BECAUSE SHE'S JUST LIKE YUU.

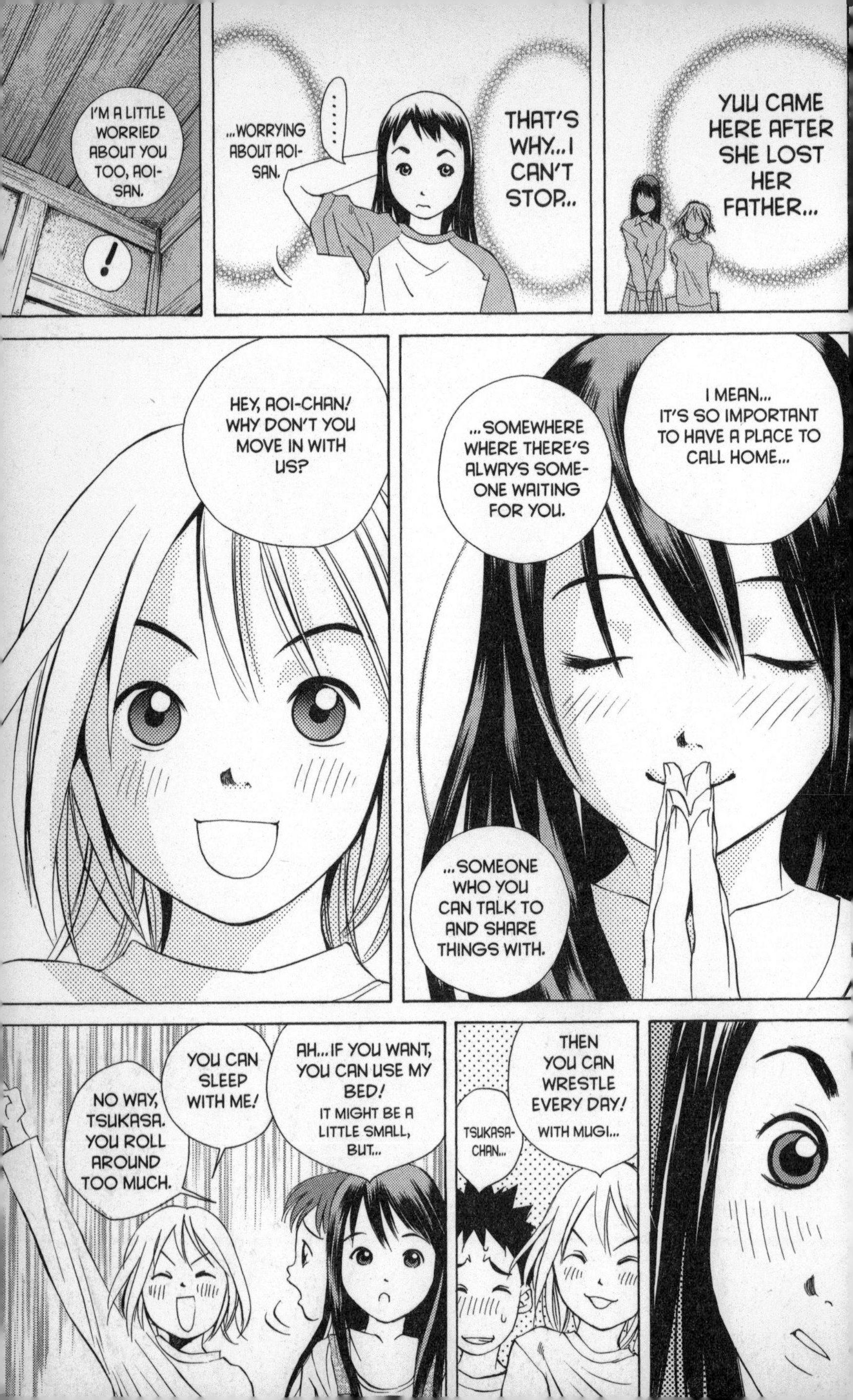
YUU CAME HERE AFTER SHE LOST HER FATHER...
THAT'S WHY...I CAN'T STOP...
......
...WORRYING ABOUT AOI-SAN.
I'M A LITTLE WORRIED ABOUT YOU TOO, AOI-SAN.
!
I MEAN... IT'S SO IMPORTANT TO HAVE A PLACE TO CALL HOME...
...SOMEWHERE WHERE THERE'S ALWAYS SOME-ONE WAITING FOR YOU.
...SOMEONE WHO YOU CAN TALK TO AND SHARE THINGS WITH.
HEY, AOI-CHAN! WHY DON'T YOU MOVE IN WITH US?
THEN YOU CAN WRESTLE EVERY DAY!
WITH MUGI...
TSUKASA-CHAN...
AH...IF YOU WANT, YOU CAN USE MY BED!
IT MIGHT BE A LITTLE SMALL, BUT...
YOU CAN SLEEP WITH ME!
NO WAY, TSUKASA. YOU ROLL AROUND TOO MUCH.

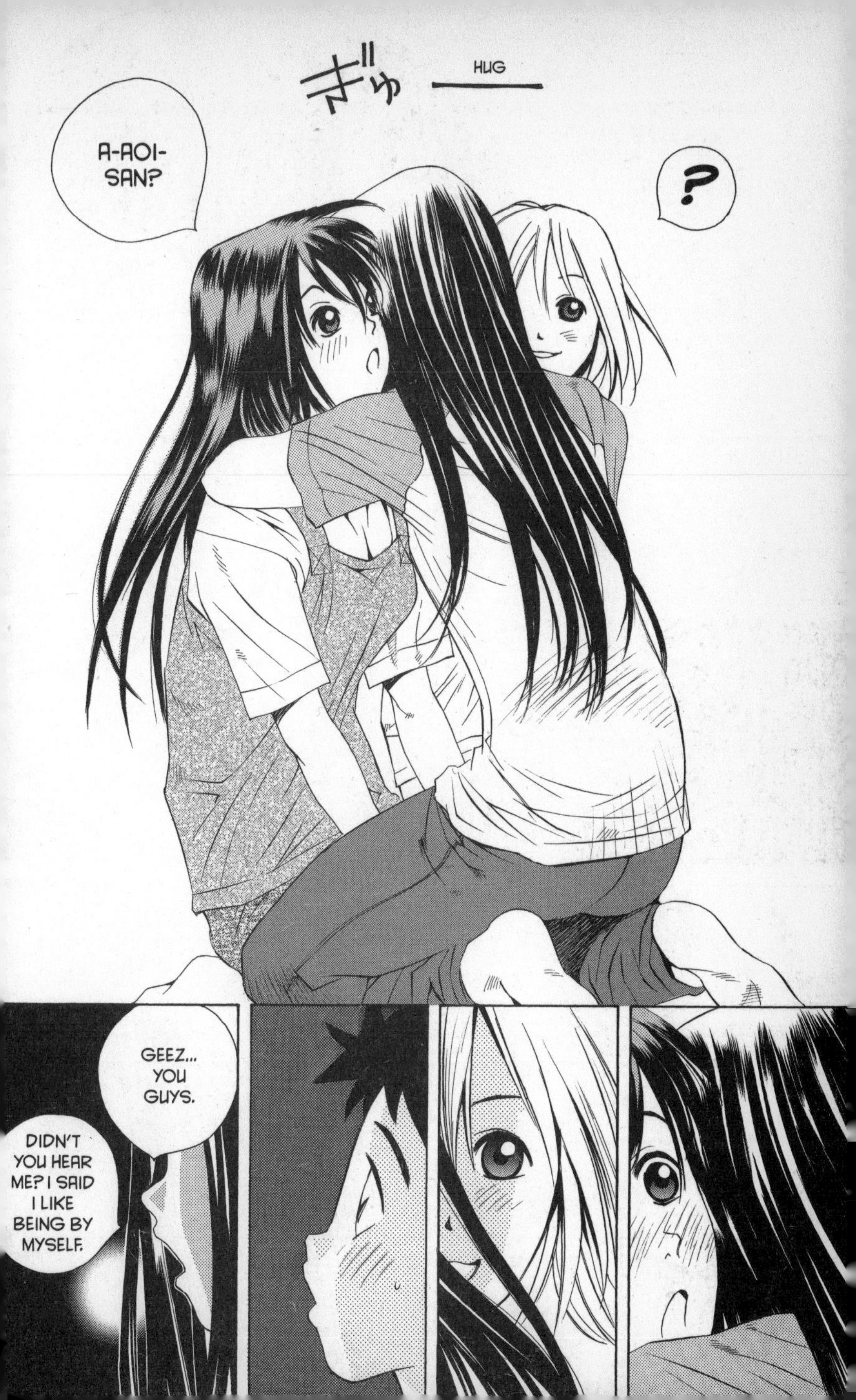
ぎゅー
HUG
?
A-AOI-SAN?
GEEZ... YOU GUYS.
DIDN'T YOU HEAR ME? I SAID I LIKE BEING BY MYSELF.

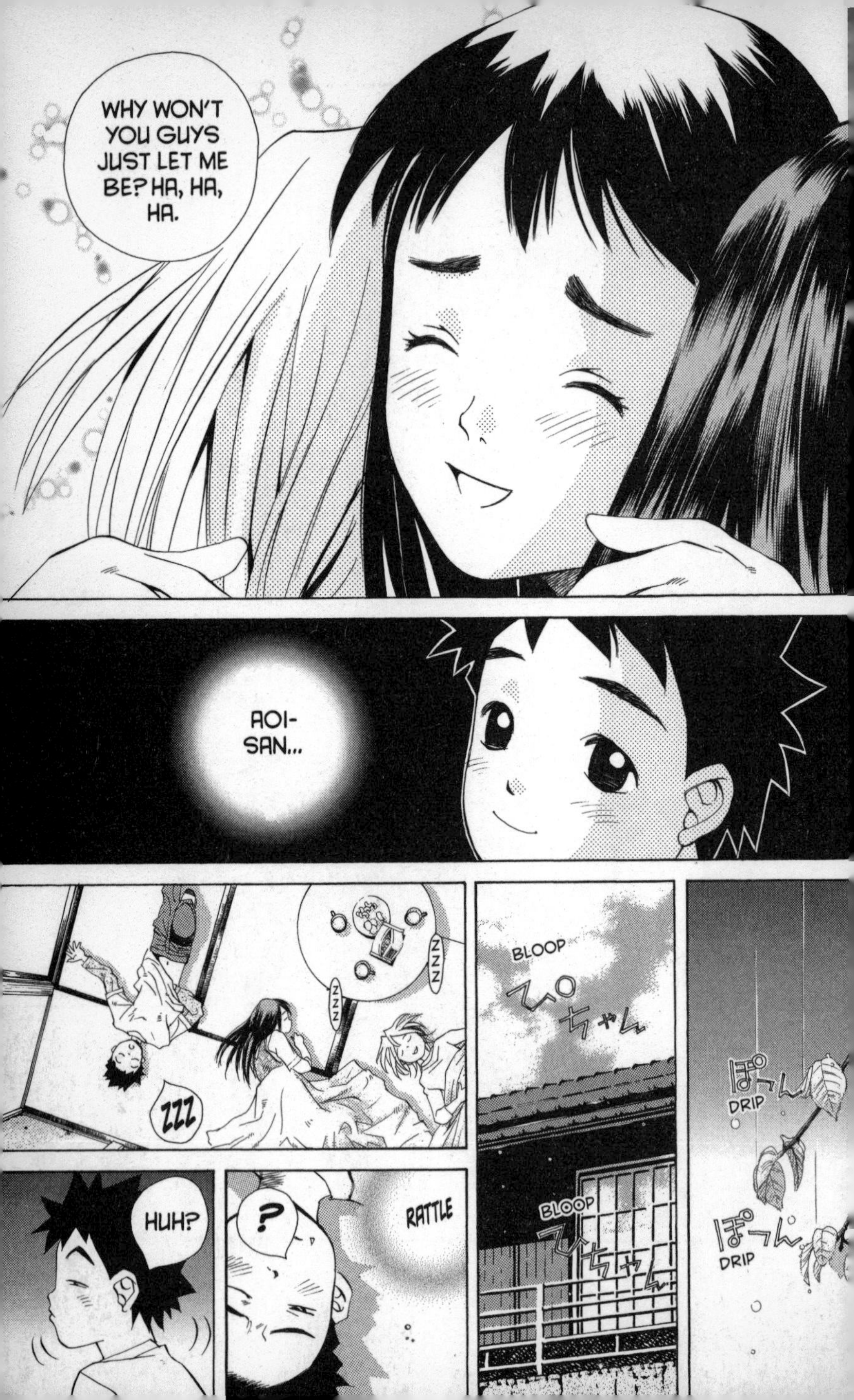
WHY WON'T YOU GUYS JUST LET ME BE? HA, HA, HA.
AOI-SAN...
ぽつん
DRIP
ぽつん
DRIP
BLOOP
ぴちゃん
BLOOP
ぴちゃん
ZZZ
ZZZ
ZZZ
RATTLE
?
HUH?

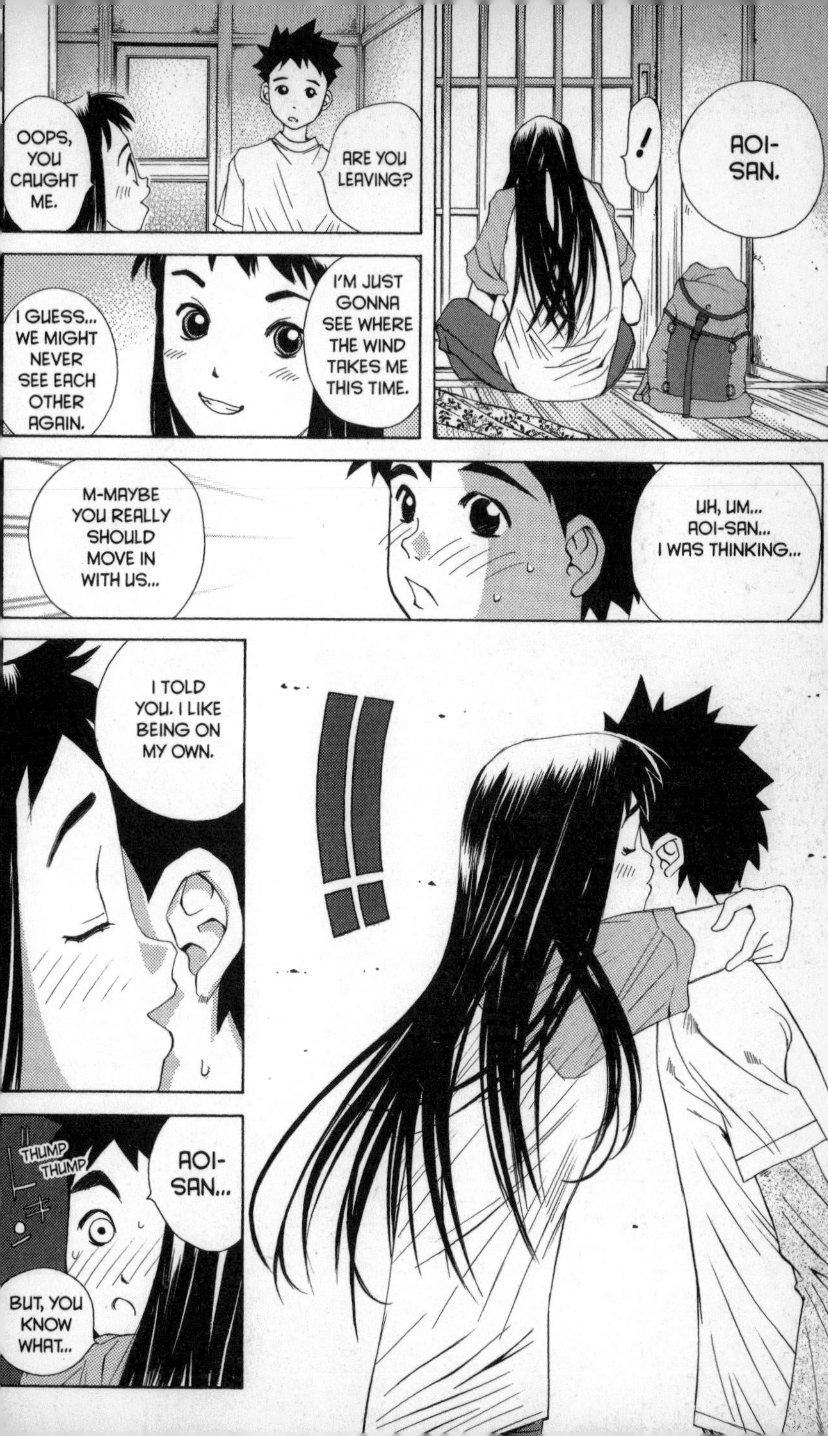
AOI-SAN.
!
ARE YOU LEAVING?
OOPS, YOU CAUGHT ME.
I'M JUST GONNA SEE WHERE THE WIND TAKES ME THIS TIME.
I GUESS... WE MIGHT NEVER SEE EACH OTHER AGAIN.
UH, UM... AOI-SAN... I WAS THINKING...
M-MAYBE YOU REALLY SHOULD MOVE IN WITH US...
!!
I TOLD YOU. I LIKE BEING ON MY OWN.
AOI-SAN...
THUMP THUMP
BUT, YOU KNOW WHAT...

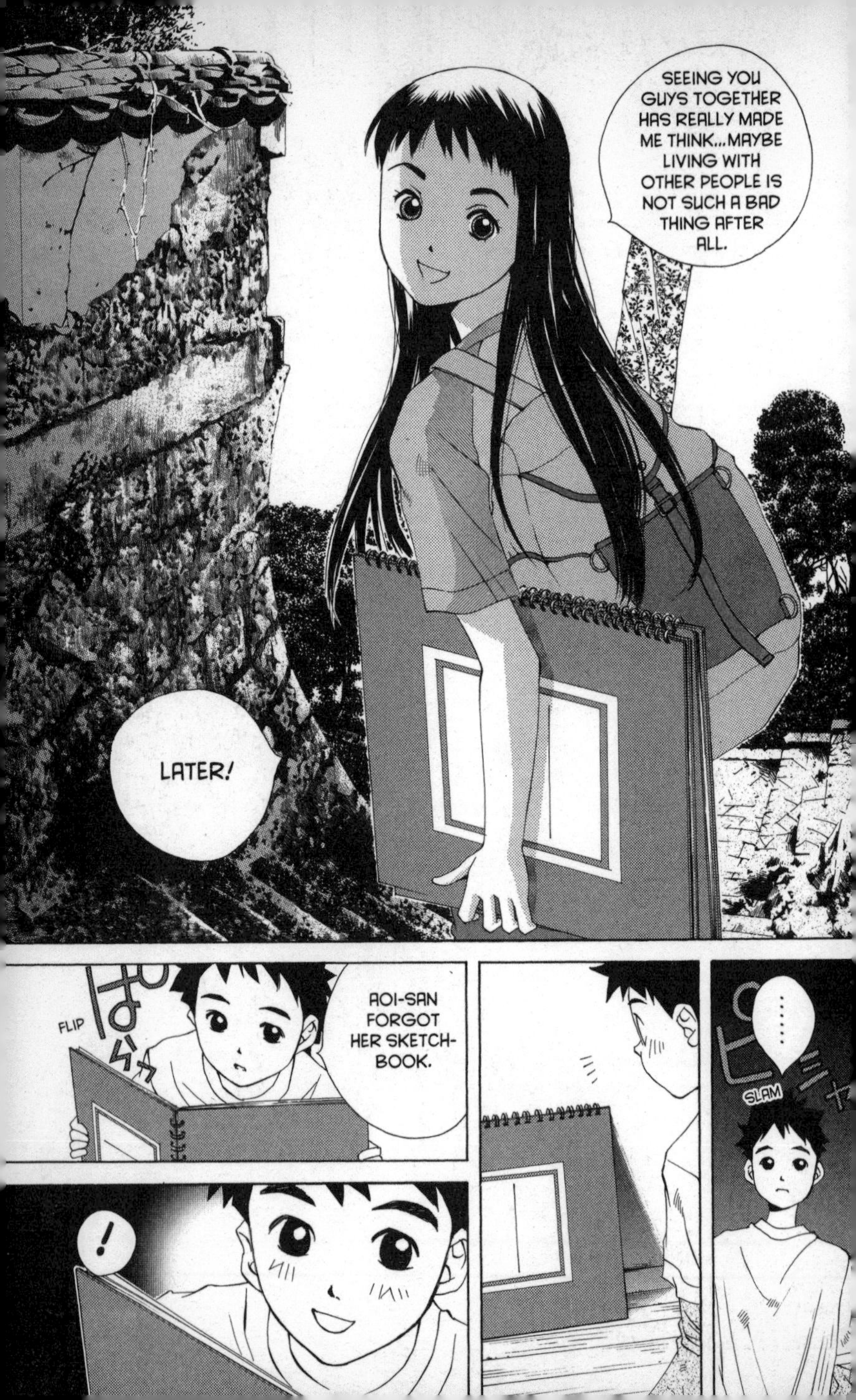
SEEING YOU GUYS TOGETHER HAS REALLY MADE ME THINK...MAYBE LIVING WITH OTHER PEOPLE IS NOT SUCH A BAD THING AFTER ALL.
LATER!
......
SLAM
AOI-SAN FORGOT HER SKETCH-BOOK.
FLIP
!

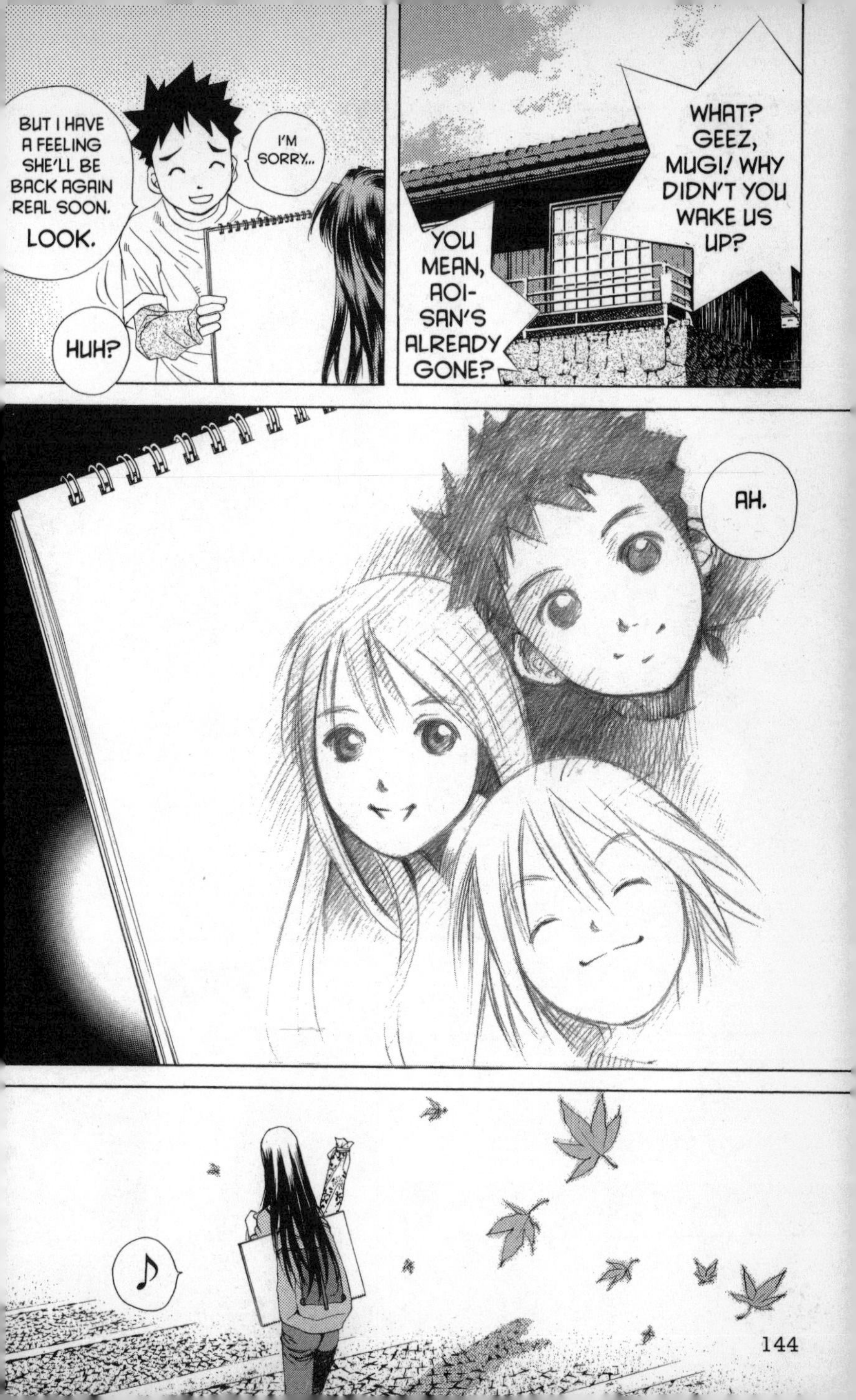
WHAT? GEEZ, MUGI! WHY DIDN'T YOU WAKE US UP?
YOU MEAN, AOI-SAN'S ALREADY GONE?
I'M SORRY...
BUT I HAVE A FEELING SHE'LL BE BACK AGAIN REAL SOON. LOOK.
HUH?
AH.
♪

Pastel

MIRACLE 39: HAPPY BIRTHDAY TO YUU!

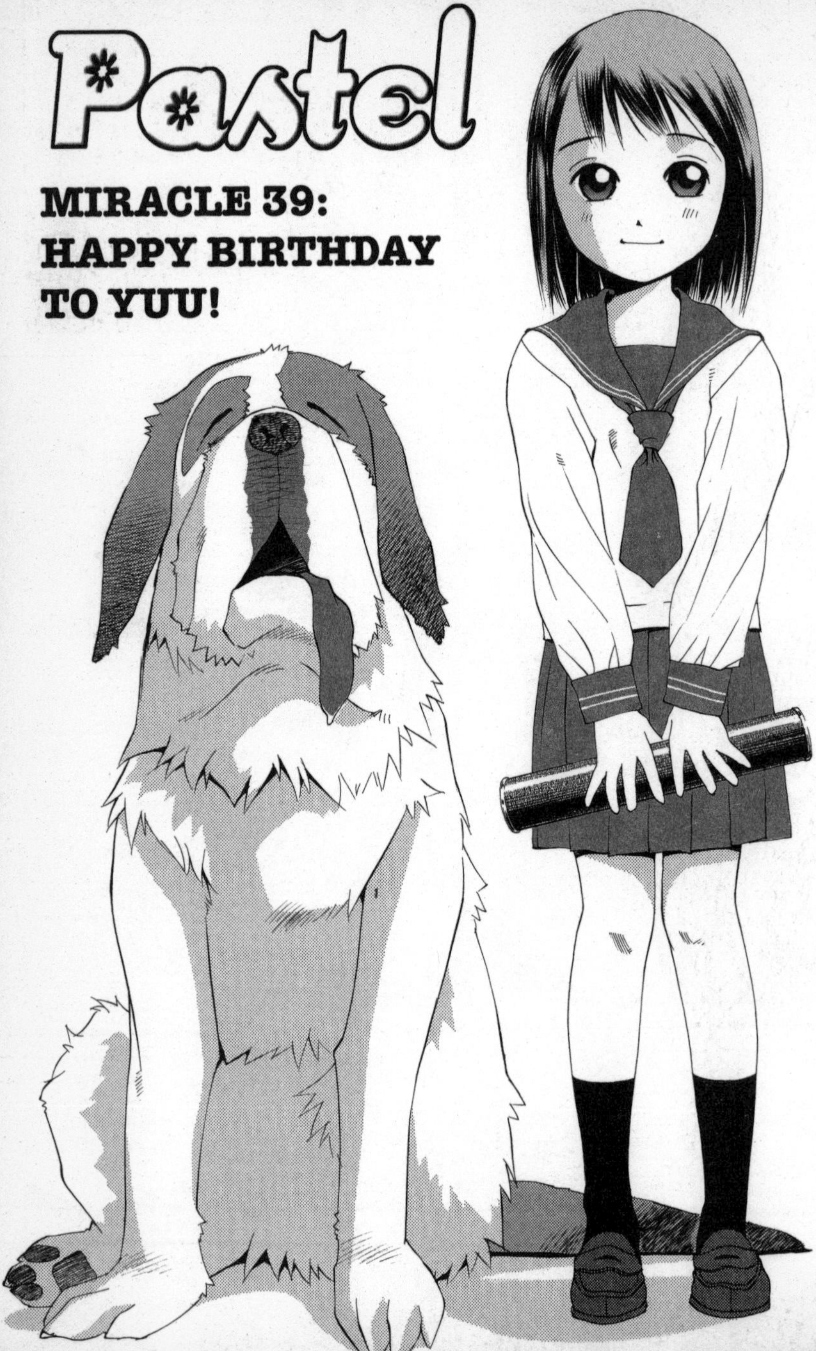

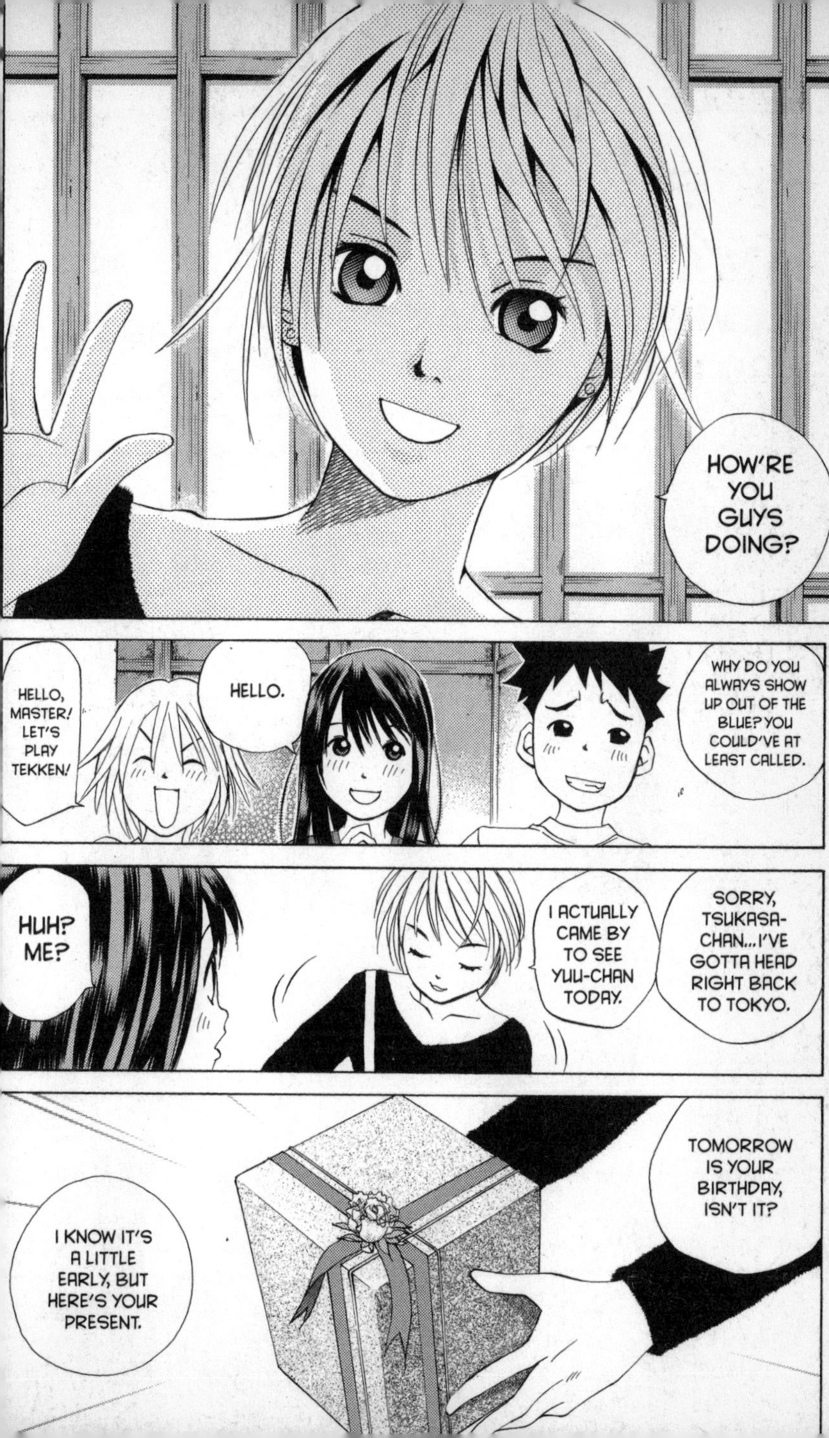
HOW'RE YOU GUYS DOING?
WHY DO YOU ALWAYS SHOW UP OUT OF THE BLUE? YOU COULD'VE AT LEAST CALLED.
HELLO.
HELLO, MASTER! LET'S PLAY TEKKEN!
SORRY, TSUKASA-CHAN...I'VE GOTTA HEAD RIGHT BACK TO TOKYO.
I ACTUALLY CAME BY TO SEE YUU-CHAN TODAY.
HUH? ME?
TOMORROW IS YOUR BIRTHDAY, ISN'T IT?
I KNOW IT'S A LITTLE EARLY, BUT HERE'S YOUR PRESENT.

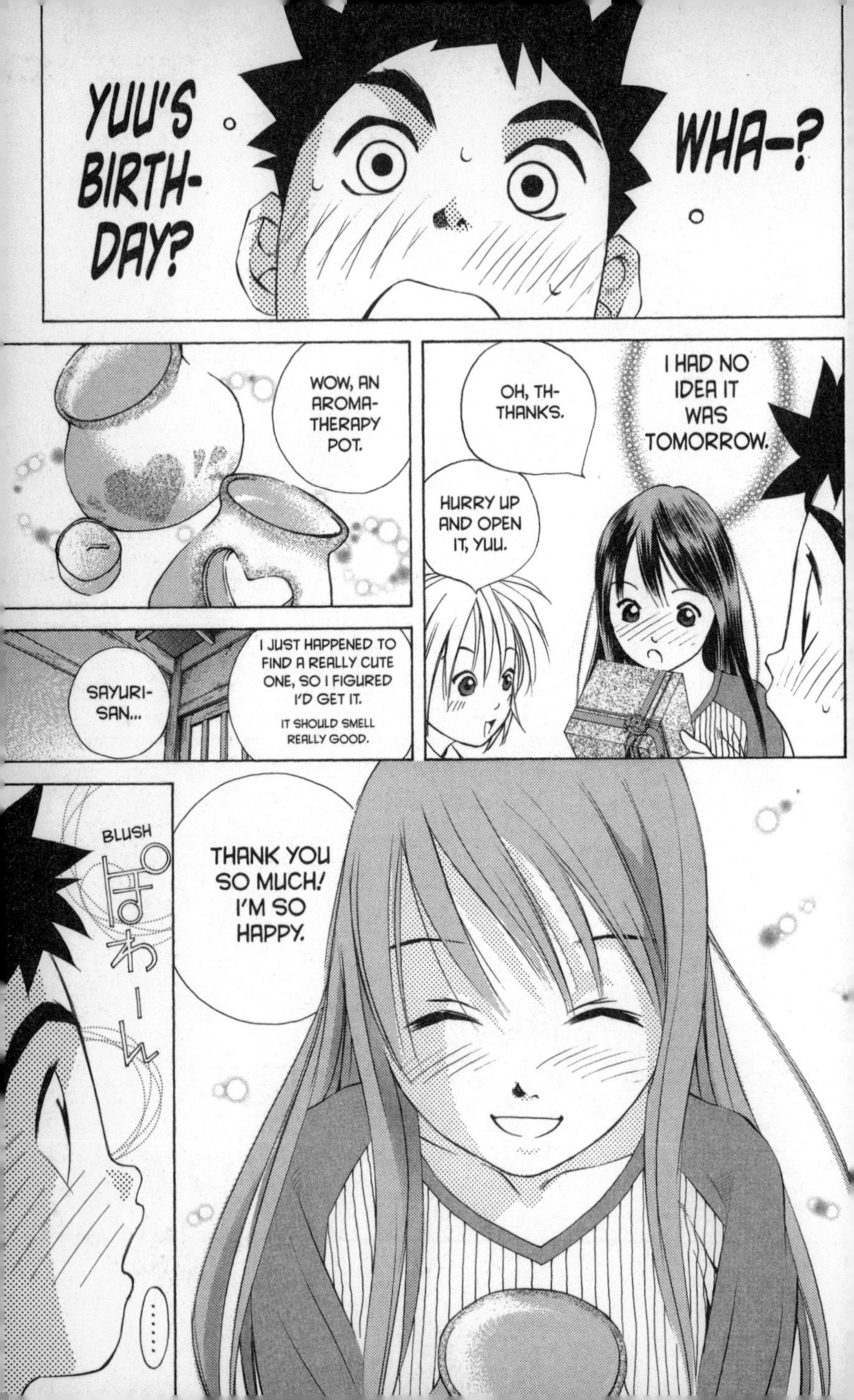
WHA-?
YUU'S BIRTH-DAY?
I HAD NO IDEA IT WAS TOMORROW.
OH, TH-THANKS.
HURRY UP AND OPEN IT, YUU.
WOW, AN AROMA-THERAPY POT.
I JUST HAPPENED TO FIND A REALLY CUTE ONE, SO I FIGURED I'D GET IT.
IT SHOULD SMELL REALLY GOOD.
SAYURI-SAN...
THANK YOU SO MUCH! I'M SO HAPPY.
ぽわーん
BLUSH
......

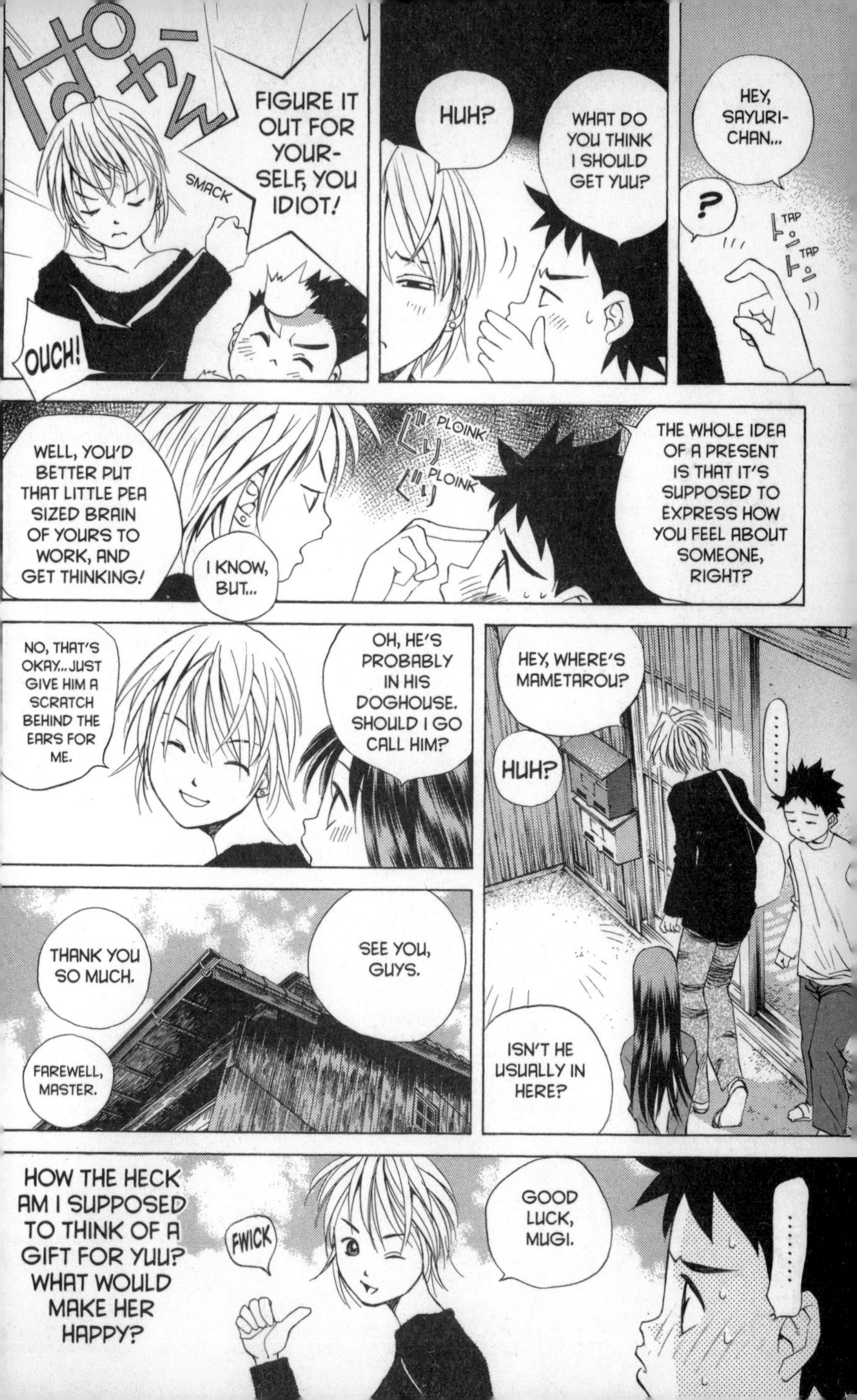
HEY, SAYURI-CHAN...
?
TAP
TAP
WHAT DO YOU THINK I SHOULD GET YUU?
HUH?
FIGURE IT OUT FOR YOURSELF, YOU IDIOT!
SMACK
OUCH!
THE WHOLE IDEA OF A PRESENT IS THAT IT'S SUPPOSED TO EXPRESS HOW YOU FEEL ABOUT SOMEONE, RIGHT?
PLOINK
PLOINK
WELL, YOU'D BETTER PUT THAT LITTLE PEA SIZED BRAIN OF YOURS TO WORK, AND GET THINKING!
I KNOW, BUT...
HEY, WHERE'S MAMETAROU?
......
HUH?
ISN'T HE USUALLY IN HERE?
OH, HE'S PROBABLY IN HIS DOGHOUSE. SHOULD I GO CALL HIM?
NO, THAT'S OKAY...JUST GIVE HIM A SCRATCH BEHIND THE EARS FOR ME.
SEE YOU, GUYS.
THANK YOU SO MUCH.
FAREWELL, MASTER.
......
GOOD LUCK, MUGI.
FWICK
HOW THE HECK AM I SUPPOSED TO THINK OF A GIFT FOR YUU? WHAT WOULD MAKE HER HAPPY?

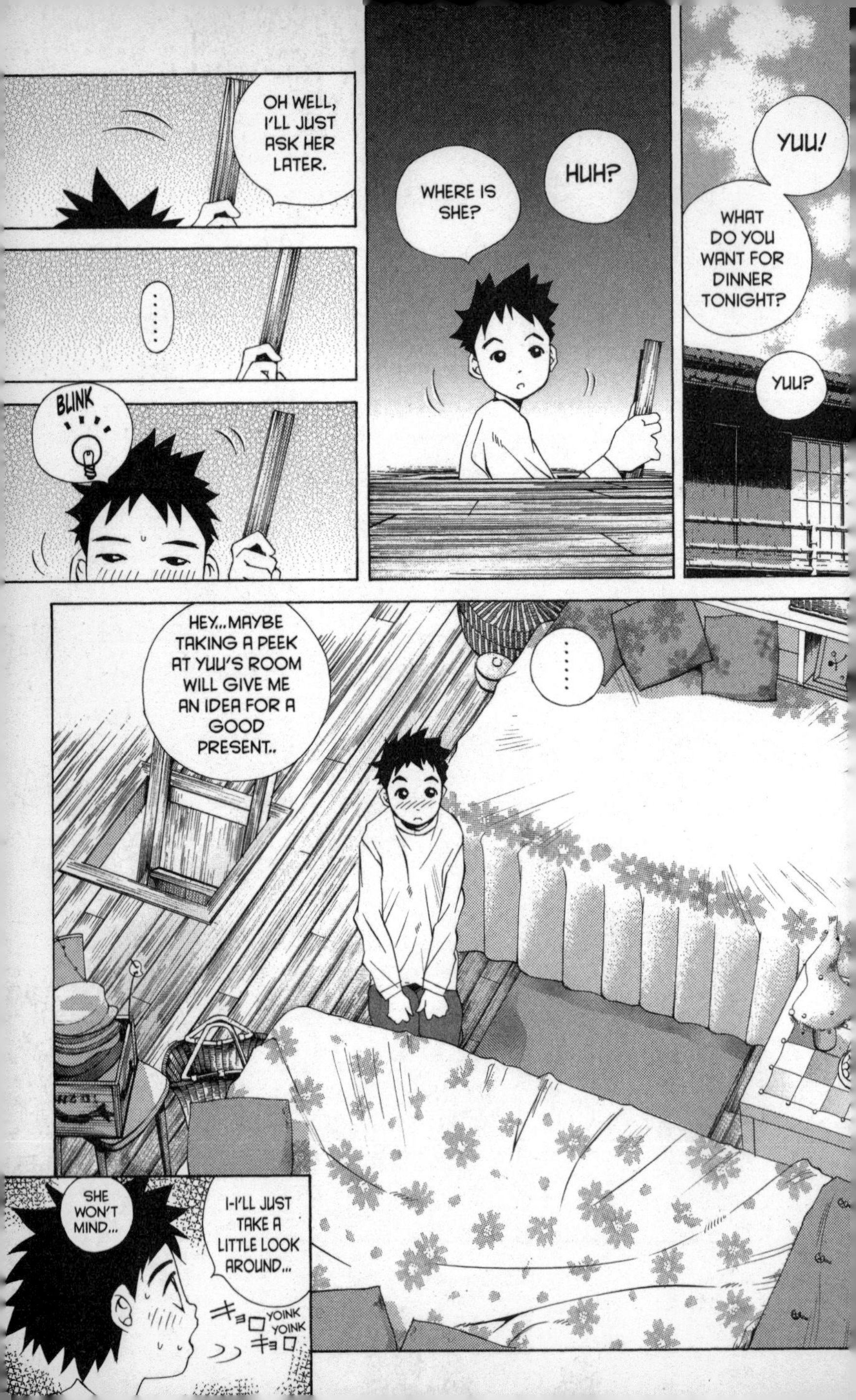
YUU!
WHAT DO YOU WANT FOR DINNER TONIGHT?
YUU?
HUH?
WHERE IS SHE?
OH WELL, I'LL JUST ASK HER LATER.
......
BLINK
......
HEY...MAYBE TAKING A PEEK AT YUU'S ROOM WILL GIVE ME AN IDEA FOR A GOOD PRESENT..
I-I'LL JUST TAKE A LITTLE LOOK AROUND...
SHE WON'T MIND...
キョロ YOINK
YOINK キョロ

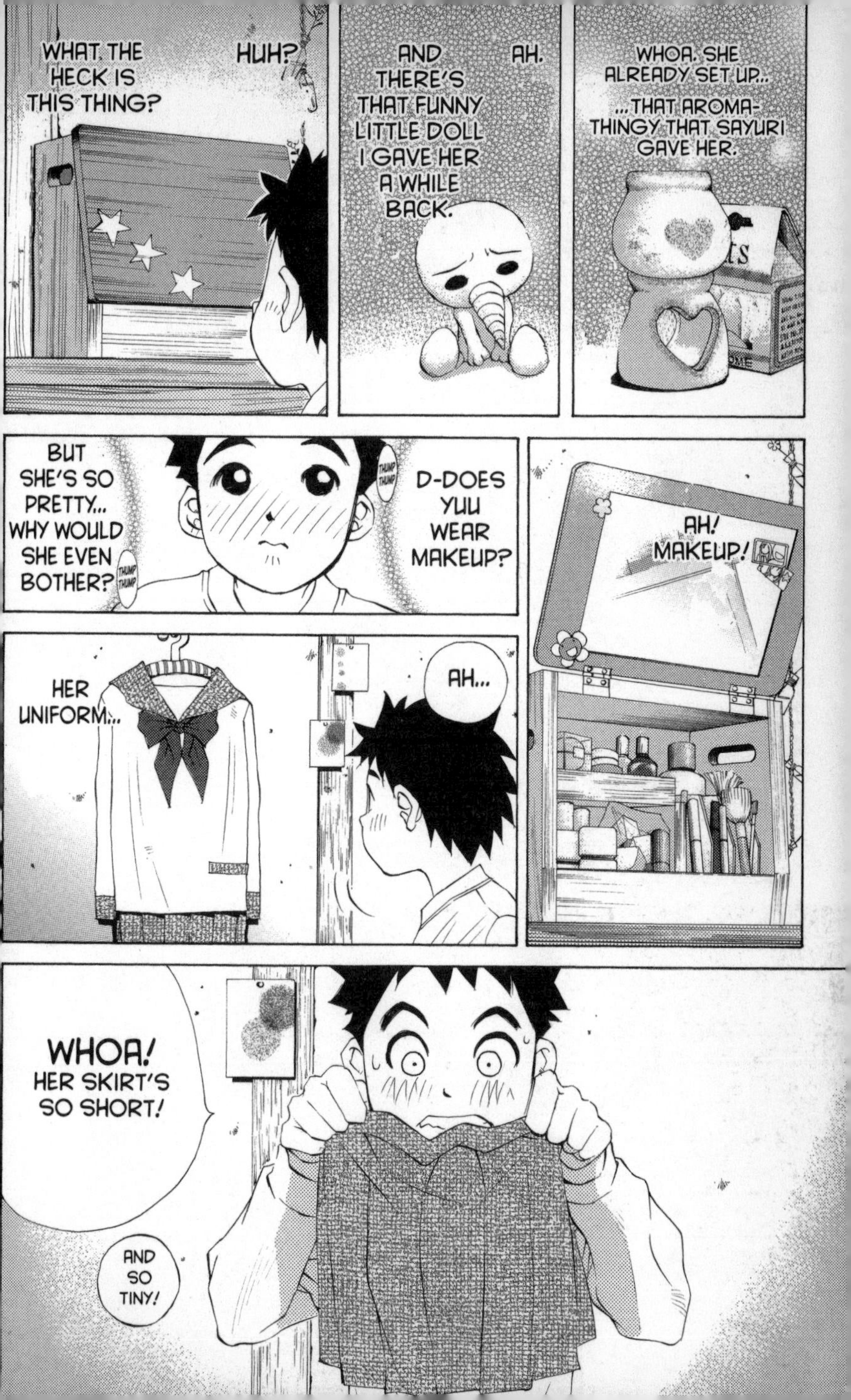
WHOA. SHE ALREADY SET UP...
...THAT AROMA-THINGY THAT SAYURI GAVE HER.
AH.
AND THERE'S THAT FUNNY LITTLE DOLL I GAVE HER A WHILE BACK.
HUH?
WHAT THE HECK IS THIS THING?
AH! MAKEUP!
THUMP THUMP
D-DOES YUU WEAR MAKEUP?
BUT SHE'S SO PRETTY... WHY WOULD SHE EVEN BOTHER?
THUMP THUMP
AH...
HER UNIFORM...
WHOA! HER SKIRT'S SO SHORT!
AND SO TINY!

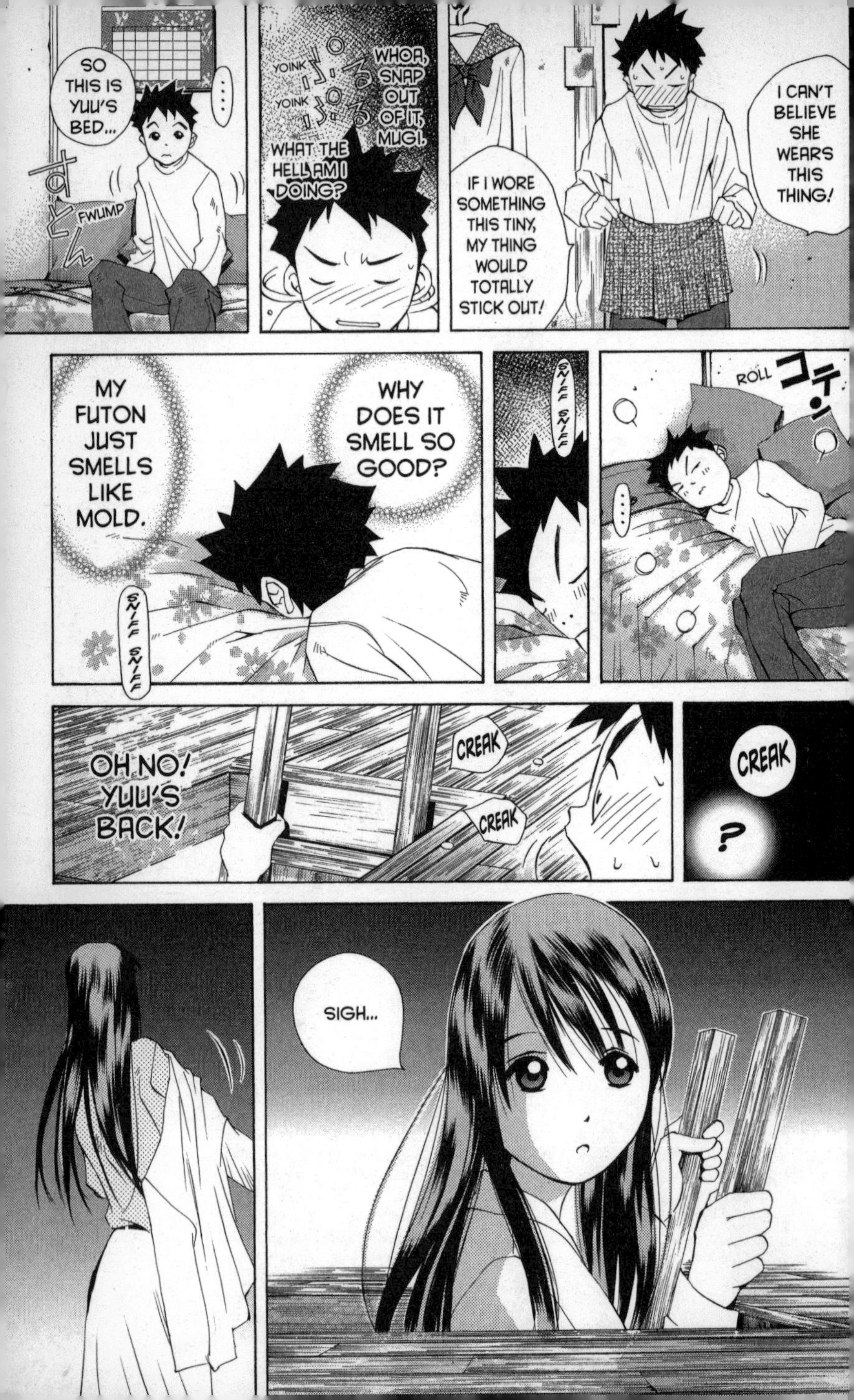
I CAN'T BELIEVE SHE WEARS THIS THING!
IF I WORE SOMETHING THIS TINY, MY THING WOULD TOTALLY STICK OUT!
WHOA, SNAP OUT OF IT, MUGI.
YOINK ぷるぷる YOINK
WHAT THE HELL AM I DOING?
SO THIS IS YUU'S BED...
....
FWUMP すとん
ROLL コテン
....
SNIFF SNIFF
WHY DOES IT SMELL SO GOOD?
MY FUTON JUST SMELLS LIKE MOLD.
SNIFF SNIFF
CREAK
?
CREAK
CREAK
OH NO! YUU'S BACK!
SIGH...

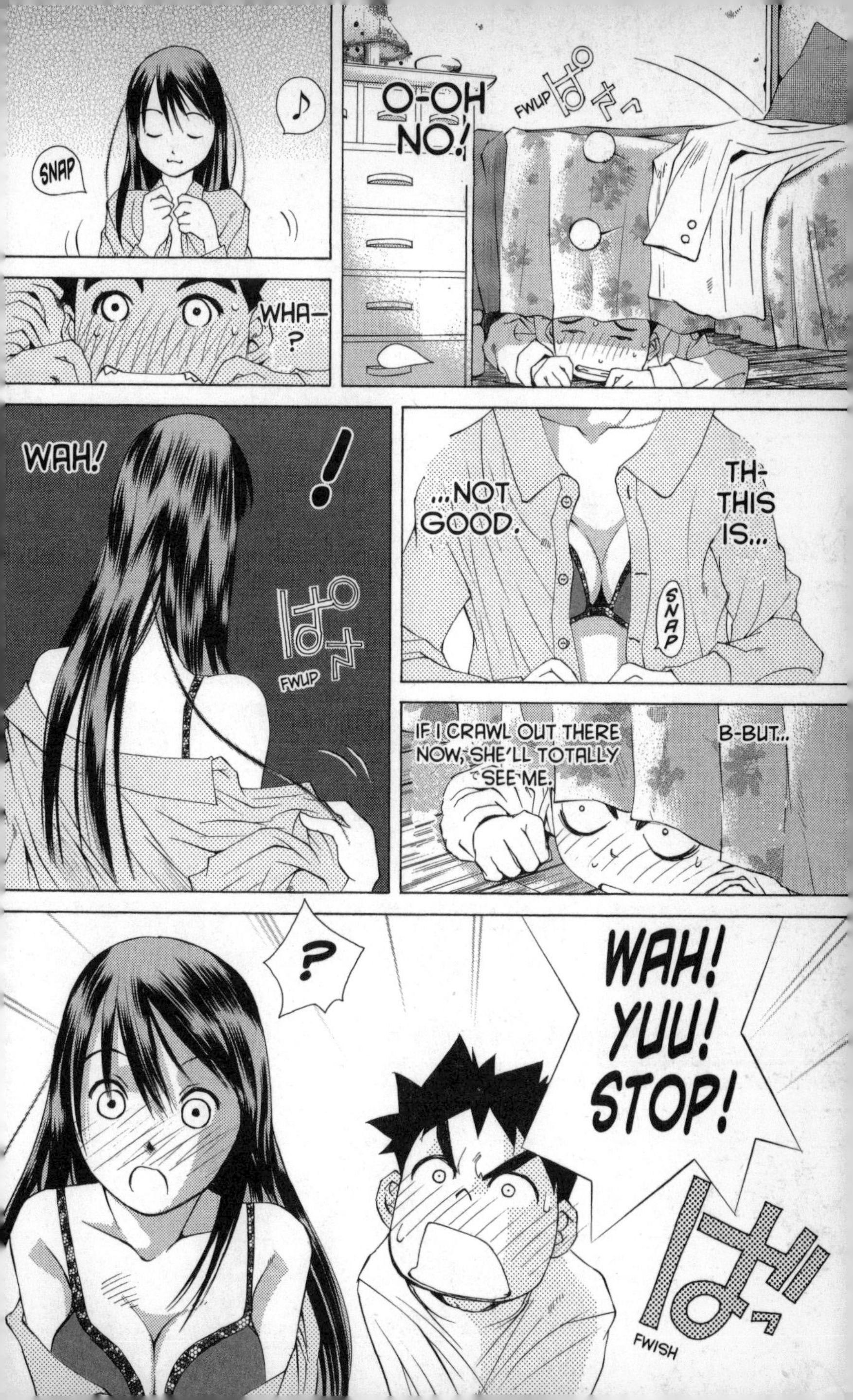
O-OH NO!
FWUP
ぱさっ
♪
SNAP
WHA-?
TH-THIS IS...
...NOT GOOD.
SNAP
B-BUT...
IF I CRAWL OUT THERE NOW, SHE'LL TOTALLY SEE ME.
!
ぱさっ
FWUP
WAH!
WAH! YUU! STOP!
ばっ
FWISH
?

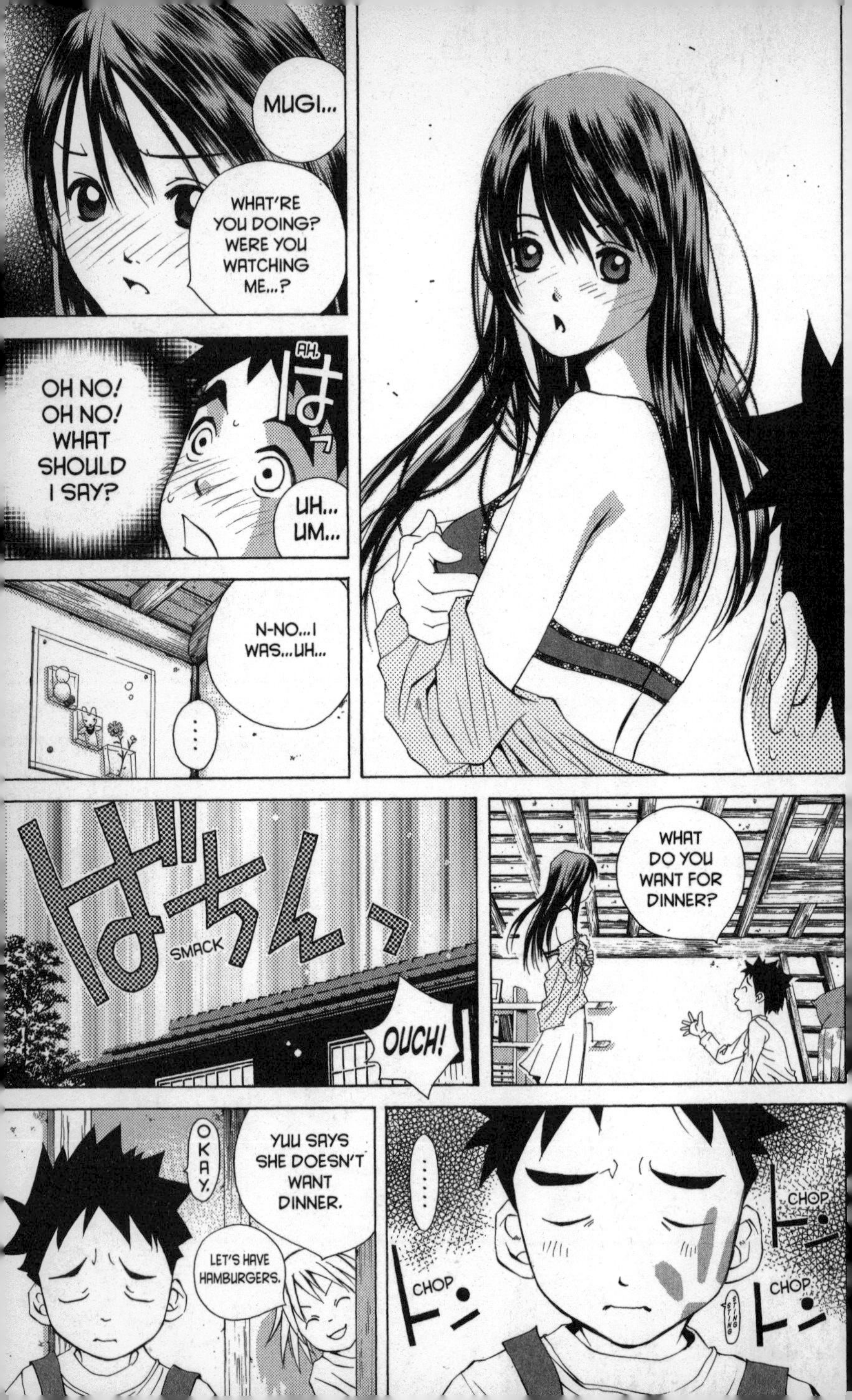
MUGI...
WHAT'RE YOU DOING? WERE YOU WATCHING ME...?
AH.
UH... UM...
OH NO! OH NO! WHAT SHOULD I SAY?
N-NO...I WAS...UH...
....
WHAT DO YOU WANT FOR DINNER?
ばちん
SMACK
OUCH!
......
CHOP
CHOP
CHOP
STING STING
YUU SAYS SHE DOESN'T WANT DINNER.
OKAY.
LET'S HAVE HAMBURGERS.

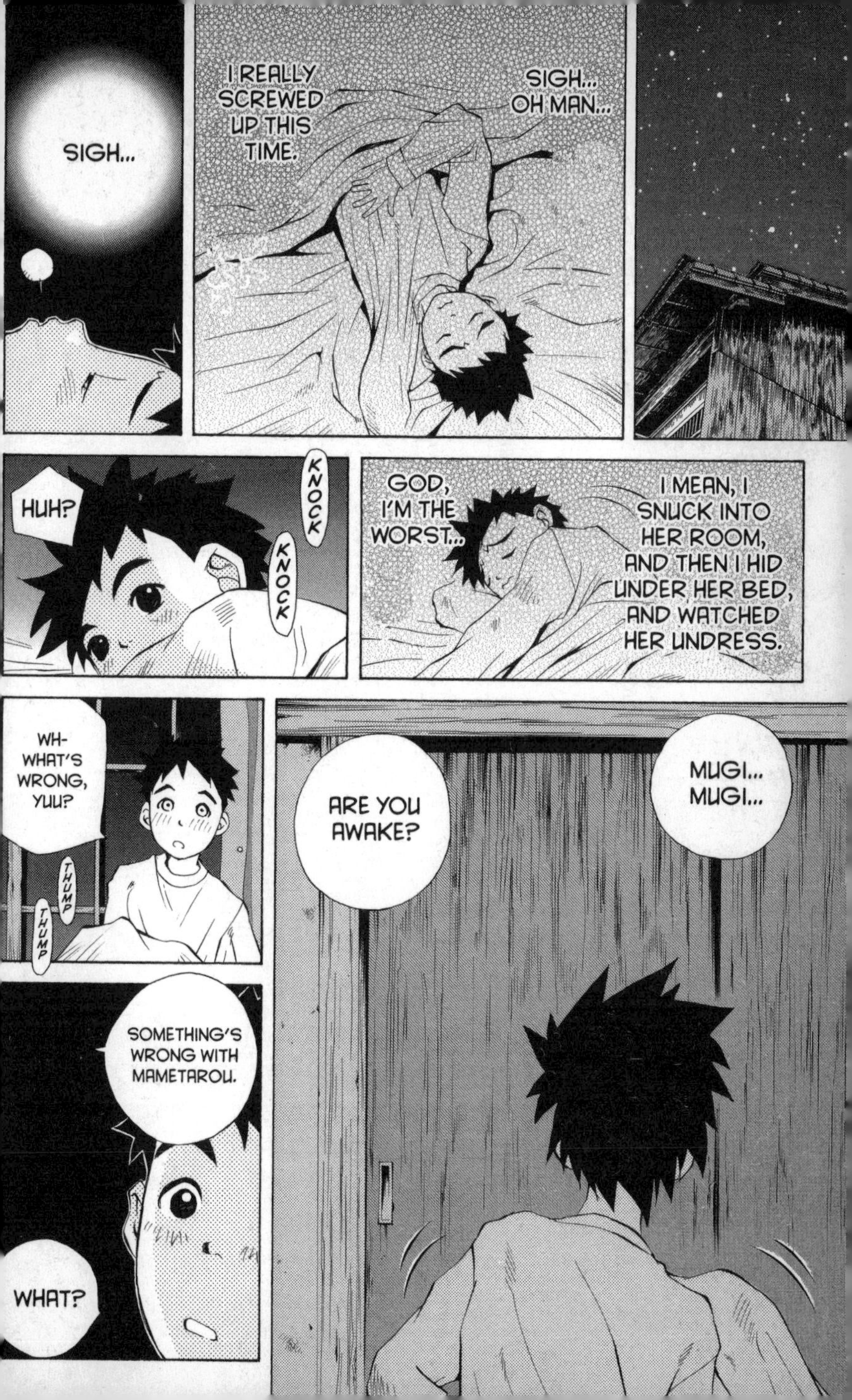
SIGH... OH MAN...
I REALLY SCREWED UP THIS TIME.
SIGH...
I MEAN, I SNUCK INTO HER ROOM, AND THEN I HID UNDER HER BED, AND WATCHED HER UNDRESS.
GOD, I'M THE WORST...
KNOCK
KNOCK
HUH?
MUGI... MUGI...
ARE YOU AWAKE?
WH- WHAT'S WRONG, YUU?
THUMP
THUMP
SOMETHING'S WRONG WITH MAMETAROU.
WHAT?

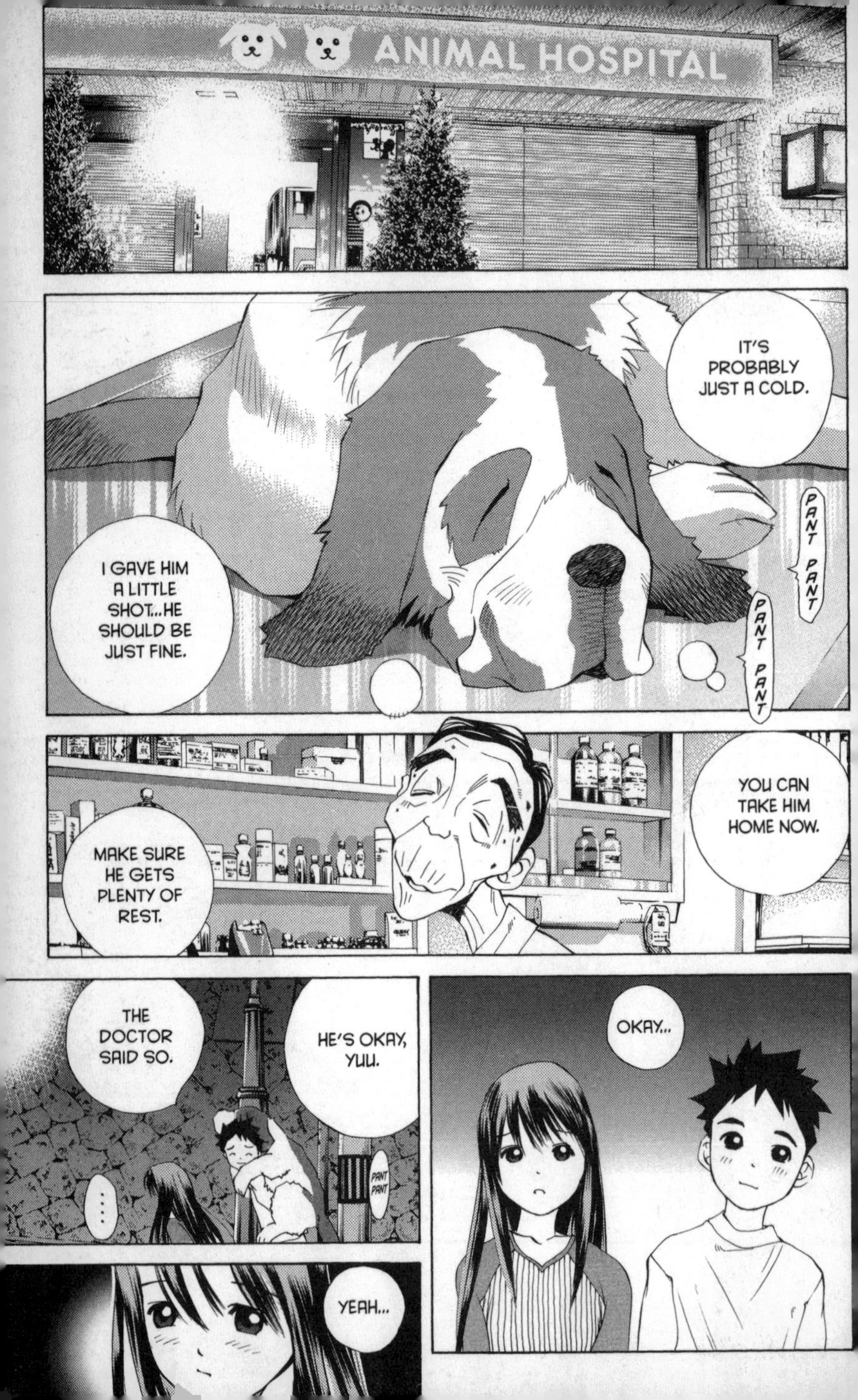
ANIMAL HOSPITAL
IT'S PROBABLY JUST A COLD.
PANT PANT
PANT PANT
I GAVE HIM A LITTLE SHOT...HE SHOULD BE JUST FINE.
YOU CAN TAKE HIM HOME NOW.
MAKE SURE HE GETS PLENTY OF REST.
OKAY...
HE'S OKAY, YUU.
THE DOCTOR SAID SO.
PANT PANT
....
YEAH...

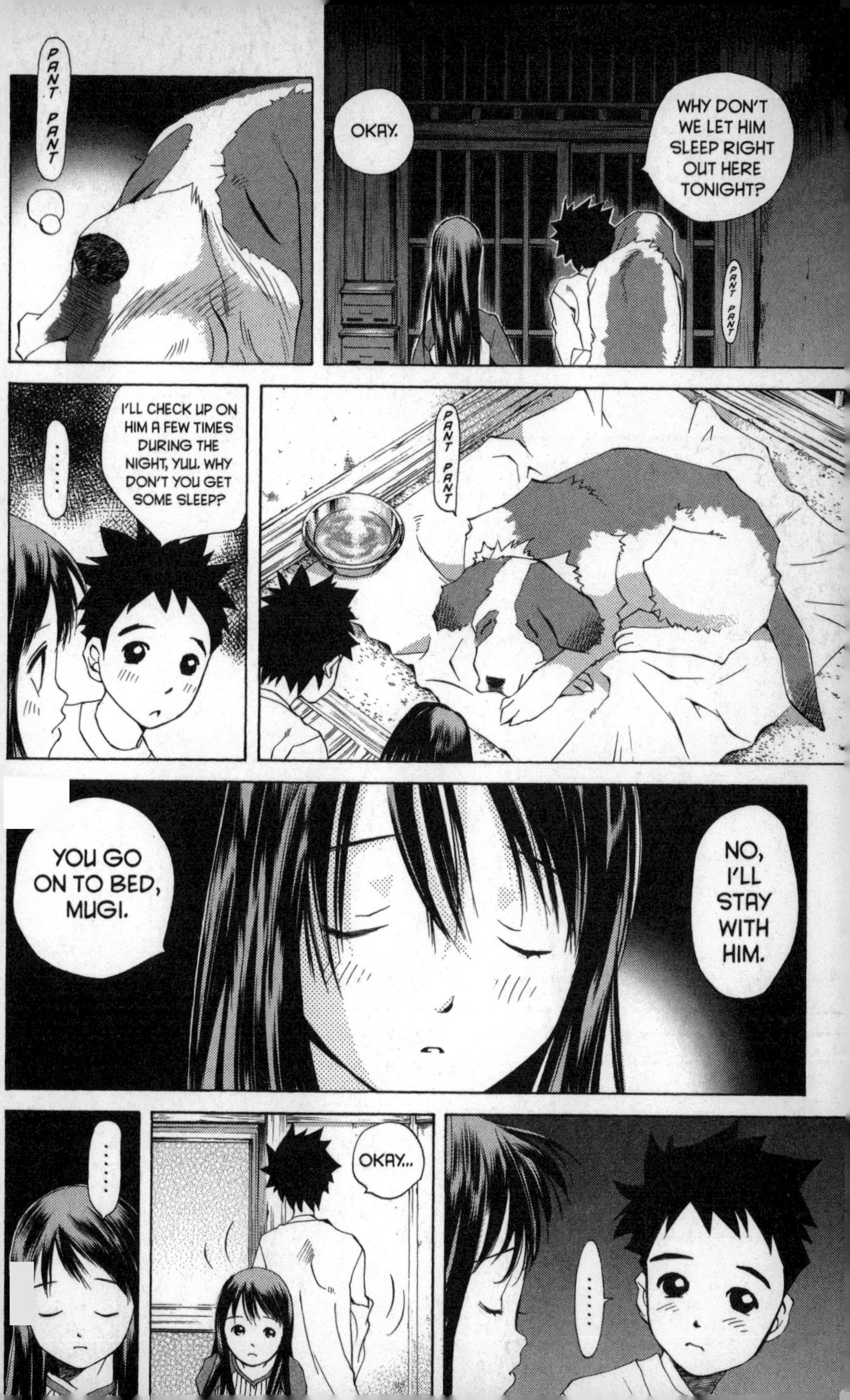
WHY DON'T WE LET HIM SLEEP RIGHT OUT HERE TONIGHT?
OKAY.
PANT PANT
PANT PANT
PANT PANT
I'LL CHECK UP ON HIM A FEW TIMES DURING THE NIGHT, YUU. WHY DON'T YOU GET SOME SLEEP?
......
NO, I'LL STAY WITH HIM.
YOU GO ON TO BED, MUGI.
......
OKAY...
......

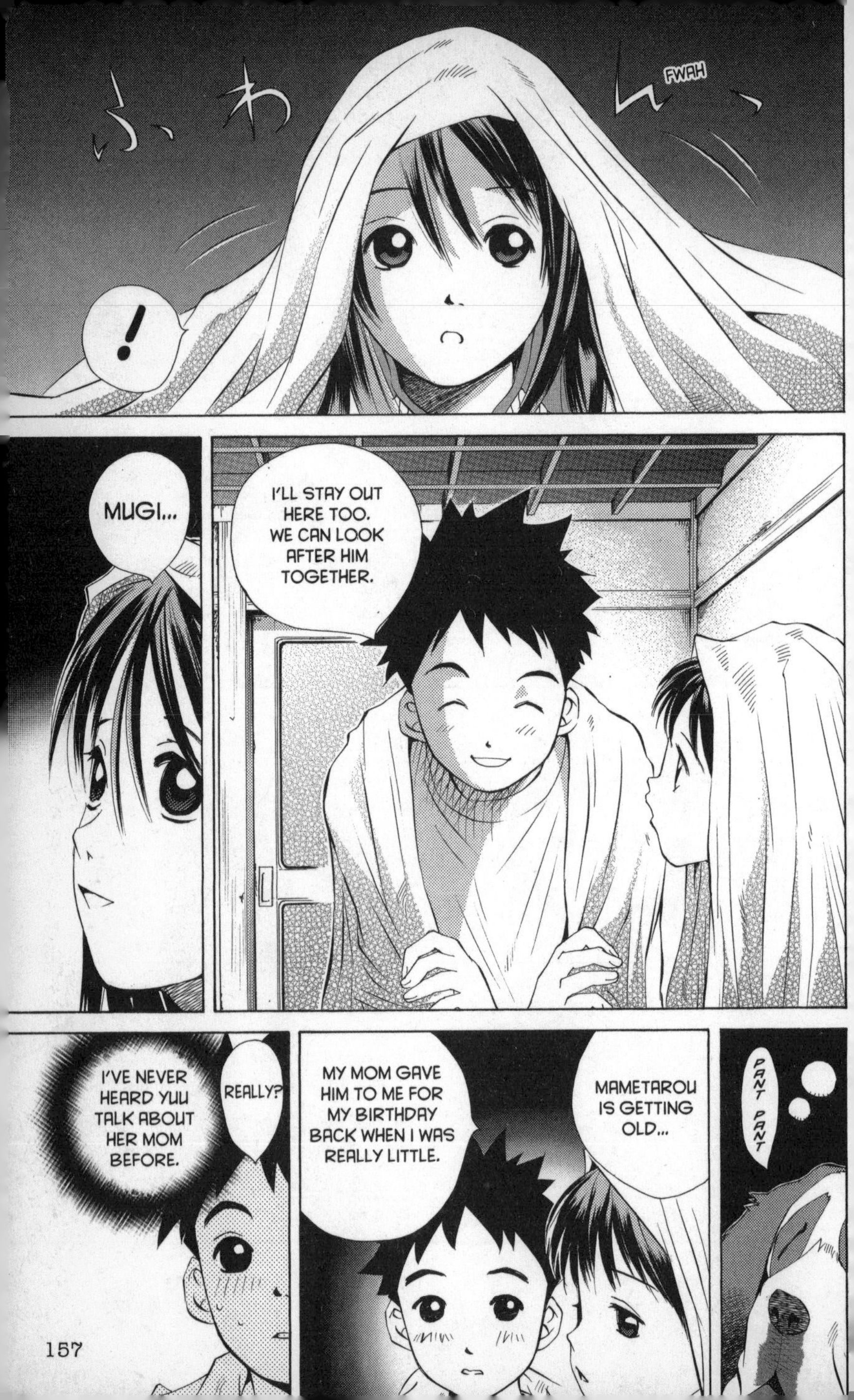
ふわ
FWAH
!
I'LL STAY OUT HERE TOO. WE CAN LOOK AFTER HIM TOGETHER.
MUGI...
PANT PANT
MAMETAROU IS GETTING OLD...
MY MOM GAVE HIM TO ME FOR MY BIRTHDAY BACK WHEN I WAS REALLY LITTLE.
REALLY?
I'VE NEVER HEARD YUU TALK ABOUT HER MOM BEFORE.

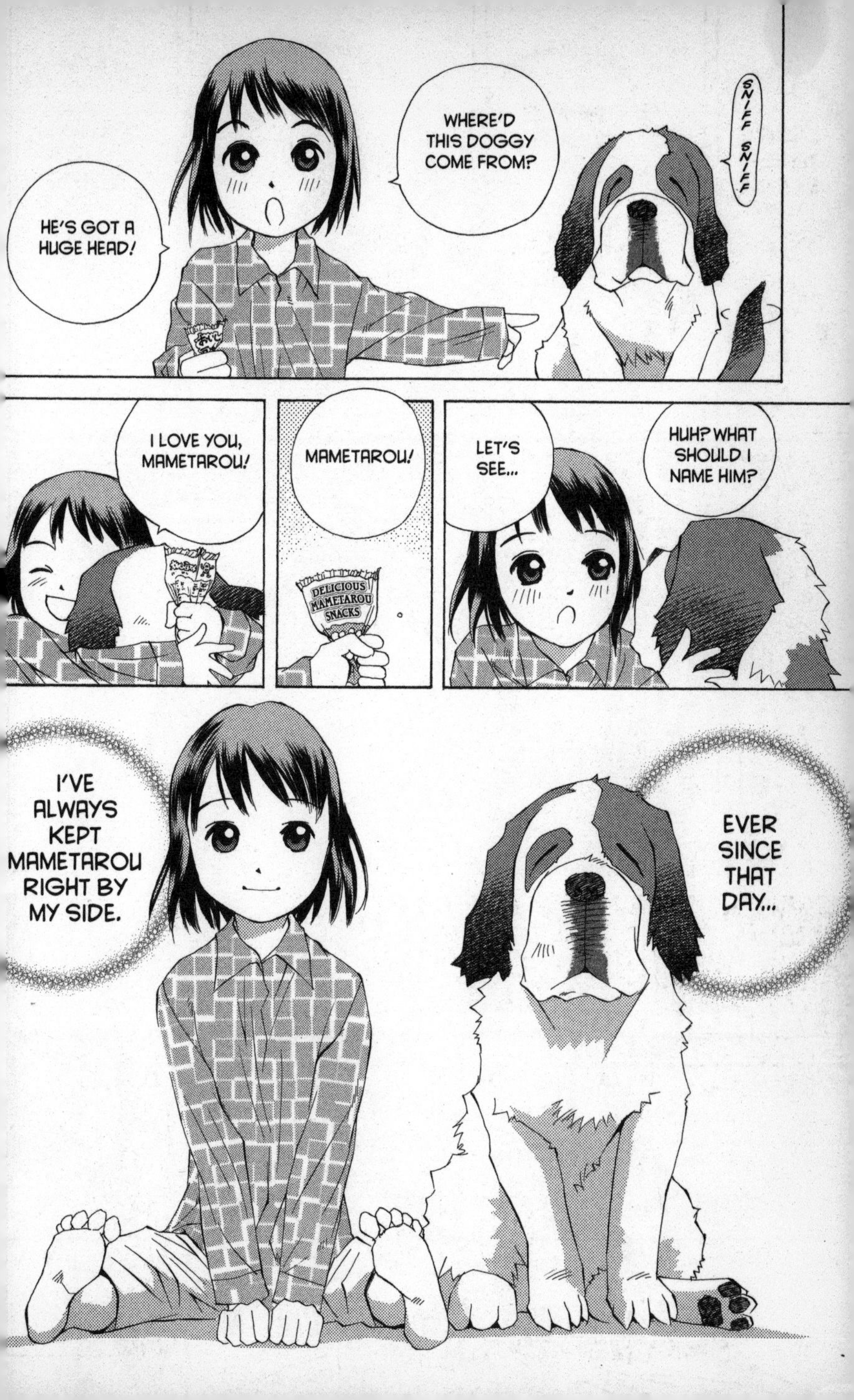
SNIFF SNIFF
WHERE'D THIS DOGGY COME FROM?
HE'S GOT A HUGE HEAD!
HUH? WHAT SHOULD I NAME HIM?
LET'S SEE...
MAMETAROU!
DELICIOUS MAMETAROU SNACKS
I LOVE YOU, MAMETAROU!
EVER SINCE THAT DAY...
I'VE ALWAYS KEPT MAMETAROU RIGHT BY MY SIDE.

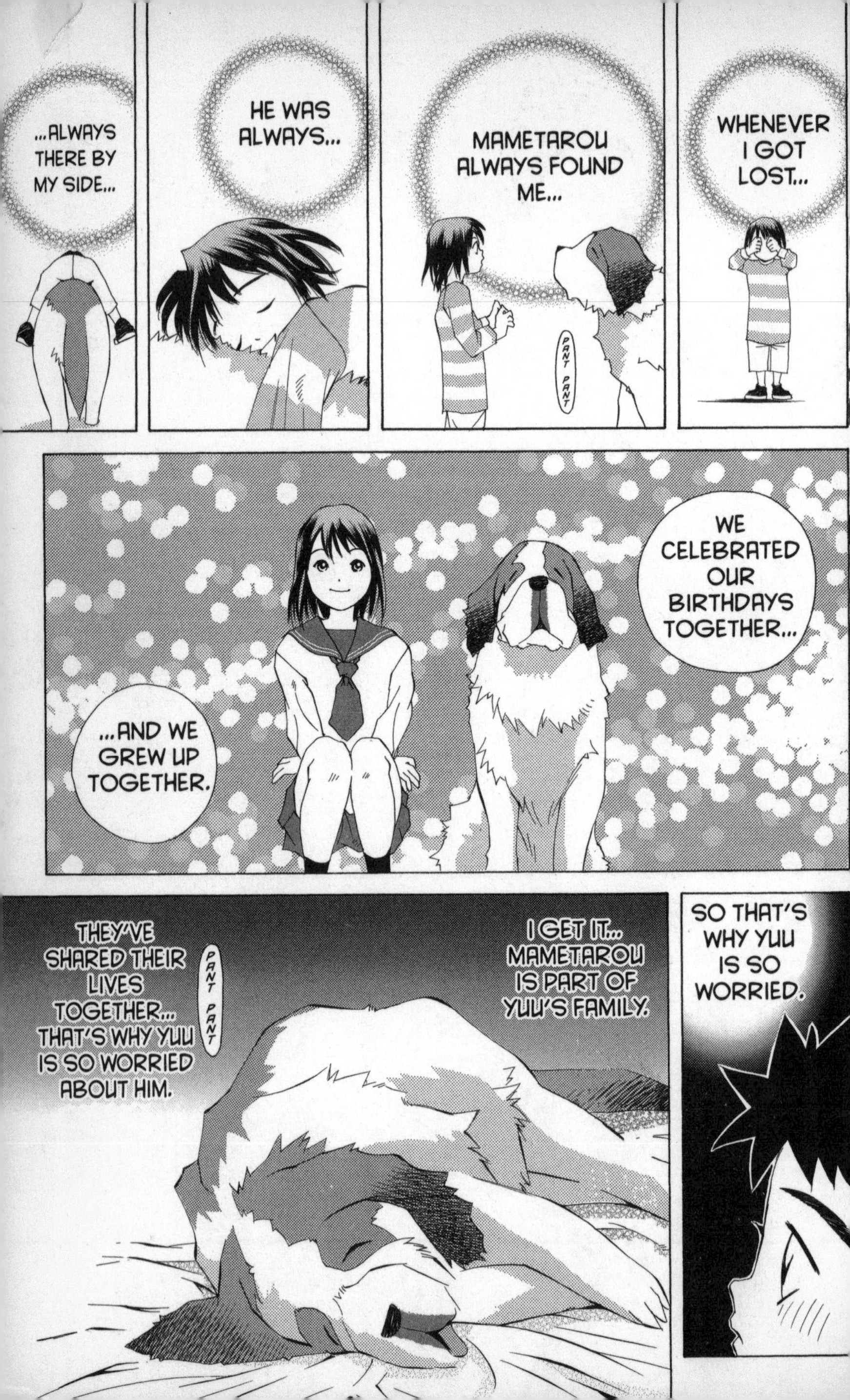
WHENEVER I GOT LOST...
MAMETAROU ALWAYS FOUND ME...
PANT PANT
HE WAS ALWAYS...
...ALWAYS THERE BY MY SIDE...
WE CELEBRATED OUR BIRTHDAYS TOGETHER...
...AND WE GREW UP TOGETHER.
SO THAT'S WHY YUU IS SO WORRIED.
I GET IT... MAMETAROU IS PART OF YUU'S FAMILY.
PANT PANT
THEY'VE SHARED THEIR LIVES TOGETHER... THAT'S WHY YUU IS SO WORRIED ABOUT HIM.

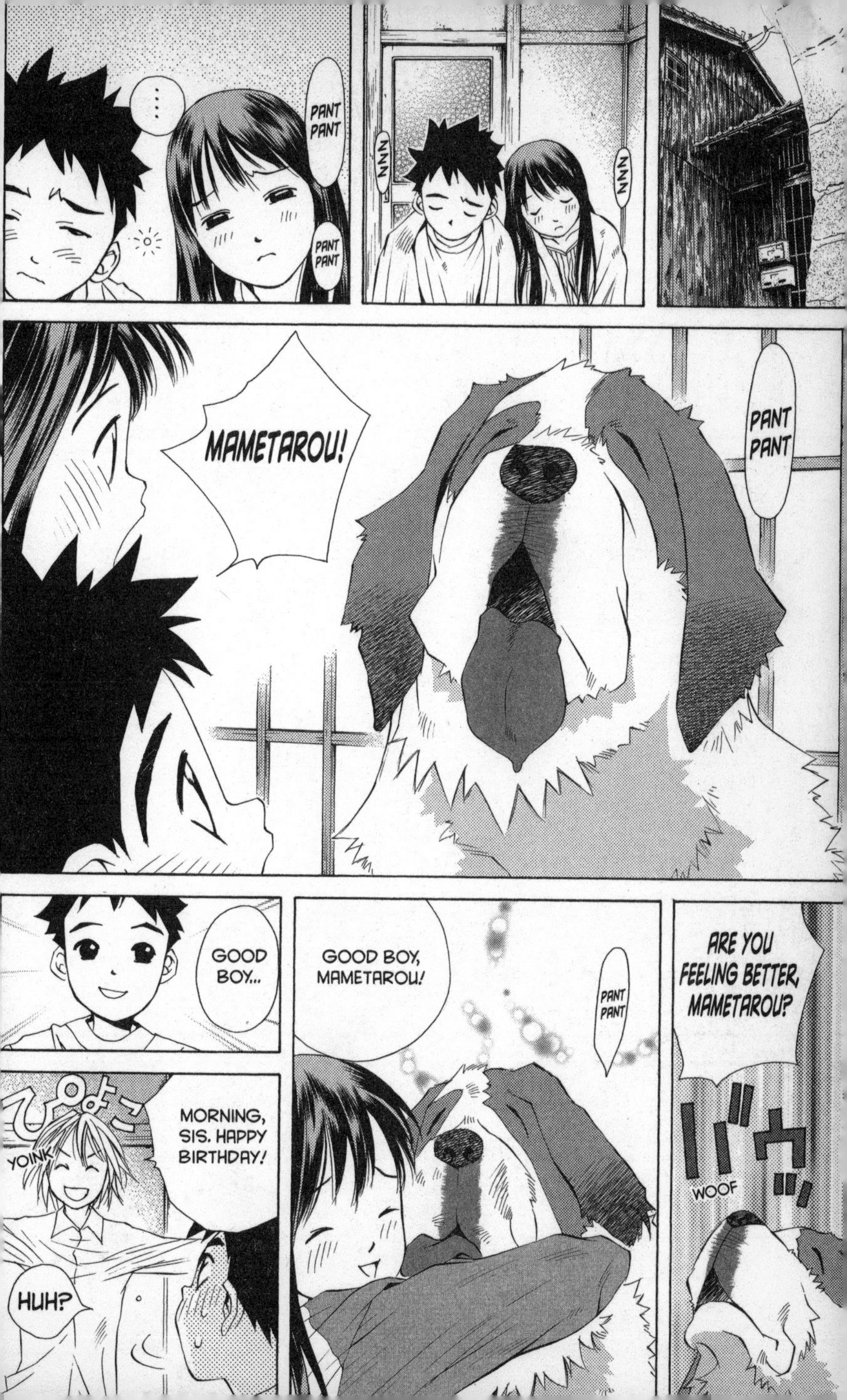
NNN
NNN
PANT PANT
...
PANT PANT
PANT PANT
MAMETAROU!
ARE YOU FEELING BETTER, MAMETAROU?
バウッ
WOOF
PANT PANT
GOOD BOY, MAMETAROU!
GOOD BOY...
MORNING, SIS. HAPPY BIRTHDAY!
ぴよっ
YOINK
HUH?

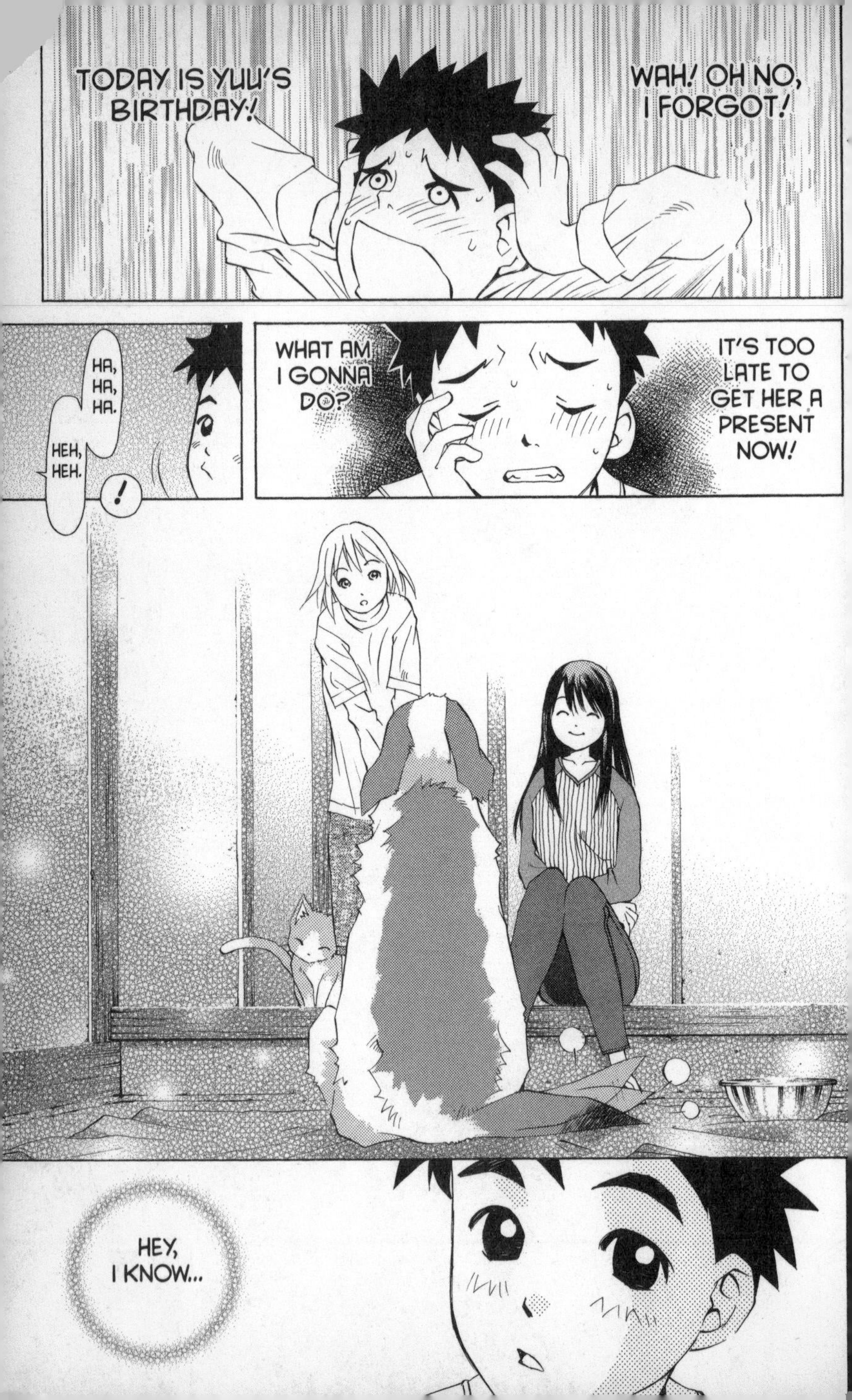
WAH! OH NO, I FORGOT!
TODAY IS YUU'S BIRTHDAY!
IT'S TOO LATE TO GET HER A PRESENT NOW!
WHAT AM I GONNA DO?
HA, HA, HA.
HEH, HEH.
!
HEY, I KNOW...

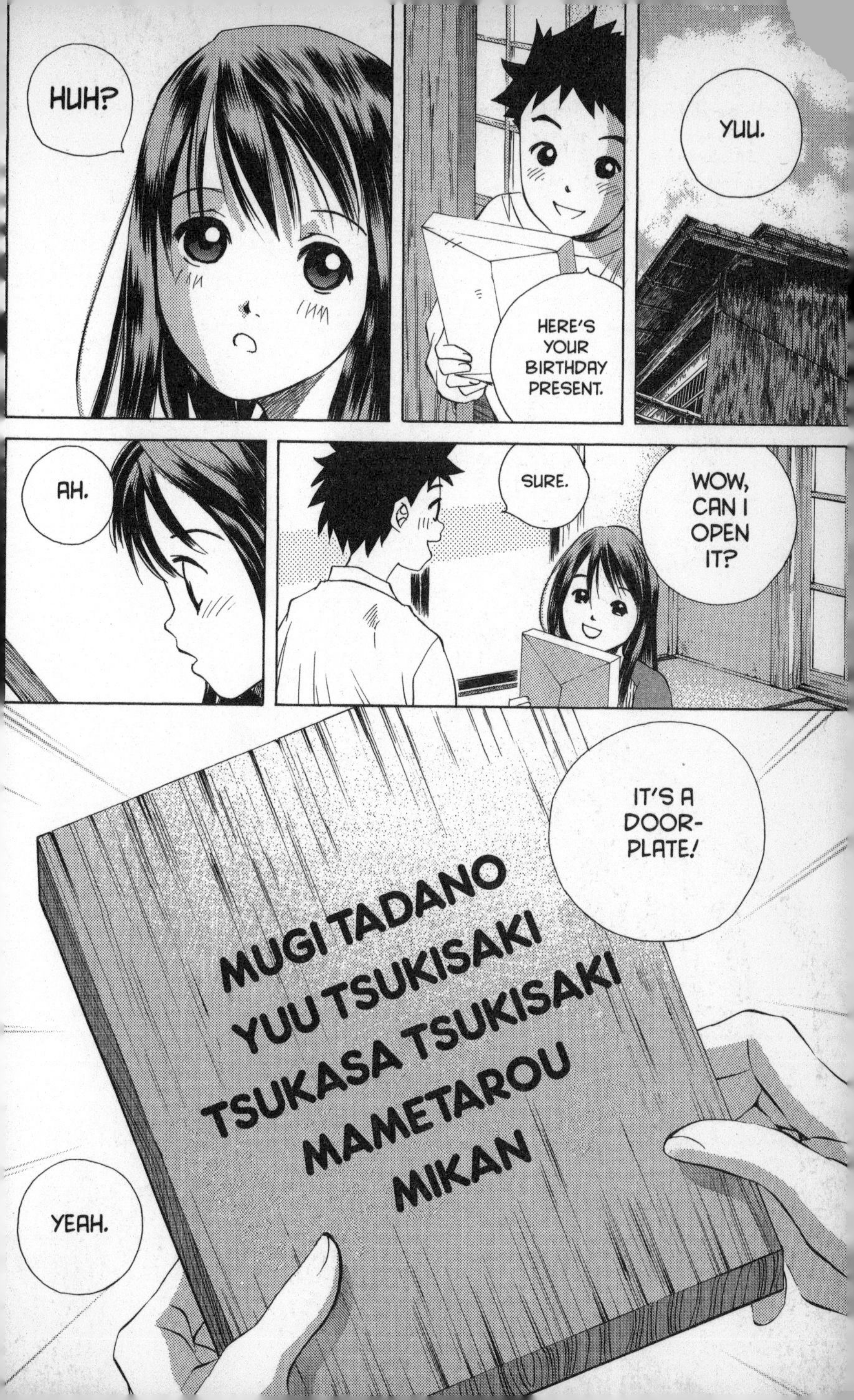
YUU.
HERE'S YOUR BIRTHDAY PRESENT.
HUH?
WOW, CAN I OPEN IT?
SURE.
AH.
IT'S A DOOR-PLATE!
MUGI TADANO
YUU TSUKISAKI
TSUKASA TSUKISAKI
MAMETAROU
MIKAN
YEAH.

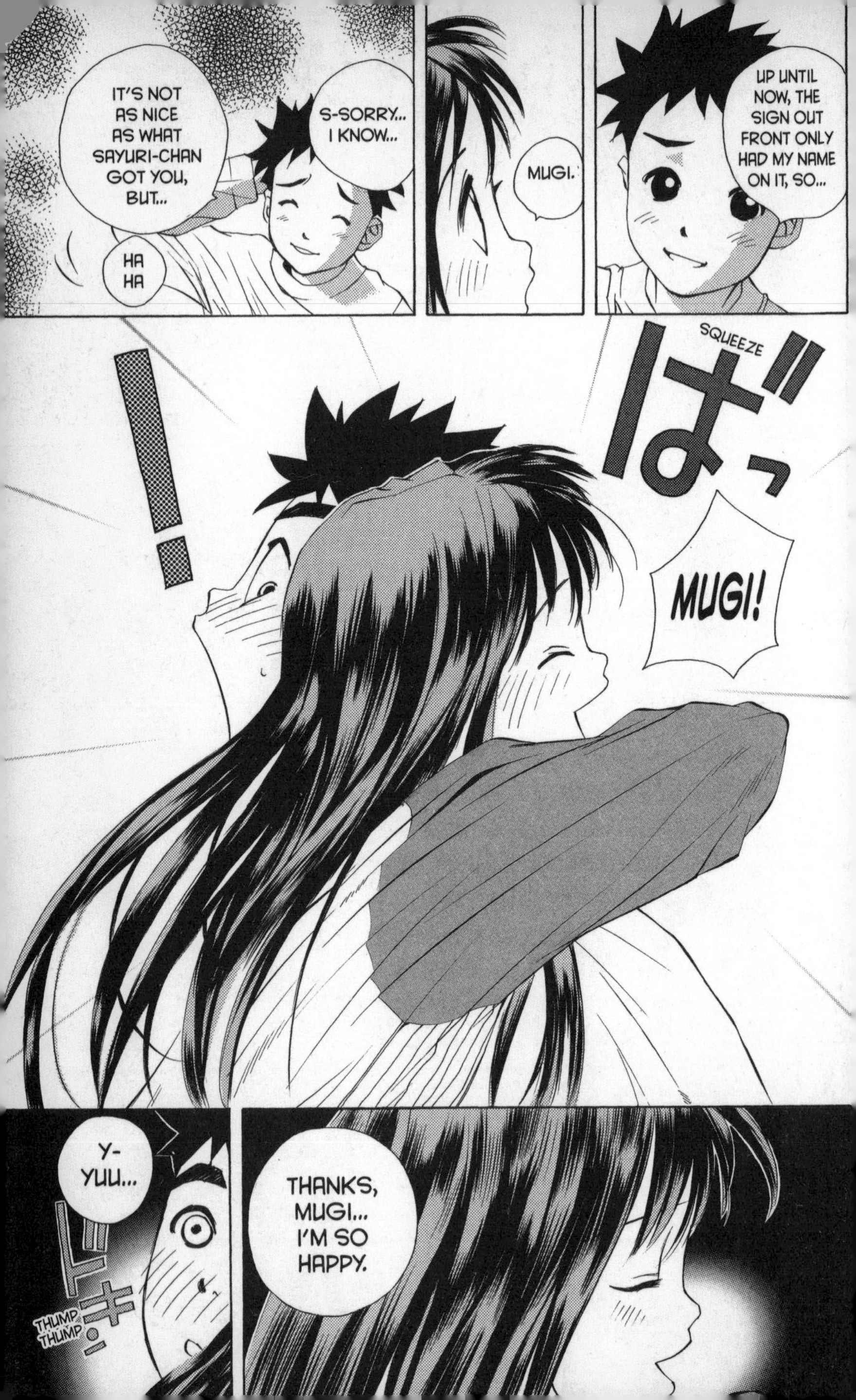
UP UNTIL NOW, THE SIGN OUT FRONT ONLY HAD MY NAME ON IT, SO...
MUGI.
S-SORRY... I KNOW...
IT'S NOT AS NICE AS WHAT SAYURI-CHAN GOT YOU, BUT...
HA HA
ばっ
SQUEEZE
MUGI!
!!
THANKS, MUGI... I'M SO HAPPY.
Y-YUU...
ドキ
THUMP THUMP

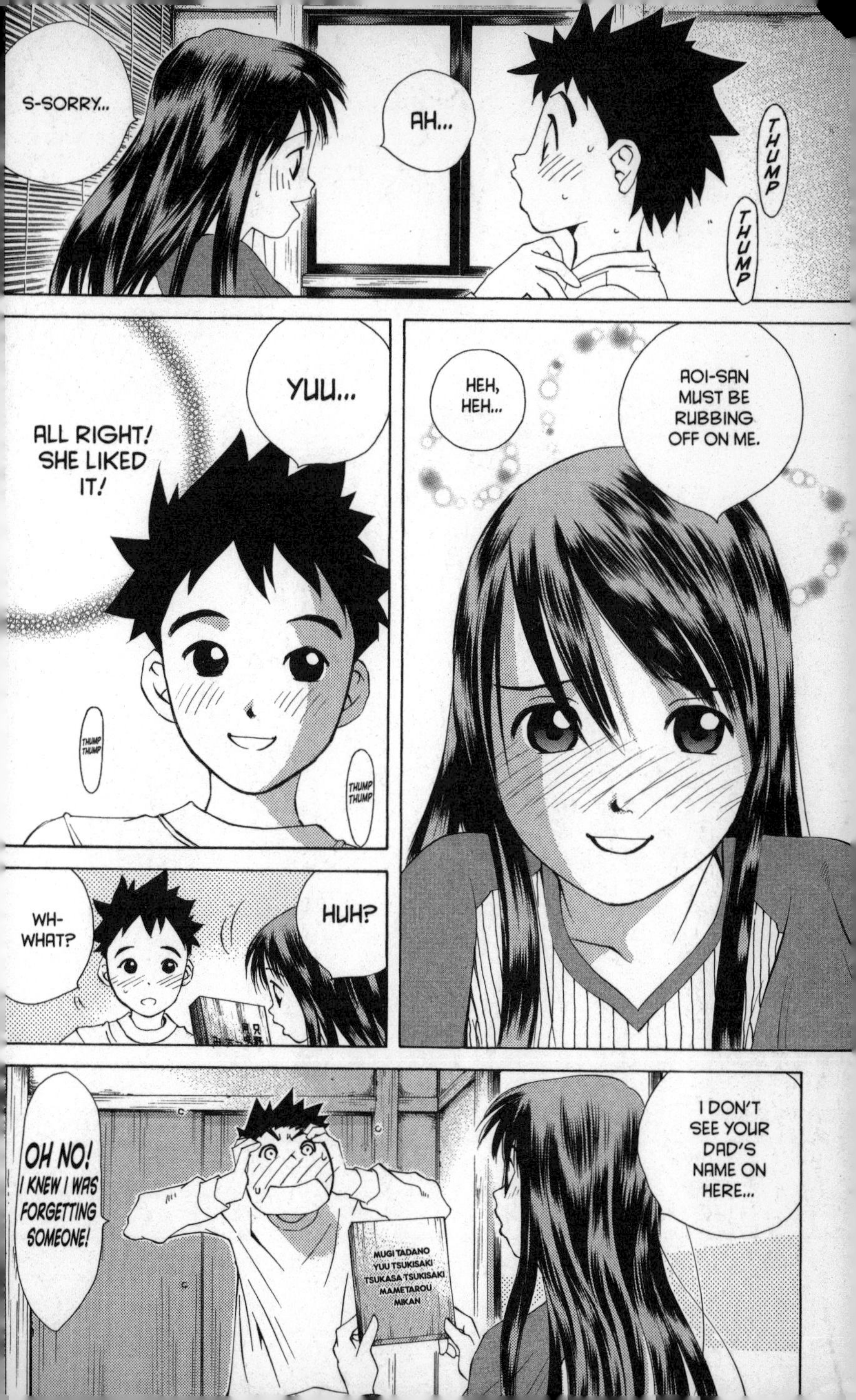
THUMP
THUMP
AH...
S-SORRY...
AOI-SAN MUST BE RUBBING OFF ON ME.
HEH, HEH...
YUU...
ALL RIGHT! SHE LIKED IT!
THUMP THUMP
THUMP THUMP
HUH?
WH-WHAT?
I DON'T SEE YOUR DAD'S NAME ON HERE...
MUGI TADANO
YUU TSUKISAKI
TSUKASA TSUKISAKI
MAMETAROU
MIKAN
OH NO! I KNEW I WAS FORGETTING SOMEONE!

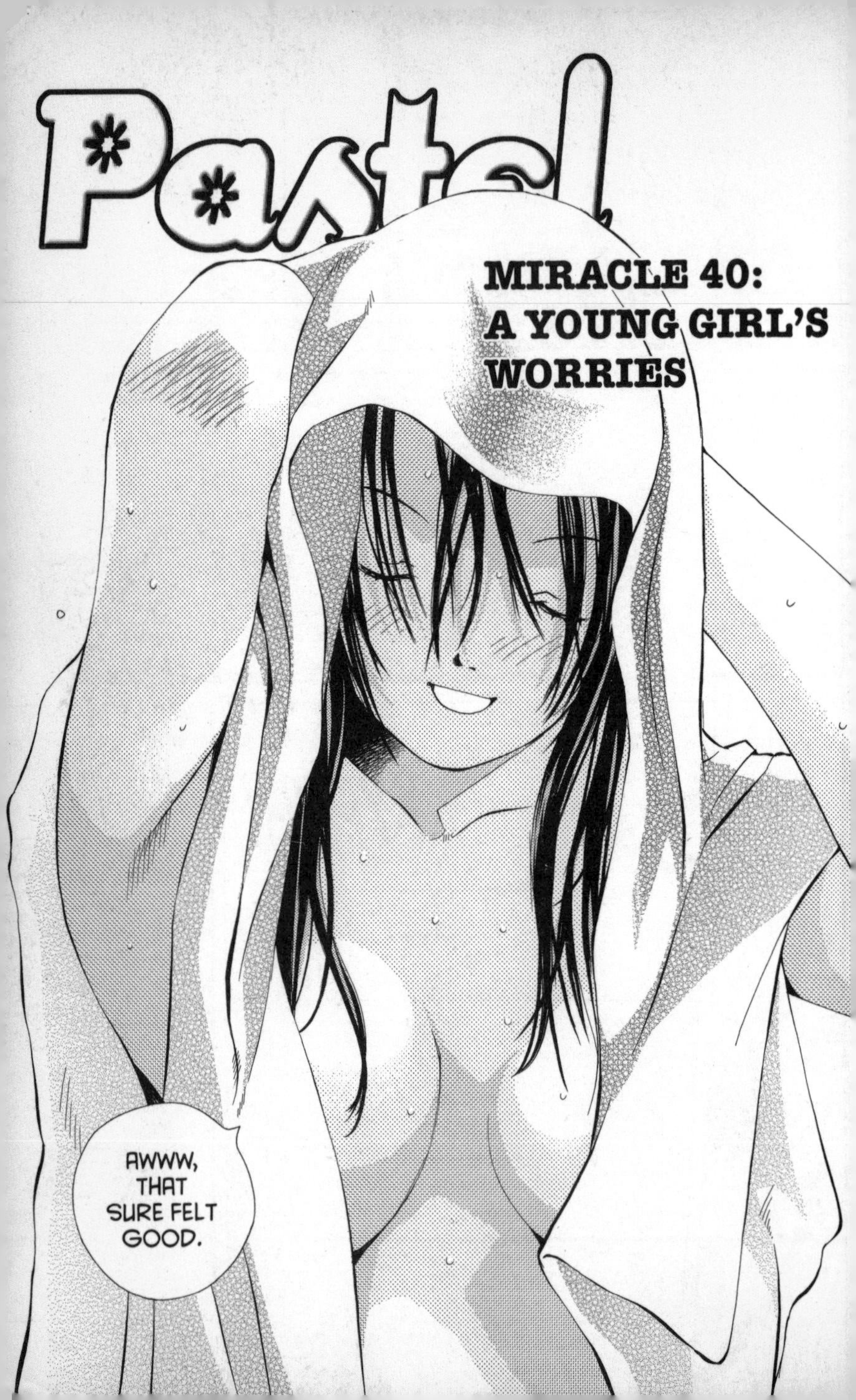
Pastel
MIRACLE 40: A YOUNG GIRL'S WORRIES
AWWW, THAT SURE FELT GOOD.

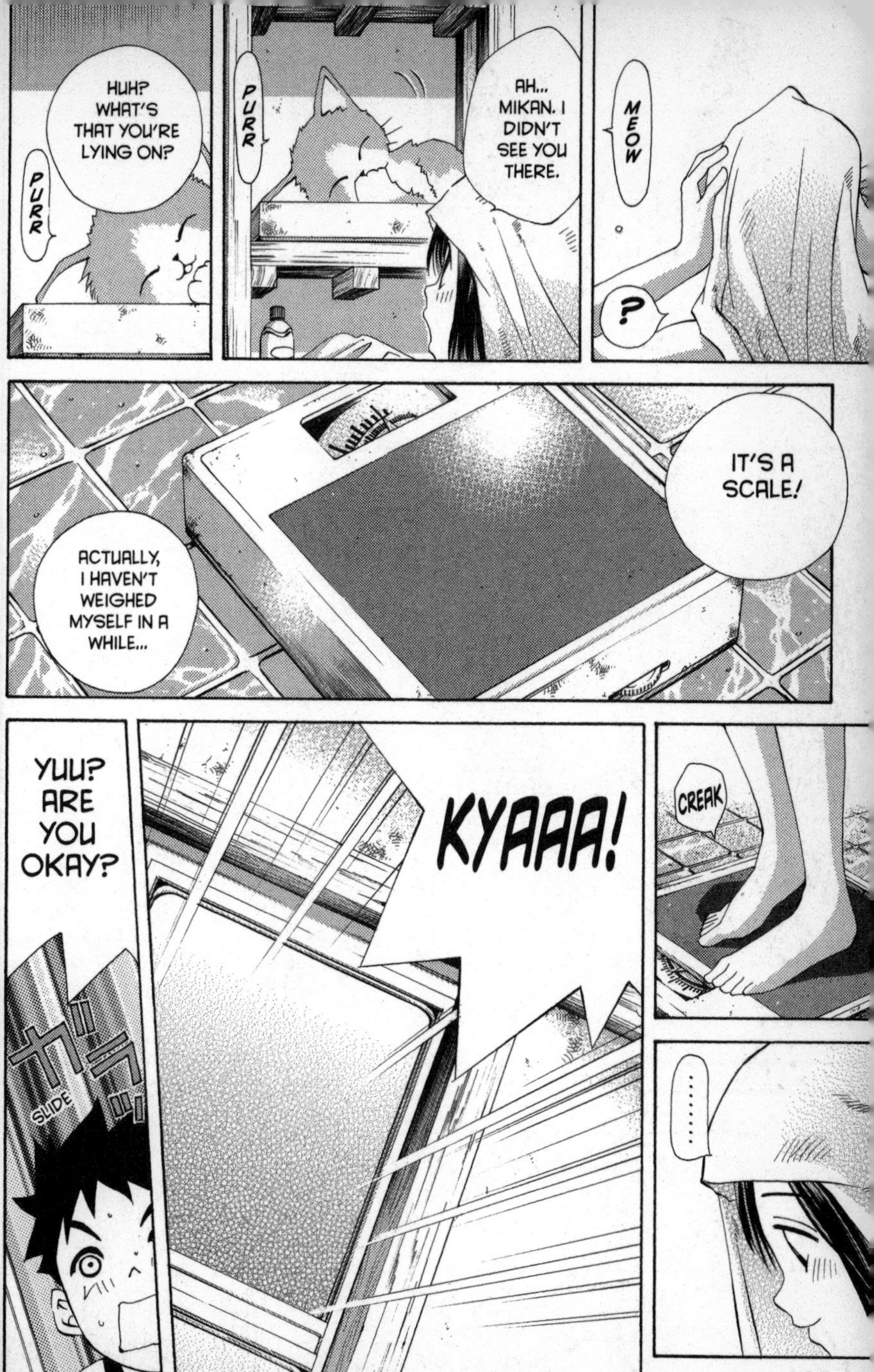
MEOW
?
AH... MIKAN. I DIDN'T SEE YOU THERE.
PURR
HUH? WHAT'S THAT YOU'RE LYING ON?
PURR
IT'S A SCALE!
ACTUALLY, I HAVEN'T WEIGHED MYSELF IN A WHILE...
CREAK
....
KYAAA!
YUU? ARE YOU OKAY?
SLIDE

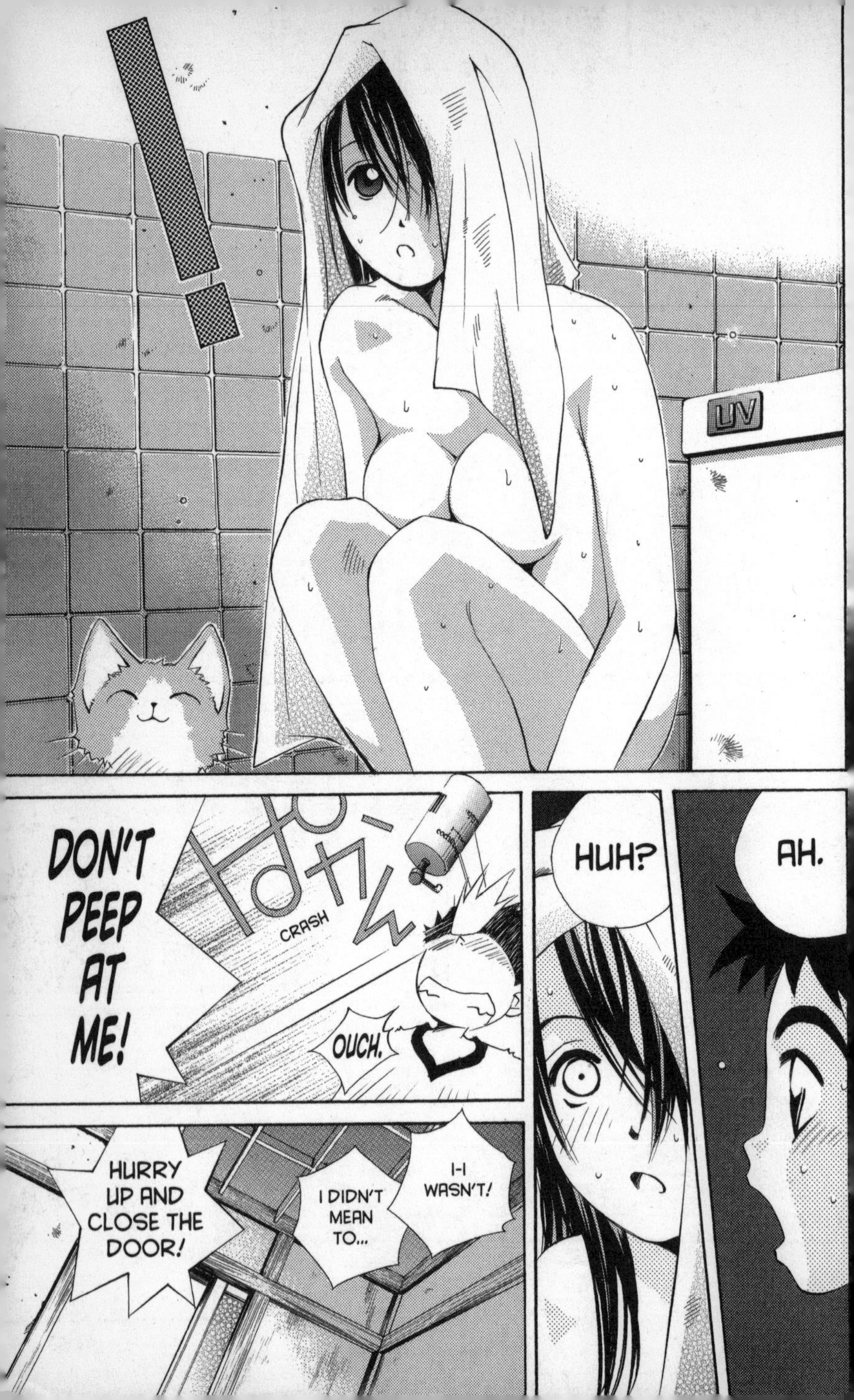
!
AH.
HUH?
DON'T PEEP AT ME!
CRASH
OUCH.
I-I WASN'T!
I DIDN'T MEAN TO...
HURRY UP AND CLOSE THE DOOR!

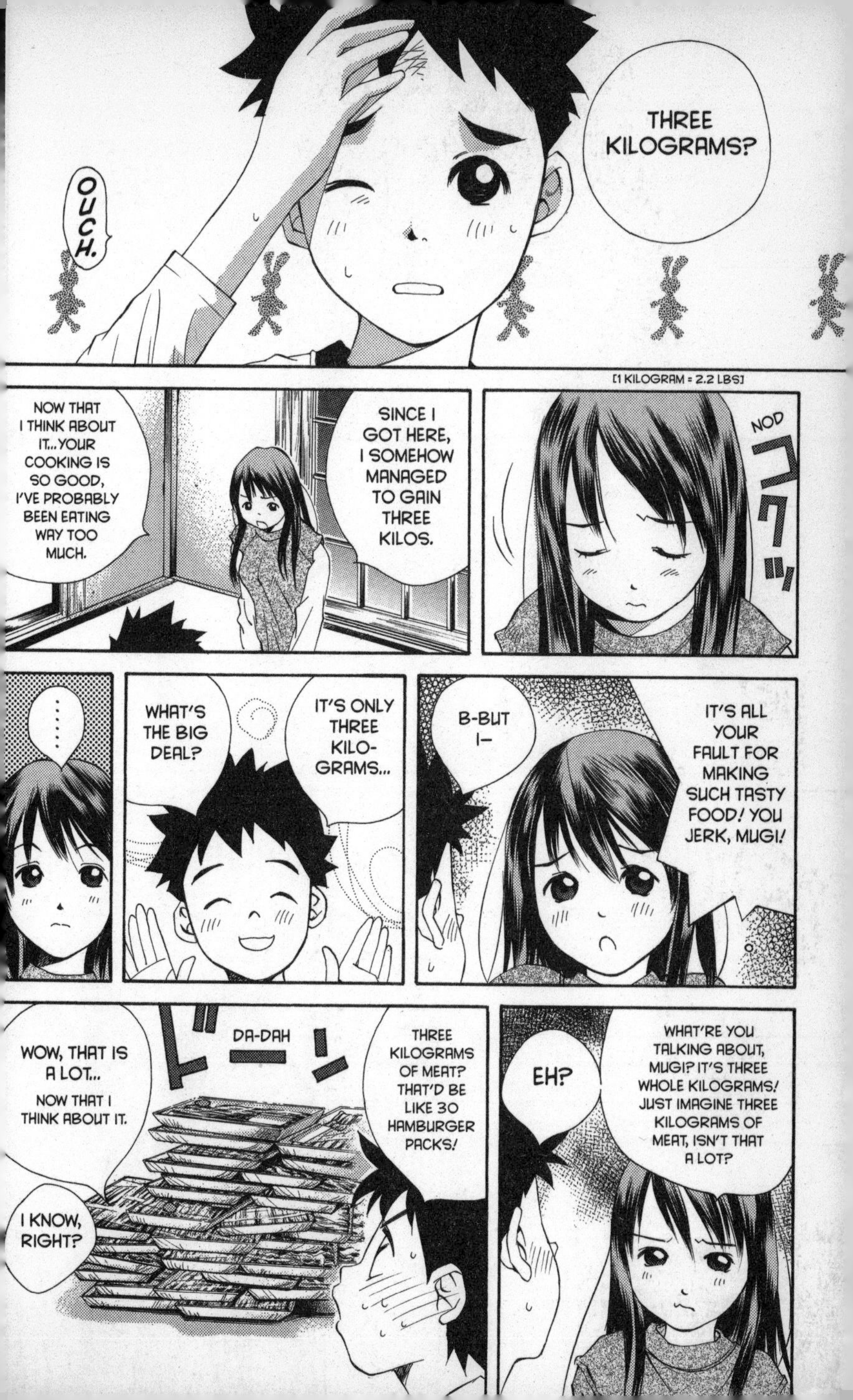
THREE KILOGRAMS?
OUCH.
[1 KILOGRAM = 2.2 LBS]
NOD
SINCE I GOT HERE, I SOMEHOW MANAGED TO GAIN THREE KILOS.
NOW THAT I THINK ABOUT IT...YOUR COOKING IS SO GOOD, I'VE PROBABLY BEEN EATING WAY TOO MUCH.
IT'S ALL YOUR FAULT FOR MAKING SUCH TASTY FOOD! YOU JERK, MUGI!
B-BUT I—
IT'S ONLY THREE KILO-GRAMS...
WHAT'S THE BIG DEAL?
......
WHAT'RE YOU TALKING ABOUT, MUGI? IT'S THREE WHOLE KILOGRAMS! JUST IMAGINE THREE KILOGRAMS OF MEAT, ISN'T THAT A LOT?
EH?
THREE KILOGRAMS OF MEAT? THAT'D BE LIKE 30 HAMBURGER PACKS!
DA-DAH
WOW, THAT IS A LOT...
NOW THAT I THINK ABOUT IT.
I KNOW, RIGHT?

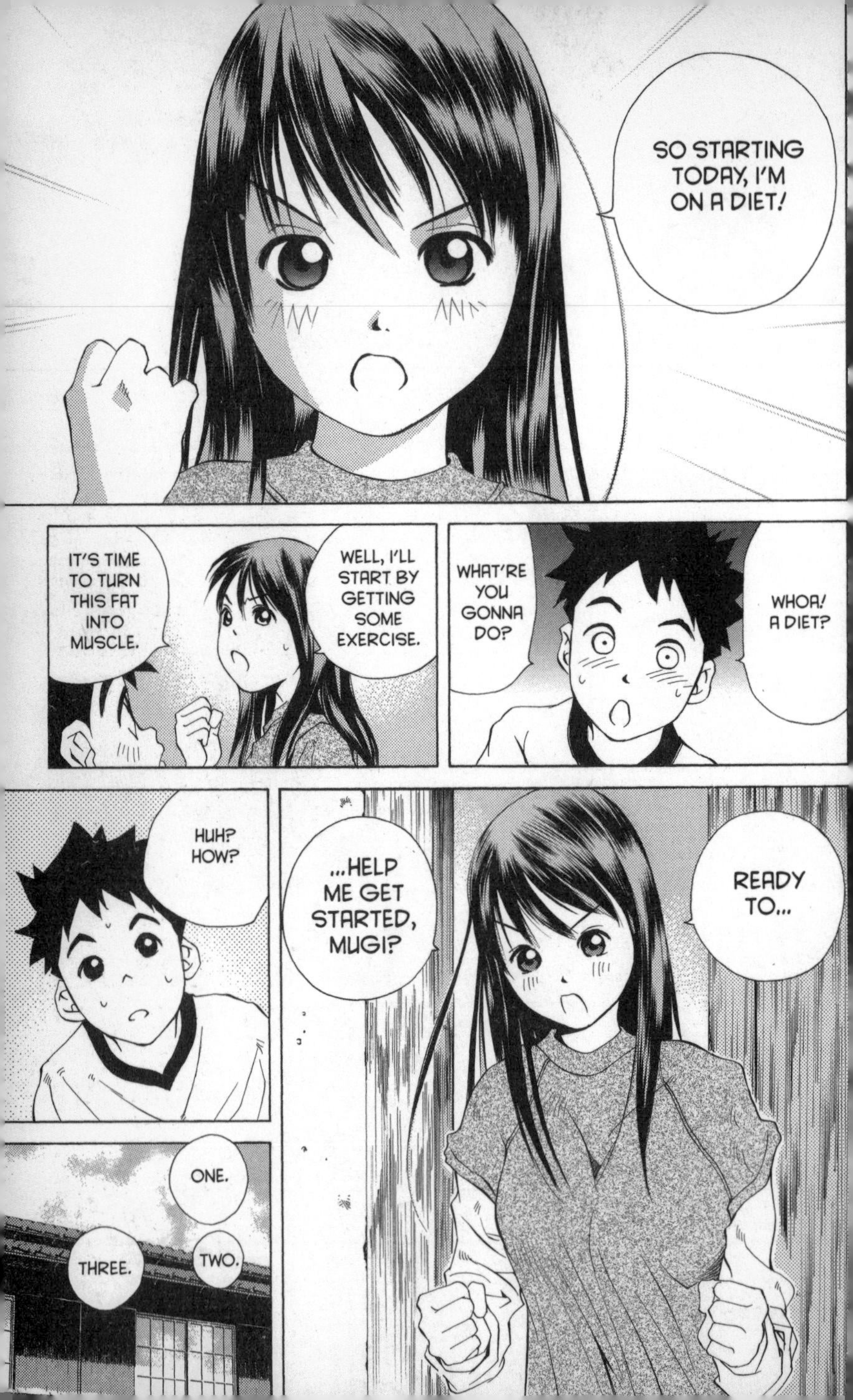
SO STARTING TODAY, I'M ON A DIET!
WHOA! A DIET?
WHAT'RE YOU GONNA DO?
WELL, I'LL START BY GETTING SOME EXERCISE.
IT'S TIME TO TURN THIS FAT INTO MUSCLE.
READY TO...
...HELP ME GET STARTED, MUGI?
HUH? HOW?
ONE.
TWO.
THREE.

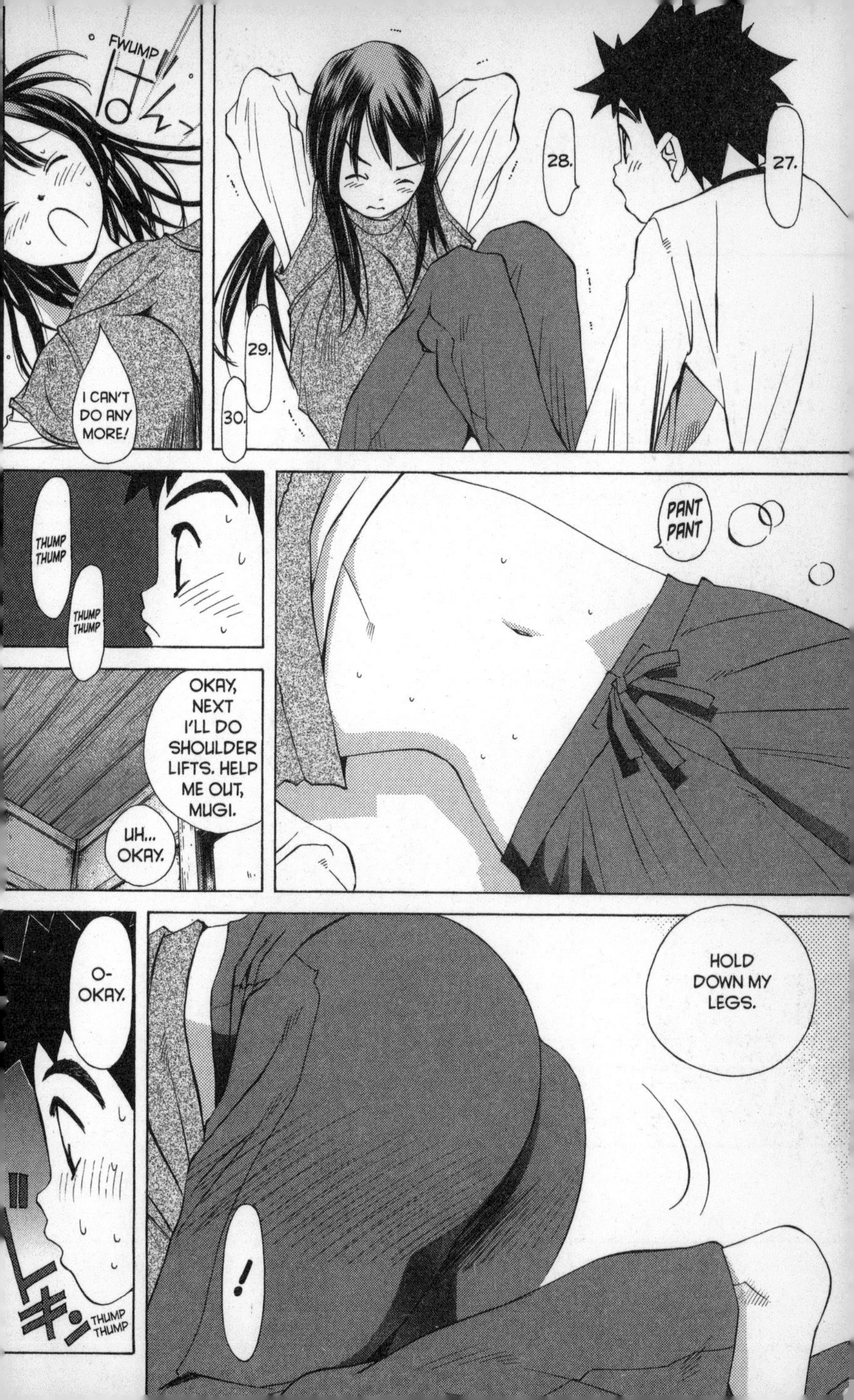
27.
28.
29.
30.
FWUMP
I CAN'T DO ANY MORE!
PANT PANT
THUMP THUMP
THUMP THUMP
OKAY, NEXT I'LL DO SHOULDER LIFTS. HELP ME OUT, MUGI.
UH... OKAY.
HOLD DOWN MY LEGS.
!
O-OKAY.
THUMP THUMP

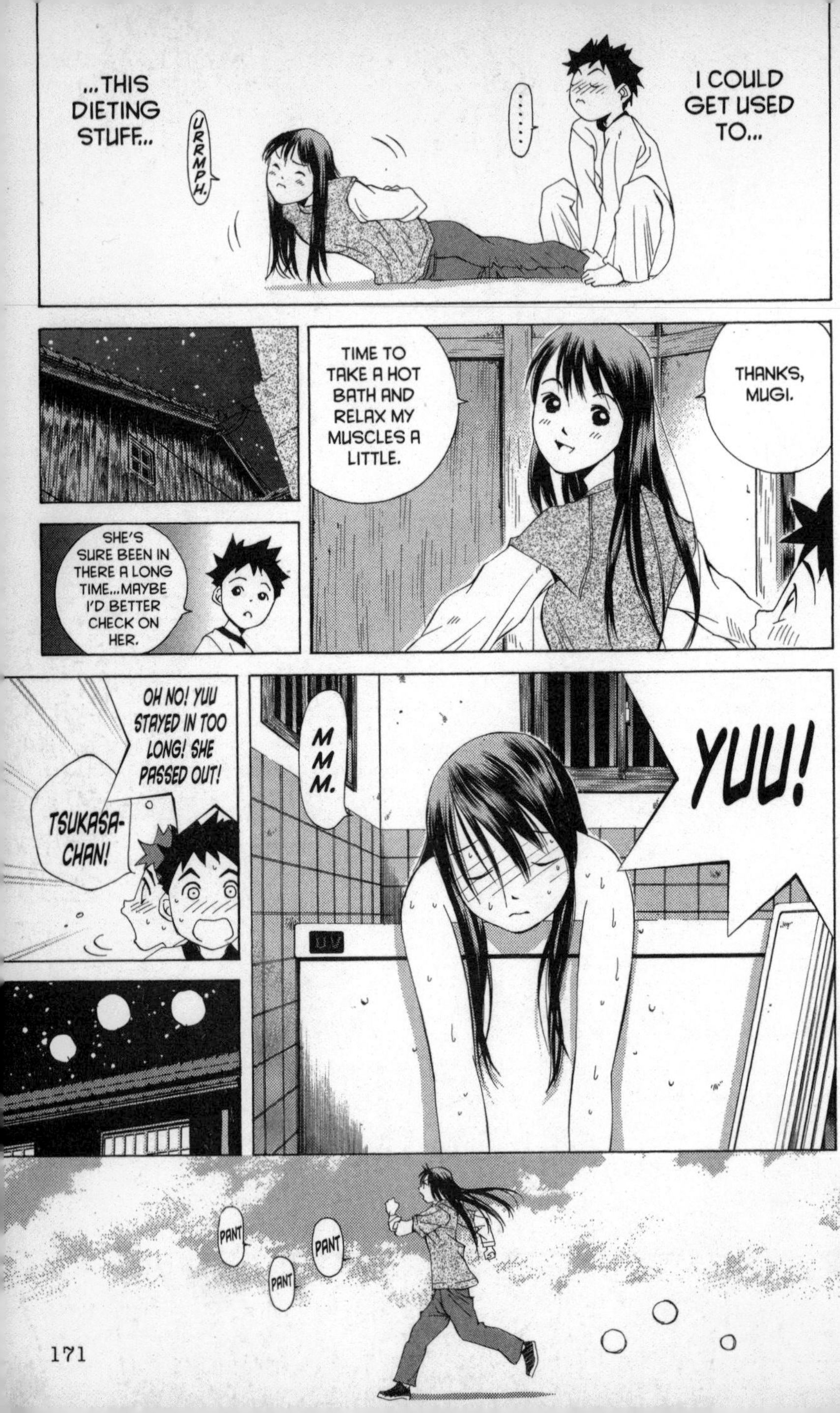
I COULD GET USED TO...
......
URRMPH.
...THIS DIETING STUFF...
THANKS, MUGI.
TIME TO TAKE A HOT BATH AND RELAX MY MUSCLES A LITTLE.
SHE'S SURE BEEN IN THERE A LONG TIME...MAYBE I'D BETTER CHECK ON HER.
YUU!
MMM.
OH NO! YUU STAYED IN TOO LONG! SHE PASSED OUT!
TSUKASA-CHAN!
PANT
PANT
PANT

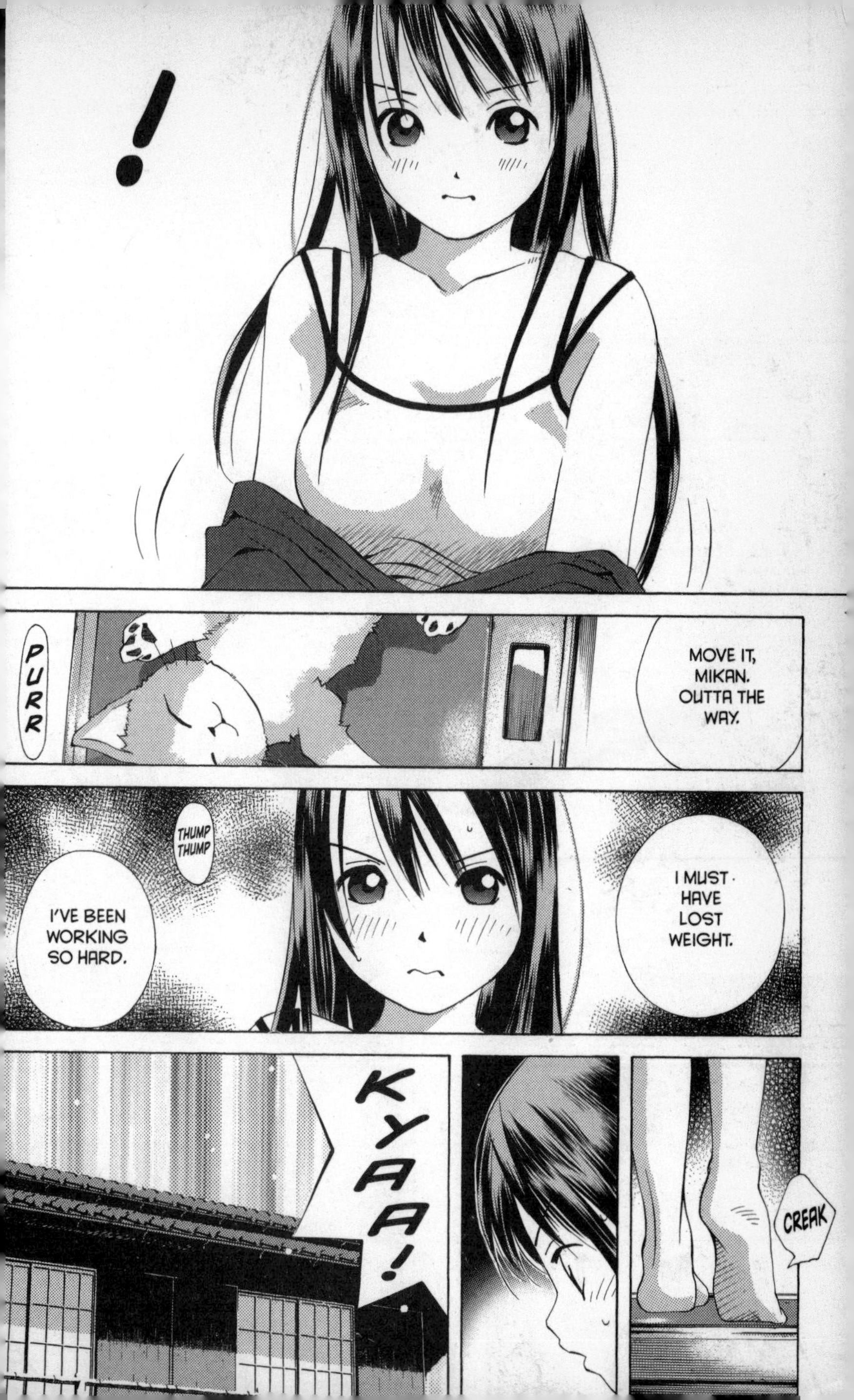
!
MOVE IT, MIKAN. OUTTA THE WAY.
PURR
I MUST HAVE LOST WEIGHT.
THUMP THUMP
I'VE BEEN WORKING SO HARD.
CREAK
KYAAA!

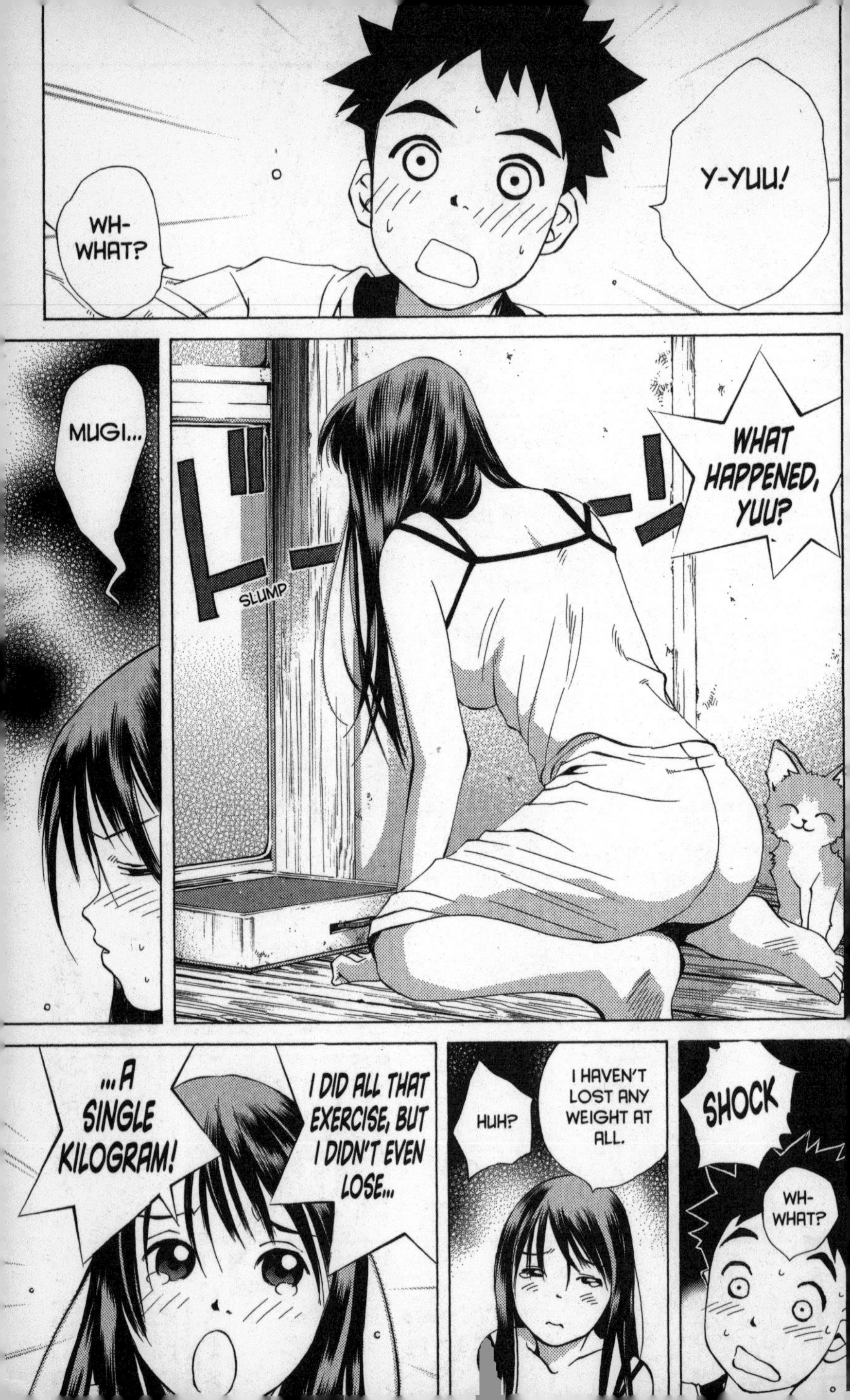

Y-YUU!
WH-WHAT?
WHAT HAPPENED, YUU?
SLUMP
MUGI...
SHOCK
WH-WHAT?
I HAVEN'T LOST ANY WEIGHT AT ALL.
HUH?
I DID ALL THAT EXERCISE, BUT I DIDN'T EVEN LOSE...
...A SINGLE KILOGRAM!

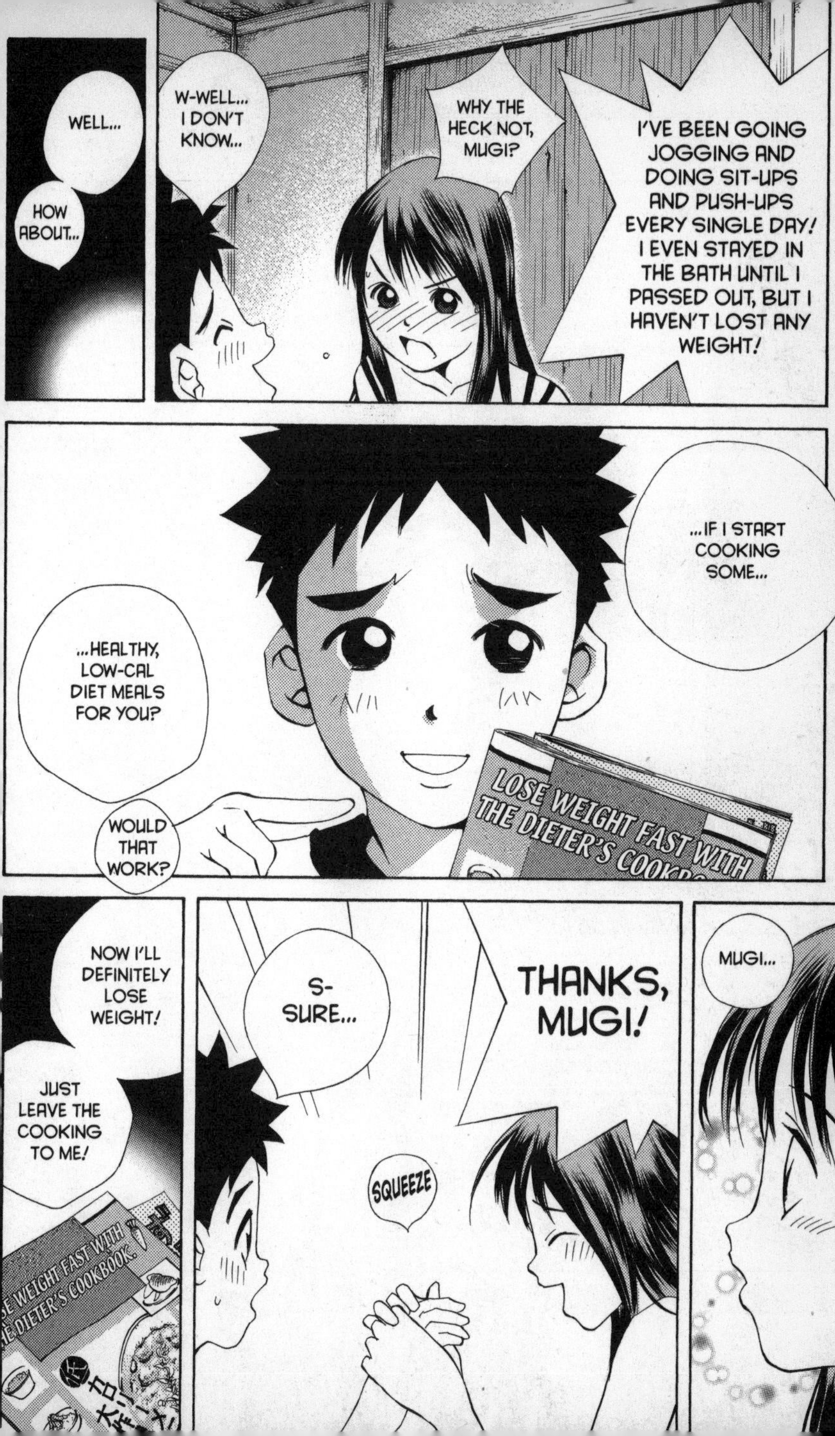
I'VE BEEN GOING JOGGING AND DOING SIT-UPS AND PUSH-UPS EVERY SINGLE DAY! I EVEN STAYED IN THE BATH UNTIL I PASSED OUT, BUT I HAVEN'T LOST ANY WEIGHT!
WHY THE HECK NOT, MUGI?
W-WELL... I DON'T KNOW...
WELL...
HOW ABOUT...
...IF I START COOKING SOME...
...HEALTHY, LOW-CAL DIET MEALS FOR YOU?
LOSE WEIGHT FAST WITH THE DIETER'S
WOULD THAT WORK?
MUGI...
THANKS, MUGI!
S- SURE...
SQUEEZE
NOW I'LL DEFINITELY LOSE WEIGHT!
JUST LEAVE THE COOKING TO ME!

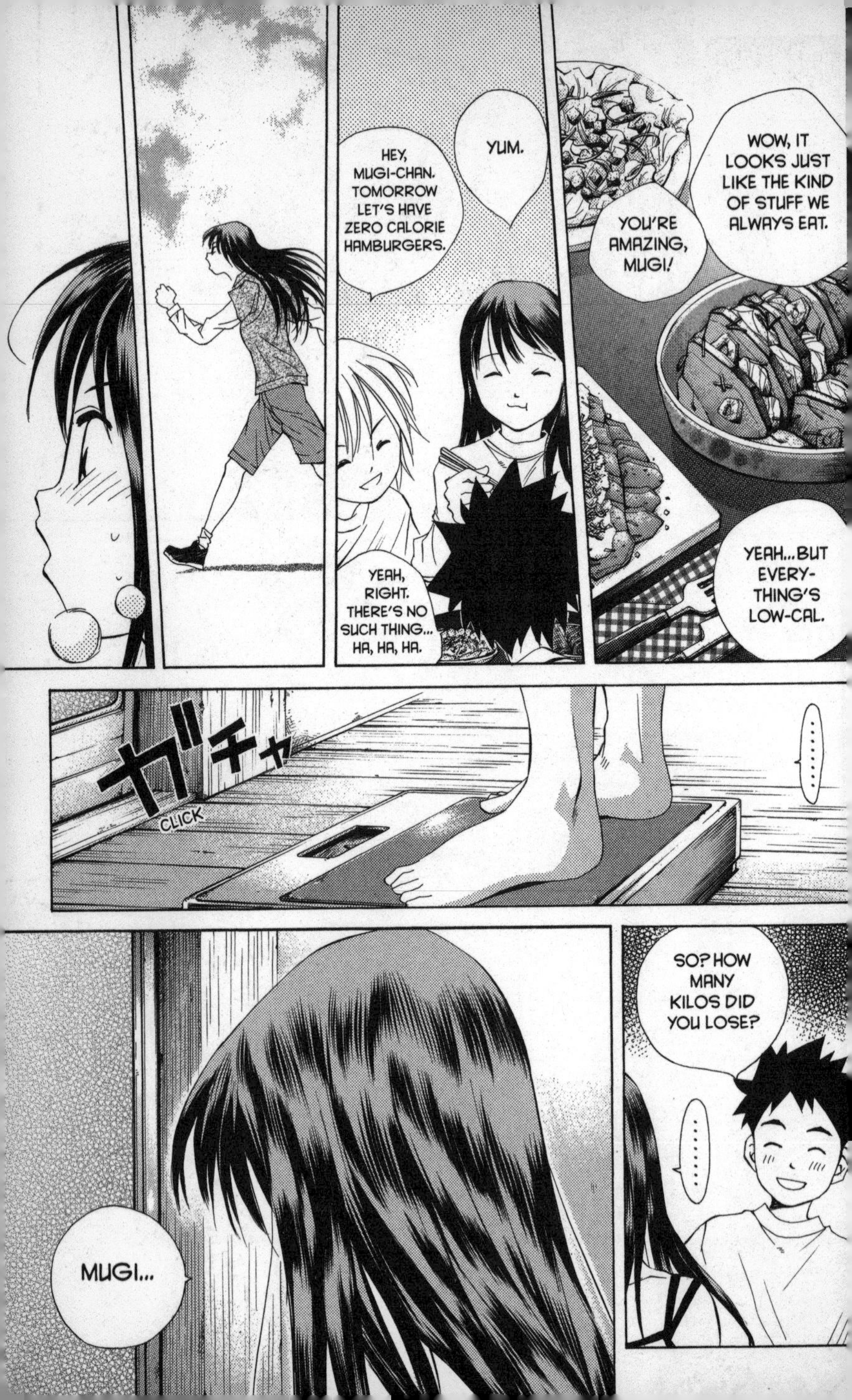
WOW, IT LOOKS JUST LIKE THE KIND OF STUFF WE ALWAYS EAT.
YOU'RE AMAZING, MUGI!
YEAH...BUT EVERY-THING'S LOW-CAL.
YUM.
HEY, MUGI-CHAN. TOMORROW LET'S HAVE ZERO CALORIE HAMBURGERS.
YEAH, RIGHT. THERE'S NO SUCH THING... HA, HA, HA.
......
ガチャ
CLICK
SO? HOW MANY KILOS DID YOU LOSE?
......
MUGI...

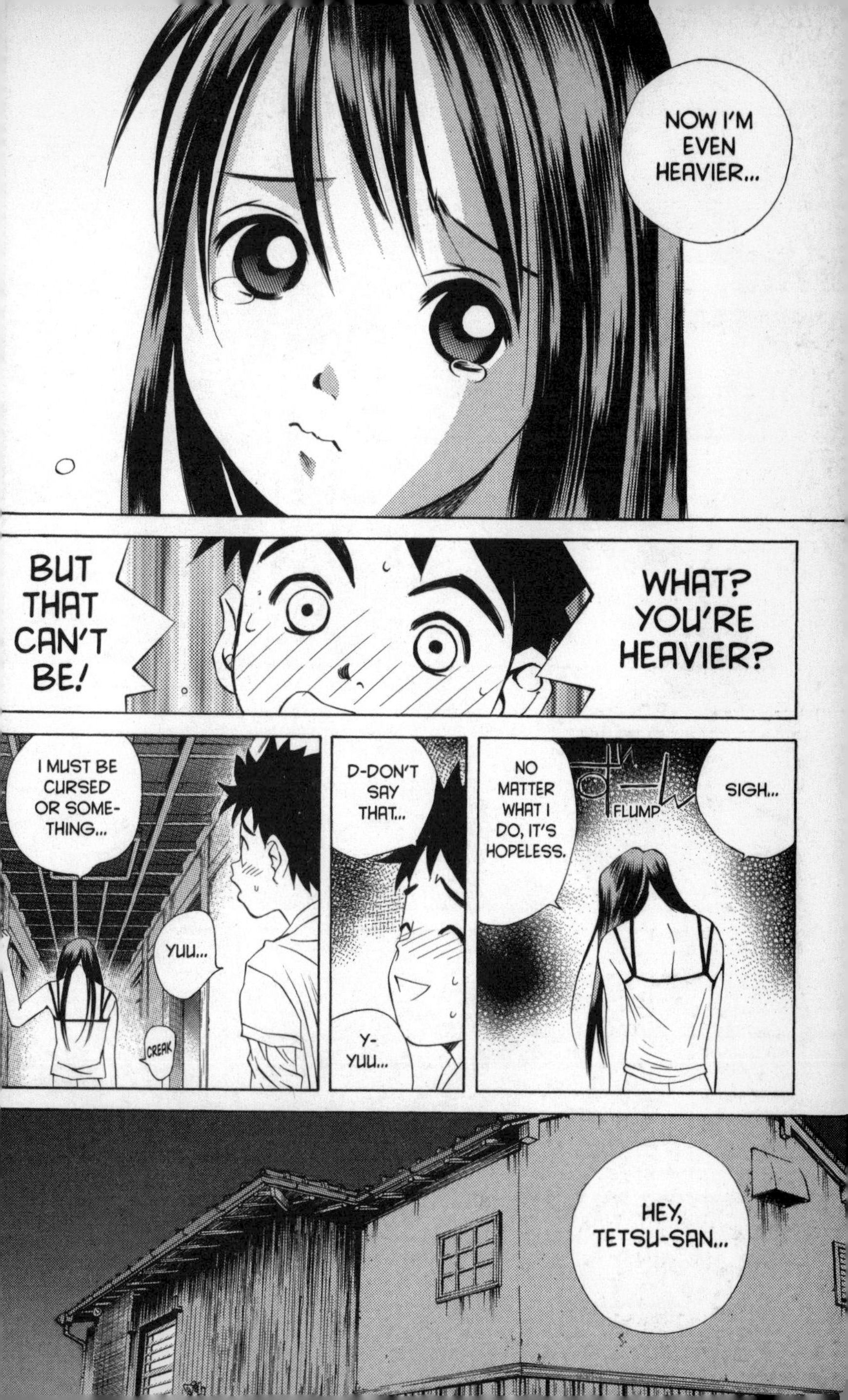
NOW I'M EVEN HEAVIER...
WHAT? YOU'RE HEAVIER?
BUT THAT CAN'T BE!
SIGH...
FLUMP
NO MATTER WHAT I DO, IT'S HOPELESS.
D-DON'T SAY THAT...
Y-YUU...
I MUST BE CURSED OR SOME-THING...
YUU...
CREAK
HEY, TETSU-SAN...

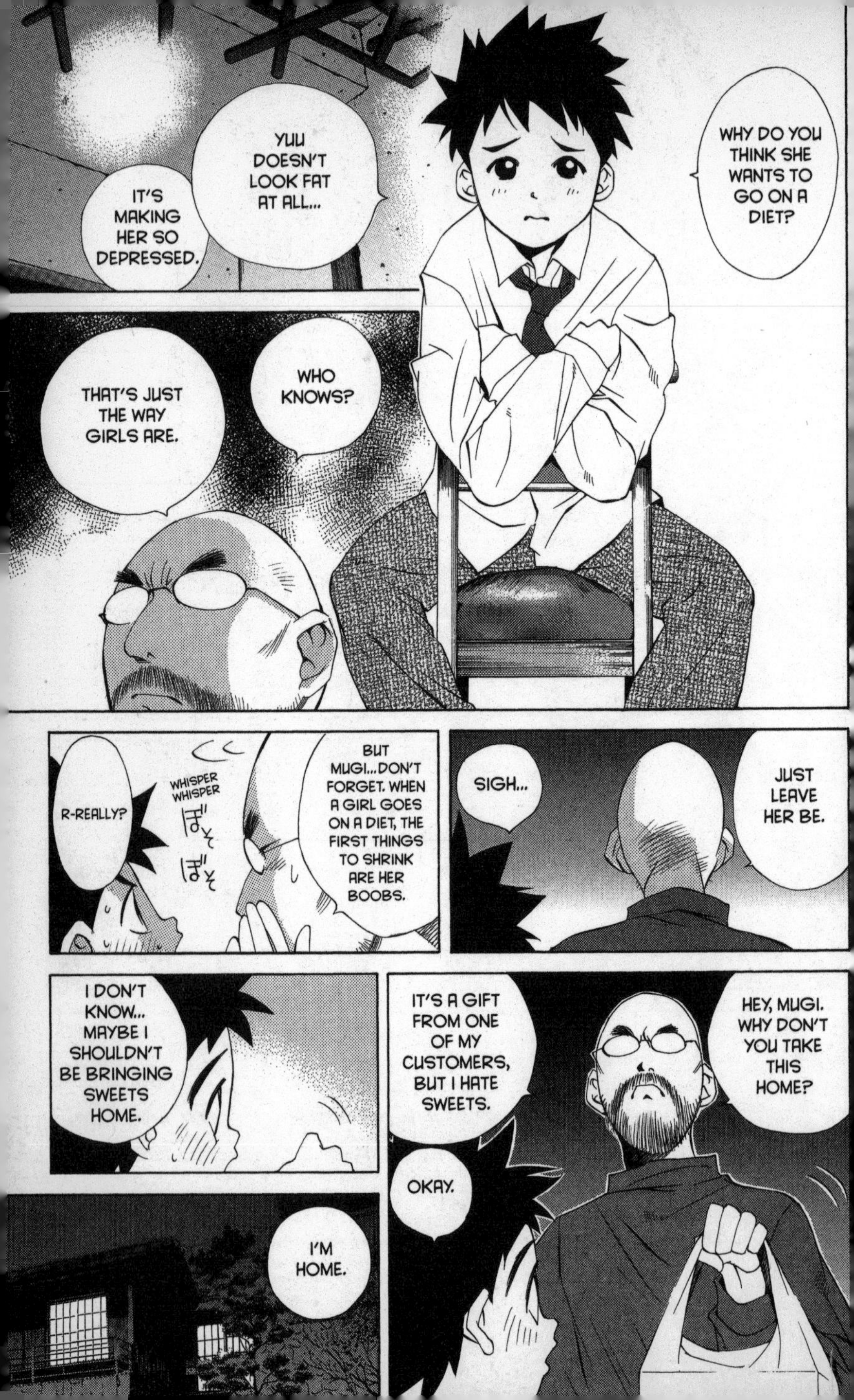
WHY DO YOU THINK SHE WANTS TO GO ON A DIET?
YUU DOESN'T LOOK FAT AT ALL...
IT'S MAKING HER SO DEPRESSED.
WHO KNOWS?
THAT'S JUST THE WAY GIRLS ARE.
JUST LEAVE HER BE.
SIGH...
BUT MUGI...DON'T FORGET. WHEN A GIRL GOES ON A DIET, THE FIRST THINGS TO SHRINK ARE HER BOOBS.
WHISPER WHISPER
ぼそぼそ
R-REALLY?
HEY, MUGI. WHY DON'T YOU TAKE THIS HOME?
IT'S A GIFT FROM ONE OF MY CUSTOMERS, BUT I HATE SWEETS.
OKAY.
I DON'T KNOW... MAYBE I SHOULDN'T BE BRINGING SWEETS HOME.
I'M HOME.

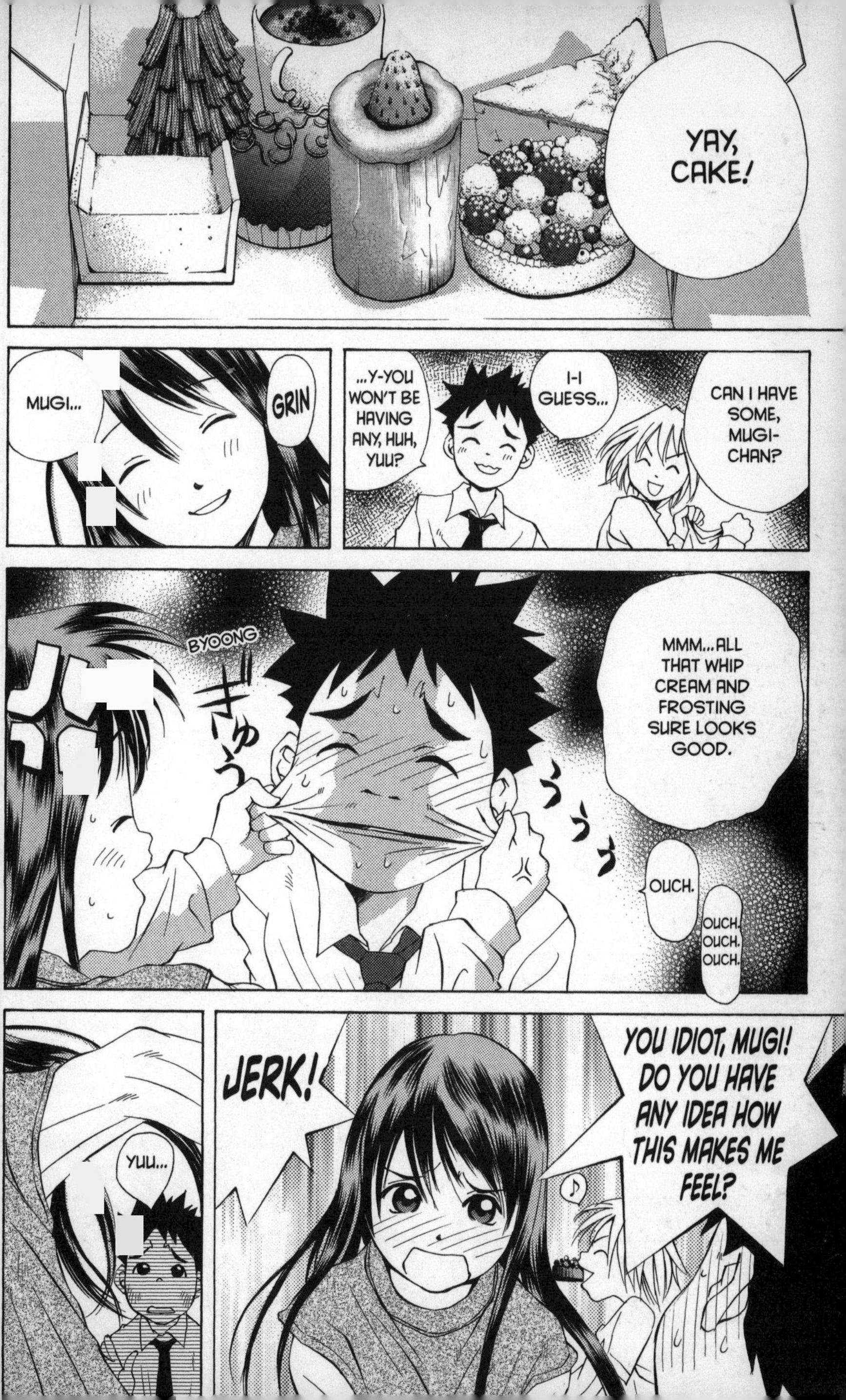
YAY, CAKE!
CAN I HAVE SOME, MUGI-CHAN?
I-I GUESS...
...Y-YOU WON'T BE HAVING ANY, HUH, YUU?
GRIN
MUGI...
MMM...ALL THAT WHIP CREAM AND FROSTING SURE LOOKS GOOD.
BYOONG
OUCH.
OUCH. OUCH. OUCH.
YOU IDIOT, MUGI! DO YOU HAVE ANY IDEA HOW THIS MAKES ME FEEL?
♪
JERK!
YUU...

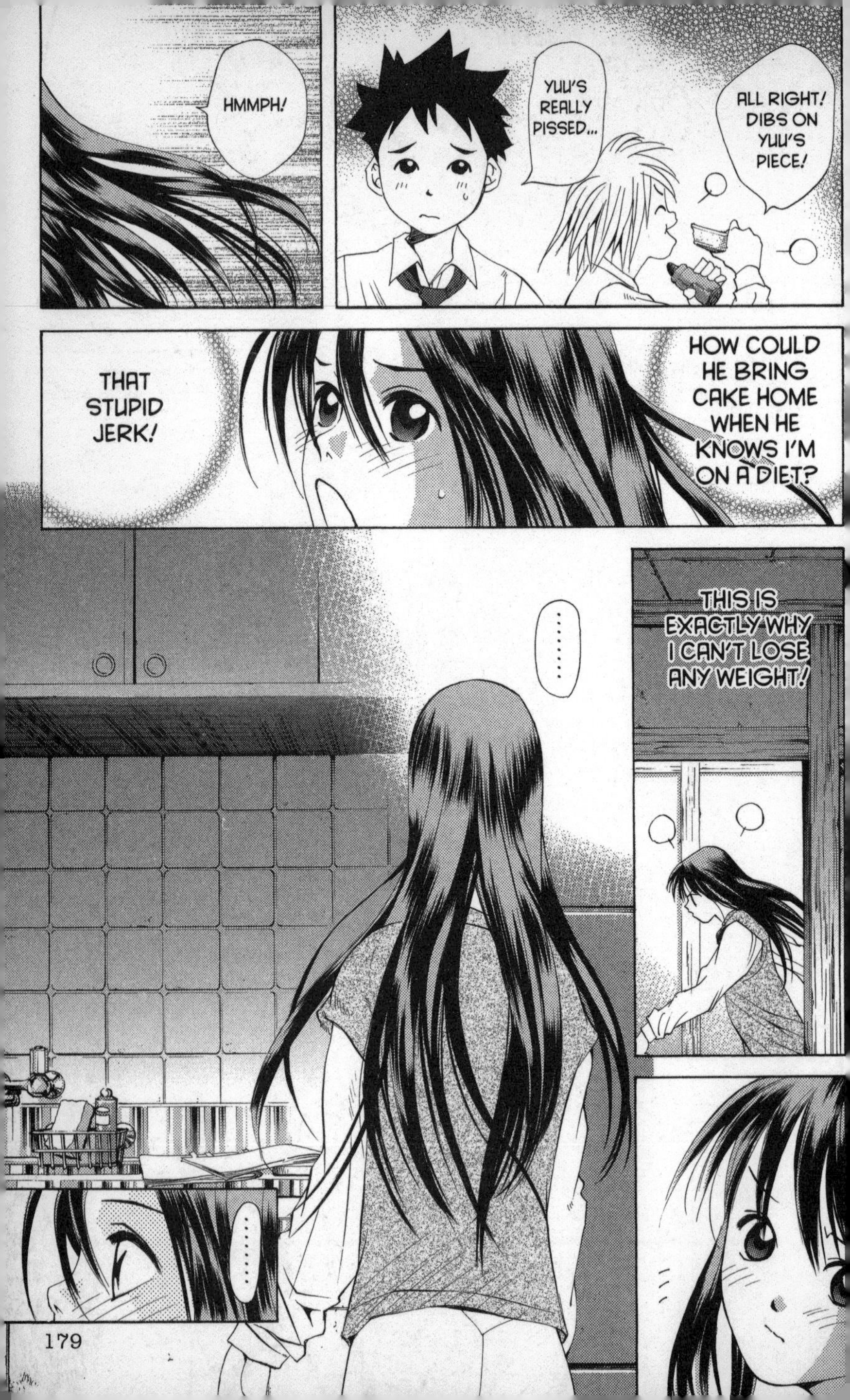
ALL RIGHT! DIBS ON YUU'S PIECE!
YUU'S REALLY PISSED...
HMMPH!
HOW COULD HE BRING CAKE HOME WHEN HE KNOWS I'M ON A DIET?
THAT STUPID JERK!
THIS IS EXACTLY WHY I CAN'T LOSE ANY WEIGHT!
....
....

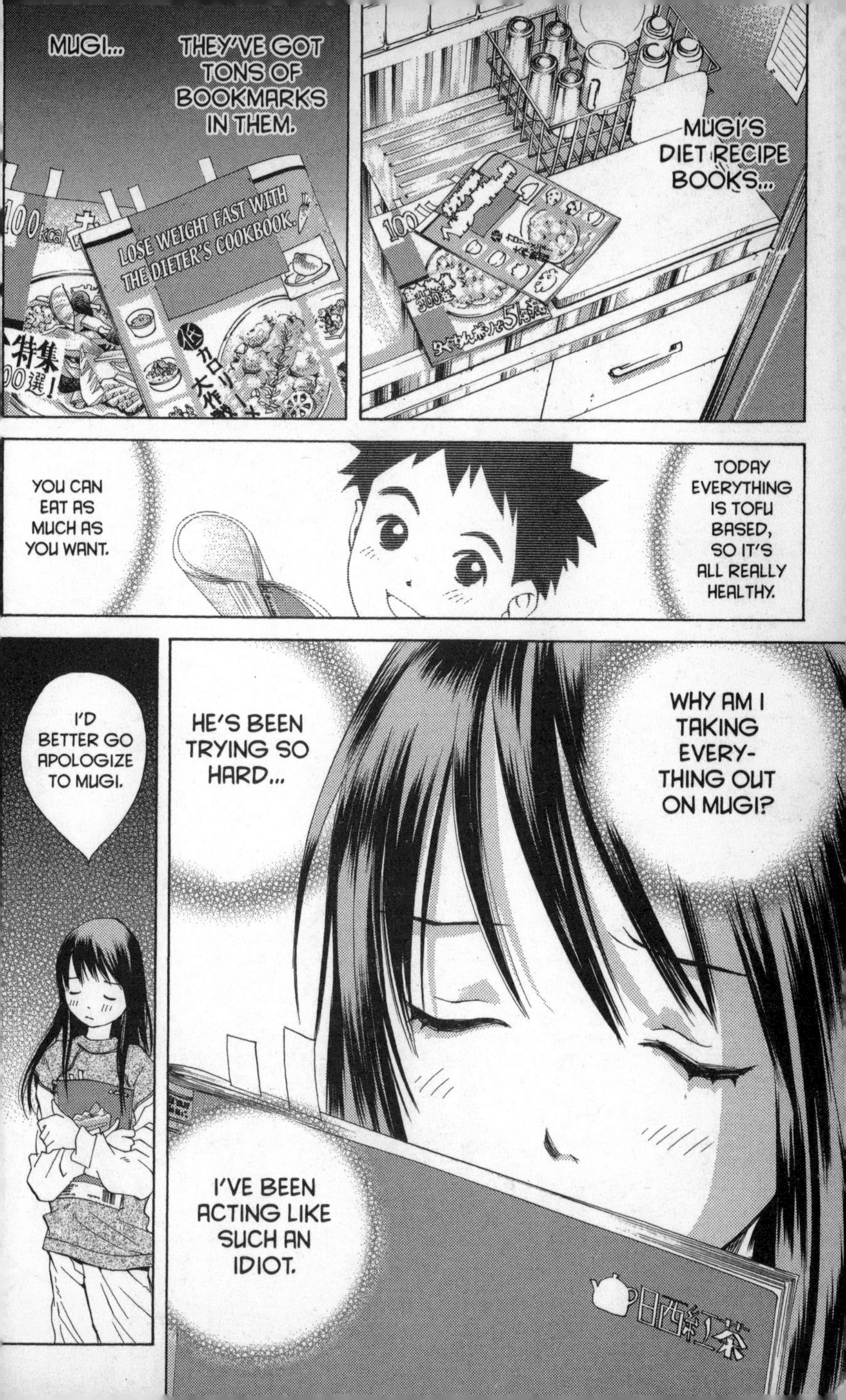
MUGI'S DIET RECIPE BOOKS...
THEY'VE GOT TONS OF BOOKMARKS IN THEM.
MUGI...
LOSE WEIGHT FAST WITH THE DIETER'S COOKBOOK.
TODAY EVERYTHING IS TOFU BASED, SO IT'S ALL REALLY HEALTHY.
YOU CAN EAT AS MUCH AS YOU WANT.
WHY AM I TAKING EVERY-THING OUT ON MUGI?
HE'S BEEN TRYING SO HARD...
I'VE BEEN ACTING LIKE SUCH AN IDIOT.
I'D BETTER GO APOLOGIZE TO MUGI.

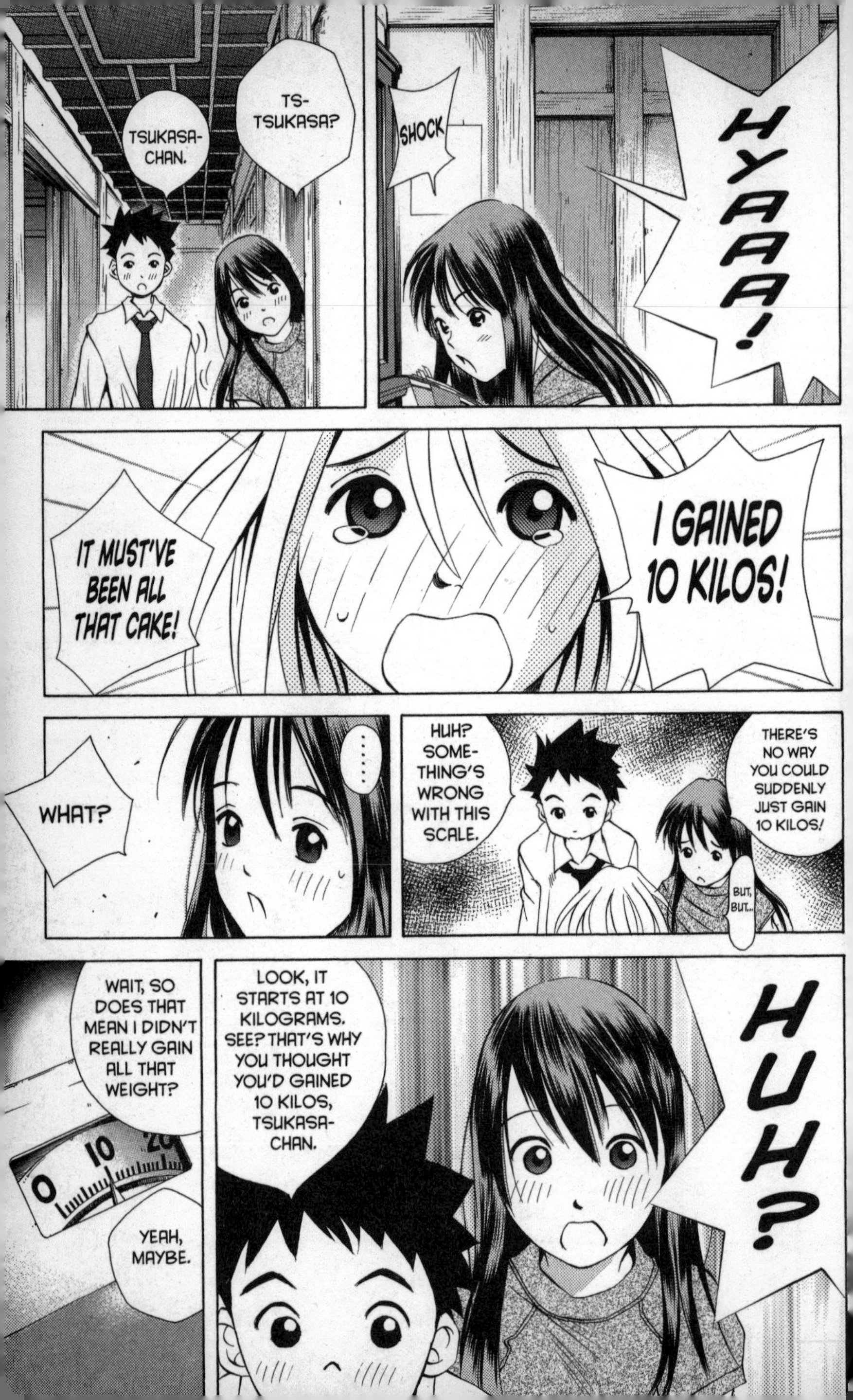
HYAAAA!
SHOCK
TS-TSUKASA?
TSUKASA-CHAN.
I GAINED 10 KILOS!
IT MUST'VE BEEN ALL THAT CAKE!
THERE'S NO WAY YOU COULD SUDDENLY JUST GAIN 10 KILOS!
HUH? SOME-THING'S WRONG WITH THIS SCALE.
BUT, BUT...
......
WHAT?
HUH?
LOOK, IT STARTS AT 10 KILOGRAMS. SEE? THAT'S WHY YOU THOUGHT YOU'D GAINED 10 KILOS, TSUKASA-CHAN.
WAIT, SO DOES THAT MEAN I DIDN'T REALLY GAIN ALL THAT WEIGHT?
YEAH, MAYBE.

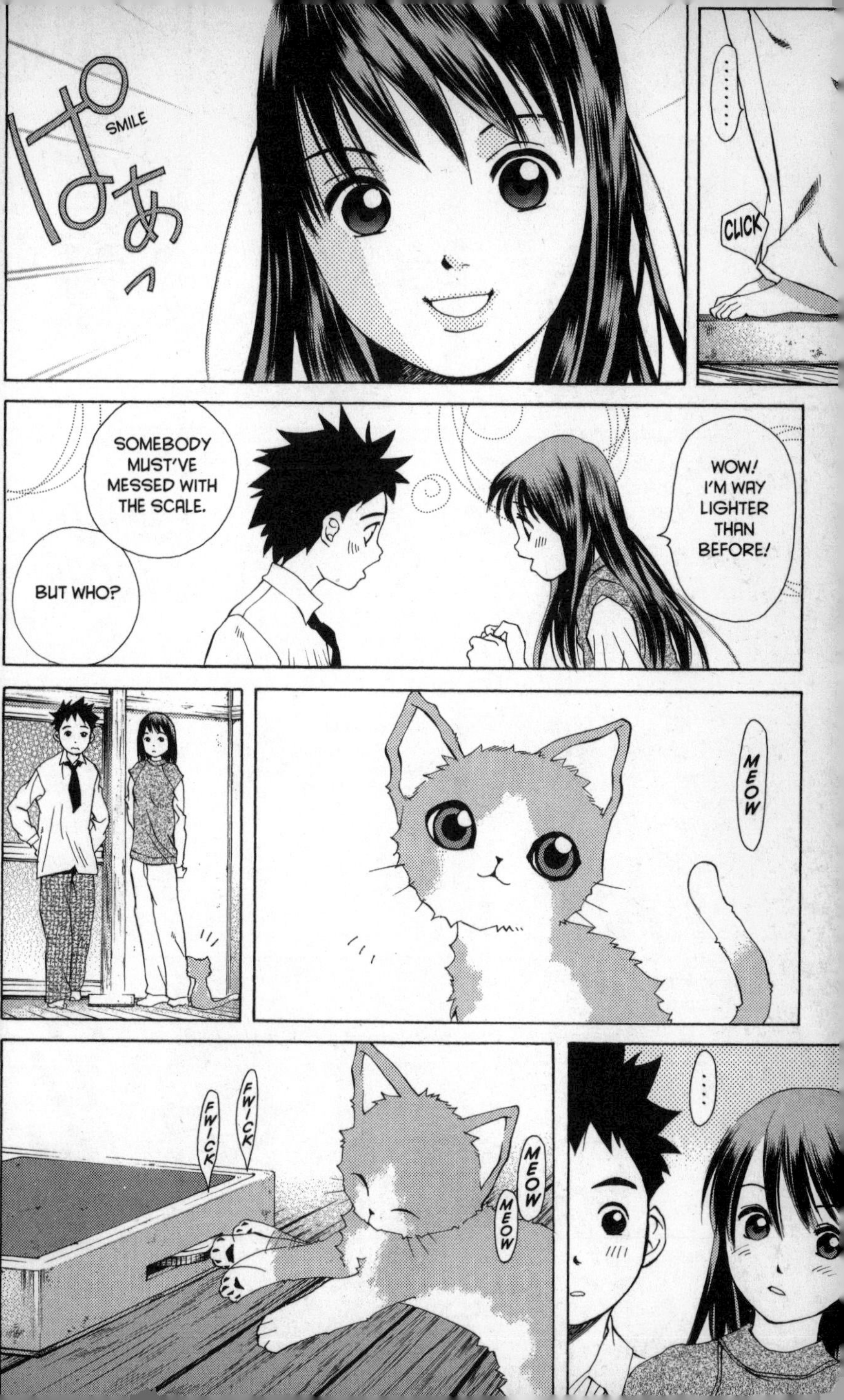
......
CLICK
ぱぁ
SMILE
WOW! I'M WAY LIGHTER THAN BEFORE!
SOMEBODY MUST'VE MESSED WITH THE SCALE.
BUT WHO?
MEOW
....
MEOW
MEOW
FWICK
FWICK

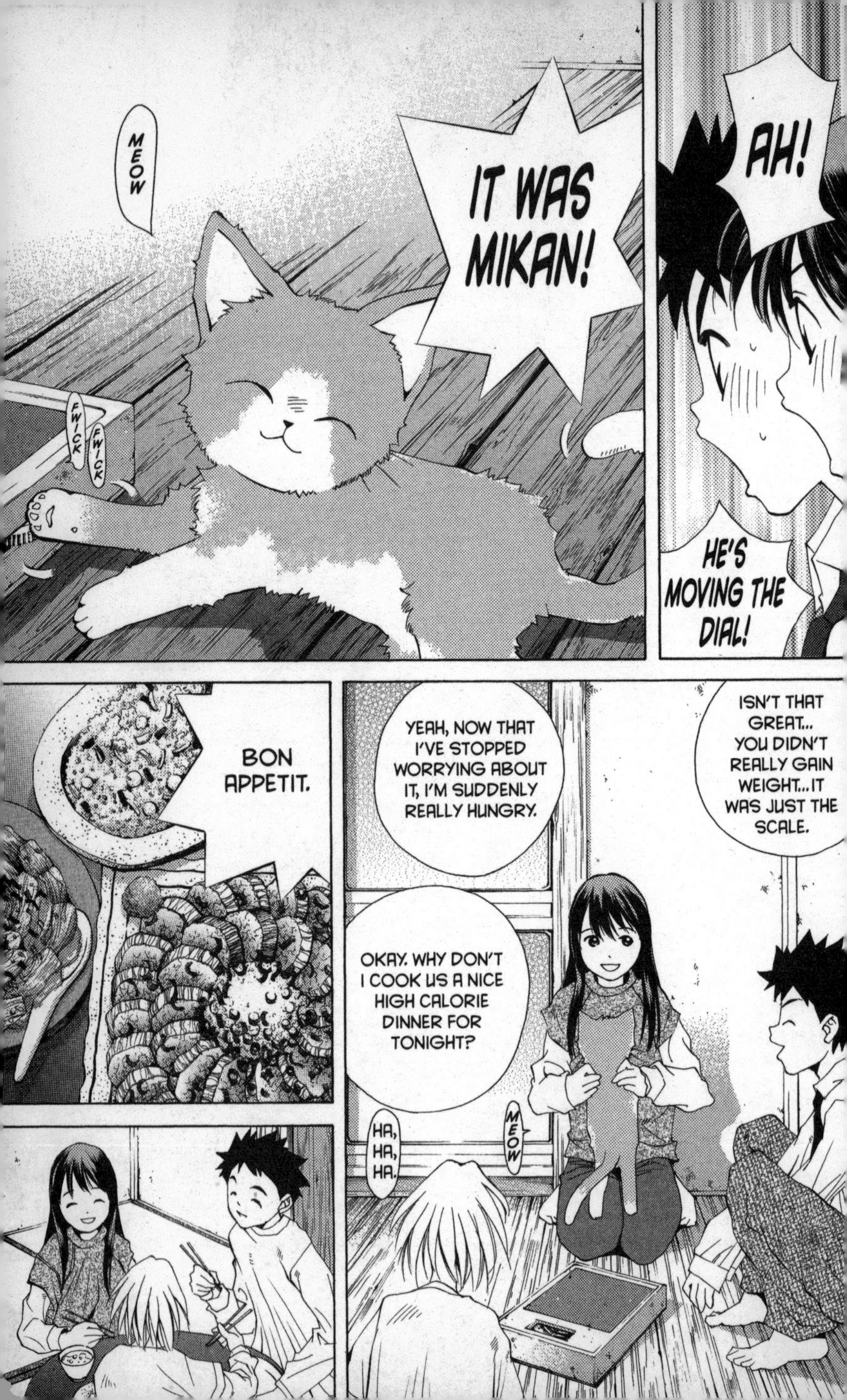
AH!
HE'S MOVING THE DIAL!
IT WAS MIKAN!
MEOW
FWICK FWICK
ISN'T THAT GREAT... YOU DIDN'T REALLY GAIN WEIGHT...IT WAS JUST THE SCALE.
YEAH, NOW THAT I'VE STOPPED WORRYING ABOUT IT, I'M SUDDENLY REALLY HUNGRY.
OKAY. WHY DON'T I COOK US A NICE HIGH CALORIE DINNER FOR TONIGHT?
MEOW
HA, HA, HA.
BON APPETIT.

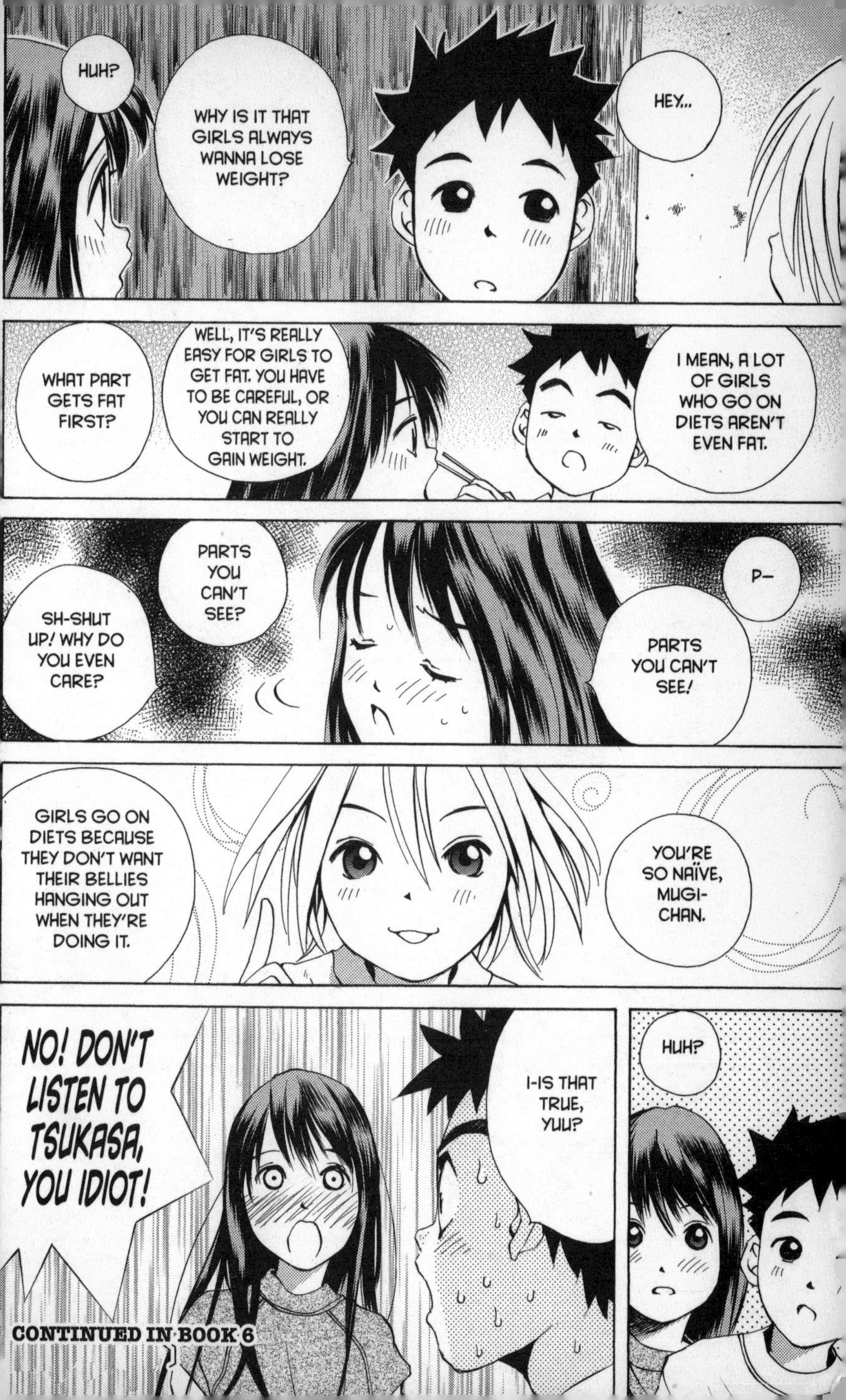
HEY...
WHY IS IT THAT GIRLS ALWAYS WANNA LOSE WEIGHT?
HUH?
I MEAN, A LOT OF GIRLS WHO GO ON DIETS AREN'T EVEN FAT.
WELL, IT'S REALLY EASY FOR GIRLS TO GET FAT. YOU HAVE TO BE CAREFUL, OR YOU CAN REALLY START TO GAIN WEIGHT.
WHAT PART GETS FAT FIRST?
P—
PARTS YOU CAN'T SEE!
PARTS YOU CAN'T SEE?
SH-SHUT UP! WHY DO YOU EVEN CARE?
YOU'RE SO NAÏVE, MUGI-CHAN.
GIRLS GO ON DIETS BECAUSE THEY DON'T WANT THEIR BELLIES HANGING OUT WHEN THEY'RE DOING IT.
HUH?
I-IS THAT TRUE, YUU?
NO! DON'T LISTEN TO TSUKASA, YOU IDIOT!

CONTINUED IN BOOK 6

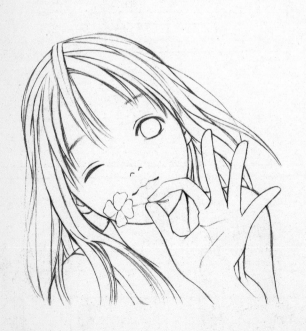

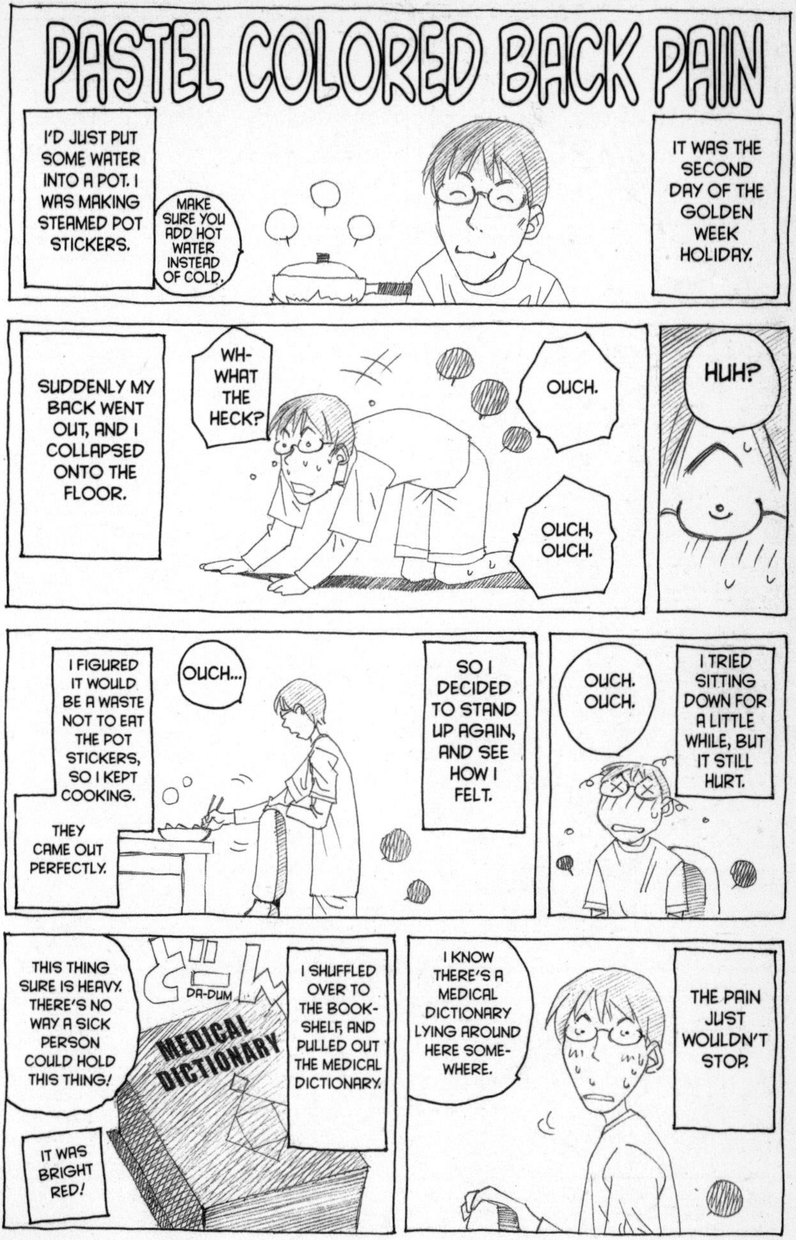
PASTEL COLORED BACK PAIN
IT WAS THE SECOND DAY OF THE GOLDEN WEEK HOLIDAY.
I'D JUST PUT SOME WATER INTO A POT. I WAS MAKING STEAMED POT STICKERS.
MAKE SURE YOU ADD HOT WATER INSTEAD OF COLD.
HUH?
OUCH.
WH-WHAT THE HECK?
SUDDENLY MY BACK WENT OUT, AND I COLLAPSED ONTO THE FLOOR.
OUCH, OUCH.
I TRIED SITTING DOWN FOR A LITTLE WHILE, BUT IT STILL HURT.
OUCH. OUCH.
SO I DECIDED TO STAND UP AGAIN, AND SEE HOW I FELT.
OUCH...
I FIGURED IT WOULD BE A WASTE NOT TO EAT THE POT STICKERS, SO I KEPT COOKING.
THEY CAME OUT PERFECTLY.
THE PAIN JUST WOULDN'T STOP.
I KNOW THERE'S A MEDICAL DICTIONARY LYING AROUND HERE SOME-WHERE.
I SHUFFLED OVER TO THE BOOK-SHELF, AND PULLED OUT THE MEDICAL DICTIONARY.
どーん
DA-DUM
MEDICAL DICTIONARY
THIS THING SURE IS HEAVY. THERE'S NO WAY A SICK PERSON COULD HOLD THIS THING!
IT WAS BRIGHT RED!

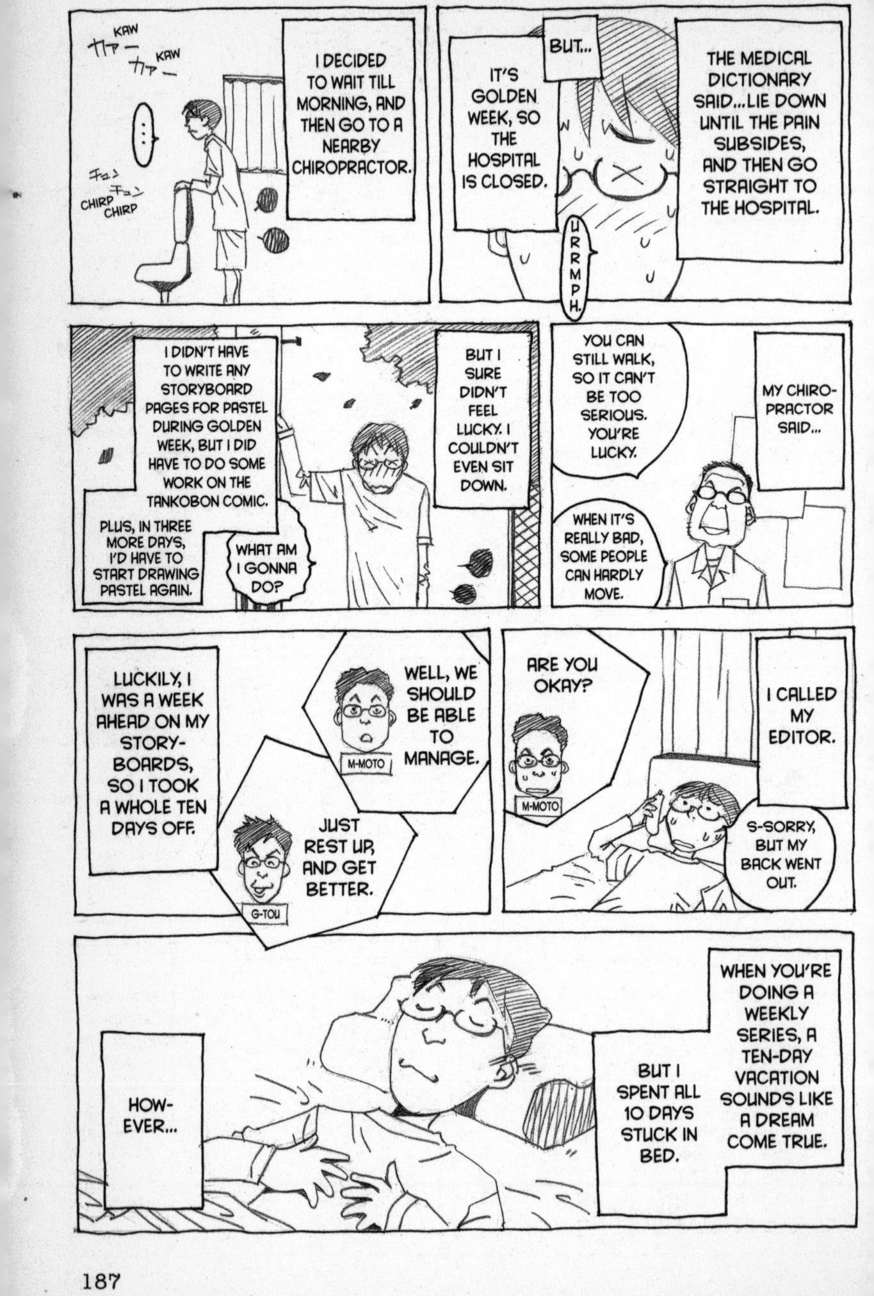
THE MEDICAL DICTIONARY SAID...LIE DOWN UNTIL THE PAIN SUBSIDES, AND THEN GO STRAIGHT TO THE HOSPITAL.
BUT...
IT'S GOLDEN WEEK, SO THE HOSPITAL IS CLOSED.
URRMPH.
I DECIDED TO WAIT TILL MORNING, AND THEN GO TO A NEARBY CHIROPRACTOR.
カァー KAW
カァー KAW
...
チュン チュン
CHIRP CHIRP
MY CHIRO-PRACTOR SAID...
YOU CAN STILL WALK, SO IT CAN'T BE TOO SERIOUS. YOU'RE LUCKY.
WHEN IT'S REALLY BAD, SOME PEOPLE CAN HARDLY MOVE.
BUT I SURE DIDN'T FEEL LUCKY. I COULDN'T EVEN SIT DOWN.
I DIDN'T HAVE TO WRITE ANY STORYBOARD PAGES FOR PASTEL DURING GOLDEN WEEK, BUT I DID HAVE TO DO SOME WORK ON THE TANKOBON COMIC.
WHAT AM I GONNA DO?
PLUS, IN THREE MORE DAYS, I'D HAVE TO START DRAWING PASTEL AGAIN.
I CALLED MY EDITOR.
ARE YOU OKAY?
M-MOTO
S-SORRY, BUT MY BACK WENT OUT.
WELL, WE SHOULD BE ABLE TO MANAGE.
M-MOTO
LUCKILY, I WAS A WEEK AHEAD ON MY STORY-BOARDS, SO I TOOK A WHOLE TEN DAYS OFF.
JUST REST UP, AND GET BETTER.
G-TOU
WHEN YOU'RE DOING A WEEKLY SERIES, A TEN-DAY VACATION SOUNDS LIKE A DREAM COME TRUE.
BUT I SPENT ALL 10 DAYS STUCK IN BED.
HOW-EVER...

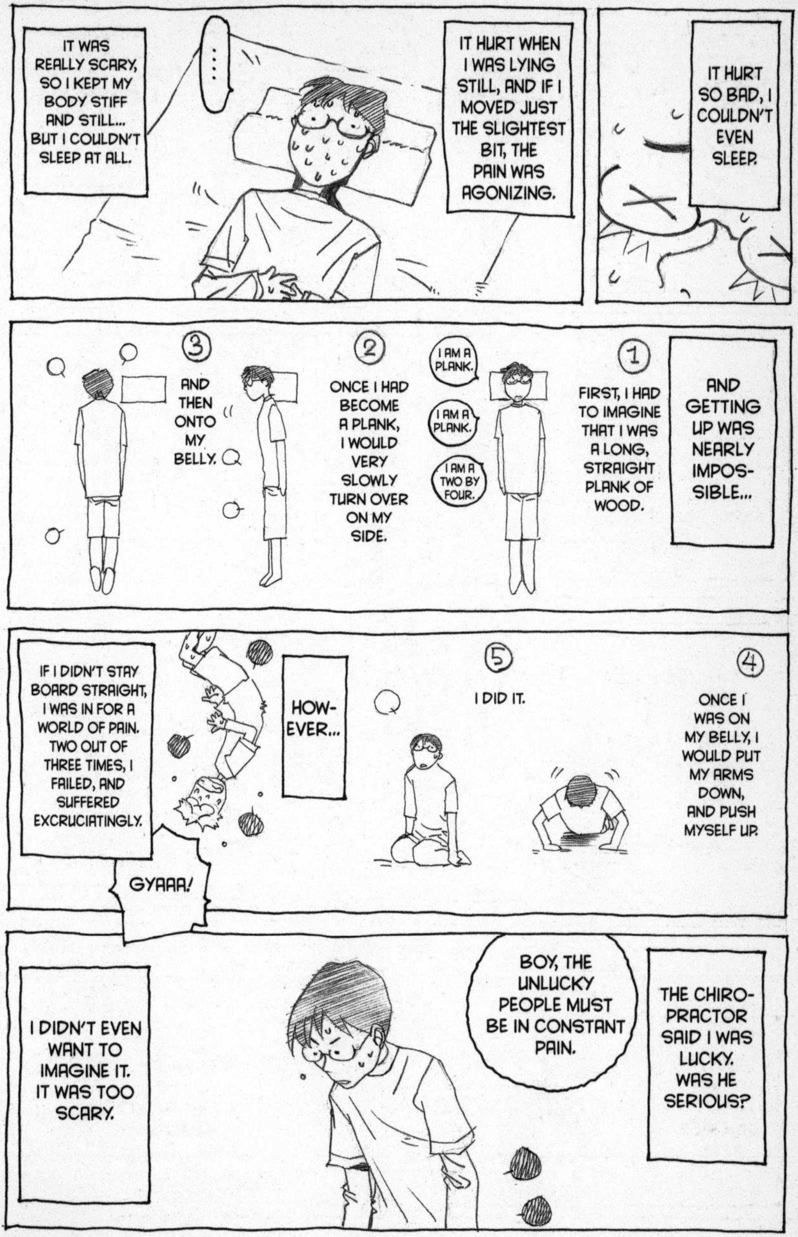
IT HURT SO BAD, I COULDN'T EVEN SLEEP.
IT HURT WHEN I WAS LYING STILL, AND IF I MOVED JUST THE SLIGHTEST BIT, THE PAIN WAS AGONIZING.
.....
IT WAS REALLY SCARY, SO I KEPT MY BODY STIFF AND STILL... BUT I COULDN'T SLEEP AT ALL.
AND GETTING UP WAS NEARLY IMPOSSIBLE...
1
FIRST, I HAD TO IMAGINE THAT I WAS A LONG, STRAIGHT PLANK OF WOOD.
I AM A PLANK.
I AM A PLANK.
I AM A TWO BY FOUR.
2
ONCE I HAD BECOME A PLANK, I WOULD VERY SLOWLY TURN OVER ON MY SIDE.
3
AND THEN ONTO MY BELLY.
4
ONCE I WAS ON MY BELLY, I WOULD PUT MY ARMS DOWN, AND PUSH MYSELF UP.
5
I DID IT.
HOW-EVER...
IF I DIDN'T STAY BOARD STRAIGHT, I WAS IN FOR A WORLD OF PAIN. TWO OUT OF THREE TIMES, I FAILED, AND SUFFERED EXCRUCIATINGLY.
GYAAA!
THE CHIRO-PRACTOR SAID I WAS LUCKY. WAS HE SERIOUS?
BOY, THE UNLUCKY PEOPLE MUST BE IN CONSTANT PAIN.
I DIDN'T EVEN WANT TO IMAGINE IT. IT WAS TOO SCARY.

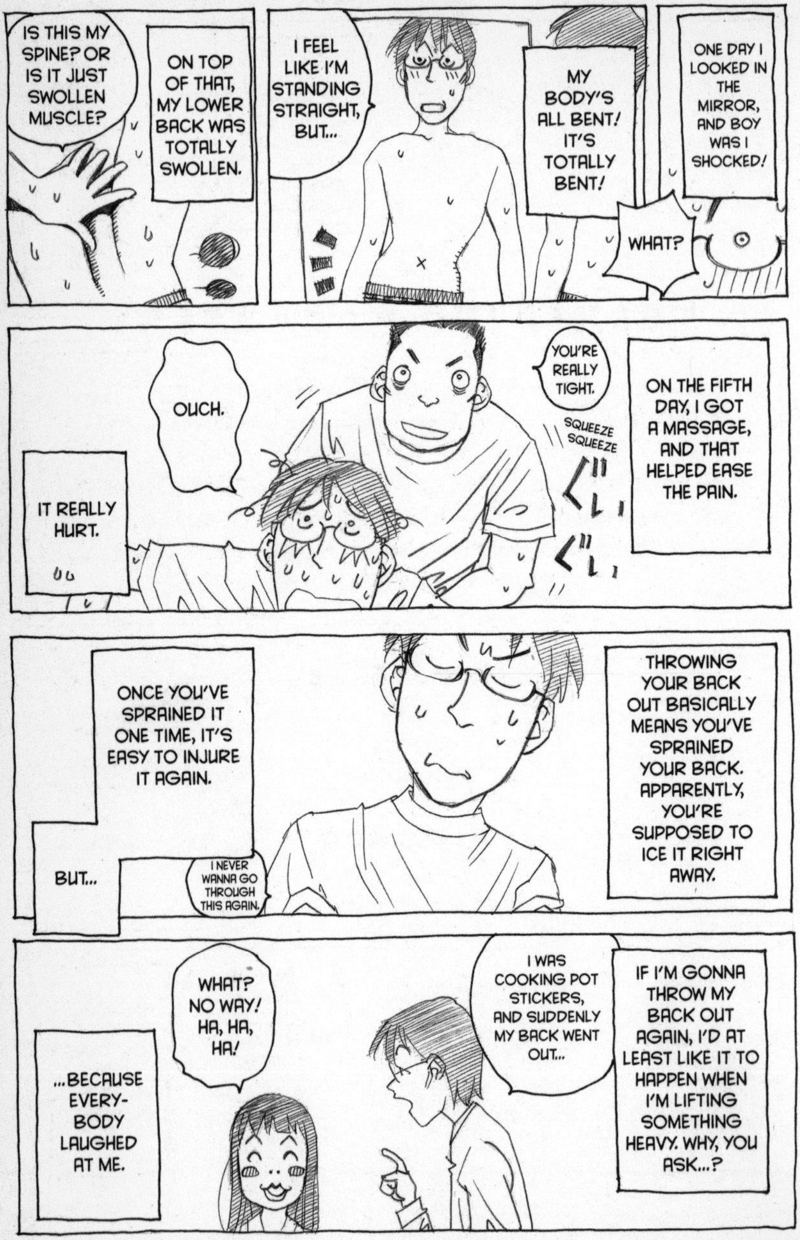
ONE DAY I LOOKED IN THE MIRROR, AND BOY WAS I SHOCKED!
WHAT?
MY BODY'S ALL BENT! IT'S TOTALLY BENT!
I FEEL LIKE I'M STANDING STRAIGHT, BUT...
ON TOP OF THAT, MY LOWER BACK WAS TOTALLY SWOLLEN.
IS THIS MY SPINE? OR IS IT JUST SWOLLEN MUSCLE?
ON THE FIFTH DAY, I GOT A MASSAGE, AND THAT HELPED EASE THE PAIN.
YOU'RE REALLY TIGHT.
SQUEEZE SQUEEZE
OUCH.
IT REALLY HURT.
THROWING YOUR BACK OUT BASICALLY MEANS YOU'VE SPRAINED YOUR BACK. APPARENTLY, YOU'RE SUPPOSED TO ICE IT RIGHT AWAY.
ONCE YOU'VE SPRAINED IT ONE TIME, IT'S EASY TO INJURE IT AGAIN.
I NEVER WANNA GO THROUGH THIS AGAIN.
BUT...
IF I'M GONNA THROW MY BACK OUT AGAIN, I'D AT LEAST LIKE IT TO HAPPEN WHEN I'M LIFTING SOMETHING HEAVY. WHY, YOU ASK...?
I WAS COOKING POT STICKERS, AND SUDDENLY MY BACK WENT OUT...
WHAT? NO WAY! HA, HA, HA!
...BECAUSE EVERY-BODY LAUGHED AT ME.

TOSHIHIKO KOBAYASHI

Born in Mihara city in Hiroshima. Birthday is February 25.
In 1995, "Half Coat" was serialized in "Magazine Special" from No.1 to No.11. After the serial publication of "Parallel" in "Magazine Special" from No.8 in 2000 to No.1 in 2002, "Pastel" was serialized in "Weekly Shonen Magazine" from the 32nd issue in 2002 to the 33rd issue in 2003. And now "Pastel" has been running as a serial ever since "Magazine Special" No.10 in 2003.

Favorites
Fruits
Sleeping
Hot green tea

Dislikes
Being scolded
Excessive expectations
Cigarette smoke

Translation Notes

Japanese is a tricky language for most Westerners, and translation is often more art than science. For your edification and reading pleasure, here are notes on some of the places where we could have gone in a different direction in our translation of the work, or where a Japanese cultural reference is used.

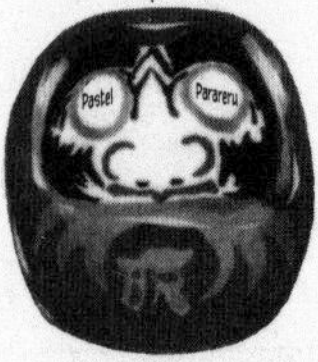
Parareru
Pastel

Daruma, author note

This little round doll is called a *daruma.* It's tradition to draw a single eye on the *daruma* and make a wish. When the wish comes true, you fill in the other eye.

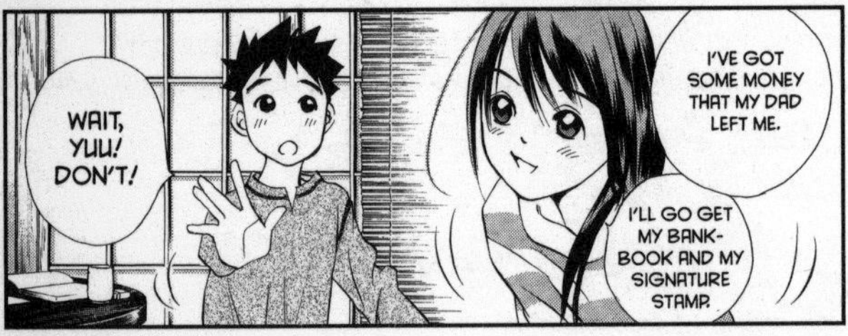
I'VE GOT SOME MONEY THAT MY DAD LEFT ME.
I'LL GO GET MY BANK-BOOK AND MY SIGNATURE STAMP.
WAIT, YUU! DON'T!

Hanko, page 5

A signature stamp, called *hanko* or *inkan* in Japanese, is a rubber stamp with a person's last name imprinted on it. These stamps are used instead of a signature when signing important documents.

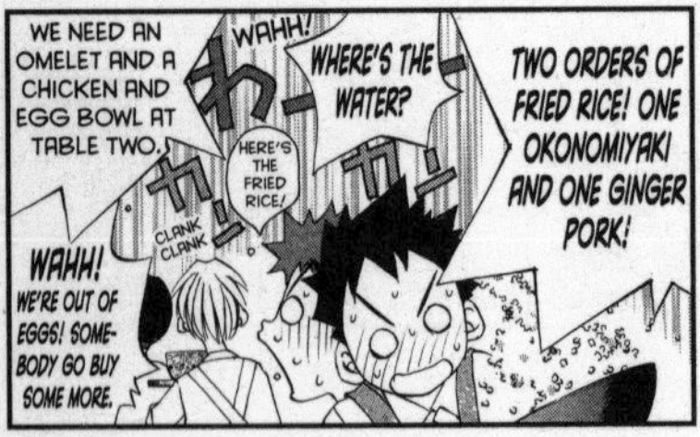
TWO ORDERS OF FRIED RICE! ONE OKONOMIYAKI AND ONE GINGER PORK!
WHERE'S THE WATER?
WAHH!
HERE'S THE FRIED RICE!
WE NEED AN OMELET AND A CHICKEN AND EGG BOWL AT TABLE TWO.
CLANK CLANK
WAHH! WE'RE OUT OF EGGS! SOMEBODY GO BUY SOME MORE.

Okonomiyaki, page 30

Okonomiyaki is commonly referred to as a Japanese style pancake. It's a concoction made up of batter and a mixture of meat, vegetables, egg, and sometimes noodles.

Takokarakusa, page 77

Takokarakusa means "octopus design," so called because the patterns are said to resemble an octopus's legs.

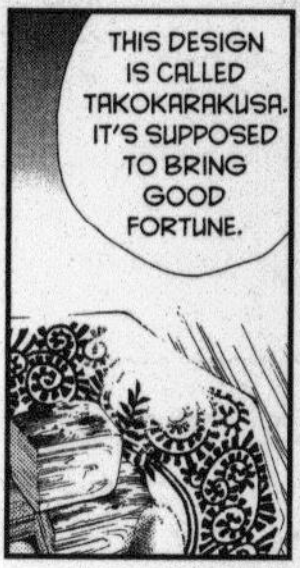
THIS DESIGN IS CALLED TAKOKARAKUSA. IT'S SUPPOSED TO BRING GOOD FORTUNE.

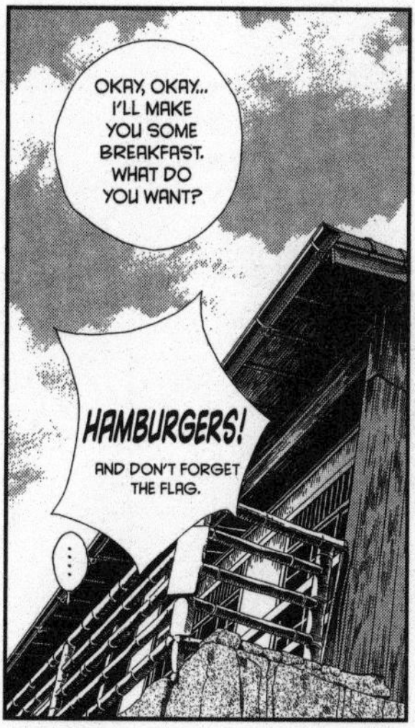
OKAY, OKAY... I'LL MAKE YOU SOME BREAKFAST. WHAT DO YOU WANT?
HAMBURGERS! AND DON'T FORGET THE FLAG.
...

Paper flags, page 84

In Japan, kid's meals are often served with a little paper flag attached to a toothpick.

Wheat, page 86

As you may recall, *mugi* means wheat in Japanese. The customer here is actually saying, "Hey, Mugi! Bring me some mugi shouchuu." *Mugi shouchuu* is a type of alcohol made from wheat.

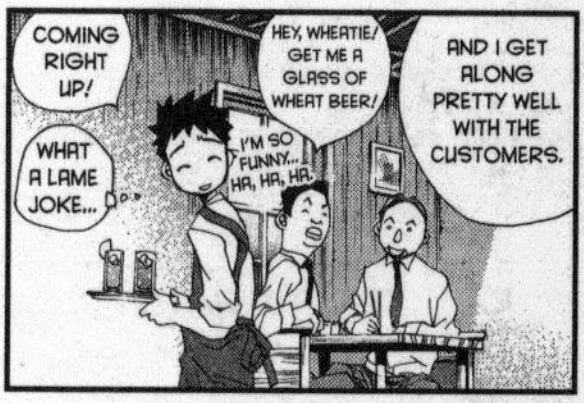
AND I GET ALONG PRETTY WELL WITH THE CUSTOMERS.
HEY, WHEATIE! GET ME A GLASS OF WHEAT BEER!
I'M SO FUNNY... HA, HA, HA.
COMING RIGHT UP!
WHAT A LAME JOKE...

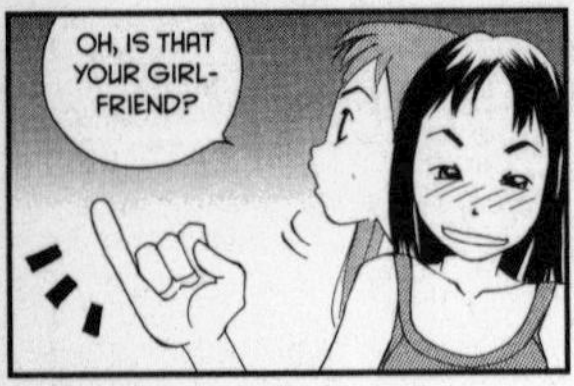
OH, IS THAT YOUR GIRL-FRIEND?

Pinky finger, page 99

Notice that Aoi is sticking her pinky finger out. In Japan, this gesture is used for "girlfriend." Aoi is literally saying, "Is that your (gesture for girlfriend)…?"

Kansetsu kiss, page 108

Mugi is excited about his *kansetsu* kiss. A *kansetsu* kiss occurs when two people's lips touch the same spot. For example, if Mugi took a sip from a straw, and then Yuu took a sip from the same straw, that would be a *kansetsu* kiss. In this case, Aoi kisses Mugi, right after she kissed Yuu, so it's almost as if Yuu and Mugi kissed directly…at least in Mugi's head.

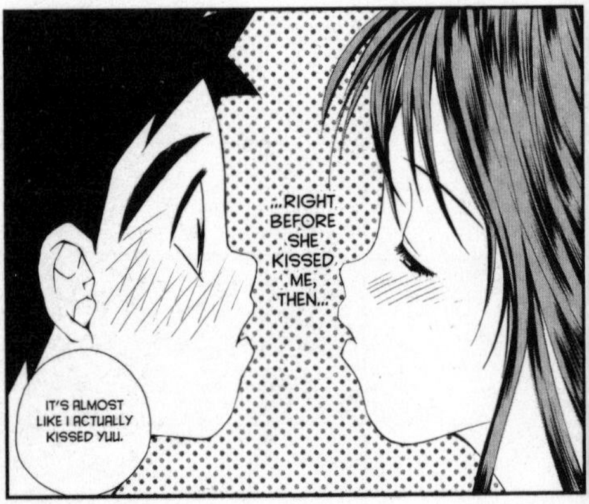
...RIGHT BEFORE SHE KISSED ME, THEN...
IT'S ALMOST LIKE I ACTUALLY KISSED YUU.

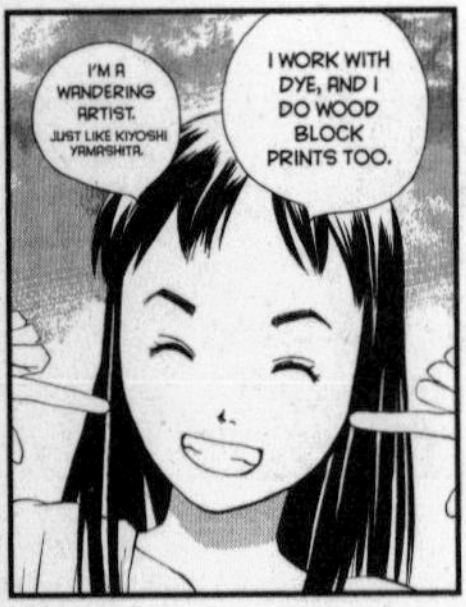
I WORK WITH DYE, AND I DO WOOD BLOCK PRINTS TOO.
I'M A WANDERING ARTIST.
JUST LIKE KIYOSHI YAMASHITA.

Kiyoshi Yamashita, page 110

Kiyoshi Yamashita, often referred to as "Japan's Van Gogh," was a famous modern Japanese artist who wandered about the country. After his death, he was made the subject of a very popular TV drama.

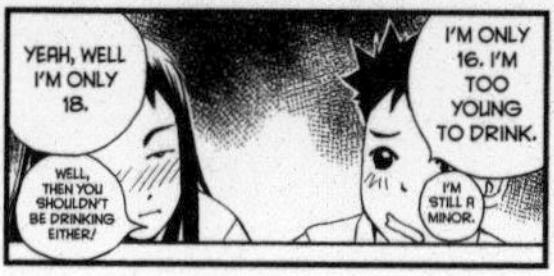
I'M ONLY 16. I'M TOO YOUNG TO DRINK.
I'M STILL A MINOR.
YEAH, WELL I'M ONLY 18.
WELL, THEN YOU SHOULDN'T BE DRINKING EITHER!

Drinking age, page 112

In Japan you must be 20 or older to partake of alcoholic beverages.

Imari, page 126

Imari is a famous type of Japanese pottery.

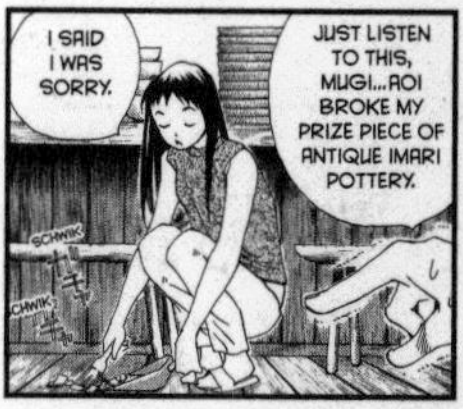
JUST LISTEN TO THIS, MUGI...AOI BROKE MY PRIZE PIECE OF ANTIQUE IMARI POTTERY.
I SAID I WAS SORRY.

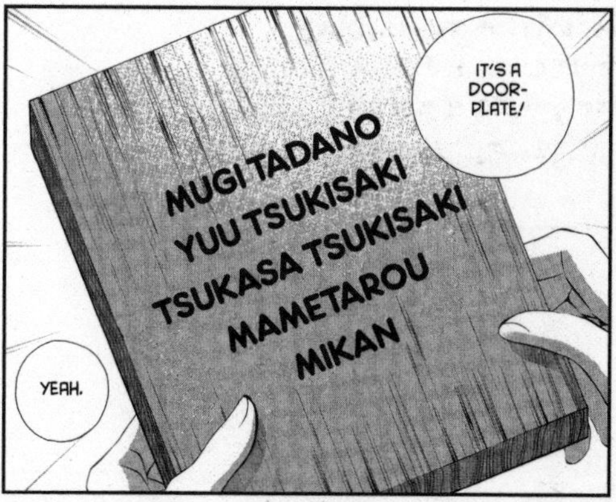
IT'S A DOOR-PLATE!
MUGI TADANO
YUU TSUKISAKI
TSUKASA TSUKISAKI
MAMETAROU
MIKAN
YEAH.

Doorplates, page 162

Doorplates, called *hyousatsu* in Japanese, are signs posted in front of houses or apartments. The signs generally show only the last name of the residents, but in this case Mugi has included every member of the household.

Preview of Volume 6

We're pleased to present you a preview from Volume 6. This volume will be available in English on March 27, 2007, but for now you'll have to make do with Japanese!

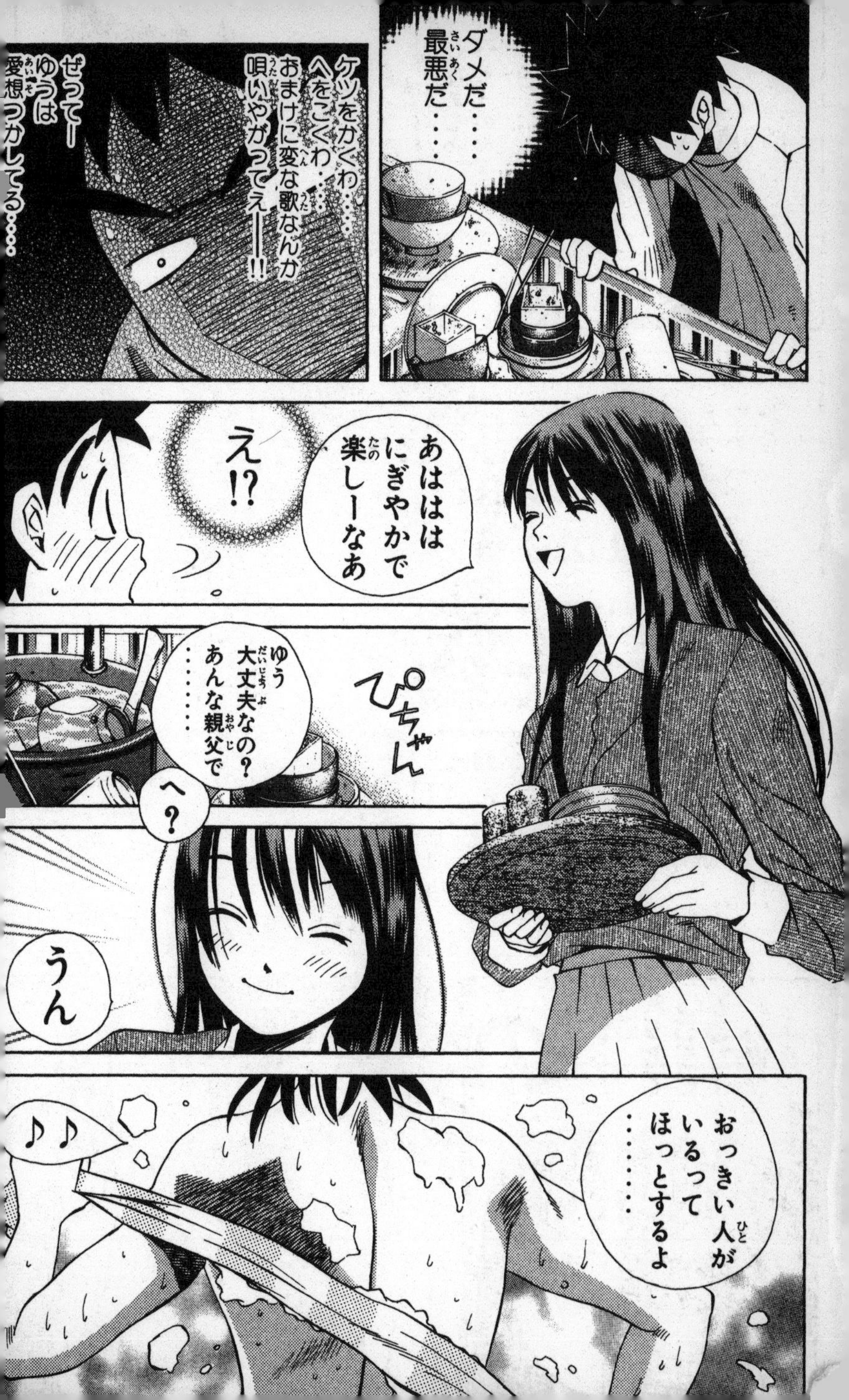
ダメだ……
最悪だ……
ケツをかくわ……
へをこくわ……
おまけに変な歌なんか
唄いやがってえーー!!
ぜってーゆうは愛想つかしてる……
あははは にぎやかで 楽しーなあ
え!?
ゆう 大丈夫なの? あんな親父で……
ぴちゃん
へ?
うん
おっきい人が いるって ほっとするよ……
♪♪

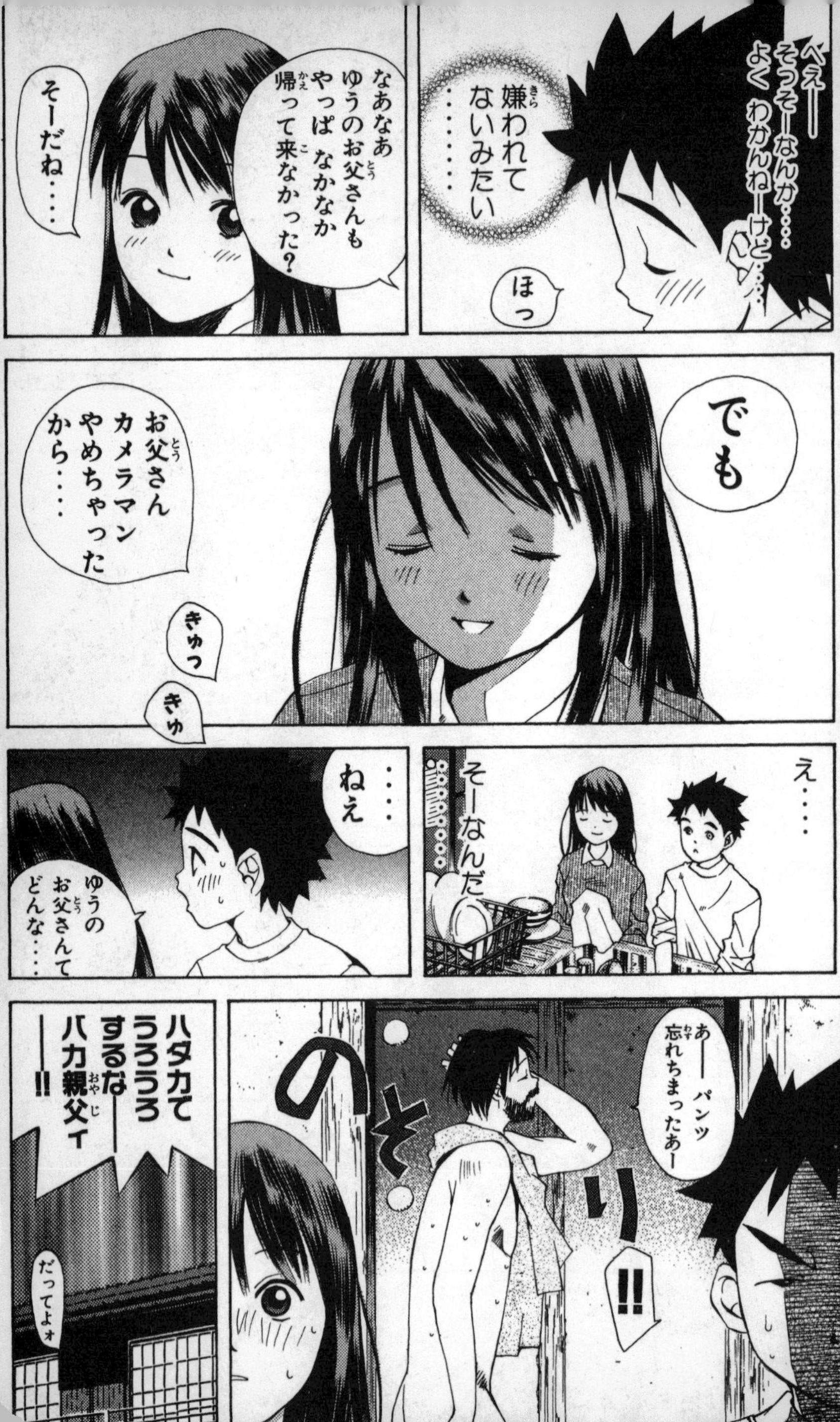

へえー そうそーなんか‥‥ よく わかんねーけど‥‥
嫌われて ないみたい‥‥‥‥
ほっ
なあなあ ゆうのお父さんも やっぱ なかなか 帰って来なかった?
そーだね‥‥
でも
お父さん カメラマン やめちゃった から‥‥
きゅっ
きゅ
え‥‥
そーなんだ
‥‥ねえ
ゆうの お父さんて どんな‥‥
あー パンツ 忘れちまったあー
のそり
!!
ハダカで うろうろ するなー バカ親父ィ ——!!
だってよォ

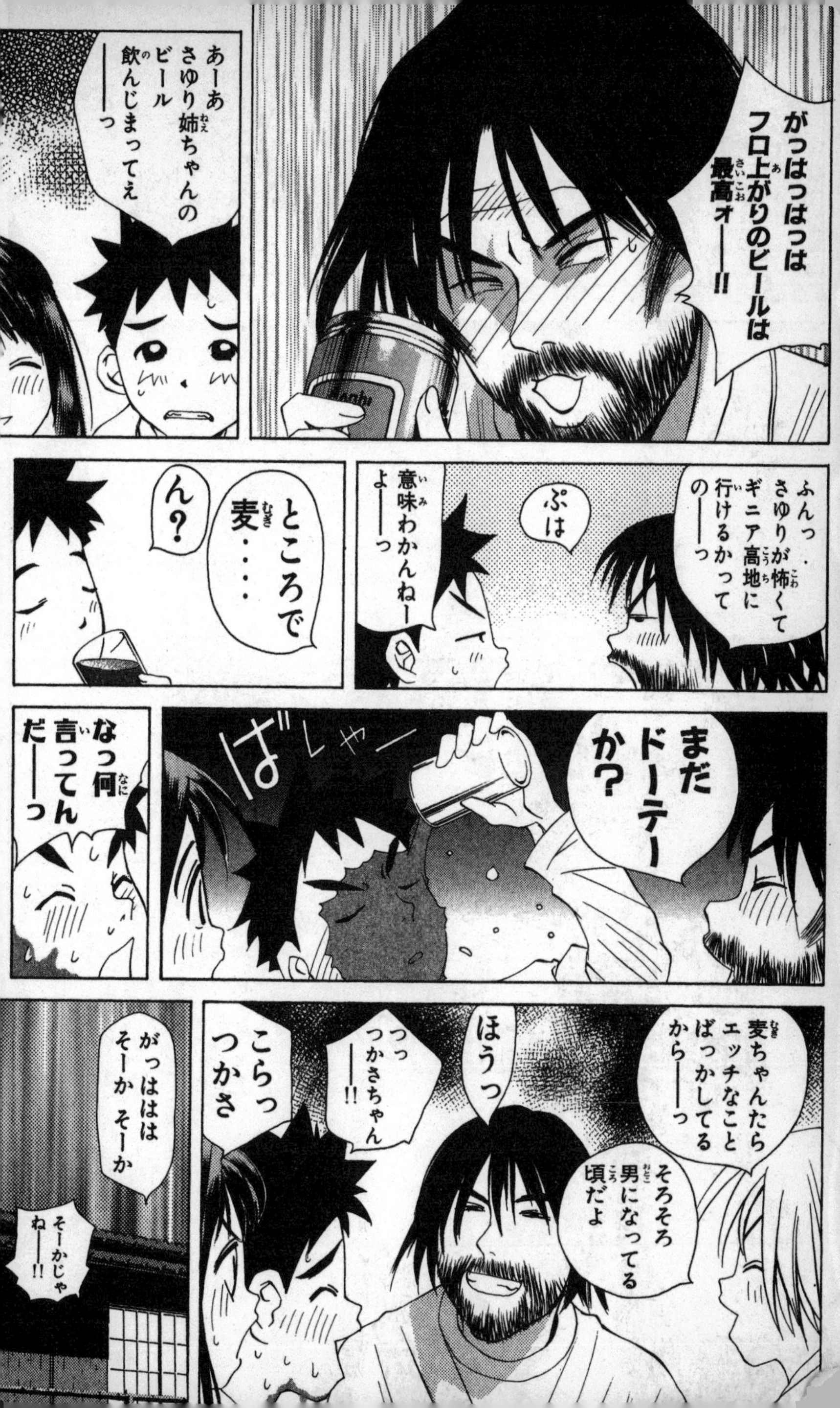
がっはっはっは フロ上がりのビールは 最高オーー!!
あーあ さゆり姉ちゃんの ビール 飲んじまってえ ーーっ
ふんっ さゆりが怖くて ギニア高地に 行けるかって のーーっ
ぷは
意味わかんねー よーーっ
ところで 麦・・・・
ん?
まだ ドーテー か?
ばしゃー
なっ何 言ってん だーーっ
麦ちゃんたら エッチなこと ばっかしてる から ーーっ
ほうっ
そろそろ 男になってる 頃だよ
つっ つかさちゃん ーー!!
こらっ つかさ
がっははは そーか そーか
そーかじゃ ねーー!!

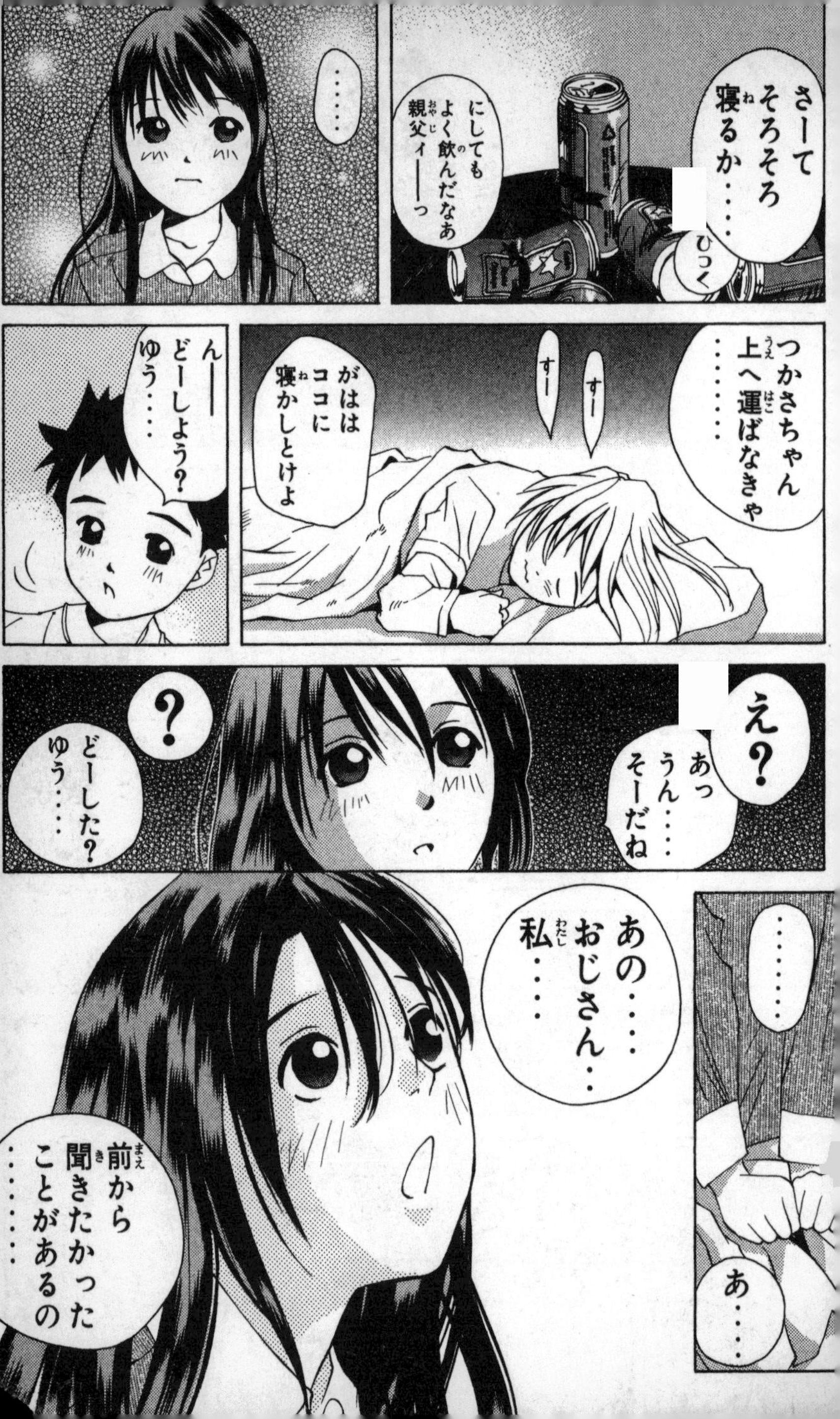
さーてそろそろ寝るか‥‥
ひっく
にしてもよく飲んだなあ親父ィ――っ
‥‥‥
つかさちゃん上へ運ばなきゃ‥‥‥
すー
すー
がははココに寝かしとけよ
んーー どーしよう？ゆう‥‥
え？
あっうん‥‥そーだね
？
どーした？ゆう‥‥
‥‥‥
あ‥‥
あの‥‥おじさん‥‥私‥‥
前から聞きたかったことがあるの‥‥‥

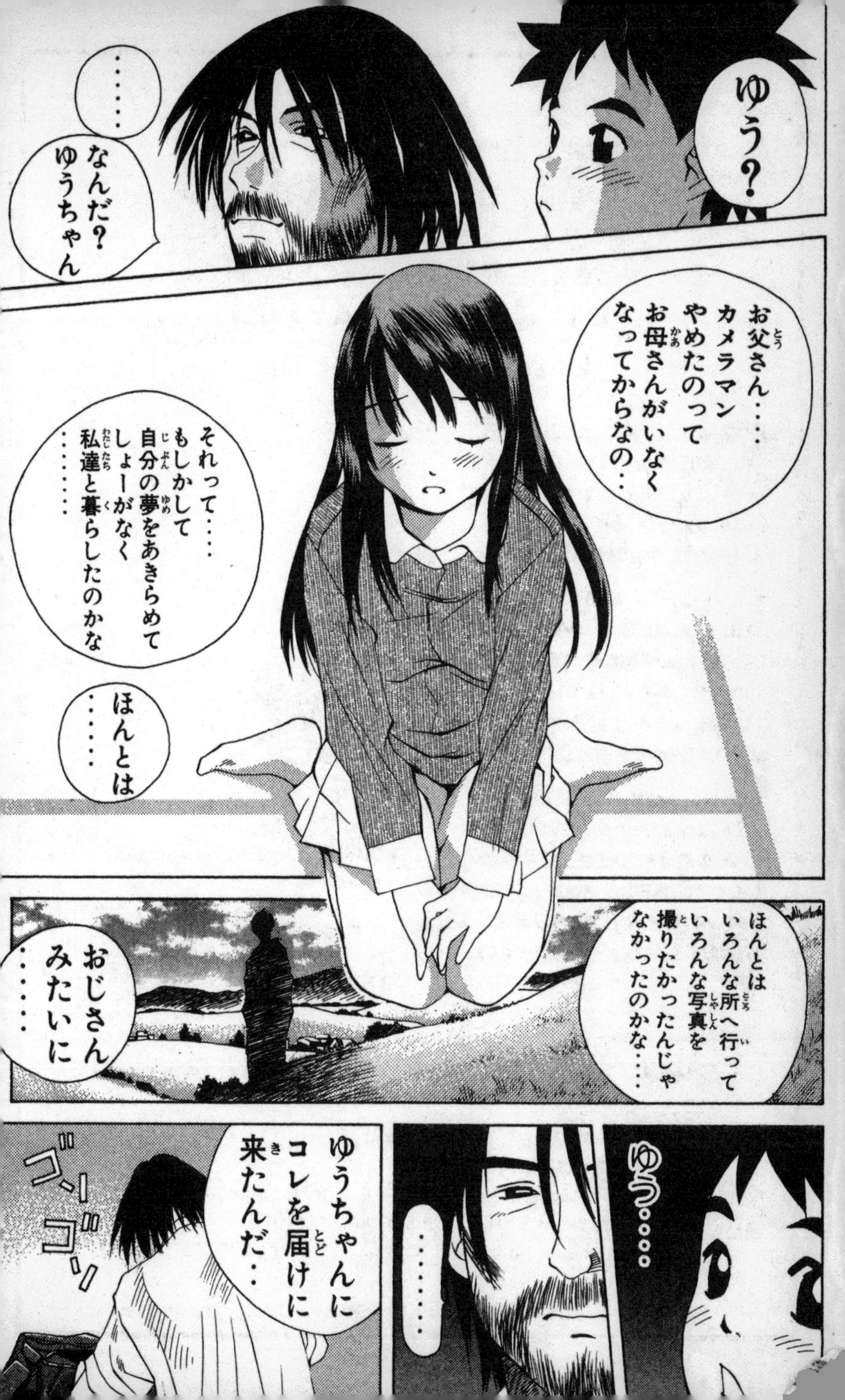
ゆう？
……
なんだ？ゆうちゃん
お父さん…カメラマンやめたのってお母さんがいなくなってからなの…
それって…もしかして自分の夢をあきらめてしょーがなく私達と暮らしたのかな……
ほんとは……
ほんとはいろんな所へ行っていろんな写真を撮りたかったんじゃなかったのかな…
おじさんみたいに……
ゆう。。。。
……
ゆうちゃんにコレを届けに来たんだ…
ゴーゴー

School Rumble

BY JIN KOBAYASHI

SUBTLETY IS FOR WIMPS!

She . . . is a second-year high school student with a single all-consuming question: Will the boy she likes ever really notice her?

He . . . is the school's most notorious juvenile delinquent, and he's suddenly come to a shocking realization: He's got a huge crush, and now he must tell her how he feels.

Life-changing obsessions, colossal foul-ups, grand schemes, deep-seated anxieties, and raging hormones—School Rumble portrays high school as it really is: over-the-top comedy!

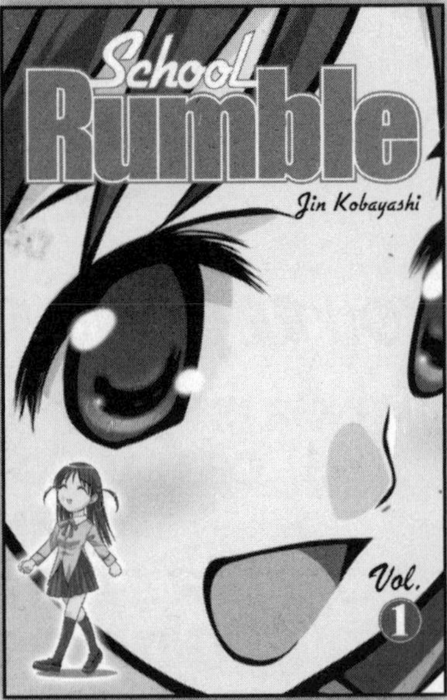
School Rumble
Jin Kobayashi
Vol. 1

Ages: 16 +

Special extras in each volume! Read them all!

VISIT WWW.DELREYMANGA.COM TO:

- Read sample pages
- View release date calendars for upcoming volumes
- Sign up for Del Rey's free manga e-newsletter
- Find out the latest about new Del Rey Manga series

TOMARE!

TOMARE!
TOMARE!

TOMARE!

STOP!

YOU'RE GOING THE WRONG WAY!

MANGA IS A COMPLETELY DIFFERENT TYPE
OF READING EXPERIENCE.

TO START AT THE BEGINNING,
GO TO THE END!

THAT'S RIGHT!

AUTHENTIC MANGA IS READ THE TRADITIONAL
JAPANESE WAY—FROM RIGHT TO LEFT. EXACTLY THE OPPOSITE
OF HOW AMERICAN BOOKS ARE READ. IT'S EASY TO FOLLOW:
JUST GO TO THE OTHER END OF THE BOOK, AND READ EACH PAGE
—AND EACH PANEL—FROM RIGHT SIDE TO LEFT SIDE,
STARTING AT THE TOP RIGHT. NOW YOU'RE EXPERIENCING
MANGA AS IT WAS MEANT TO BE.